MAIN STREET, SALT LAKE CITY.

NEW AMERICA.

BY

WILLIAM HEPWORTH DIXON,

EDITOR OF THE "ATHENÆUM," AND AUTHOR OF "THE HOLY LAND," "WILLIAM PENN," ETC.

With Illustrations from Original Photographs.

COMPLETE IN ONE VOLUME.

Third Edition.

PHILADELPHIA:
J. B. LIPPINCOTT & CO.
1867.

TO

CHARLES WENTWORTH DILKE, Esq.

OF

TRINITY HALL, CAMBRIDGE,

MY FELLOW-TRAVELLER IN THE GREAT WEST,

This Volume

IS AFFECTIONATELY INSCRIBED.

ILLUSTRATIONS.

PREFACE.

SOME studies of past times, which have long occupied my pen, led me last summer to the James River and to Plymouth Rock. I went out in search of an old world, and found a new one. East, west, north, and south, I met with new ideas, new purposes, new methods; in short, with a New America.

The men who planted these Free States — doing the noblest work that England has achieved in history — were spurred into their course by two great passions: a large love of Liberty; a deep sense of Religion; and, in our Great Plantation, liberty and religion exercise a power over the forms of social and domestic life unknown at home. In the heart of solid societies and conservative churches, we find the most singular doctrines, the most audacious experiments; and it is only after seeing what kind of forces are at work within them, that we can adequately admire the strength of these societies and churches.

What I saw of the changes now being wrought in the actual life of man and woman on the American soil, under the power of these master passions, is pictured in these pages.

6 ST. JAMES' TERRACE,
New Year's Day, 1867.

CONTENTS.

NEW AMERICA.

CHAPTER I.

THE WESTERN COUNTRY.

"GUESS these Yanks must look alive on this side the River, unless they should happen to enjoy having their eye-teeth drawn—eh, Judge?"

The man to whom this appeal is made as judge lifts up his chin from a dish of hominy and corned beef, glances first at myself, then at my fellow-traveler, and after winking an eye to the right and left, says slowly, "Guess you are right there, Sheriff."

Spoken, as it is, across the table of a tiny hotel in the City of Atchison—the only wonder about which hotel is, how a place so diminutive can hold so much dirt and feed so much vermin—this passage of legal wit may need a few words of explanation.

The Yanks now warned by the Sheriff that they must look alive, under penalty of having their eye-teeth drawn, are my friend Charles W. Dilke and myself; two men of undeniable English birth and blood. English faces are not seen every day in the State of Kansas; and these Western boys (every man living beyond the Missouri is a Boy, just as every woman is a Lady—in her own right), these Western boys, having dim notions of ethnology and accent, set down every man who crosses the River, with a white face and without a bowie-knife, as a Yankee—a traveler from the

New England States in quest of gold dust, reservations, and corner lots. "The River" means the Missouri; here flowing between the settled State of that name and the wild unpeopled region, known in maps as Kansas, in poetry and fiction as Bleeding Kansas. To a Western boy, the Missouri is the Thames, the Rhine, and the Seine; his stream of commerce, beauty, luxury, and art; and every man and woman, that is to say, every boy and lady, living in the western uplands, beyond this margin of bluff and forest, talks to you about going down to the River just as a Picardie peasant boasts of going up to Paris, as a Marylebone grocer speaks of running down to Brighton and the Isle of Wight. The River divides him, as he says, from the East, from the States; and the current jest, everywhere to be heard from Atchison to Salt Lake, says, that a man who means to cross the Missouri is going on a trip to America. Dressed in his high boots, his slouch hat, his belt, his buffalo-skin, his bowie-knife, and his six-shooter, a Western boy feels for the unarmed, sober, unadventurous men dwelling on the opposite bank of the River, the sort of proud contempt which an Arab beyond Jordan cherishes for the settlers in Galilee, spiced with the fierce hatred which a Spanish hidalgo dwelling east of the Duero feels for the Portuguese peddlers crawling on the western bank.

Now, that question of drawing the eye-teeth is one about which I hold to an extreme opinion. Five or six years ago, when calling on my old friend Landor in his Florentine house, and expressing my joy at finding him so hale and bright (he was then eighty-four), I heard in reply to my congratulations, these noticeable words: "My dear fellow, say no more about it; I have lost four of my teeth." When I smiled, the veteran added, "Do not laugh at me; I would rather have lost all my intellect than one of my teeth." On the whole, I should hardly go Landor's length, though the threat of having your "eye-teeth" drawn for you, willy nilly, is certainly one to disturb a saint. But we have crossed our Jordan, and on this side the River we must take our chance.

Early yesterday, a sultry August morning, we left St. Louis; a bright and busy city, full of a fierce and tameless life, half Saxon, half Latin; a city which has been smitten to the heart by panic, such as will sometimes fall upon Cairo and Aleppo in a time of plague. For a month of burning heat—the heat of a great plain, lying low down in the drain of a great continent, three hundred miles from the nearest hills, eight hundred miles from a mountain range—cholera has been sweeping off her countless victims from those quays on which the poor Irish labor, from those slums in which the improvident negroes lodge.

No Howard Society sprang up this year to assist the poor, as on a former visitation of the pest, when fifteen hundred of the young, rich, able men of the city had put their hearts into the helping work. Nothing had been done to meet a calamity which is always threatening such a city as St. Louis, built on one of the deepest sewers in the world. With a lack of wisdom hardly to be matched beyond the walls of Gotham, the council had ceased to make daily returns of the dead, the number of which could only be guessed from the march of funerals through the streets, and from the register of interments in the ten or twelve busiest graveyards. The rate of deaths ran high, and it was grossly extended by the arithmetic of fear. Fires were burning in every street; lime was being forced into every gutter; no one dared to enter a public conveyance; horrible tales, the offspring of a

Southern brain, were whispered in your ears at table, where you heard that every officer had flown from the cemeteries, even the felons and murderers who had been promised their pardon on condition of interring the victims of cholera; that the unburied corpses were heaped together in the island; that coffins and sear-cloths had been set on fire by the runaways; that a thousand nameless horrors had been committed in the dead-houses and in the graveyards. The death-bells were tolling day and night.

We left the city early. Noon saw us at Macon, picking grapes and sucking melons; midnight brought us to St. Joseph (affectionately called St. Joe), on the Missouri River, some dozen miles above Atchison, and of course on the eastern bank. At two o'clock, in the night, we came to the end of our iron-track, when the car in which we rode emptied itself into a field, at no place in particular, but in a patch of waste land overgrown by stinkweed, and in a situation generally supposed to be occupied by a ferry-boat.

When we came alongside the last plank of the railway, the night being bleak and chilly, it was sweet to hear the cry of the hotel-runner (a tout is here called a runner), "Any one for Planter's House?" Yes: we were all for Planter's House; and away we huddled, with our sacks and sticks, our wraps and overcoats, into an omnibus, which stood ready by the plank to swallow us up. Ugh! what monster is lying among our feet? Something like a huge black dog was sleeping on the floor; which, the moment we pushed into the doorway, began to snort and kick. It seemed too big for a dog; perhaps it was a bull, that, finding the omnibus open, had crept in from the Missouri chills. Presently, it began to swear; such oaths as Uncle Toby heard in Flanders; and on waking into consciousness, the strange beast proved to be the driver, coiled up, concealed, and snoring in a buffalo's hide. Getting into our seats, with a dozen sleepless wretches like ourselves, we cried, "All right," and bade the driver "go ahead."

"Guess you'll wait for the ferry," said he, with a volley of adjectives and objurgations, such as ladies and clergymen would consider somewhat high in flavor.

"When will the ferry-boat come over?" some one asked.

"Well, I guess about seven o'clock."

It was now two; the night raw and cold; the omnibus choked with passengers; and we were lying out in an open field. Shaking the hotel-runner from a doze—both he and the driver had again tumbled off into sleep, in the cosiest corner of our coach—we learned that the river might be crossed, at that point, even in the night, if we liked to venture upon it in a small rowing-boat. Venture upon it! Away we trudged, through the stinkweed, lugging our traps, which no one could be got to carry for us to the river side; feeling our feet down the bank, listening to the lap of the stream, and crying for help to the opposite bluffs. The bank was steep and soft, the black loam slipping beneath our shoes, while a dense yellow fog lay heavily on the swift and whirling flood. On the opposite heights we could trace the outlines of a little town; a few white houses scattered here and there; below these ran the dark outline of the river bank. But where was the rowing-boat? Not on our side of the river; for Bill, the waterman, lodged in his wifeless cabin on the Kansas side; and a "Yep, yep"—a war-whoop raised by the runner, which ought to have

2

roused the seven sleepers from their trance—came back to us only in echoes from the Kansas bluffs. No boat came over with it; and after hanging by the waterside for an hour, seeing the fog grow thicker, and fancying the stream grow wider, we turned away from the muddy bank, not wholly displeased at our war-cry having failed to disturb the boatman's rest.

Going back to the omnibus, we found the driver snorting in his nook. We shall never forget the volleys of oaths and growls which he fired off during the next four hours; neither shall we forget the rude and ready kindness with which he thrust upon us one of his blankets and his buffalo-hide. My friend lay down and slept; sleep comes to you easily in youth; for myself, I walked on the plank; made a second trip to the river; watched the stars pale out; railed against the stinkweed; smoked a cigar.

At seven the ferry-boat came steaming over; at eight we are seated at table in the Planter's House, in the midst of these rough aristocrats of Kansas; a jolly set of dogs, each dog with a bowie-knife in his pocket, a six-shooter in his belt.

"Can you tell me, sir, at what hour the Overland Mail leaves Atchison for Salt Lake?" is the simple inquiry to which the Sheriff answers, as above, with that suggestion about our eye-teeth being hardly safe in Kansas. Not taking the reply so quickly as might be, I look the man steadily in the face, and repeat my question; this time with extreme deliberation; on which the company break into a pleasant burst of Satanic laughter. Then we hear from the Judge that the Overland Mail (to travel by which, on our way to Denver and Salt Lake, we have come from St. Louis to Atchison, its starting-point) has ceased to run by the Platte route, and that the officers and stages have been sent down the river to Leavenworth, whence the mail is in future to be sent across the Plains by an easier and shorter line.

Mail, mail-agent, stock, mules, wagons, all have been sent down the river to Leavenworth, and we have no choice left us but to take up our traps and follow in their wake. These folks make merry at our expense, with a brutal kind of good nature; for a transfer of the Overland Mail from Atchison to Leavenworth is a big blow to their town, such as people who have put their money in it, and who are bound either to stand by it or fall with it, may be forgiven for not seeing in the light of a joke. Being regarded as companions in their misery, it is expected in the town that we shall consider ourselves generally as victims of a plot, and as having had one at least of our eye-teeth drawn.

In a hundred phrases we are told that the mail is leaving the best route through the prairies for the worst. The Platte route, we hear, is safe and easy; a good road, well stocked and stationed; the military posts on which are strong, the Indians all through which are friendly to white men. In a word, it is the route. The new route is called the Smoky Hill route, from a rolling mist which runs along it for a hundred miles.

"Well, gentlemen," says the Sheriff, "you will see it, and then you will judge. Perhaps you like having your remaining eye-teeth drawn?"

One of these citizens takes from his pocket a gazette of the current date, in which there is news from the Smoky Hill country; showing that Black Kettle, Roman Nose, Spotted Dog, and some other worthies of the red race, are out on the war-path; telling how this and that lonely ranch has been plundered and fired by the Cheyennes; and giving lists of white men who have been killed by these savages. By the same gazette we learn that in the North the state of affairs is rather worse than better. A party of white men, coming down the Missouri, has been attacked by Blackfeet Indians, who exchanged shots with them, and swam after them, but were distanced by the rapidity with which the white men plied their boats. The party thus escaping from the tomahawk report that seven white men, coming in a boat down the same river, have been captured and killed by Crows, an Indian tribe who have recently made a treaty of peace with the Government; but in consequence of some slight, as they allege, have burned their treaty, put on ochre and vermilion, and gone out, like their brethren the Cheyennes and Sioux, on the war-path.

A tall, swashing fellow, bickering with rifle, bowie-knife, and six-shooter, lounges into the room, and is introduced to us as Captain Walker; "the famous Captain Jem Walker, sir, who has crossed the plains seven-and-twenty times; after whom Walker's Creek is named"—a creek of which we blush to think that we know nothing, not even the famous name. Captain Walker is of opinion that we shall be fools if we trust our scalps along the Smoky Hill route. The Platte road is the only safe one. When we object that, as the mail no longer runs along that safer path, we can hardly travel by it, he opines that we shall do well to stay a few days in Atchison, during which he will put us up to the ropes, and fix us generally in prairie politics. If we don't know what is best for ourselves, he has no objection to our being damned, as we certainly shall be after making unpleasant acquaintance with a Cheyenne knife.

It is clear that these men of Atchison have but a

poor opinion of the Leavenworth route when compared against their own.

Hearing that a small steamer is going down the river to Leavenworth in the afternoon, we send for our bills, and have our boxes put on board. It is now nine in the morning, and as we have nothing to do, our new friends think proper to stay and help us; a courtesy on their side to which we should offer no objection if it were not for their frequent and sardonic allusions to the fact of our having been taken in. About noon an accident raises us in their good opinion to a height yet higher than that from which we had evidently fallen; enabling us to quit the town, morally speaking, sword in hand and with flying colors.

Sauntering down the street, enjoying our gossip and cigar, we note the word post-office on a shop-front, and on going inside we find there is one letter with my name on the cover, written in an unknown hand, on which three cents are due. Paying the money, and breaking the seal, I find the letter is not for me; on which I fold and restore it to the postmaster, saying it is not mine, and should be kept for the owner, to whom it is perhaps of moment. Eyeing me in a queer way, the postmaster takes the letter, and gives me back my change of three cents. "Do you see?" says the Sheriff to his nearest friend; "damned smart that—read his letter and got his money back! Hang me if I think they are Yanks, after all."

One touch of roguery, it would seem, is enough to make the whole world kin!

CHAPTER II.

BLEEDING KANSAS.

"WELL, Sam," say I to a blithe young negro of thirty-five years, a boy with quick eye and delicate razor-hand, as he powders my face and dabs the rose-water on my hair, in the shaving-room of Planter's House, Leavenworth, "where were you raised?"

"Me riz in Missouri, sar."

"You were born a slave, then?"

"Yes, sar, me slave in Weston; very bad boss; always drunk and kicking poor nigger boy."

"And how did you get your freedom, Sam—did you go and fight?"

"No, sar; me no fight; tink fighting big sin; me swim."

"Swim! Oh, yes; you mean you swam across the Missouri into Kansas, from a slave State into a free State?"

"Dat true, sar. One bery dark night, me slip away from Weston; run through the wood along river bank, down stream; get into de water by dem trees, and push ober to de mud bank" (pointing to the great ridge of slime which festers in front of Leavenworth when the water runs low); "there wait till morning, looking at de stars ob heaven and de lights in dese houses all about; and when daylight come, creep out of de rushes and wade ober to the levée."

"Then you were free?" Sam answers with a smile.

"Had you any help, in your escape, from men on this

side the river?"—the slaves had always good friends in Kansas.

"No, sar; me got no help to 'scape; for me neber tell no one; 'cause me neber know afore the moment when me slip away. The Lord put it in my head. Me Methodist, sar; most nigger boy in Missouri, Methodist; me just come home from chapel, tinking of de wonderful ways of de Lord, when some one say, close in my ear, 'Rise up, Sam; run away and be a man.' It was de voice of de Lord; I know it well. At first, I not see what to do; me tink it quite wrong to run away and steal myself from boss—twelve hundred dollars. Den me tink, it must be right to obey de voice of de Lord, for me belong more to de Lord than to boss, and den I slip away into de woods."

"Of course you were followed?"

"Yes, sar," says Sam, putting the last of his fine flourishes upon my face; "boss come ober into Leavenworth, where he find me in de street. 'Come here, you damned nigger,' he say, pulling out his revolver, and catching me by de neck. He got a boat all ready; den some people come up. 'You let dat nigger go alone,' say one; 'Put a knife into de damned nigger,' say another. Den come a big row; dey fight for me all day; and my side win."

The date of this little history was six short years ago. Missouri, the fertile State beyond the river, the forests of which I have before me as I write, was then a slave State, with a sparse but fiery population of slave-breeders and slave-dealers. Nine years before that time—that is to say, so late as 1851, when the world was gathering for its jubilee of progress in Hyde Park—all this wide region, lying westward of the Missouri, from this river bank to the Rocky Mountains, was without a name. A host of wild Indian tribes,

Kansas, Cheyennes, Arappahoes, hunted over the great plains; following the elk, the buffalo, the antelope, to their secret haunts. Two great lines of travel had been cut through the prairies; one leading southward to Santa Fé in New Mexico, the other running westward, by the Platte River, toward Salt Lake and San Francisco; but the country was still an Indian hunting-ground, in which the white man could not lawfully reside. Half a dozen forts had been thrown up by the Government in this Indian country—Fort Bent, Fort Laramie, Fort Leavenworth, Fort Calhoun, Old Fort—but rather with a view to guarding the red man's rights than to helping the white traveler and trader in their need. But while the people of all nations were assembling in Hyde Park, and wondering at the magnificent country which had even then to be represented by an empty space, a swarm of settlers crossed the Missouri on rafts and in canoes, seized upon the bluffs between Fort Calhoun and Fort Leavenworth, threw up camps of log-huts, staked out the finest patches of land, especially those on the banks of creeks and pools, and so laid the foundation of what are now the populous and flourishing towns of Omaha, Nebraska, Atchison, and Leavenworth—cities of the free Territory of Nebraska, of the free State of Kansas.

Then commenced along the whole line of the Missouri River, that fitful, sanguinary strife, which earned for this region the mourning epithet of Bleeding Kansas. It lasted six years, and was a prelude to the Civil War.

Lawrence and Leavenworth were the results of this battle, of which Sam's little story may be taken as a sample.

Every one is aware that in the great feud between the free-soilers and the slaveholders of America, a truce had been made in 1820, which is known in history as the Missouri Compromise; by which act it was arranged between the parties that slavery should never be introduced into any western region lying beyond 36° 30′ of north latitude, excepting into such portion of Missouri as happened to stand above that line. For thirty years that truce held good, and even when the war of freedom raged against slavery on other fields, the Missouri Compromise was respected in the West. As the final conflict neared, the two parties in the struggle showed an equal discontent with that act of truce. The slaveowners in Missouri, having an exceptional advantage in their State of settling with their slaves above the prohibited line, desired to carry their domestic institution straight backward through the country in their rear to the foot of the Rocky Mountains, even if they should not be able to carry it thence to the Pacific Ocean. All the South went with them in their plans, though their action was in open conflict with the law. Secret societies sprang up in many States—Blue Lodges, Social Bands, Sons of the South, and many more, all pledged to aid these planters in carrying slavery westward of the Missouri River, in the teeth of their own compromise, in violation of their own truce.

The slaveholders of Missouri won one victory without a shot, in quietly, by a local act, which attracted no attention either in Boston or in New York, extending their own frontier westward, from the line drawn north and south through Kansas City, up to that of the river bank; adding six large and now populous counties to their State, and consequently to the area of the slave empire. This act was absolutely illegal; but no one in the eastern cities noted it until the bills effecting the change had become law, and the district had been peopled with masters and their slaves. The game appeared to be wholly in their hands. From this new slave soil, which lies on the opposite bank, in front of my window, Blue Lodges, Social Bands, and Sons of the South streamed over into these Delaware reserves, into these Kansas hunting-grounds; each boss, accompanied by his sons and his negroes, proceeding to help himself to the choicest lots. From St. Louis to New Orleans, their courage was applauded, their success predicted. In Washington, the slave-dealing senators, instead of calling these Missourian planters to account, and carrying out the law against them, sustained them in this outrage on the free States. By a course of partisan agitations they procured a fresh compromise, in which it was agreed that the question of slavery should be referred back, generally, to the people of any unorganized country claiming to come within the Union either as a Territory or as a State. Such an act was supposed by the planters of Missouri and Kentucky to be an open declaration that Kansas and Nebraska were to be organized as slave territories. But now New England came into the field. The conversion of Nebraska from free soil into slave soil, would have carried the line of slavery, in the western country, as high north as Boston! A Northern Emigrant Aid Society was founded in Massachusetts; sturdy farmers, fervent professors, youthful poets, yoked horses to their wagons and pushed across the continent toward the Missouri, sworn to settle on the new Indian lands, to accept the compromise of Congress, and, in their quality of free citizens, to vote a free constitution for Kansas. The Blue Lodges were already hutted at Leavenworth and Atchison; and when the first New Englander crossed the stream, being unable to answer these sentinels that he owned any niggers, they placed him in an open boat, without food, without oars, and sent him floating down the river amid derisive shouts and threats. A meeting of Sons of the South was called in Westport, on the Kansas border, but within the limits of Missouri, at which, after fiery eloquence, the following resolution was unanimously carried:

"That this association will, whenever called upon by any of the citizens of Kansas Territory, hold itself in readiness together to assist and remove any and all immigrants who go there under the auspices of the Northern Emigrant Aid Society."

The "Squatter Sovereign," a news sheet, published in the town of Atchison (founded and named by David Atchison, Senator of Missouri), put forth in an early number this declaration of the planters:

"We will continue to lynch and hang, tar and feather, and drown any white-livered abolitionist who dares to pollute our soil."

In July, 1854, thirty New England free-soilers crossed the river in open boats; they were well armed, and brought with them tents and provisions. Pushing up the Kansas River, they rested at the foot of a fine bluff, in the midst of a rolling prairie, covered with flowers. Pitching their tents, and beginning to fell wood for shanties, they called the place at which they camped the City of Lawrence, from the name of their popular purse-holder. In August, they were joined by seventy more, men, like themselves, well armed and resolute, prepared to found that city and to free that soil. Now had arrived the time for the Missouri men to show their spirit; a hundred Yankees, separated from their friends by six great States, had come into their midst, daring them to carry out their threat of either hanging, lynching, or drowning every one who should cross into Kansas without a negro slave in his train. Three hundred and fifty Sons of the South took horse, dashed over the shallow stream, and, having early in the morning formed a camp and thrown out pickets, sent word into Lawrence that these new settlers must quit the Territory, promising never to return. Three hours were given the free-soilers in which to pack their things and get ready to march. A Yankee bugle summoned the immigrants to arms; a civil but decisive answer was returned to the Missouri camp; and when the Sons of the South perceived that the Yankees were ready for the fray, and would be likely to fight it out so long as a man could hold his piece, they began to suspect each other, to doubt the goodness of their carbines, and to steal away. Dusk found their camp much thinned; dawn found it broken up and gone.

From that day Lawrence has grown and prospered. More than once it has fallen into Missourian hands, and the marks of grape and canister are seen upon some of its buildings; but its free-soil people have never been driven out, and it is now a charming little city, with the brightness of a New England town. It is the capital of a free State.

In these streets of Leavenworth many a fierce battle has been fought; the Sons of the South living close at hand, in a score of villages on yon wooded banks. Blood has been shed in almost every lane, especially at the voting times, when thousands of the Missourians used to come across in boats, take possession of the polling-booths, and return an overwhelming but fictitious majority in favor of a slave constitution. One good citizen, William Phillips, an advocate, was seized by Sons of the South for having signed a protest, as a lawyer, against the frauds which had disgraced the election; was forced into a boat and pulled up the river to Weston, on the Missouri side, where he was first tarred and feathered, then ridden on a rail, afterward put up to auction as a slave, and finally knocked down, amid frantic yells and menaces, to a negro-buyer. On his escape from Weston, Phillips returned to Leavenworth, resolute in his free-soil faith, and ready for the post of danger in every fray.

In another week from this date, it will be just ten years since a gang of Blue Lodges started from the opposite bank, landed on this levée, took possession of the town, which lay completely at their mercy for many hours, and under pretense of searching for arms—an utterly illegal search on their part—plundered and insulted the free-soilers in every house. Phillips refused to allow these fellows to come inside his door, on which the house was attacked and its owner killed. Before he fell, Phillips had shot two of his assailants dead. His house was burned to the ground, along with many other dwellings; and every free-soiler who could be found in Leavenworth was put on board a steamer and sent down the river.

Yet the New Englanders rallied to their flag, with growing numbers and glowing passions, becoming genuine settlers on the land, which the Missouri men were not. Here, and elsewhere, it has been shown that slavery, as a social system, lacked the solid fiber of a colonizing power. Slaves could not work the prairie land to profit; negroes, toiling under a master's eye and whip, required the rich soils of Mississippi and Alabama. With a pistol in one hand, a hoe in the other, these stout New Hampshire and Massachusetts lads fought on, toiled on, not only until they had gained a fair majority in the ballot-boxes, but won a full ascendency in the open field.

One of the comic incidents of this war was the bat-

3

tle of Black Jack, when Captain Clay Pate (ominous name!), a Virginian, who gave himself airs as a professional soldier, put himself at the head of fifty-six Sons of the South, and threatened to eat up old John Brown, of Osawatomie (afterward, unhappily, of Harper's Ferry), and his band of twenty-seven free-soilers. Pate had organized his force like a little army, with its horse and foot, its camp equipage, and its luggage train; and having just then been plundering Palmyra, a free-soil city, his baggage mules were heavily laden with the spoils of war. Brown made a fair fight by going out into the open plains. After a lusty tug, Clay Pate surrendered to the tough old fellow—himself, with his sword, his luggage train, all the spoils of Palmyra, twenty-one hale men, the whole of his dead and wounded, and his gorgeous tent.

In 1861, a few months after these citizens of Leavenworth had fought the battle for my friend Sam on this levée under my windows, the wounds of bleeding Kansas were stanched and healed by her admission into the Union as a free State.

CHAPTER III.

OVERLAND MAIL.

THE Overland Mail is one of the many great facts of the Great Republic. The postal returns tell you how many, you can imagine how important, are the letters going westward from the Atlantic cities to the Pacific cities. This mail is an Imperial institution.

While we were yet in London, dreaming of the details of our trip to the Rocky Mountains, it was always comforting to know that in going out among the wild Cheyennes and Sioux, we should find ourselves traveling in company with the Imperial Mail. Glancing at maps, scanning the vast spaces over which Cheyenne, Sioux, Comanche, and Arappahoe roam, one is apt to think there may lurk some spice of danger in such a journey; but then comes in the assuring thought that all along this route across the Prairies, across the Mountains, the American mails are being daily sent under powerful escorts of mounted men. Magic lies in this word "daily." That which is daily done must be safely done. Would he not be considered a sorry fellow who should fear to travel, even along a road infested by Sioux and rattlesnakes, under escort of United States troops in company with the Imperial Mail? When Speaker Colfax drove across the Plains last fall, to study the Indian question, the Mining question, and the Mormon question, among living Indians, Miners, and Mormons, instead of reading about them in government reports, he had only one general officer, one colonel, and twenty-four sabers galloping round his coach; yet he has publicly confessed that—although the redskins frightened him a little, and delayed his journey much, by plundering the stations in his front, and threatening every moment to have his scalp—he got safely through to Denver and Salt Lake.

Colfax, it is true, was a State official, and besides having his escort, he had also with him a considerable party of well-armed men. We are strangers, only two in number (so far as we can see); we are but slightly armed with Colts—since we have all along been dreaming, that if any fighting is to be done, it will be the work of our gallant escort, riding by our sides in defense of the Imperial Mail.

At Leavenworth we find the mail-agents, to whom we have letters from their chief in New York—as we have to every one employed by the Overland Mail Company along these tracks. Nothing can be more polite, more teasing, than their answers to our questions. Everything shall be done for us that can be, under the circumstances. We have come at an unlucky time. If we had only started a month sooner—if we had only stayed a month later—all would have been right. As it is, they will do their best; we may find things a little rough in the plains, but the agents have hardly any doubt that we shall get through to our journey's end.

Such words rather pique our fancies; since our health, our comfort, nay our lives, depend on the state of these plains. The fact is, the old road by way of the Platte River has been changed, by order of Congress, for a shorter cut through the vast Indian region of the Smoky Hill Fork; a shorter course, perhaps a better one, if the road had only first been made, bridged, and leveled; and if the Indian tribes who hunt buffalo and antelope across it had been either driven away or negotiated into peace. None of these things have yet been done.

Two great lines of travel have been driven by the white men through these plains: (1) the Platte road from Omaha and Atchison, by way of Kearney, Denver, and Salt Lake City, to San Francisco; (2) the Arkansas route, starting from Kansas City, and running by Fort Atkinson and Fort Wise to Puebla, the gold regions of Colorado, and thence to San Francisco. To the existence of these two roads the Indians seem to have submitted in despair. To the Platte road, they have ceased to show any strong opposition; having fought for it and lost it; first to the Mormon pilgrims, afterward to the gold-seekers, men who came into their country, driving before them trains of wagons, in bands of eighty or a hundred, and being armed with rifles and revolvers. To the Arkansas road, they nurse a sharper antipathy; since it is mainly a trial road, the right to travel over which has been purchased from their chiefs. Still, though it may be with a bad grace, and with many murmurs and protests, they have shown, and they still show, themselves ready to respect the white man as he passes through their lands by either of these two routes. But in the vast prairies between these tracks lie the great buffalo-runs, with the pastures feeding nearly all that remains in the Indian territories of the elk, the antelope, and the black-tailed deer. The buffalo-runs are also theirs, say the Cheyennes and the Arappahoes, and they must either keep them free from whites or else die like dogs. They say they will not die before the pale-faces; therefore, they must keep the buffalo-runs of Kansas and Colorado (as the white men have begun to call the plains—on paper) free from intrusion of mail and train.

Now the new route chosen by Congress for the Overland Mail, beyond all question a shorter line from St. Louis to San Francisco, cuts these buffalo-runs, these elk and antelope pastures, into two halves, and, as the Cheyennes and their allies, the Comanches, Arappahoes, Kiowas, Sioux, and Appaches, know very well, a railway is being built in the rear of this new mail; a railway which has already reached Wamego, near Fort Riley. Now the red men, knowing that the Mail is only a herald of much worse, and that the railway bell will quickly follow the crack of a driver's whip, have called a counsel of their tribes, and some say have concluded to try war against the whites for the possession of these buffalo-runs. When a railway engine, say the braves, shall have whistled away buffalo and antelope, it will be idle to raise the hatchet and draw the bow. Now is the time for them to strike; now or never; and, even if a few of the old men, gray with years and sad with sorrow, should recommend peace with their white neighbors, resignation to the will of their Great Spirit, the young braves, proud of their own strength, ignorant of the white men's numbers and resources, are said to be all for war. If the pale-face will not come into the buffalo-runs, they will keep the peace; if he will build his ranch, dig his well, and crop his grass, in these runs, the Cheyenne and the Arappahoes, aided by their brethren of the prairie and the hill country, will burn his shanty and take his scalp.

Such are the rumors that we hear from every mouth in Kansas. A small party, it is true, affects to regard the alarm of Leavenworth, Lawrence, and Wamego, as a panic having little or no foundation; partisans of the new route by way of Smoky Hill Fork, who wish to see it opened and kept open. They are few in number; and I do not hear that any of these heroes propose to settle, as yet, along the line of road though the Cheyenne country.

Now, as we gather from the mail-agents in Leavenworth, this is the line along which we are to go a journey of thirteen hundred miles; through a country the greater part of which has never been surveyed, through which there is no road, in which there are many streams and gullies, but not a single bridge; a country in which the hills, the creeks, the rivers, have as yet received no names, and in which the small military posts of the United States, themselves only corrals of logs and planks, lie two hundred miles apart.

Still, a line along which a mail so magnificent as that sent off from New York to San Francisco, not to speak of the thousand inferior cities which help to feed it, has been running its daily course, must be at least as safe as the line from Damascus to Banias. But on our saying this, or something like this, to a friend in Leavenworth, we learn, to our surprise, that there has never been a daily mail running along that line; that no such thing has ever yet been attempted; that there are neither men nor mules along the road to carry a daily mail; that, in point of fact, only one wagon, an empty wagon, has gone out in advance of us; that no one knows where that empty wagon is, or whether it will arrive in safety beyond the plains.

We look at our pistols, and feel the hair on our polls; the aspect of affairs is at once tragic and comic; and the kindly jokes of our friends in Pall Mall, as to the best way of enjoying a scalping-knife, are coming rather near and hot. We find, too, that we are the only passengers booked for the trip; so that the number of revolvers coming into play, in case of a scrimmage with the Cheyennes and Comanches, in aid of the military escort, seems to be reduced to two. All our acquaintance in this city urge us to get more and better arms; a suggestion in which the mail-agents cordially agree. The new arm of the West, called a Smith and Weston, is a pretty tool; as neat a machine for throwing slugs into a man's flesh as an artist in murder could desire to see. Bowie-knives, and such like, being useless to a Britisher who may have seen, but never practiced, the art of ripping up an adversary's side, like a Livornese and a Valentian, we buy a couple of these Smith and Westons, and then pay our fare of five hundred dollars to Salt Lake. An escort of veterans from the Potomac, aided by these six-shooters, will surely scare away all the Cheyennes, Arappahoes, and Sioux, who may be found clamoring about the rights of man, especially about the rights of red men, in the buffalo-runs.

The rail has been laid down so far west as Wamego—the Clear Springs—so called from the fact of there being no water in the village; and there we are to join the stage for our long ride; the stage being an old and much-worn Concord coach; a vehicle unknown in Europe, though its shapelessness and inconvenience might be hinted by cutting off the coupé of a French diligence, and bellying out the rotundo, until it could be supposed by its proprietor big enough to hold nine persons. This coach, when we come to it, is jammed full of mail-bags—forty-two hundredweight in all—State dispatches, love-letters, orders, bills of exchange, invoices of account, all sorts of lively and deadly missiles, the value of which to governor, maid, clerk, banker, emigrant, and dealer must be far beyond price; and here are five passengers on the books to take their chances of the road (three of them being a young woman and two babies), who, having duly paid their fares and got their tickets, have a right to be taken on. But this going on is a thing impossible, as a glance at the coach and the mail-bags tells the experienced eye of the Wamego agent. What shall be done? The mail must go, even though the passengers should have to wait in Wamego for a month; and as the driver is already cracking his whip, and belching out volleys of oaths, which the lady and her two babies are obliged to hear (poor things!), the agent quickly makes up his mind, bids us get aboard—men and revolvers—says one sharp word to the driver, when away we plunge into the dust, leaving our female fellow-traveler, astonished, protesting, in the cloud of mud and sand. We look at each other wonderingly; for in this Paradise of Women, a petticoat is accustomed to carry all things before it—the best room at a hotel, the highest place at table, the first seat in a coach, in spite of your prior right. Ha! the revolvers have done it. As we are dashing off, we look out of window for the troops who are to be our companions in the Cheyenne country. None are in sight! "The escort," says the agent, "will join you at Junction City, if there should seem to be any need; you must consider the mail as starting from Junction City;" and as he courteously waves his hand, we roll away into the dust.

In a couple of hours we pass Fort Riley; in two or three more we are at Junction City; a city of six wooden shanties, where we alight to sup off hot cake, tea, and tomatoes; and about an hour later, in the midst of a pleasant chat with the landlord of our hostelry, we hear the driver's cry, "On board!" Rushing out into the night, our belts swung round us, our pistols loaded for the fray, we find that our big Concord coach has been exchanged for a light prairie wagon, smaller in size, frailer in build, without a door, with very bad springs, and with canvas blinds for windows. Into this wagon, the letter-bags have been forced by an ingenious violence, the art of which is only known in the Western country, with so neat a finish that it would seem impossible to insert two human beings between the mail-bags and the wall. But, in time, by doubling our legs across each other, by craning our necks, by slinging our elbows into straps, the feat is accomplished; the two human beings aforenamed having been persuaded, much against their grain, to wriggle themselves between the bags, under a promise that the said bags will shake down in a few minutes so as to give plenty of room. This is not easy, we suggest to each other, since we have our own small litter of pistols, books, maps, brandy-flasks, shawls, night-caps, potted meats, cigar-cases, sticks, umbrellas, and the like, about our feet. We begin to fear, that unless the load shall happen to shake down considerably, we may chance to have a bad week of it.

But see, this fellow is about to start, though the escort is not in sight!

Whew! We speak to the agent: "Well," says he, in effect, "the officer in charge will not lend us any troops; his command is very low just now; the country is disturbed by Indians in his front and flank; he has enough to do to hold his own in the post. But," the good-natured agent adds, for our comfort, "you will find the road all right; some troops went up the plains yesterday; you will pass them ahead; good-by!" And we are off.

The truth now flashes on our minds like a revelation:

We are the escort!

Not a soul goes out with the mail, either now or

through the journey, except the boy who drives the mules (changed every forty or fifty miles on the road); no escort, no mail-agent, nobody save ourselves. I cannot say that in my travels I have ever seen the fellow of this prairie mail. In the most dangerous district crossed by traveler and trader west of Chinese Tartary, the New York and St. Louis people trust the most important mail leaving any city in the world excepting that from London, without a guard. No one doubts that the Cheyennes and Sioux are now holding council on these plains, even if they have not as yet gone out upon the war-path; nay, that they have given notice, after their Indian manner, of an intention to stop the road; yet, the mail is going into their buffalo-runs, in spite of all warnings, without a single guard, even such an old fogie as used to blow his horn and shoulder his blunderbuss on Hounslow Heath.

Perhaps I am forgetting the confidence which they place in their English guard. They know that we are armed; they feel a reasonable certainty that we know how to use our tools. "The road is a little rough," says one of the stock-keepers as we roll from his station into the black midnight and the unknown prairie; "but the Government will do nothing for us, until it has been roused by a great disaster; they care nothing for a few lives, especially for the lives of poor teamsters and drivers." One passing friend rather hopes that we may be scalped, as he thinks that such an event might create a pleasant and profitable sensation in New York.

We have paid five hundred dollars for escorting the United States mail to Salt Lake. It is a high price, but the privilege might be worth the cost, if we had a mind to use the facilities which fall about our feet and court us to see them. This mail is wholly at our mercy. Six nights and days we are shut up with our pistols and the United States correspondence; our sole companion being the boy outside, who cannot see into the wagon when the flaps are down. In one place a bag falls out of the wagon, and would certainly be left behind on the plain, but that we call the driver to stop and pick it up. In another place one of the bags bursts open, when a stream of letters comes flowing about our feet. We have only to help ourselves; read what we like, pocket what we like. Might not the secrets of a single letter be worth, in some hands, more than the five hundred dollars we have paid to guard them?

CHAPTER IV.

THE PRAIRIES.

Of all the States and Territories which still exist on paper, Kansas may be described as the Prairie State. Nebraska, Colorado, and the Indian territory are covered by prairies; great grassy plains, not level, as many persons think, but rolling uplands, rising from the river to the mountains in a series of ascending billows, always of gentle grade, often of enormous sweep. But Kansas is beyond dispute the region in which these plains display themselves on the largest scale, and with their points most perfect.

On the old maps, which show the natural history of each section of the Great Republic, the district now called Kansas will be found figured by a buffalo, as Nebraska is marked by an antelope, Iowa by a beaver, Utah by a bear. Across these plains, up from the Indian territory on the south, come the wild and multitudinous herds on which the Cheyennes, the Arappahoes, the Comanches, and the Kiowas feed.

For two hundred miles westward from the Missouri, the plains are green with trees, most of all so along the lines of the Kansas River and its many creeks and inlets. The wood is hickory, walnut, oak, and water-elm. Maple and chestnut are not found in the plains. The land is alive with shrubs and flowers; among which flourish wild marigolds, shamrock, water-lily (in the pools), rosin-weed, stink-weed, and sunflowers. These sunflowers of the West are not the tawny gauds of our cottage gardens; big and brazen bachelors, flourishing on a single stock; but little golden flowers, clustering in bunches, and, like our buttercups, numberless as the stars of heaven. In many parts, the prairie is alive with their golden light. A white frame house—on this side of the river called a ranch—peeps out here and there from beneath the foliage, having its green blinds, its bit of garden, its sheep-fold. Herds of horses can be seen on the rolling plateau. Here you have a drove of cattle, there a long wagon train. Anon we pass an Indian village, where some families of Delawares, sent out from those Atlantic forests now occupied by the quays and palaces of Dover, Baltimore, and Philadelphia, have taken a fitful and precarious root in the soil. These Delawares have long since buried the hatchet, put on pantaloons, forgotten the use of war-paint. Some of them make farmers; living on friendly terms with their pale neighbors; even marrying their sons into the families of whites. We pass a Shawnee village, of which the same things may be said. White men's ranches stand among them; dangerous neighbors to these natives; for the pale-face, finding his way through the cracks and crannies of Indian character, making himself first useful, then formidable, to the tribe, commonly ends the connection with them by becoming lord and owner of their lands.

The air is warm and sweet; a perfume of prairie flowers mingling with the distant snows of the sierras. The sky is intensely blue, with none of that golden haze which frets the eye in our own southern landscapes. A patch of cloud, intense and vivid in its whiteness, dots and relieves the grand monotony of azure, so as to combine in one field of view the distinctive beauties of a Sicilian and an English sky.

As we draw away from the river, the woodland scenery disappears; the country opens to the right and left; the plains swell languidly into greater breadths of upland. About the creeks and pools, for the most part dry on the surface, there are still some shrubs; the wild convolvulus is common; also the Virginian creeper; more than all others, a plant called the rosin-weed. This rosin-weed appears to be Nature's choice in the way of verdure and adornment. When the ground is either cleared by fire, or cut by the prairie breaker, the rosin-weed disappears; the fire-weed springs up in its place, and dies in its turn after two or three crops, in some places after one crop; when this second weed is succeeded by the tickle-grass. (P. S.—Don't let the tickle-grass get up your legs—for it seems to be alive; to know you don't like it—and to creep up your pantaloons the faster you fret and worry.) After this grass come three or four species of wild grasses; and after these fertilizers sown by Nature have dropped their decaying blades into the ground, the farmer may come with his rake and his seed to a soil made ready for his use.

Driving on night and day (as men must drive who have charge of an imperial mail), we begin to leave all trace of man and his arts, save one, behind. A prairie hen clucks in the wild sage; a rattlesnake coils among the sunflowers; a wolf steals noiselessly along the road; dead mules, dead horses, dead oxen, strew the path, on which the carrion-crow, the raven, and the wolf, find food; these white horns and skeletons of man's servants being often the only traces of his ever having found his way across the plains.

By daring ingenuity and patience, the Western trader has pushed a way for himself across this difficult trail of land; making an opening for trade and travel between the Atlantic and Pacific Oceans. He has done this feat as a private man, without help from the State, without cheers from any learned body, at a cost of blood and money which can never be counted upon earth; and for this reason; the Western man thinks nothing of blood, not much of treasure, when he regards them as being invested in a business that will pay. Holding his life in his hand, this reckless, jovial fellow, swearing overmuch, brimming with help when help is of use, is careless of blood—either his own or yours—far beyond an Arab, almost beyond a Chinese. This path through the prairie has been paved by him, again and again, with bones; but the trace of his passage, of his suffering, dies away out of sight with the autumnal flowers. Nature is here too strong for man to do more than throw a trail upon her landscape, which may show itself for a day in the bunch-grass, among the gray sand, and then vanish from sight like the track of a ship at sea. The prairie is not man's home. Even if he had time to plant and reap it, he could hardly grow a blade of grass, a stalk of Indian-corn, on these open flats, where myriads of locusts clatter through the air, devouring in their hunger every green leaf and twig. We ride past a lonely ranch, near which the daring and hopeful tenant had planted a field with corn, for his winter food. Look at the poor man's harvest! Legions of locusts are upon his crop; and every ear that should have made him bread has been picked away.

In these uplands, Nature is lord and king. Snipes and plovers abound; blackbirds, carrion-crows, ravens, and vultures are also seen. Flowers are still common; most of all, the dwarf sunflower, which is sown so thickly through the landscape as to give it a shimmer of burning gold. The dwarf sunflower is, in fact, *the* prairie flower; lighting up the face of Nature everywhere in our route, from the Missouri River to the Great Salt Lake; in some parts growing low and stunted, the stalk not a foot long, the flower not higher than a common marigold, in others rising ten or twelve feet high, with clusters of flowers each as big as a peony. Ants are toiling in the ground; the little prairie dogs—comedians of the waste—sit crowing on their mounds of earth, until we drive close up to them, when they utter a quick laugh, and with a shout of mockery plunge into their holes head downward, disappearing from our sight with a last merry wag of their tails. Owls, prairie-dogs, and rattlesnakes live on the most friendly terms with each other; the owls and snakes dwelling in the prairie-dogs' holes, and sometimes, I fancy, eating the dogs when they happen to be short of food. It may only be a superstition; but the teamsters and drivers across the plains have a fixed belief that flesh of the prairie-dog is poisonous in a peculiar way, and that men who eat of it become insane. Once, in a stress of hunger, I was obliged to kill one.

"Lord!" cries the boy at the ranch, "you will never eat that, sir?"

"Why not? I am hungry enough to eat a Cheyenne."

"Well, sir," says the lad, "we prairie folks consider the owl, the rattlesnake, and the prairie-dog to be all of a kith and kin, the Devil's own spawn, and that anybody who eats them will go mad."

"Put him in the pan; I must take my chance." The flesh proved to be delicious, with something like the taste of squirrel; and on seeing me suck the savory bone, the prairie-boy instantly seized and devoured a leg. I hope the teamsters and drivers will continue in their want of faith as to the wholesomeness of prairie-dogs; for the antics of these little animals should make them dear to every man who has to cross these plains, in which the supply of comedy is extremely scant.

After passing Fort Ellsworth—a collection of wooden shanties, in which lie a hundred men, not very well armed (we hear), and careful to keep their feet within bounds, leaving the Cheyennes and Arappahoes alone —we have before us a stretch of two hundred and twenty miles of dangerous country, without a single post for its protection; a country in which there is no town, no camp, no ranch, except the log stables, now being built for the overland mules. We are alone with Nature and the imperial mail. Around us, we have many signs that the Cheyennes and Arappahoes are hovering nigh; at times we catch visible evidence of a scout on some distant ridge of the Smoky Hill, and see the curl of blue smoke from some neighboring creek.

We are now between Big Creek and Big Timber Station, in the very heart of the wild game country; a country of long, low, rolling hills, covered with a short sweet grass—bunch-grass—on which the buffalo loves to feed. We have ceased firing at rattlesnakes and prairie chickens; reserving our cartridges for the nobler uses of self-defense; though we are tempted, now and then, to try a shot at some elk, or antelope, or black-tailed deer. The great game being buffaloes, against the tough hides of which our small six-shooters are of no avail, we sit quietly in our wagon watching the herds troop by; in lines, in companies, in droves, in armies, the black and shaggy beasts go thundering in our front; sometimes from north to south, sometimes from south to north; but always scudding in our front, and always across our line of march. The plains are teeming with life; most of all with buffalo bulls and cows. For forty hours we have now had them always in our sight; thousands on thousands, tens of thousands after tens of thousands; a countless host of untamed animals; all of them fit for human food; enough, we should think, to stock Arappahoe, Comanche, and Cheyenne wigwams to the end of time. Once or twice the driver tries a shot; but fear of the red-skins commonly checks his wish to fire.

This buffalo, which is the white man's sport, is also the red man's food; and a Cheyenne warrior cannot be made to see why a pale-face should come into his country and destroy the buffalo for the sake of a little amusement. A white man who has to kill buffalo to live, the Indian can comprehend, though he may have to suffer in estate by that white man's rifle; but a man who shoots buffalo for sport, having no wish to eat it, is a mystery of conduct to which any red-skin would gladly put an end by tomahawk and scalping-knife.

As we ascend the plains, a series of rolling steppes, in no part level for a dozen miles, the sun grows fiercer overhead, the sands hotter beneath our feet. Snakes, lizards, locusts, swarm on the ground and in the air; the heat of noon is terrible; sometimes, in the breathless noon, reminding me of the Jordan valley. Water is scarce and bad, and the dry, hot fever of external nature creeps into and corrupts your blood.

The fourth day of our journey on the plains is one of tropical warmth. That short, sweet grass on which the buffalo loves to feed, is now behind us in the lower plains, where moisture, though it may be scant, is not unknown, as it seems to be here for many a league on league. Our path is strewn with skeletons of oxen, mules, and horses; waste of the life that helps to keep up an overland trade from the river to the sea. Ravens and wolves are seen fattening on these remains of mule and ox; tame enough to be hardly scared from their meal by the crashing of our wagon wheels through the burning sand. A golden haze, the effect of heat, envelops the earth, and the mirage tantalizes our parching throats with a promise of water,—never to be reached. A stillness as of death is round about us. In the west we see a little cloud, not bigger when we see it first, than a prairie-dog; anon it is the size of a fox, of a buffalo, of a mountain; in a few minutes it has covered the sky with one black and sulphurous pall, out of which the lightnings begin to leap and dance.

A flash comes through the still and silent air, like a gunshot, suddenly, with a sharp surprise. It is followed by a wail of wind and rain, which lifts the sand from the ground into the air, and drives it into the canvas flaps of our mountain wagon, splashing us with mud and mire. No care can keep the deluge out; and in a few minutes we are drenched and smothered. Four or five hours that storm of sand and rain drives heavily against us. Two or three times the mules stand still in fear; turn their backs to the heavenly fire, refusing to go forward under any encouragement of either voice or whip. Were they not fastened to the coach, they would fly before the tempest; bolting for their lives until the hurricane should have drooped and died. Being chained to the wagon, they can only stand and moan. When the storm is spent, the stars come peeping out; the air is chill and sweet; and we drag our way along the wet and smoking plain.

Want of sleep, want of food, want of exercise—or we are jolted over the unmade tracks all night, all day, stopping at the creeks for a little water, at the log-stables for the change of mules, but a few moments only—have made us ill. We obtain no proper supplies of food and drink, and we are cooped up in a wagon designed (one might suppose) by some infernal genius as a place of torture; a machine in which you can neither sit, nor stand, nor lie down. My friend is suffering from bilious sickness; I am tormented by eruptions on the skin; yet, even with these quick monitors of evil in us, we are every day astonished by the sudden gush of life, which comes with the morning light. We crawl from our miserable den—a den without a door, without a window, without a step—with nothing save a coarse convas cover for a roof, coarse canvas flaps for sides,—into the dust and filth of a stable; banged and beaten and jolted, until our heads are swollen, our faces bruised, our hands lacerated; sleepless, hungry; our temples racked by pain, our nostrils choked with sand, our limbs stiffened and bent with cramps; but after rinsing our mouths and dipping our heads in some little creek, the water of which we dare not drink, and pushing on three or four miles ahead of the stage, winding up the long prairie swells, and breathing the morning air, we pause in our brisk step, look at each other, and smile. The effect is magical; all pain, all cramp, all languor, have disappeared; the blood flows freely, the lungs act softly, the nostrils seem to open from within, and the eyes appear to cast out sand and dust by some internal force. If we could only now get food, we feel strength enough to defy all other forms of pain.

But food is a thing we cannot get.

CHAPTER V.

PRAIRIE INDIANS.

THE red men of these prairies have been taking counsel together in a field near Fort Ellsworth, as to the policy of allowing the white men, headed by their Big Father in Washington, to open a new road through their country by way of this Smoky Hill Fork; and the warlike tribes of this region, the Cheyennes, and Arappahoes, aided and supported by allies from the South and from the North, the powerful Sioux, the savage Kiowas, the clever Comanches, and the swift Apaches, are said to have resolved on war.

These Indians say they have been deceived by the white men; this they always say when going out on the war-path; for a red man's pride will not suffer him to acknowledge, even to himself, that he has done any wrong—that he has broken any pledge. In these frontier quarrels, the Indian, by his own confession, is always right. So far as we can learn from these Cheyennes and their allies, it would seem that early in the spring of this present year (1866) Major Wyncoop, an officer of Government, employed in the task of making treaties—a brisk and profitable branch of the public service—had been among these prairie hunters, giving them arms and blankets, flour and whisky, in exchange for a promise of good behavior on the roads in respect to emigrant wagons and merchants' trains. Wyncoop, they say, had told them, by word of mouth, to have no fears about the safety of their buffalo-runs, since the Big Father in Washington had no intention of opening any new road by way of the Smoky Hill. After Wyncoop left them, they began to fear that he had been a bearer of lies; for they heard that, even while he was sleeping in their lodge, eating elk with Roman Nose, Black Hawk, and Spotted Dog, Cheyenne chiefs and warriors, the white men had been laying their plans for cutting a road straight toward the heart of these buffalo lands.

Of course they have heard from the pale-faces that all roads should be free and open. They have been told that the road from St. Louis to New York is just as free to a red man as to a white man; and they have been also told, as though this second thing followed from the first, that the path from St. Louis to Salt Lake should be as free to the white man as it is to the red; but Roman Nose, Black Hawk, and Spotted Dog are men too subtle to be taken in by what they call baby-talk. They answer, that in their sense of the word yon road from St. Louis to New York is not open. Would Black Hawk be allowed to hunt through the fields of Ohio? Would Spotted Dog be suffered to pitch his lodge in the streets of Indianapolis? Could Roman Nose, on that road from St. Louis to New York, kill and eat sheep and cow, animals which have replaced his own buffalo and elk? If not, how, they ask, can the track be called open to them, dwellers in wigwams, hunters of wild game? These Cheyennes, these Arappahoes and Sioux, are as well aware as any pale-face in Washington, that their laws are not our laws, their liberties not our liberties. If it were one of their Indian fashions to have a party-cry, they would probably raise the shout of "The hunting-ground for the hunter!"

Roman Nose and Spotted Dog tell us that the very best hunting-grounds now left to the red man are these prairie lands, lying along and around the Smoky Hill Fork; a dry and sandy ravine, more than a hundred miles in length, stretching at the foot of this high ridge or bluff, called Smoky Hill from the cap of mist which commonly floats above its crest. Here grow the sweet bunch-grasses which the buffalo loves to chew, and hither come those herds of game on which the Indian lodge depends for its winter store. Disturb these herds in their present quarters, and whither can they flee? Southward lies the Arkansas road from St. Louis to Santa Fé; northward lies the Platte road from Omaha to Salt Lake. No game will linger on the white man's track; and to make a path for the mail by way of Smoky Hill Fork is simply to drive away the red man's food. Elk and antelope may wander into close vicinity to a trader's and an emigrant's trail; buffalo, a bolder and fiercer, but more cautious animal, never.

"White man come, buffalo go," says Black Hawk, with his sharp logic; "when buffalo gone, squaw and papoose die."

From Black Hawk's point of view, the policy of resisting our encroachments on their hunting-fields is beyond dispute.

A second cause has helped to create the trouble which besets us on these plains.

One of the great feuds which divide Eastern America from Western America—the States lying east of the Mississippi from the States and Territories lying west of the Big Drink—has its birth in the question, What line of policy should be followed by the Government in dealing with the red men? The Eastern cities are all for rose-water and baby-talk; the Western cities are all for revolvers and bowie-knives. Each section has its sentiment and its passion. In Boston, no one believes that a red Indian can do wrong; in Denver, no one believes that a red Indian can do right. Each party accuses the other of ignorance and petulance; Massachusetts looking on the red-skin solely in his romantic lights, as a representative of tribes and nations, dear to art and poetry, which are rapidly passing into the land of dreams; Colorado looking upon him solely in his prosaic aspects of a thief, a beggar, an assassin, who may have stolen white women and scalped white men. In Massachusetts, in Rhode Island, in New Hampshire, almost everybody has either made a sketch, composed a song, or read a romance, about the Indian; while in Colorado, in New Mexico and California, almost everybody has had a kinsman butchered, or a kinswoman carried off by that romantic personage—a difference which may very well account for the radical opposition of ideas as to a true Indian policy regarding him in the East and in the West. Being strong in Washington, Massachusetts has commonly had her own way in Kansas, and wherever a judge's writ will run; being near to the plains, Colorado has sometimes had her own way in the lonely grass land and the nameless creek.

One sudden blow Colorado dealt last year at her savage enemy, when a body of volunteer horse, under Colonel Shevington, broke into a Cheyenne camp at Sand Creek, a little way in our front, where a thousand Indians had encamped, under the command of White Antelope, an aged and renowned Cheyenne warrior. The Colorado volunteers, raised by orders from Washington, rode in upon these Indians, shooting down brave and squaw and papoose in undistinguishing hate and wrath. White Antelope fell like the hero in a poet's tale; for, seeing that defense was idle, that escape was impossible, he sprang up a mound of sand, and, throwing open his embroidered jacket, bade the pale-faces fire. With twenty slugs in his body, he rolled upon the earth. Most of his followers fell around his corpse—old and young, men and women, wrinkled warriors and puling infants. Sixteen of the volunteers were slain; and their comrades rode back into Denver, covered, as they imagined, with the glory of their deed.

In New England, this raid upon the Cheyenne camp is everywhere denounced as the Indian massacre; in the ranches of these prairies, in the cities near the mines, it is everywhere celebrated as the big fight. Your opinion on the point is held to be a test of your good sense. In Boston, any approval of the big fight would subject you to a social ban; in Denver, any denunciation of the Indian massacre would bring a bowie-knife into your side. After saying so much, I need scarcely add, that westward of the Missouri I have never met a man who does not say that the Sand Creek affair, though terrible enough in some of its details, was a good and wholesome act of severity, an act that ought to be repeated twice a year, until every Indian tribe has been swept away from these plains.

Eastern men assert, that when Shevington attacked the Indian camp the Cheyennes were at peace with the whites, and that the American flag was floating above White Antelope's tent. Shevington denies these facts, asserting that the Cheyenne camp had been the refuge of dog soldiers, a band of red-skin outlaws and assassins, who had been plundering settlements and murdering teamsters and emigrants for many months, a fact which he and his Colorado friends assert was proved: in the first place, by the Indians having had a white girl, of sixteen, and three young white children in that very camp, whom they sold, after much palaver, to the citizens; in the second place, by their boast of having two other white women in their lodges, whom they would neither give away nor sell; in the third place, by the white men finding, when their camp was taken, a heap of rings, ribbons, photographs, and human scalps.

One act of atrocity, committed by these Indians, is said to have roused, in a peculiar manner, the indignation of Denver. In a ranch on Running Creek, near that city, lived with his wife and two children, a man named Hungate—an honest man, a good farmer, who stood well with his neighbors. The red men had swept down upon his lonely farm, had driven off his cattle, had burnt his ranch, had violated his wife, had massacred his children, and shot himself. The heads of all the Hungate family were scalped, the bodies hacked and pounded. When they were found in this mutilated state, they had been borne into Denver City, and made a public show, like the wounded men of Paris in '48, rousing the hot blood of Colorado into madness.

White Antelope was made to answer for the blood of Hungate.

Two of the scalps, which the volunteers under Shevington found at Sand Creek after the fight, are said to have been fresh: one, a white man's scalp, was hardly cold; a second, a white woman's scalp, was declared by the army surgeon to have been drawn within ten days.

Feud begets feud, and the strife of last year can only be answered by strife in the coming fall. A son of White Antelope is now going about the plains calling on the tribes and nations to rise and avenge his father's death, which Roman Nose, Black Hawk, Tall Buffalo, Lance, and Little Blanket, all powerful chiefs, are said to be willing enough to do, since they may gain a rare opportunity of gratifying their passion for blood while clearing these favorite buffalo-runs of all white disturbers of the Indian game.

CHAPTER VI.

THE RED MAN.

A LONG line of poems and novels leads an English reader into habits of looking on the red man as a picturesque figure of the prairie and the lake, rather than as a living force in the midst of American cities. We have lodged the Indians in our minds as we have the men who exist for us only in tales and plays. When we recall either an Iroquois or a Mohican, he presents himself to our vision in his war-paint, in his hunting gear; he is sitting in council under the Treaty tree, seeing God in clouds and hearing Him in the wind. We note him stealing forth with Hawk-eye on the war-path, watching over Minnehaha in the wigwam, tearing himself from his old hunting-grounds on the Ohio, starting for his new home in the unknown West. We connect him with aged hemlocks, running waters, and silent valleys. But whether he comes before us in his hunting gear or in his paint and feathers, with a pipe of peace in his mouth, or a scalping-knife raised in his hand, he is ever the same for us: a being of the mind, a picture, a poem, a romance; not a man of flesh and blood, endowed with senses, rich in passions, fruitful in ideas, one strong to resist, one swift to impress, all men who may come into contact with him.

In the United States people know him better. The red man lives among them like the black man: less ductile in genius, more prolific in ideas; having his own policy, his own arts, his own traditions; with a power, which the black man has not, of giving back, no less than taking, in the way of thought. They have to deal with him from day to day as with a man having rights in the soil which no Yengee can deny, which no honest Yengee feels the wish to dispute.

No race of men ever yet drove out another race of men from any country, taking their lands and cities from them, without finding on the spot which they came to own, a local genius, which affected their polity, their usages, and their arts. Man is a living power, acting and reacting on his fellow, through a natural law. All force is relative. If the strong act upon the weak, the weak react upon the strong. Numbers are strength; and if the higher race should have the disadvantage of being few in number, they will fall in some measure to the level of their slaves, in spite of their first superiority in physical gifts and in moral power. Thus, the Roman masters of Greece adopted the art, the language, the religion, and at length the country they had won by the sword. The Norman hero became an English gentleman, helping to make that name the proudest title borne on earth. After three generations, the settlers under Strongbow proved themselves more Irish in feeling than the Celts. Duke Rollo's soldiers softened into Sicilians. The Mantchoo Tartars have become Chinese. Even in cases where fire and sword have been used to thin off the original people, the effect has been pretty much the same. The Israelites were told to cut down the Hittites and Amorites, the Canaanites, Perizzites and Jebusites; and they slew the men of these nations without mercy, as they had been commanded from God. Yet the customs and ideas of these heathens clung to the soil, and generation after generation of the chosen people fell into sin by running after the native gods. Dagon, Moloch, Ashtaroth, drew men away from Jehovah; and the arts of Tyre and Sidon acted upon those whom the sword of Jabin could not drive from the land. In like fashion, those red men whom our fore-comers found on the Atlantic seaboard, and whom they have been pushing back, at first toward the Alleghanies, then to the Ohio and the Wabash, afterward to the Mississippi, and at length beyond the great river as far west as the Kansas and the Arkansas, have left the traces of their former presence in the national mind; in the popular politics, in the popular science, in the popular life. They have done so in places from which they have wholly disappeared, as well perhaps as in districts where they still exist; among the Spiritualists of New England, among the Mormons of Salt Lake valley. Man is what he eats; and a nation grows into the likeness of that which it absorbs. Where the Indian has been destroyed by assimilation, the pale-face must have undergone a change, to be measured by the amount of resisting power; a quality in which some tribes of these red-skins are pre-eminently rich. When the Indian has survived the shock of conflict with the pale-face, as at Oneida Creek, at Wyandotte, at St. Mary's Mission, and in many other places, the power of acting and reacting on the whites is still in force, affecting the national character in a way which no man could have foreseen, and no one will now deny.

The Anglo-Saxon power of assimilation is very great; but the Cheyenne and the Dakota present to it, perhaps, the very hardest meal it has ever been called upon to digest. The Anglo-Saxon has not gone far in the process of eating up the red man; yet he shows by a hundred signs the effect of that indigestible meal upon his health. The Indian fiber is exceedingly tough. Can any one say whether, up to this moment, though the white men have an easy mastery, the action of the white men on the red has been stronger than that of the red men on the white?

Let those who think so come into these Western plains, into the lands where red and white men live together in anything but harmony. They will find that each has acquired the other's vices; that while the Indian has learned how to beat his pale brother in debauchery, the white man has only come to equal his red brother in ferocity and craft. If the Yengee has taught the Indian to drink whisky, the Indian has taught the Yengee to keep squaws. Nearly all the old trappers and teamsters, who have lived among Indians, are polygamists: Jem Baker, of Clear Creek, has two squaws; Mageary, of South Platte, has three; Bent, of Smoky Hill, is said to have married six. As an Indian chief said to Colonel Marcy, "The first thing a Yengee wants in the plains is plenty wife." If Little Bear drinks and beats his squaw to death, Jem Smithers has learned to make a jest of taking scalps. I hear anecdotes in these plains to make the blood run cold. Jack Dunkier, of Central City, scalped five Sioux in the presence of his white comrade. The same Colorado boy is said to have ridden into Denver with the leg of an Indian warrior slung to his saddle; a leg which he had cut from the trunk, and on which he reported that he had been living for two whole days. No one believed his story; but a boast is in its way a fact, and there is no doubt that in Denver City a white man openly boasted of having boiled and eaten steaks from a human thigh. A Pawnee would glory in such a deed; vaunting it afterward in the meetings of his tribe. The Yengee quickly learns to imitate the red man's crimes. One of the Sand Creek volunteers returned to Denver with a woman's heart on the head of a pole; having shot the squaw, ripped her breast open, and plucked out her heart. No one blamed him, and his trophy was received with shouts by a rabble in the public streets. I am glad to say, that white opinion underwent a change, even in the rough mining districts, with respect to this man's doings; not that any one dreamed of arresting him for his crimes, not that his comrades in the ranks thought any worse of him for his lark; but the jokes of the grog-shop, the gaming-house, and the smoking-room turned rather freely on his deed, and the fellow being deficient in wit and patience, fled away from the town, and never came back. In a Cheyenne brave, such a crime as his would have raised a warrior to the rank of a chief. One offence, though it implied no loss of life, appeared to me more revolting than even the murder of a squaw, of a papoose — the violation of Indian graves by the Yengees. A Government train, passing through the Indian territory, came upon a heap of stones and rocks, which the knowing trapper who accompanied the train pointed out as the burial-place of some great chief: when the Western boys ripped it open, kicked the bones of the dead warrior, and picked up the bow and arrows, the spoon of buffalo horn (an officer of the United States army gave me that horn as a keepsake!), the beads and ornaments, the remnants of a buffalo robe in which the chief had been wrapped for his final rest.

Along with many of their vices, the Yengees have borrowed from the Indians some of their simple virtues — a spirit of hospitality, a high respect for the plighted word, a sovereign contempt for pain and death.

The red men have taught the whole world how to smoke the Indian weed. Have they received from the pale-face any one boon to compare with this gift from the savage to the civilized man?

It is no figure of speech to say that in White America red influence is very widely spread and very strongly felt, alike in the sphere of institutions and in the sphere of thought.

The confederacy of the Five Nations was the type adopted by the whites when framing the confederacy of the Thirteen Colonies; not only as regards the principle of their Union, but also in respect to its most original details. The Iroquois had invented the theory of State Rights, which the colonists borrowed from them; an indefinable and dangerous theory, implying a power of separate action, perhaps of withdrawal, from the Union; leading to a thousand quarrels, and to a civil war, of which the end has not yet been reached. These Iroquois had adopted the theory of extending their power and territory, not by adding to the limits of any existing nation of the confederacy, but by bodily introducing new tribes and nations into union; a novel principle of political growth, which the white men also borrowed from them. Under these two principles, the Five Nations had grown into Eight Nations; and the Thirteen Colonies, following in their wake and carrying on their work, have expanded into Forty-six States and Territories.

In the conference of 1774, when commissioners from Pennsylvania, Maryland, and Virginia, went to consult the Iroquois sachems at Lancaster, the great chief Casannatego addressed them in terms which a Greek member of the Achaian League might have used: "Our wise forefathers established union and amity between the Five Nations. This union has made us formidable. This has given us great strength and authority with our neighboring nations. By showing the same method, you will acquire fresh strength and power. Therefore, I counsel you, whatever befalls you, never to fall out with one another." Official reports to Congress from the Indian bureau confess that this Iroquois confederation was the true political germ of the United States.

The men of the Five Nations had very high notions of liberty, and that on both the public and the domestic side. Every man was considered equal to his fellow. The sachem, even when he came of a ruling stock, was elected to his office. They had no hereditary rank, and no other titles than the names which described their function, such as warrior, counselor, and seer. They said that all men of Iroquois race, together with their allies, were born free and equal with each other; and that no man, thus freely born, could ever be made a slave. Indeed, they set their faces against slavery in any form. No Iroquois could own his fellow. If enemies were taken by him in war, they were either put to death or naturalized and adopted into his tribe. Nay, the sentiment of freedom was so strong in the Five Nations that they declared the soil itself free, so that no slave could be found within the districts hunted by these red men, even when negro slaves were everywhere being bought and sold in the streets of Boston, Philadelphia, and New York. In time, however, some of the less noble tribes of Indians—Cherokees, Choctaws, and Chickasaws—learned from the white men to buy and to steal their negro brother, and to hold him in bondage, like a mule or a dog.

Among many of the Indian tribes, though less in these savage western provinces than among the Delawares, Mohicans, and Senecas, the women have a singular degree of power; not only in the wigwam, where they occupy the seats of honor, but in public places and in public life; even the right of holding meetings and discussing questions of peace and war. Among the higher class of Indian tribes, the braves take a pride in paying to their squaws a measure of respect exceeding the mere courtesies of city life; often rising into what, for lack of a better name, might be called chivalry; a fine feeling of the strong toward the weak, as such; a softening of the hard toward the gentle; a bending of the warrior toward the hus-wife. Of course, in a settled society, where rights are guarded by law, not left to the caprice of individual will, there should be little need for this open and avowed protection, on the part of men toward women. It is a virtue of the savage and the semi-savage, of the hunter and the herdsman, of the Seneca Indian and the Anezi Arab, which has not failed to touch with moral and poetic beauty the manners of a people of far nobler grade.

What man can doubt that Indian ideas on witchcraft, on polygamy, on plurality of gods, on the migration of souls, on the presence of spirits, on future rewards, have entered deeply into the popular mind, and are now affecting for good or ill the course of American religious thought?

One of the first things to strike an English eye about these red-skins (after their paint and feathers, perhaps), is their division into tribes; the oldest form in which men were organized into societies. It is an Oriental system, found in Media and India, in Arabia and Scythia, among all the wandering and pastoral nations. In the first step from savage toward civil life, all races are divided into tribes, of either the family or the clan. In Sparta there were three of these original tribes, in Athens four, in Palestine twelve, in Rome three; in each of which states one tribe would appear to have had some sort of regal superiority—the Hyllean at Sparta, the Eupatrid in Athens, the house of Judah in Palestine, the Ramnes in Rome. Among these multitudinous tribes of the red race, no such regal character appears to obtain; the Cheyenne admits no moral superiority in the Sioux, the Mohican in the Seneca; each nation is a separate body; and the chief policy of the red natives is that of maintaining their tribal independence. From them the white settlers have borrowed the sentiment of State Rights.

CHAPTER VII.

INDIAN LIFE.

The story of Minnehaha, Laughing Water, has made known the fact that there exists, among these sons of the lake and prairie, a body of tradition available for art. The life of a red Indian—as he starts on a trail, as he hunts the bison and the elk, as he courts his mistress with the scalp of an enemy slain in battle or by stealth, as he leaps in the war-dance, as he buries the hatchet and lays by the knife, as he harangues his fellows in council, as he defies the malice of his captors, as he sits down under his hemlock and smokes the pipe of peace—is nothing less than a romance. His presence is a picture, his conduct a poem. The forest in which he dwells, the plain on which he hunts, the river along which he floats, are full to him of a myriad spirits. His canoe is an ark, his wigwam is a tent. On every side, he is in contact with the innermost soul of things, and nature speaks to his ear out of every leaf and from every stone. What marvel, then, that his unwritten poetry should be of a wild and daring kind; new in its character, fresh in its colors, like and yet unlike to the Homeric, the Ossianic, and the Gothic primitive romance?

A young hunter fell in love with a beautiful girl whom he sought for his wife, and being the pride of his tribe, both for swiftness in the race and for courage in war, his suit was accepted by her father, and she was given to him in marriage. On her wedding-day she died. Tearing a trench in the soil, the women swathed her limbs in a cloth, and after wailing over her body, laid her down in the bunch-grass. But the young hunter could not leave her. His bow was unstrung in the wigwam, his club lay idle on the ground, for his heart was buried in that forest grave, and his ears were no longer awake to the sounds of war and the chase. One joy was left to him on earth:—to sit by himself, near that mound under which his love lay at rest, pondering of his lost bride, and following her in fancy to the spirit-land. Old men of the tribe had told him, when a child, that souls go after death to the Blessed Isles, lying far off to the south, in a sunny clime, upon the bosom of a placid lake, under a sky of unfreckled blue; and one day, as he sat on the cold ground, with snow in the trees above him, the thought came into his mind that he would go in search of that Island in which the soul of his mistress dwelt. Turning his face to the south, he began his journey, which, for a long while, lay through a country of lakes, hills, valleys, much like his own; but in time, there appeared to be less snow in the trees, less frost on the streams, more brightness in the air, more verdure on the earth; then he came upon buds and blossoms, he saw flowers in the field, and heard warblings in the bush. Seeing a path into a thick grove, he followed it through the trees until it led him to a high ridge, on the top of which stood an Indian lodge. At the door of this lodge, an old man, with white hair, a pale face, and fiery eyes, covered with skins of wild beasts, and leaning on a staff, received him with a sad smile. The hunter was beginning to tell his story:—"Hush!" said the old man; "I expected you, and have risen to give you welcome. She whom you seek has been here; she rested for awhile, and then went on. Come into my lodge." When the hunter was refreshed with food and sleep, the old man led him forth of the lodge and said: "See you that gulf and the plain beyond? It is the land of souls. You stand upon its confines, and my lodge is the gate of entry. But only souls can pass beyond this gate. Lay down your bundle and your quiver; leave behind your body and your dog; now, pass into the land of spirits." The hunter bounded from the earth, like a bird on its wings. Forest, lake, mountain, were the same, but he saw them with new eyes, and felt them with a strange touch. Nature seemed to have become luminous and vocal. The air was softer, the sky was brighter, the sward was greener, than they seem to our mortal senses. Birds sang to him out of trees, and animals came frisking past him. No creature was afraid of him, for blood is never shed in the spirit-land. He went forward without effort, gliding, rather than walking, along the ground; passing through trees and rocks as a man in the flesh might walk through a wreath of spray and a cloud of smoke. At length he came to a wide and shining lake, from the midst of which sprang a lovely isle. A canoe of white stone lay close in shore, with paddles laid ready to his hand. Stepping into this boat, and pushing from the bank, he became conscious, as in a dream, that another white canoe was at his side, in which, pale and beautiful as he had last seen her, sat his bride. As he put forth from the bank, she put off also; answering to the motion of his oars like the chords in music. A tranquil joy was in the hunter's heart as they pushed their way toward the Blessed Isle. On looking forward toward the land, he was seized with fear for his beloved; a great white line of surf broke angrily in their front, and in the clear deep waters he could see the bodies of drowning men and the bones of thousands who had perished in that surf. His thews being strong and his courage calm, he had no fears for himself; but he yearned for her, exposed to the surf in that glittering shell; but when they pushed boldly into the breakers, they found their canoes go through them as through air. Around them were many boats, each freighted with a soul. Some were in sore distress, some wrecked and lost. The boats which bore young children glided home like birds. Those containing youths and maidens met with gusts and rollers. Older men were beaten by storms and tempests, each according to his deeds; for the calm and storm were not in the spirit-lake, but in the men who sailed upon it. Softly running to the shore, the hunter and his bride leaped lightly from their canoes upon the Golden Isle. What a change from the dull, cold earth on which the hunter lived! They saw no graves. They never heard of war. No gales ever vexed the air, no fogs ever hid the sun. Ice was unknown to that Blessed Isle. No blood was ever shed; no hunger and thirst were felt; for the very air which they breathed was food and drink. Their feet were never tired and their temples never ached. No sorrowing was endured for the dead. Gladly would the hunter have remained forever with his bride in this spirit-land; but a great presence, called the Master of Life, came near to him, and speaking in a voice like a soft breeze, said to the young man:—"Go back to the land from which you came; your day is not yet. Return to your tribe, and to the duty of a good man. When that is done, you will rejoin the spirit which you love. She is accepted; she will be here forever; as young, as happy as when I called her from the land of snow." When the voice ceased from its speaking, the hunter started in his sleep—to find the little mound at his feet, snow in the trees overhead, and a numb sorrow in his heart.

Ah me, it was all a dream!

The red man believes in a god, or rather he believes in many gods; also in a life after death, to be shared by his horse, his hawk, and his dog. He thinks there is a good spirit and a bad spirit, equal in dignity and strength to each other; that, under them, live a multitude of gods; spirits of the rock, the tree, the clouds, the river, and the frost; spirits of the wind, of the sun, and of the stars. No Greek shepherd ever peopled Hymettus and Arcadia, Orion and the Bear, with such swarming multitudes of shapes and radiances as the Cheyenne, the Pawnee, and the Snake believe to inhabit their plains and mountains, their creeks and woods, their lakes and skies. But the Indian has never yet learned to erect temples to his deities; being content to find them in tree and flower, in sunshine and in storm, in the hawk, the beaver, and the trout. His only religion is that of nature, his only worship a kind of magic. He believes in witches and in sorcerers; in their power to degrade men into beasts, to elevate beasts into men. Sleep is to him but another side of his life, and dreams are as real as his waking deeds. In his fancy all space is teeming with gods and spirits, which are close to him as he hunts and fights, capable of hearing his call to them, of making known to him their presence and their wishes by signs and sounds. He is the original source of all our spirit-rapping, all our table-turning; and in the act of invoking demons to his aid, he is still beyond the reach of such puny rivals as the Davenports and Homes.

His religious rites are few and cabalistic; thus, he will sing for the sick, and offer meat to the dead; he will put a charm in his ear, in his nose, and around his wrist—commonly a shell from the great sea—as a defense against evil spirits. He has no priest, as we understand the word, but he submits himself abjectly to his prophet (jossakeed) and seer; and he does so, not only as regards his soul but his body. In fact, his prophet is his doctor also; disease being in his opinion a spiritual as well as physical defect, only to be conquered by one who has power upon sin and death. Brigham Young has very much the same function to perform at one end of Salt Lake that a Shoshonee seer may have to discharge at the other.

The red men have no settled laws. Their government is patriarchal, the chief power being exercised, as in every savage horde, by the old men of the tribe, except in war time, when the bravest and most cunning take the lead. They know nothing about votes, either free or open, but in electing leaders they declare their preference with a shout. They have no conception of the use and power of work, and it is only with a slow and sullen heart that even the best among them will consent to practice a trade. They have about them a sense of having always been a wild tribe; a race of hunters and warriors, lords of the arrow and the club; and they are too proud to moil and toil, to do the offices of squaws and cowards. If they were not driven by hunger to the chase, they would do nothing at all, except drink and fight. In these things the Creeks and the Dakotas excel the most accomplished rowdies of Denver, Leavenworth, and New York.

I cannot say that their domestic life is either noble or lovely. A prairie brave, mounted on a strong pony, with a rifle on his saddle, a blanket strapped behind him, dressed in a handsome skin jacket, adorned with beads and tags, with his squaw trudging heavily by his side on foot, carrying her papoose on her back, and a parcel of provisions in her hands, was one of my earliest illustrations of the chivalries of Indian life. A mob of Ute warriors, tearing through the streets of Denver, rushing into shops and painting their faces, while the squaws and papooses tumbled after them in the mire, laden with cabbages, buffalo-skins, and miscellaneous domestic fry, was another A listless, insolent crowd of Pawnees, smoking and drinking on the Pacific road, while their squaws were laboring on the railway line as navvies, hired out by the braves at fifty cents a day and a ration of corn and meat uncooked, was a third. As such examples grew in strength upon me, I began to think the noble Indian was not so much of a gentleman as a believing reader of the Last of the Mohicans might suppose. "Why don't these fellows work for themselves, instead of lounging in groceries and grog-shops, while their wives are digging earth and carrying wood?" An Omaha friend who stood near me smiled: "Don't you see, they are warriors and gentlemen; they cannot degrade themselves by work."

The Sioux, the Pawnee, the Cheyenne squaw, though she may have a certain power in the wigwam, and an uncertain liberty of speech in the council, when her character as a woman happens to be great, is, in many respects, and as a general rule, no better than a slave; such rights as she may exercise belonging to her rather as a member of the tribe than as a mother and a wife. Her husband has probably bought her for a blanket, for an old carbine, for a keg of whisky; and it depends wholly on the man's humor, on his fondness, whether he shall treat her as a lady or as a dog. He can sell her, he can give her away. The squaw's inferiority to the hunter is like that of the horse to his master. She is one of the man's chattels; one of many like herself; for the Indian is a polygamist, and keeps a harem in the prairie. She has to perform all in-door, all out-door labor; to fix the wigwam in the ground, to fetch water from the stream, to gather billets from the bush, to dig roots and pick up acorns, to dress and cook the food, to make the clothes, to dry the scalps, to mend the wigwam, to carry her children on the march. And while she has a thousand toils to endure, she has scarcely any rights as either a woman or a wife. The man may put her away for the most trifling fault. Her infant may be taken from her lap. Her modesty is not always spared. While the sins into which her own fancies may have led her are visited with revolting punishment; she may be forced by her husband into acts of immorality which degrade her as a woman, not only in her own eyes, but in those of the companions of her shame. If she commits adultery without her husband's leave, his custom allows him to slit her nose; yet when the whimsy takes him, he may sell her charms to a passing guest. In the freedom of his forest life, it is common for the Shoshonee and the Comanche to offer his squaw to any stranger visiting in his lodge. The theory of the wigwam is, that the female member of it is a chattel, and that her beauty, her modesty, her service, belong to her lord only, and may be given as he lists. For her there is nothing save to hear and to obey.

And the Indian squaw is what such rules of life must make her. If her mate is cruel in disposition, she is savage; if he is dirty in person, she is filthy; if he is lax in conduct, she is shameless. When anything base and monstrous has to be done, it is left to the squaws. If an enemy is to be tortured, the women are set upon him. A brave might club his prisoner to death by a blow, but the sharper and slower agonies caused by peeling off his skin, by tearing out his nails, by breaking his finger-joints, by putting fire under his feet, by gouging out his eyes, are only to be inflicted by the demons who have taken up their dwelling in female forms.

All the men who fought against the Indians at Sand Creek, to whom I have spoken, describe the squaws as fighting more furiously than the braves; and all the white women (as I hear) who have had the double misfortune of falling into Indian hands, and surviving to tell the tale of their dishonor, exclaim against the squaws as deeper in cruelty and iniquity than their lords. The story of a white woman's captivity among the Sioux and Arappahoes is one that ought never to be told. In Colorado there are fifty, perhaps a hundred, females who have undergone the shame of such a passage in their lives; and it is fearful to see the flashing eyes, to hear the emphatic oaths, of either father, lover, or son to one of these wretched creatures, when a Cheyenne is spoken of otherwise than as a dog, whom it is the duty of every honest man to shoot.

It would be a dangerous trial for a Yengee to say one word in favor of the Indians either in the streets of Denver and Central City, or along the route through the Rocky Mountains traveled by the wagon trains and the mail.

Yet with all their faults, the Indians have some virtues and many capacities. They are brave. As a rule, they are chaste. In patience they have few equals; in endurance they have none. They are affectionate toward their children; moderately faithful to their squaws. Their reverence for age, for wisdom, and for valor, is akin to religious feeling, and is only a little lower in degree than that which they pay to their Great Spirit. In war time, and against an enemy, they consider everything fair; but the first and worst of all vices in the savage, the habit of lying, is comparatively rare in these red men.

CHAPTER VIII.

CARRYING THE MAIL.

In bands from fifteen to forty, well armed and well mounted, the Cheyennes and their allies are moving along our line, plundering the stations, threatening the teamsters and drivers with fire and lead. A red-skin war is never sudden in its coming; for, as many tribes and nations must be drawn into it, there is much running to and fro, much smoking of tobacco, and a vast amount of palaver. When a man desires to have war, he must first persuade his chief and his tribe to dare it; next he must ride round the country into other tribes, whispering, haranguing, rousing, till the blood of many of the younger braves boils up. Meetings must be held, councils compared, and a decision taken by the allies. If the palavering, in which the aged and timid warriors have a principal share, is going on slowly, some of the younger braves steal off into the enemy's land, where they provoke bad blood by plundering a ranch, driving away mules, if possible carrying off women. They know that the white men will turn out and fight, that two or three braves may happen to get killed, and they are pretty sure that the nations which have suffered in the fray will then cry loudly for revenge.

As a rule, the white men, being few in number, unsupported by their Government, never resist these Indian attacks, unless life is taken or women are captured; short of these crimes being committed, the pale-face says it is cheaper to feed the red men than to fight them, since he must always meet them with a halter round his neck. A white man dare not fire on a band of Sioux, of Comanches, though he may be perfectly sure that they are enemies, bent on taking his life. If he killed an Indian, he would be tried for murder. The red man, therefore, has his choice of when and where he will attack, and the grand advantage of being able to deliver his volley when he pleases. It is only after some one has been killed that the white man feels himself safe in returning shot for shot. So, when parties of Indians come upon lonely ranches and stations on the plains, the white men have to kill, as it were, the fatted calf; that is to say, they have to bring forth their stores of bacon, dried buffalo-tongue, beans, and potted fruit, set the kettle boiling, the pan frying, and feed the rascals who are going to murder them, down to the very last pound of flesh, the very last crust of bread; only too happy if they will then go away into their wilds without taking away women and scalps. Of course, few women are to be found in these perilous plains; not a dozen between Wamego and Denver, I should say.

Now, these small bands of Cheyennes and Arappahoes in our front have come from the great camp of the Six Nations, lying near Fort Ellsworth, under the command of Roman Nose. They are going forward as a party of feelers and provokers, a little way in advance of us, insulting the whites and eating up the road. At every station, after passing Fort Riley, we hear of their presence and of their depredations.

Red-skins, however, will not permit themselves to be seen, unless they are friendly and mean to beg. In going over one of the long, low ridges of Smoky Hill, we observe a small party of Cheyennes moving along the opposite ridge; they are mounted, and leading spare horses, and, as we catch the gleam of their rifles, we know they are well armed. Unlike the Bedouin, every red-skin has a revolver of his own; some of them have two or three revolvers in their belts; almost every one slings a rifle across his horse. They seem to be crossing our path. "Who are these Indians?" I ask the driver, by whose side I am sitting on the box. "Well," says he, in the deliberate Western fashion, "guess they are some cuss." They seem to have halted; for the moment, as I think, they are trying to prevent our seeing a white horse, which one of them is leading. "Guess I can't make them out,' adds the driver, after taking time to consider his want of opinion; "if they were friendly, they would come to us and beg; if they were thieves, they would hide in the creek, so as not to be seen; guess they are out on the war-path." When they draw up we can count them; they are only five men in number, with four led horses in addition to their own. Five men would not dream of attacking the mail, in which there might be a dozen men and guns; especially not when the blinds are down, and they cannot from their coign of vantage see into the coach and count the number of their foes. A sure knowledge of the enemies to be met in fight is a cardinal point in the system of an Indian warrior, who prides himself more on his success than even on his valor. Rich in stratagem, he is always afraid of ambuscade; and he rarely ventures to attack an enemy, when, from either want of light or any other cause, he cannot see into every element of his game.

This Indian fact is of use to us now. In the presence of our Cheyenne neighbors, we draw the curtains of our wagon pretty close, so that the red-skins, who can see that we are two outside, the driver and myself, cannot tell how many more may be sitting inside with revolvers. They know, in a general way, that no one rides outside the stage in the burning heat of these plains, unless the inside seats are filled. The rule is not good for us, our seats being occupied with mail-bags; but the Cheyennes and Comanches have no notice of our straits. Now, five red-skins, though they might rush upon a single man, or even upon a couple of men, no better armed than themselves, against whom they would enjoy the privilege of firing the first volley, will always pause before pulling a trigger on a foe of invisible and unknown strength. It is, therefore, without surprise, though with much inward satisfaction, that we see them break up their council, fall into line, and move along the creek in such a way as to increase the distance between us at every stride.

At the next log-hut we find that this party of Cheyennes, with the led horses, stolen from some wagon train, have been here; very insolent and masterly; not mincing words; not concealing threats. They have eaten up everything in the station: the dried elk, the buffalo-tongue, the fat bacon, the canned fruits; have compelled the boys to boil them coffee, to fetch clean water, to mend their horses' shoes; and have left the place with a notice that the mail must be stopped, the stock removed, and the shanties burnt.

Having tasted a little putrid water, seasoned with a few drops of cognac, happily carried from New York, we push out of the station, following in the track of these menacing braves. We crash through ravines, in which our driver believes they lurk, and we pass little mounds, under which the scalpless heads of white men, murdered in the recent frays, have scarcely yet grown cold. The long green line of the Smoky Hill is on our left, not half a mile from our course, which lies for two or three days and nights along the bank of Smoky River. As we dash into Low Creek, we find the men in a scare, though they are only a few miles distant from Ellsworth. A party of Cheyennes have been to the station, have eaten up their food, have taken away what they wanted, and promised to return in fifteen days to burn down the shanty and murder the men. The boys say these Indians will come back before the end of their fifteen days. They notice many signs of the red man's anger which are invisible to us. The blacksmith went out in the morning; but he saw enough in an hour to induce him to scamper back. A farmer, living in a ranch close by, has called in his man and horses from the plains. Every one is belted and on guard; in all, five men against as many thousand red-skins. With some satisfaction, we hear of seven United States soldiers, from the fort, having ridden on in front of us, looking after buffalo and red-skins. The mules having been yoked, our revolvers fired off and reloaded, and a can of bad water swallowed, we light our cigars and jump on the wagon.

Just as we are sallying from the station, a riderless horse comes sweating and panting into the yard, and is instantly recognized as belonging to one of those soldiers who had passed through in the early day, looking after buffalo and red-skins. One or other he seems to have found. Bill the driver pulls at his reins, doubtful whether he ought to go out; but on second thoughts, with an ugly twist of the jaw and resolute scowl on his brow, he whips his team into a rage, and plunges out with them upon the hot and arid plains.

Half a mile from the station, we come upon a dying horse, which the driver says had belonged to one of those soldiers who had gone before us. The beast is ripped through the belly; but whether he has been gored by a buffalo horn or slit open with a knife, we cannot decide as we roll swiftly by. Saddle and trapping have been taken away; but there is nothing to tell by whom, or for what end.

With fingers laced on our revolvers, we keep a keen eye upon objects, both far and near. At Chalk Bluff we find Kelly and Walden, the two stockmen, horribly scared. Kelly, an Irish lad, makes a wry face and a joke about the dirty vermin, who have just been here; but Walden, a Yankee, who has been through the war, is painfully white and grave. They believe these Cheyennes mean mischief. We give the brave lads a little cognac, wring their hands, and bid them be of good cheer, as we rattle off in the wagon.

(I am sorry to say, that three weeks afterward these men were murdered by the Cheyennes. The Indians came to the hut, and, as usual, asked for food and tobacco. Kelly put their dinners on the table, which they instantly devoured. I cannot say how the poor men came to be so careless as they must have been, when the Cheyennes, catching them off their guard, lanced Kelly through the heart, and shot Walden in the bowels. Kelly fell dead, and Walden only lived a few hours. A wagon came up, and a white man heard the story from his lips.)

The whole road is unarmed, unprotected; for the two forts, Ellsworth and Wallace, each with a couple of weak companies, stand at a distance from each other of two hundred and twenty miles. If they are able to defend themselves it is thought enough. Pond Creek lies a mile from Fort Wallace: a woman and her daughter, Mrs. and Miss Bartholomew, live here; and when a party of Cheyennes came into the station yesterday, eating it up, and threatening to burn it down, the woman sent a driver up to the fort, which contains a garrison of one hundred and fifty men, with two field-pieces, and begged for help; but Lieutenant Bates, the gentleman in command, replied to her cry of distress, that if she and her daughter need protection, they must seek it in the lines, as he cannot spare a man to defend the road along which we are guarding the imperial mail!

She is packing a few things in a handkerchief, and as we drive out of the yard, we see the two women start off for the military post.

From Big Timber station, a place where we find a few trees, most welcome to our sight, the red-skins have hardly gone, as we roll in; they have been here three days, a party of twenty-eight, with Little Blanket at their head; eating the fat bacon, sipping the hot coffee, and lording over the stockmen like kings over conquered slaves. The country, they said, is theirs, and everything brought into it is theirs. When about to go away, they counted these trees, fifty-one in number. "No cut down trees," they said, "we like them to stand there, in the creek." Pointing to a stack of hay, laid up for the mules, they added, with a grim and smiling humor, "Cut grass,—cut plenty grass,—make big fire;" and, as they rode away, the chief turned round, and said, "Fifteen days we come back; you gone, good; you not gone—ugh!" accompanying his threat with a horrible pantomime, expressive of lapping flames.

At Cheyenne Wells we have another domestic scene. Long before coming to this station, we heard from drivers and trainmen of Jack Dunbar, the station-keeper, as a reckless Colorado devil, one of those heroes of Sand Creek who had sent a slug into the heart of White Antelope, when the aged red-skin had bared his breast and called on the troops to fire. We hoped to find one man, at least, unscared by this Indian raid along our line; but on our wheeling into his yard, we see that everything is wrong, for Dunbar has a wife at Cheyenne Wells, and his own share in the exploit of Sand Creek being well known to the Indians, he is fearful that the first sharp blow of the coming war may fall upon her head. A glance at the way bill tells him that the stage is full, that passengers who have paid their hundreds of dollars have been left behind for want of room; but then, as he says, it is a question of life and death,—of a woman's life and death,—and he comes to us, cap in hand, with a prayer that we will carry on his wife into a place of safety. For himself, he is willing to stand by his stock, defending himself and his stable to the last; but the poor woman cannot fight, and in case of his own death, before he should have time to kill her, her fate would be revolting, far beyond the power of an English imagination to conceive.

What can we do, but offer to comply? A fresh disposal of the mail-bags; a new twist of our limbs; and a hole is made in the vehicle, into which the hero's wife inserts her slim and plastic body. A pillow thrust behind her head, protects her from many a bump and blow; but when we lift her, thirty hours later, from the wagon, it is hard to say whether she will live or die.

In the night, we rougher fellows get a little rest and relief by climbing to the box, breathing the cold air, and occasionally curling up our legs in the boot. It is only the fiery day that kills.

As the sun works westward toward his setting, the

air grows cooler to the skin, softer in the lungs; and a spring of life comes back as it were into the veins. Our pulses quicken, our chests dilate, our limbs put out new strength. The weird and pensive solitude of the prairie grows into our souls as the stars peep out; and when the ancient moon lifts up her head from the horizon, bathing the vast ocean of rolling grass in her tender light, we feel in the beauty and majesty of Nature such a sovereign balm, that unless the scalping-knife were in his hand, we could salute either a Cheyenne or a Sioux as a man and a brother.

CHAPTER IX.

RED COMMUNITIES.

Between the great lakes and the Gulf of Mexico, there may be two hundred tribes and tribelets of the red men: Creeks, Dakotas, Mohicans, Cheyennes, Pawnees, Shoshones, Cherokees, Sioux, Comanches, and their fellows, more or less distinct in genius and in shape: men who once roamed over these hills and valleys, danced in their war-paint, hunted the elk and the bison, and left their long and liquid names to many American rivers and American States.

What to do with these forest people has been the thought of colonist and ruler from those early days when the first Saxon came into the land. At times, perhaps, an adventurer here and there has plied them too freely with the carbine and the cruse; but his better nature and his higher principle have brought him to regret this use of powder and whisky, the destroying angels of civilization; and from the days of Penn, at least, the red man's right in the country has been commonly assumed by writers, and his claim to compensation for his lost hunting-ground has been recognized by the laws.

This policy of paying money for the land taken by the white men from the red was the more just and noble, as Indians, like the Senecas and the Walla-Wallahs, have no clear sense of what is meant by rights in the soil. The soil? They know no soil. A Seneca comprehended his right to fish in the Hudson River; a Walla-Wallah understood his right to hunt bison in the plains at the feet of the Blue Mountains; but as a thing to plow and plant, to dig wells into, to build houses upon, the soil was no more to them than the sea and the sky are to us. A right to go over it they claimed; but to own it, and preserve it against the intrusion of all other men, is a claim which the red men have never made, and which, if they should learn to make it, could never be allowed by civilized men. No hunting tribe has any such right; perhaps no hunting tribe *can* have any such right; for, in strict political philosophy, the only exclusive right which any man can acquire in land, the gift of nature, is that which he creates for himself by what he puts into it by way of labor and investment alike for his own and for the common good. Now, a slayer of game does nothing for the land over which he roams; he clears no forest, he drains no marsh, he embanks no river, he plants no seed, he cultivates no garden, he builds no city; what he finds at his birth he leaves at his death; and no more property would, under such conditions, accrue to him in the soil than in the air. But, in dealing with such men as the Sioux and the Delawares, is it wise to be always bringing our political logic to the front? A law which the strong has to enforce, and which weighs upon the weak, may be tempered with mercy, even when it cannot be generally set aside. A little love, say the philanthropists, may go a long way. The land is here; we come and seize it; gaining for ourselves a possession of untold wealth, while driving the hunter from rivers and forests which before our coming had yielded his family the means of life. Ours is the profit, his the loss. Our wants can hardly be the measure of our rights; and if the Walla-Wallah has few rights in the soil, the stranger who displaces him has, in the first instance, none at all, beyond that vague common right which every human being may be supposed to possess in the earth on which he is born. A compromise, then, would appear to these reasoners to offer the only sound issue out of such conflicting claims: and an Englishman, jealous — for family reason — of everything done by his brethren in the United States, may feel proud that, as between Yengees and Indians, the strong have dealt favorably with the weak.

Washington laid down a rule for paying to each tribe driven back from the sea by settlers a rental for their lands; arrangements for that purpose being made between a Government agent and a recognized chief; and these payments to the Apalachian and Algonquin tribes and tribelets have ever since that day been made by the United States government with unfailing good faith.

But a legal discharge of this trade obligation was far

from being enough to satisfy conscientious men, who felt that in coming upon the Indian plain and forest they were driving a race of hunters from their fields, and cutting away from them the means by which they lived. Could nothing else be done for the red man? These white men saw that the past was past. A tribe of hunters, eating the flesh of antelope and buffalo, could not dwell in a province of farms and pastures. The last arrow had been shot when the homestead rose; it was only a question of years until the bow must be broken and the archer cast aside. A hunter needs for his subsistence an area wide enough to feed thousands of men who can make their living by the plow and the spade. In a planet crowded like ours, no room can be found to grow the hunter's food; for the wild buck which he traps, the elk which he runs down, the bison which he slays, will only breed in a country that is seldom disturbed by man. The smoke of a homestead drives away buffalo and deer. Even a pastoral tribe can find room enough only in the wilds of Asia and Africa, where the feuds between tent and city burn with consuming heat; yet a people living by pasturage, driving their flocks before them in search of herbage, require very little ground for their sustenance compared against a people living by the chase. What then? Must the red man perish from the earth? Should he die to let the white man live upon his land? Thousands of voices cried out against such sentence; at least until the white man, who had brought his law upon the scene, could say that every effort to save the Indian had been made, and that every experiment had failed.

Then came the question (only to be laid at rest by trial), whether the Seneca, the Delaware, the Oneida, and the Chippewa could be trained in the arts of life; could be persuaded to lodge in frame-houses, to live in one place, to plant corn and fruit-trees, to wear trowsers and shoes, to send their little ones to school? A number of pious persons, full of zeal for the red race, though lacking true knowledge of the course through which Nature works, put themselves to much cost and trouble in trying these experiments. These reformers had a strong belief in their power of doing things, so to say, by steam—of growing habits of life under glass, and of grafting civilization with the knife. They fell to their work with unflinching spirit. Lands were given up to the red-skins; teachers were provided for them; schools, chapels, saw-mills, houses, were built for them; all the appliances of farming—plows and flails, corn-seed and fruit-trees, horses and oxen, poultry and pigs—were furnished, more or less freely, from the white man's stores. A true history of these trials would be that of a great endeavor, an almost uniform failure; fresh proof that Nature will not suffer her laws to be broken, her order contravened, and her grades disturbed.

A tribe of Senecas was placed upon the Alleghany River in a fine location; a tribe of Oneidas settled on a reservation, in the center of New York, called Oneida Creek. Care and money were lavished on these remnants of red nations; farms were cleared, houses built for them; but they would not labor with their hands to any purpose; not with the caution, the continuity, needful to success in growing grain and stock. A good harvest made them lazy and improvident; a bad harvest thinned them by starvation and disease. One or two families, in whom there was a tinge of white blood, made pretty fair settlers; the rest only lived on the land so long as they could sell the timber and the game. As wood grew scarce, and game disappeared, they began to sell the land; at first to appointed agents; and to move away into the wild country of Green Bay. Most of the tribe have now left Oneida; — with the exception, perhaps, of the Walkers, all will quit their ancient Creek in time. Bill Beechtree, one of the remnants, cut me some hickory sticks, and showed me some bows and arrows which he makes for sale. He can do and will do nothing else. Though he never drew bow against an enemy in his life, and has a very nice voice for a psalm-tune, he considers any other occupation than cutting sticks and barbing arrows unworthy of the son of a brave.

The Delawares whom we saw near Leavenworth, the Pottawottamies whom we found at St. Mary's Mission, are in some respects better off than the Oneidas, being settled in the midst of friendly whites, among whom they continue to live, but only in a declining state. Both these tribes have engaged in farming and in raising stock. The Delawares rank among the noblest nations of the red men; they have finer forms, cleaner habits, quicker senses, than the Cheyennes and the Pawnees. A fragment of this people may be saved, by ultimate amalgamation with the surrounding whites, who feel less antipathy for them than for Sioux and Utes. The Pottawottamies have been lucky in attracting toward their settlement in Kansas the wise attentions of a Catholic bishop. At St. Mary's Mission, half a dozen priests have founded schools and chapels, taught the people religion, and trained them to habits of domestic life. Two thousand children are receiving lessons from these priests. The sheds are better built, the stock better tended, and the land better tilled at St. Mary's than they are in the reservation of any Indian tribe that I have seen—except one.

At Wyandotte, on the Missouri River, some Shawnee families have been placed; and here, if anywhere in the Red Land, the friends of civilization may point the moral of their tale. Armstrong, their chief and their richest man, has English blood in his veins; indeed, many of these Shawnees can boast of the same high title to respect among their tribe. They farm, they raise stock, they sell dry goods; some of them marry white girls, more give their daughters to whites; and a few among them aspire to the mysteries of banking and lending money. A special act endows these Shawnees with the rank of citizens of Kansas, in which capacity they serve on juries and vote for members of Congress.

But the Shawnees of Wyandotte, being a people mixed in blood, can hardly be used as set-off against a score of undoubted failures.

CHAPTER X.

THE INDIAN QUESTION.

Now, the blame arising from these failures to found any large red settlement in the old countries once owned by Iroquois and Algonquin has been constantly charged against the red man. Is this charge a just one? Is it the Delawares' fault that he cannot pass in one generation from the state of a hunter into that of a husbandman? If a man should have his lodge built with a green shoot instead of with a strong tree, whose fault would it be when the lodge came down in a storm?

Every one who has read the annals of our race — a page of nature, with its counterfoil in the history of everything having life — is aware that in our progress from the savage to the civilized state, man has had to pass through three grand stages, corresponding, as it were, to his childhood, to his youth, and to his manhood. In the first stage of his career, he is a hunter, living mainly by the chase; in the second stage, he is a herdsman, living mainly by the pasturage of goats and sheep, of camels and kine; in the third stage, he is a husbandman, living mainly by his cultivation of corn and maize, of fruits and herbs. These three conditions of human life may be considered as finding their purest types in such races as the Iroquois, the Arabian, and the Gothic, in their present stage; but each condition is, in itself and for itself, an affair of development and not of race. The Arab, who is now a shepherd, was once a hunter; the Saxon, who is now a cultivator of the soil, was first a hunter, then a herdsman, before he became a husbandman. Man's progress from stage to stage is continuous in its course, obeying the laws of physical and moral change. It is slow; it is uniform; it is silent; it is unseen. In one word, it is growth.

No one can step at his ease from the first stage of human existence into the second; still less can he step from the first stage into the third. All growth is a work of time, depending on forces which are often beyond the control of art; work to be helped perhaps, not to be hurried, by men. As in the training of a vine, in the rearing of a child, a wise waiting upon nature seems our only course.

These three stages in our progress upward are strongly marked; the interval dividing an Iroquois from an Arab being as wide as that which separates an Arab from a Saxon.

The hunter's habits are those of a beast of prey. His teeth are set against everything having life; every beast on the earth, every bird in the air, being an enemy against which his club will be raised and his arrow will be drawn. On passing into the stage of a herdsman, he becomes used to the society of horses, dogs, and camels, animals of a tender breed; he finds himself charged with the care of sheep and goats, of cattle and fowls, creatures which he must pity and tend, bearing with their humors under penalty of their loss. If he would feed upon their milk and eggs, if he would clothe himself in their wools and skins, he must study their wants, and care for them with a parent's eye. It will become his business to serve and guard them; to seek out herbage and water for them; to consider their times and seasons; to prepare for them a shelter from the heats of noon and the frosts of night. Thus, a man's relation to the lower world of life must undergo a change. Where, in his savage state, he sharpened his knife against every living thing, he has now to become a student of nature, a nursing father to an ever-increasing family of beasts and birds.

Such cares as occupy all pastoral tribes — the Arab in his tent, the Caffir in his krall, the Kirghis in his hut — are utterly unknown to the Seneca, the Shoshonee, and the Ute; the softer manners which result from the paternal relation of men to domestic animals having no existence in any hunting tribe. To advance from the stage of a Seneca into that of an Arab, is a march requiring many years, perhaps many generations, to accomplish; and even when that stage of pastoral existence shall have been gained, with all its changes of habit and of thought, the hunter will be only halfway on his path towards the position occupied by a grain-growing Saxon. After the second stage of this journey has been accomplished by the red man, those who have visited Nahr Dehab in Syria, and watched the trials there being made by the Turks in settling the Ferdoon Arabs on the soil, will feel inclined to wait for any further results of his effort in a very calm and dispassionate frame of mind.

The Cheyenne is a wild man of the woods, whom neither cold nor hunger is strong enough to goad into working for himself, his children, and his squaws. How should it? A man may die of frost and snow, and even for lack of food, without bringing dishonor upon his tribe; but to labor with his hands is, in his simple belief, a positive disgrace. A warrior must not soil his palm with labor, seeing that his only duties in the world are to hunt and fight. If maize must be planted, if roots must be dug, if fires must be lit, if water must be carried, where is the squaw? Not much work is ever done in a Cheyenne lodge; but whether it be much or little, the man will take no part of the trouble upon himself. To kill his enemy and to catch his prey—that, in a line, is the Cheyenne's whole duty of man. Starvation itself will not drive him into treating industry as a duty; the neglect of which, even in another, is never, in his eyes, an offence. In some of the western tribes, where game is running scarce and the beavers evade the trap, the squaws and little ones throw a handful of grain into the soil; but the hunters give no heed to their work; and if, on their return to the spot, later in the year, the men find that their squaws have omitted to sow the maize, the idea of anybody working and waiting for a crop to grow is so foreign to their Indian taste, that they sit down and laugh at the neglect as a passing jest. If the tribe runs short of food, the hunter's remedy is to march against his neighbor, and by means of his bow and his tomahawk, to create a fresh balance between the mouths to be fed and the quantity of buffalo and elk which may be found to feed them. This rude remedy for want is his only art. Any thought of making the two ends of his account meet by setting up beehives and multiplying herds, would never present itself unbrought to his simple mind. His fathers having always been hunters, the only resource of his tribe, when their food runs short, is the original one of breaking through every obstacle to a fresh supply with his club.

Can we marvel, then, that when the Senecas were placed upon such land as the Alleghany reservation, in a bountiful and fruitful country, rich in white pines, and in other valuable trees, they should have done little or nothing in the way of planting and sowing; that they should have sold their timber to the whites; that they should have rented their saw-mills and ferries to the whites; that they should have let out their rafting yards and landing-places to the whites; in short, that they should have starved on a few dollars derived from rent, while the more eager and industrious Yankee, placed in the same location, would have coined the real riches of the country into solid gold? Like his Arab brother at Nahr Dehab, the Seneca on the Alleghany could not defile his hands with work—the business, not of warriors, but of squaws.

It is only fair, then, to remember, that the failure of so many attempts to convert the hunter into a husbandman at a single step was due to great laws of nature, not to the perversity of man. The chasm could not be bridged; but your eager and well-meaning friends of the red race, having no science to guide them, had to work this truth for themselves out of vague ideas into visible facts. In their ignorance of the general laws of growth, they saw their very sympathies and generosities changed into destroying powers; for the Indians who gave up their lands to the white men, receiving rentals or annuities in return for them, had to abandon their old habits of life without being able to enter on any new employments. And what was the end of this change for them? Hanging about the skirts of towns, they ate and drank, rioted and smoked, themselves into premature old age. Of a hundred millions of dollars which have been paid to the red man, it is said that fifty millions at least have been spent in grog-shops and in houses of evil name. The misery is, that in their savage state the red men have to live in the light of a high civilization. The ferns which grow in their native forests would not more surely perish if they were suddenly planted out in the open sun.

The same hasty desire to bring the red savage into close relation with white civilization affects the policy pursued by government agents in these Plains. In the American part of Red India failure of justice is the rule; in the Canadian part of Red India failure of justice is extremely rare; and the reason is this, the trappers and traders living beyond the Canadian frontier deal with robbery and murder with a promptness and simplicity unknown to American judges. My friend, Jem Baker, a sturdy old trapper, who resides with his squaws and papooses on Clear Creek, near Denver, put the whole case into a few words. "You see, colonel," says Jem, to whom every gentleman is a colonel, "the difference is this: if a Sioux kills a white man near Fort Ellice, you English say, 'Bring him in, dead or living, here 's two hundred dollars;' and when the Indians have brought him in, you say again, 'Try him for his life; if he is guilty, hang him on the nearest tree.' All is done in a day, and the Indians have his blood upon themselves. But if a Sioux kills a white man near Fort Laramie, we Americans say, 'Bring him in with care, along with all the witnesses of his crime;' and when the Indians have brought him in, we say again, 'He must have a fair trial for his life; he must be committed by a justice and sent before a judge, he must have a good counsel to speak up for him, and a jury to try him who know nothing about his crime.' So most times he gets off, has a present from some lady perhaps, and goes back to his nation a big chief."

I have heard the details of cases in which Indian

assassins, taken all but red-handed, have been sent to Washington for trial, three thousand miles away from the scenes and witnesses of their crimes; who, on being acquitted from the lack of such evidence as complicated legal methods require, have come back into these prairies, bearing on their arms and necks gifts of philanthropic ladies, and taking instant rank as leaders in their tribes. A simpler and swifter form of trial is needed on these Plains—on penalty of such irregular acts of popular vengeance as the battle of Sand Creek.

The truth is, the eastern cities have always shirked the Indian question; fearing to face it boldly, hoping it would drop out of light and vex their spirits no more. "We push our way," said Secretary Seward to me, condolingly; "ninety years ago, my grandfather had the same sort of trouble with Indians, only sixty miles from New York, that you have now been suffering six hundred miles beyond St. Louis." I am often surprised by the splendid confidence which Americans express in their power of living down everything which they find unpleasant; but I am not convinced that this policy of pushing the red man off this continent is the only method of procedure.

If policy compels this people to make a new road from St. Louis to San Francisco, policy suggests that the road should be made safe. Thus much will be admitted in Boston as well as in Denver. But how is a path through the buffalo-runs to be made safe? By the white men going out every spring to beg a treaty of peace from Roman Nose and Spotted Dog, paying for it with baby talk, blankets, fire-arms, powder, and whisky? That is the present method of proceeding, and no one, except the agents, finds it much of a success. My own impression is, that such a method can have only one result, to deceive the red man into an utterly false impression of the white man's weakness. These Cheyennes actually believe that they are stronger, braver, and more numerous than the Americans. If one of these fellows, who may have been at St. Louis, reports to his tribe that the white men of the sunrise are many beyond counting, like the flowers on the prairie, they say that he has been seized by a bad spirit, and made into a speaker of lies. Thus, they hold the white men in contempt.

If these new roads are to be kept open, and blood is to be spared, this position of the white and red man should be reversed, and the order of things in this country made to correspond with the actual facts. The Indians must be driven into suing for treaties of peace. If you admit their right to the land, buy it from them. When they come to you for peace, let them have it on generous terms, and then compel them to observe it with religious faith. A little severity may be necessary in the outset; for the Cheyenne has never yet felt the white man's power; but a policy at once clear, clement and firm, would soon become intelligible to these sons of the prairie. If the policy of leaving things alone, and letting the trader, emigrant, and traveller, push their way through these deserts, is continued, the American will never cease to have trouble on their Indian frontiers.

CHAPTER XI.

CITY OF THE PLAINS.

At the head of these rolling prairies stands Denver, City of the Plains.

A few months ago (time runs swiftly in these western towns; two years take you back to the middle ages, and a settler of five years' standing is a patriarch) Denver was a wifeless city.

"I tell you, sir," exclaimed a fellow-lodger in the wooden shanty known to emigrant and miner as the Planter's House, "five years ago, when I first came down from the gulches into Denver, I would have given a ten-dollar piece to have seen the skirt of a servant-girl a mile off."

This fellow was sitting at a lady's feet; a lady of middle age and fading charms; to whom, an hour or so afterwards, I said, "Pray, madam, is the gentleman who would have given the ten-dollar piece to see the skirt of a girl's petticoat, your husband?"

"Why do you ask, sir?"

Having had no particular reason for my query, I replied, with a bow, "Well, madam, I was rather hoping that so good a lover had met with a bright reward."

"No," she answered with a smile, "I am not his wife; though I might be to-morrow if I would. He has just buried one lady, and he wants to try on with a second."

On alighting at the Planter's House I noticed, swinging near the door, a little sign, on which these words were painted —

"MADAME MORTIMER,
"CLAIRVOYANT PHYSICIAN."

In the shop-windows of Main Street I had seen a hand-bill, which appeared, from its ragged look, to have done service in some other house, of dirty habits, announcing that the celebrated Madame Mortimer had arrived in Denver, and might be consulted daily (no address being given) on what I may, perhaps, be allowed to call diseases of the heart. Her room in the hotel stood next in the corridor to mine, and as a large panel over her door (door discreetly locked) leading from my room into hers was open, I could at any time of the last three or four nights and days have made her personal acquaintance by simply standing on tip-toe and looking through. Strange to say, I have not thought of arming myself against the wiles of my neighbor, even by a cursory inspection of her camp; and when I spoke just now to the faded woman in the parlor, I was utterly unaware that she was the celebrated Madame Mortimer, who could tell everybody's fortune — show every man a portrait of his future wife, every woman a picture of her future husband — for the low charge of two dollars per head!

Poor sorceress? there is not much poetic charm in her; not a tradition of the art, the grace, and suppleness of spirit which made the genuine witch. This afternoon, in passing my door in the lobby, with the adoring lover at her heels, she saw me looking on the ground for something. It was only a match, which I had dropped while drawing on the wall for a light.

"You have lost something?"

"Madame, it is only a match; can you make me a new one?" said I, looking from her face to that of the miner.

"We do not make matches in Denver," she replied, in the saddest spirit.

"Surely they cannot help making them wherever you are," I said with a bow.

She looked quite blank, though the lover began to chuckle. "How?" she asked, still simpering.

"How! by gift and grace of heaven, where all matches are made."

At last she smiled. "Ha! thank you, sir; I like that, and will keep it;" on which she and the lover slipt away into the parlor, and I lit my cigar with a fusee. Yet this poor sorceress is a feature in the City of the Plains; and I am told that, while the bloom of her coming was fresh among these mining men, the curiosity about her was keen, the flow of dollars into her pocket was steady. But the charm appears to be nearly spent; the landlord, properly protected by a wife, and not being of a romantic turn, is said to be dunning her for bills; and she is consequently being driven by adverse fates to trifle with the affections on her own account. Her life in this city of rakes and gamblers must have been a very hard one; the nearest town is six hundred miles away; the price of a seat in the stage is about two hundred dollars. Poor artist in fate—the stars appear to be very hard on her just now.

(*Note.* On my return from Salt Lake City to Denver, I found that her little sign had been removed from the house-front, and I began to fear that she had been driven off by adverse angels to either Leavenworth or Omaha; but in skipping upstairs to my room, I met the poor creature on the landing-stage, and made her my politest bow. From a friend in the house I learned that she had retired from her profession into domestic life; but only, I am grieved to add, with what, in this City of the Plains, is described as the brevet rank of lady and wife.)

The men of Denver, even those of the higher classes, though they have many strong qualities—bravery, perseverance, generosity, enterprise, endurance—heroic qualities of the old Norse gods—are also, not unlike the old Norse gods, exceedingly frail in morals; and where you see the tone of society weak, you may always expect to find aversion to marriage, both as a sentiment and as an institution, somewhat strong. Men who have lived alone, away from the influence of mothers and sisters, have generally but a faint belief in the personal virtue and fidelity of women; and apart from the lack of belief in woman, which ought to be a true religion in the heart of every man, the desire for a fixed connection and a settled home will hardly ever spring up. Men may like the society of women, and yet not care to encumber themselves for life. The worst of men expect, when they marry, to obtain the best of wives; but the best of women do not quit New England and Pennsylvania for Colorado. Hence it is a saying in Denver,—a saying confirmed by practice, that in these western cities, though few of the miners have wives, you will not find many among them who can be truly described as marrying men.

On any terms short of marriage these lusty fellows may be caught by a female snare. They take very freely to the charms of negresses and squaws. One of the richest men of this city, whose name I forbear to give, has just gone up into the mountains with a couple of Cheyenne wives. Your young Norse gods are nervously afraid of entering a Christian church.

Denver is a city of four thousand people; with ten or twelve streets laid out; with two hotels, a bank, a theatre, half a dozen chapels, fifty gambling-houses, and a hundred grog-shops. As you wander about these hot and dirty streets, you seem to be walking in a city of demons.

Every fifth house appears to be a bar, a whisky-shop, a lager-beer saloon; every tenth house appears to be either a brothel or a gaming-house; very often both in one. In these horrible dens a man's life is of no more worth than a dog's. Until a couple of years ago, when a change for the better began, it was quite usual for honest folks to be awakened from their sleep by the noise of exploding guns; and when daylight came, to find that a dead body had been tossed from a window into the street. No inquiry was ever made into the cause of death. Decent people merely said, "Well, there is one sinner less in Denver, and may his murderer meet his match to-morrow!"

Thanks to William Gilpin, founder of Colorado, and governor elect, aided by a Vigilance Committee; thanks also to the wholesome dread which unruly spirits have conceived of the quick eye and resolute hand of Sheriff Wilson; thanks, more than all, to the presence of a few American and English ladies in the streets of Denver, the manners of this mining pandemonium have begun to change. English women who have been here two or three years, assure me it is greatly altered. Of course Gilpin is opposed—in theory, at least—to all such jurisdiction as that exercised by the Vigilance Committee; but for the moment, the society of this city is unsettled, justice is blind and lame, while violence is alert and strong; and the Vigilance Committee, a secret irresponsible board, acting above all law, especially in the matter of life and death, has to keep things going by means of the revolver and the rope. No one knows by name the members of this stern tribunal; every rich, every active man in the place is thought to be of it; and you may hear, in confidential whispers, the names of persons who are supposed to be its leaders, ministers, and executioners. The association is secret, its agents are many, and nothing, I am told, escapes the knowledge, hardly anything escapes the action, of this dread, irresponsible court. A man disappears from the town:—it is an offence to inquire about him; you see men shrug their shoulders; perhaps you hear the mysterious words—"gone up." Gone up, in the slang of Denver, means gone up a tree—that is to say, a cotton-tree—by which is meant a particular cotton-tree growing on the town creek. In plain English, the man is said to have been *hung*. This secret committee holds its sittings in the night, and the time for its executions is in the silent hours between twelve and two, when honest people should be all asleep in their beds. Sometimes, when the storekeepers open their doors in Main Street, they find a corpse dangling on a branch; but commonly the body is cut down before dawn, removed to a suburb, where it is thrown into a hole like that of a dead dog. In most cases, the place of burial is kept a secret from the people, so that no legal evidence of death can be found.

Swearing, fighting, drinking, like the old Norse gods, a few thousand men, for the most part wifeless and childless, are engaged, in these upper parts of the Prairie, in founding an empire. The expression is

William Gilpin's pet phrase; but the congregation of young Norse gods who drink, and swear, and fight along these roads, are comically unaware of the glorious work in which they are engaged.

"Well, sir," said to me, one day, a burly stranger, all boots and beard, with a merry mouth and audacious eye; "well, what do you think of our Western boys?"

Remembering Gilpin, and wishing to be safe and complimentary, I replied, "You are making an empire." "Eh?" he asked, not understanding me, and fancying I was laughing in my sleeve—a liberty which your Western boy dislikes—he brought his hand, instinctively, a little nearer to his bowie-knife. "You are making an empire?" I put in once again, but by way of inquiry this time, so as to guard against giving offence and receiving a stab.

"I don't know about that," said he, relaxing his grim expression, and moving his hand from his belt; "but I am making money."

Gilpin, I dare say, would have laughed, and said it was all the same.

William Gilpin is perhaps the most noticeable man on the Plains, just as Brigham Young is the most noticeable in the Salt Lake Valley; and it would hardly be a figure of speech to say that his office in Denver (a small room in the Planter's House, which serves him for a bedroom, for a library, for a hall of audience, for a workshop, and the upper ten thousand of Colorado, generally, for a spittoon) is the high school of politics for the gold regions and the mountain districts. By birth, Gilpin is a Pennsylvanian; by nature and habit, a state founder. Descending from one of the best Quaker families of his State, (his ancestor was the Gilpin who came out with Penn and

Logan,) taught by history the need of that large and graceful tolerance of religious sentiment which Penn displayed in the court of Charles the Second, which the Friends have put into practice on the Susquehanna, and armed by nature with abundant gifts of genius,—patience, insight, eloquence, enthusiasm,—he has played, and he is now playing, a singular and dramatic part in this western country. He describes himself to me as in sympathy a Quaker-Catholic: that is to say, as a man who embraces in his single person the extremes of religious thought—the feeling of personality with the dogma of authority—the laxest forms of liberty with the sternest canons of order; an unusual blending of sentiments and sympathies, one not made in a day, not springing from an individual whimsy, but the result of much history, of a long family tradition, and nowhere, perhaps, to be found in this generation except on the frontier-land which unites Quaker Pennsylvania with Catholic Delaware. Gilpin abounds in apparent contradictions. A Quaker, he is also a soldier—a West-Pointer—and of singular distinction in his craft. He bore a prominent part in the Mexican war; was the youngest man in the army who attained the rank of lieutenant-colonel; and but for his resignation, on moving out West, would have been the superior officer of Grant and Sherman. It is a happy circumstance for him that no call of duty made it necessary for him to hold prominent command against any section of his countrymen during the civil war. Gilpin's work is in another field, in the Great West, of which he is the champion and the idol; and which he has given his mind to explore, to advertise, to settle, and to subdue.

Under this man's sway, the city is changed, and is changing fast; yet, if I may believe the witnesses, the advent of a dozen English and American ladies, who came out with their husbands, has done far more for Denver than the genius and eloquence of William Gilpin. A lady is a power in this country. From the day when a silk dress and a lace shawl were seen in Main Street, that thoroughfare became passably clean and quiet; oaths were less frequently heard; knives were less frequently drawn; pistols were less frequently fired. None of these things have ceased; far, very far, is Denver yet from peace; but the young Norse gods have begun to feel rather ashamed of swearing in a lady's presence, and of drawing their knives before a lady's face.

Slowly, but safely, the improvement has been brought about. At first, the ladies had a very bad time, as their idiom runs. They feared to associate with each other; every woman suspected her neighbor of being little better than she should be. Things are safer now; and I can testify, from experience, that Denver has a very charming, though a very limited society of the better sex.

ROBERT WILSON, SHERIFF OF DENVER.

CHAPTER XII.

PRAIRIE JUSTICE.

THE chief executive officer of this city is Robert Wilson, sheriff, auctioneer, and justice of the peace; though he would hardly be recognized in Colorado under such a description. As Quintus Horatius Flaccus, poet and good-fellow, is only known as Horace, so Robert Wilson, sheriff and auctioneer, is only known as Bob, in polite society as Bob Wilson. The Sheriff, who is said, like our Judge Popham of immortal memory, to have been a gambler, if nothing worse, in his wild youth, is still a young-looking man of forty or forty-two; a square, strong-chested fellow, low in stature, with a head like the Olympian Jove's. The stories told in the Prairies of this man's daring make the blood freeze, the flesh creep, and the pulse gallop. To-day he came and sat with me for hours, talking of the city and the territory in which his fortunes are all bound up. One of his tales was that of his capture of three horse-stealers.

According to the code in fashion, here in Denver, murder is a comparatively slight offence. Until two or three years ago, assassination — incidental, not deliberate assassination — was a crime of every day. At the door of some gambling-house — and every tenth house in Main Street was a gambling-house, openly kept, with the stimulants of drinking, singing, and much worse — it was a common thing to find a dead man in the streets each daybreak. A fight had taken place over the roulette-table; pistols had been drawn; and the fellow who was slowest with his weapon had gone down. No one thought of searching into the affray. A ruffian had been shot, and the city considered itself free of so much waste. Human life is here of no account; and what man likes to bring down upon himself the vengeance of a horde of reckless devils by seeking too particularly into the cause of a fellow's death?

A lady, whom I met in Denver, wife of an ex-mayor of that city, told me that when she first came out into the West, four or five years ago, there were sixty persons lying in the little grave-yard, excluding criminals, not one of whom had died a natural death. Exact inquiry told me this account was somewhat beyond the mark; but her statement showed the belief still current in the best houses; and indeed it was only a little beyond the truth. Men quarrel in the streets and fight, but no one dreams of going to the help of the weaker side. One night, when I was writing in my room, a pistol-shot exploded near my window, and, on looking out, I saw a man writhing on the ground. In a few moments he was carried off by his comrades; no one followed his assailant; and I heard next day, that the assassin was not in custody, and that no one knew for certain where he was. Opposite my window there is a well, at which two soldiers were drinking water late at night; an English gentleman, standing on the balcony of the Planter's House, heard one soldier say to the other, "Look, there is a cobbler, bang at him!" on which his comrade raised his piece and fired. Poor Crispin jumped up into his shop and shut the door; he had a near escape with life, for the ball had gone through the boarding of his house, and lodged itself in the opposite wall. Nothing was done to those two soldiers; and every one to whom I expressed my surprise at such negligence on the part of their commanding officers, marvelled at my surprise.

Unless a ruffian is known to have killed half a dozen people, and to have got, as it were, murder on the brain, he is almost safe from trouble in these western plains. A notorious murderer lived near Central City; it was known that he had shot six or seven men; but no one thought of interfering with him on account of his crimes until he was taken red-handed in the very act. Some persons fancied he was heartily sorry for what he had done, and he himself, when tossing off cocktails with his rough companions, used to say he was sick of shedding blood.

One day, on riding into Central City, he met a friend whom he invited to take a drink. The friend, not wishing to be seen any more in such bad company, declined the offer, on which the ruffian drew his pistol in the public street, in the open day, and saying, with a comic swagger of reluctance, "Good God, can I never come into town without killing some one?" shot his friend through the heart. Seized by the indignant crowd, the callous ruffian had a stern trial, a short thrift, and a midnight escape up the famous cotton-tree in the city ditch.

But with respect to theft, most of all the theft of horses, public opinion is far more strict than it is with respect to murder. Horse-stealing is always punished by death. Five good horses were one day missed from a corral in Denver; and on Wilson being consulted as to the probable thieves, the Sheriff's suspicions fell on three mining rowdies, gamblers, and thieves, named Brownlee, Smith, and Carter, men who had recently come into the city from the mines and the mountain roads. As inquiry in the slums and grog-shops could not find these worthies, Wilson, feeling sure that they were the men he wanted, ordered his horse, and, after looking well at his revolver and bowie-knife, jumped into the saddle and turned toward the Platte road. The time was early spring, when the snow was melting and the water high. Coming to the river, he stript and crossed the rapids, holding his clothes and pistols above his head, and partly swimming his horse across the stream. Riding on all day, all night, he came upon the thieves on a lonely prairie, one hundred and fifty miles from Denver, and five miles from the nearest ranch. Carter and Smith were each leading a horse, in addition to the one he rode; Brownlee rode alone, bringing up the rear. It was early day when he came up with them, and as they did not know him by sight, he entered into conversation, chiefly with Brownlee, passing himself off with the robbers as a broken miner going home to the States; and riding with them from eight o'clock until twelve in the hope of meeting either the public stage, or some party of traders who could lend him help. But he looked in vain. At noon he saw that no assistance could be got that day, and feeling that he must do his perilous work alone, he suddenly changed his air and voice, and reigning in his horse, said,—

"Gentlemen, we have gone far enough; we must turn back."

"Who the h—— are you?" shouted Brownlee, drawing his weapon.

"Bob Wilson," said the Sheriff, quietly; "come to fetch you back to Denver. You are accused of stealing three horses. Give up your arms, and you shall be fairly tried."

"You go to h——!" roared Brownlee, raising his pistol; but before he could draw the trigger, a slug was in his brain, and he tumbled to the ground with the imprecation hot upon his lips. Smith and Carter, hearing the loud words behind them followed by the exploding pistol, turned round suddenly in their saddles and got ready to fire; but in the confusion Smith let drop his piece; and in an eye-blink, Carter fell to the ground, dead as the dust upon which he lay. Smith, who had jumped down from his horse to get his pistol, now threw up his hands.

"Come here," cried Wilson, to the surviving thief; "hold my horse; if you stir a limb, I fire; you see I am not likely to miss my mark."

"You shoot very clean, sir," answered the trembling ruffian.

"Now, mind me," said the Sheriff; "I shall take you and these horses back to Denver; if you have stolen them, so much the worse for you; if not, you are all square; any way, you shall have a fair trial."

Wilson then picked up the three pistols, all of them loaded and capped. "I hesitated for a moment," he said to me, in this part of his tale, "whether to draw the charges; on second thought I resolved to keep them as they were, as no one could tell what might happen." Tying the three pistols in a handkerchief, and carefully reloading his own revolver, he then bade Smith get on one of the horses, to which he then made the fellow fast by ropes passed round his legs. Leaving the two dead men on the ground, and turning the horses loose to graze, Wilson led his captive along the road as far back as the ranch. A French settler, with an English wife, lived at this prairie ranch, and on Wilson stating who he was, and what his prisoner was more than suspected of being, the brave couple entered into his plans. After lashing Smith to a post, and telling the woman to shoot him dead if he struggled to get free (an order which her husband said she would certainly carry out, should the need for it arise), the two men rode back to the scene of execution, buried the two bodies, recovered the four horses, and brought away many articles from the dead men's pockets, which might serve to identify them in evidence. Returning to the ranch, they found the woman on guard, and Smith in despair. In their absence, Smith had used all his arts of appeal upon the woman; he had appealed to her pity, to her vanity, to her avarice. At length she had been forced to tell him that she would hear no more, that if he spoke again she would fire into his mouth. Then he grew white and silent. Next day brought the Sheriff and his prisoner to Denver, when Smith had a short shrift and a violent escape up the historical tree.

CHAPTER XIII.

SIERRA MADRE.

From Denver City up to Bridger's Pass, the highest point of the Sierra Madre (Mother Crest, or saw-line) over which trapper and trader have worn a track, the ascent is easy as to gradients, though it may be most uneasy in the matter of ruts, creeks, sand and stones. So far a traveller finds but little difference between the mountains and the prairies, which are also rolling uplands, rising between Leavenworth and Denver upwards of four thousand feet, the height of Snowdon above the sea. Yet Bridger's Pass is the water-parting of a great continent; the eastern slopes shedding their snow and rain towards the Atlantic Ocean, the western slopes towards the Pacific Ocean.

For ninety miles the road runs quietly north of Denver, along the base of a lower range of mountains known as the Black Hills, in search of an opening through the towering wall of rock and snow. At Stonewall, near Virginia Dale, it finds a gorge, or canyon, as the people call it, leading into a pretty woodland district, full of springs and streamlets, in which the trout are so abundant you may catch them in a creel. The scenery is not yet wild and grand, though it is picturesque, from the strange rock formation and the brilliance of its body color. The moment you enter into the mountain land, you see why the Spaniards called it Colorado. The prevailing tint of rock, of soil, of tree (especially in the fall), is red.

Between Virginia Dale and Willow Springs, the country lying south of our track may be called beautiful. The road runs high, commanding a sweep of many valleys, bright with welcome foliage, therefore blessed with water; broken by cols and ridges, with long dark intervals of space between; the whole landscape crowned in the distance by the mighty and irregular range from Long's Peak to Pike's Peak. This is a true Swiss scene; the hills being clothed with pine, the summits capped with snow; a scene as striking in its natural features as the more famous view of the Oberland Alps from Berne.

At Laramie we lose this mountain picture. Low mounds of earth and sand, covered with the wild sage, peopled by prairie dogs, coyotes, and owls, shut out the snow-line from our sight.

Here and there along the track we pass the shoulder, we cross the summit, of a height which may be called a mountain (out of courtesy) such as Elk Mountain, the Medicine Bow Mountain, and the ridge of North Platte, before we descend upon Sage Creek and Pine Grove; but we see no peaks, we climb no alps; jog jog,—trot trot,—grind grind,—we rumble in the light wagon over stones, over grass, over sand, across creeks and water-ruts, with a uniform misery, day after night, night after day, that would murder any man outright, from sheer exhaustion of his animal spirits, were it not for the strong reaction caused by the ever-expected appearance of Ute, Cheyenne, and Sioux.

The life is hard at its best, intolerable at its average. Only twice in the night and day we are allowed to eat. The food is bad, the water worse, the cooking worst. Vegetables there are none. Milk, tea, butter, beef, mutton, are commonly wanting. Even the talismanic letters from New York are useless in these high and desolate Passes through the sage-fields. If there were food it would be sold to us; but, as a rule, there is simply none at all. Hot dough, which they call cake, you may have, though you will find it hard to eat, impossible to digest—you who are not to the material and the method born, and who have been pampered and spoiled by the *chefs* in Pall Mall. No beer, no spirit, sometimes no salt, can be found. As a luxury, you may get dried elk and buffalo-flesh, seasoned with a dash of powder; and for these horrid dainties you are charged a dollar and a half, in some places two dollars, per meal.

But if the life seems hard to us, who get through it in a dozen days and nights, what must it prove to the trapper, the teamster, the emigrant? Spite of its perils and privations, this mountain road is alive with trains of people going to and fro between the River and Salt Lake. Hundreds of men, thousands of oxen, mules, and horses, climb these desolate tracks; bearing with them, in light mountain wagons built for the purpose, the produce of eastern fields and cities,—green apples, dried corn, salt beef, flour, meal, potted fruits and meats,—as well as tea, tobacco, coffee, rice, sugar, and a multitude of dry goods, from caps and shoes to coffin-plates and shrouds,—bearing them to the mining districts of Colorado, Utah, Idaho, Montana, where such things find a ready sale. The trainmen march in bands for safety, and a train from Leavenworth to Salt Lake resembles in many ways the great caravan of commerce on a Syrian road. A trader on the river,—at Oma, in Nebraska,—at Leavenworth, in Kansas,—hears, or perhaps suspects, that some article, such as tea, cotton, fruits,—it may be molasses, tanned leather,—is running short in the mountains, and that in a few weeks a demand for it is likely to spring up at high rates. Buying in a good market, he takes the risk of being wrong in his conjecture. With his one prime article of trade he combines a dozen minor articles; say, with a huge bulk of tea, a little cutlery, a little claret, a little quinine and other drugs, store of blankets and gauntlets,—perhaps a thousand pairs of top-boots. He buys fifty or sixty light wagons, with a dozen oxen to each wagon; engages a train boss, or captain, hires about a hundred men,—packs up his goods,—and sends the caravan off into the plains. No actuary in his senses would ensure the arrival of that train in Denver, in Salt Lake, in Virginia City. The journey is considered as an adventure. The men who go with it must be excellent shots, thoroughly well armed; but they are not expected to defend their cargo against the Indians; and should the red-skin plunderers show in force, the teamsters are allowed to cut the traces, mount on the fleetest mules, and fly to the nearest post or station, leaving their wagon, stock, and cargo, to be plundered as the Indians list. No man likes his poll to be scalped; and the teamster, with a wife and child, perhaps, lying in Omaha, in Leavenworth, loves to keep his hair untouched. Murder will happen in the best conducted trains; but the bravest Western boy sets his life above a hundred chests of tea and a thousand sacks of flour.

Some of these trains haul passengers along the road at the rate of fifty dollars a-head for the journey—(in the stage it is two hundred and fifty)—the passenger finding himself in food, herding with the teamsters, and cooking his own meals.

The trip, when it is done at all, is made in about ninety days, from the River to Salt Lake; a journey of more than twelve hundred miles; with the city of Denver as a resting-place, six hundred miles from the starting-point and from the end. The average rate is fourteen or fifteen miles a day; though some of the train-men will push through twenty miles on the plains.

Four or five hours in the middle of the day they rest to let the cattle graze, and to cook their food; at nightfall they encamp near to fresh water, if possible in the vicinity of a little wood. They corral the wagons; that is to say, they set them in the form of an ellipse, open only at one end, for safety; each wagon locked against its neighbor, overlapping it by a third of the length, like the scales on plate armor; this ellipse being the form of defence against Indian attack, which long experience in frontier warfare had proved to the old Mexican traders in these regions to be the most effective shield. When the wagons are corralled, the oxen are turned loose to graze, the men begin to cut and break wood, the women and children (if there be any in the party) light the fires, fetch water from the spring or creek, boil the kettle, and bake the evening bread. Some of the young men, expert with the rifle, tramp across gully and creek in search of plover, prairie dog, and chicken; and on lucky days these hunters may chance to fall upon antelope and elk. Luck going with them, the evening closes with a feast. Others hunt for rattle-snakes, and kill them; also for stray coyotes and wolves, many of which, driven mad by hunger, infest the neighborhood of a camp. I saw a huge gray wolf shot within two yards of a wagon, which had been lifted from the wheels and set on the ground, and in which lay a sleeping child. When supper is done, the oxen, having had their mouthful of bunch-grass, are driven for safety into the corral of wagons; or otherwise the morning light would haply find them miles away in an Indian camp. A song, a story, perhaps a dance, winds up the weary day. In warm weather, train-folks sleep in the wagons, to escape the rattle-snakes and wolves. When the snow is deep in the gully, when the wind comes sweeping down the ice, a wagon on wheels is too cold for a bed, and the train-men prefer a blanket on the ground, with a whisky-bottle for a pillow. Long before dawn they are up and about; yoking the cattle, hitching up the wagons, swallowing their morning meal. Sunrise finds them plodding on the road.

Sometimes the owner travels with his train; not often; for the boss can manage these unruly, drunken, quarrelling teamsters better than the actual owner of the cargo. If the rations should run short, if the whisky should turn out bad, if the wagons should break down, the boss can join chorus with the teamsters in swearing at his chief. A strong outburst of abuse is said to do the men much good; and as the owner does not hear it, he is none the worse. When the chief is present, every man in the train has a complaint to make; so that time is lost by the way, and a spirit of insubordination shows itself in the camp. When anything goes wrong,— and every day, in such a country, something must go wrong,—if the real master is not present, the boss can say, *he* cannot help it, they are all in one boat, and they must make the best of a bad job. In this way — grumbling, drinking, fighting — they get through the mountain-passes; to end their ninety days of stern privations by a week's debauchery, either in the secret slums of Salt Lake City, or in the solitude of some mountain ranch.

The owner travels in the mail, more swiftly, not more pleasantly, than his servants, and is ready in Denver, in Salt Lake, in Virginia City, to receive his wagons; when he may sell the whole train, tea, drugs, hosiery, wagons, oxen, in a lump or lumps.

The ranch-men are of two classes: (1), the enterprising class, who go out into the mountains — much as eastern farmers go into the backwoods — to clear the ground, to grow a little corn, to feed a few sheep and kine; fighting the battle of life, on one side against reluctant nature, on the other side against hostile red-skins; living on bad food and bad water, in the hope of getting a first footing on the unoccupied soil, and laying the foundation of a fortune for their sons and grandsons; (2), the more reckless class, who build a log-hut by the roadside, in the highway of teamster and emigrant, with a view of selling whisky and cordials to the passers-by, and even to the tipsy Cheyenne and Sioux, making in a brief season a fortune for themselves. Both classes lead a life of much peril and privation. Even more than the teamster and the emigrant, the ranch-man bears his life in the palm of his hand; for every ruffian on the road who calls for drink, with a bowie-knife and a revolver in his belt, has the quick, quarrelsome spirit of the Western boy, and often wants whisky to drink when he has never a dollar in his pouch to pay for the delicious dram.

But the chief peril comes to the ranch-man in the shape of Indians; most of all, when a powerful tribe, like that of the Sioux, that of the Pawnees, sets out on the war-path. The red-skin loves whisky more than he loves either wife or child; in peace he will sell anything to obtain his darling poison; his papoose, his squaw, even his captive in war: but when a Sioux has put the red paint on his cheek, and slung the scalping-knife to his side, he no longer thinks of buying his dose of fire-water from the white man; he sweeps down upon the ranch, takes it by force, and with it, not unfrequently, the life of its vendor.

Yet the spirit of gain tempts the ranch-man to rebuild his burnt shed, to replenish his plundered store. If he lives through two or three seasons of successful trade in whisky and tobacco, he is rich. Paddy Blake, an Irishman, from Virginia city, keeps a ranch near the summit of Bridger's Pass, in a field which is the very model of desolation. He lives at Fort Laramie; by trade he is a suttler; but he finds it pay better to sell bad spirits to the teamsters at three dollars a bottle, and cake-tobacco for chewing at six dollars a pound, than to deal in decent stores among soldiers and civilians at the fort. A small log-hut contains his stock of poisons, which he vends to the passer-by, including Utes and Cheyennes, about four months in the year, while the roads are open and the snow is off the ground; taking buffalo and beaver skins from the red men, dollars and kine (the kine too often stolen) from the whites.

Along this mountain road, in every train, among the callous teamsters, among the raw emigrants, among the passing strangers, among the resident stockmen, there is one topic of conversation night and day,—the Indians. Every red man moves in this region with the scalping-knife in his hand. Spottiswood, one of the smart agents of the Overland mail, told me that he saw a white man taken by the Sioux from his wagon, and burnt to death on a pile of bacon. The antelope-hunter of Virginia Dale was killed only a few weeks ago. Between Elk Mountain and Sulphur Springs a train was stopped by Cheyennes, and eighteen men, women, and children, were massacred and muti lated. Two young girls were carried off, and, after being much abused by the Indians, were sent into Fort Laramie, and exchanged for sacks of flour from the quartermaster's store.

Near the top of the first pass, stands a lonely mail-station, called, by a pious and permissible fiction, Pine Grove; two stockmen occupy the log-hut; one of them, named Jesse Ewing, is the hero of a tale more striking than many a deed that has earned the Victoria Cross.

In the spring of this year a party of Sioux, then out on the war-path, came to Pine Grove, and by accident found Jesse there alone. As usual, they made free with what was not their own; ate up the bread and coffee, the dried elk, and the salt bacon; and having gorged their stomachs, they told Jesse to light a big fire, as they meant to roast him alive. Burning their captives is a common pastime with the Sioux; not their Pawnee enemies only, but the Swaps (as they call the Yengees) or Pale-faces also. Up to this time Jesse had contrived to keep his knife and his revolver hidden in his clothes, and neither of these weapons being seen, the Indians supposed that he was quite unarmed and at their mercy. At first, he refused to light a fire, knowing they would carry out their threat; and on their saying they would set their squaws to skin him if he did not swiftly obey their chief, he said he could not make a big fire unless he were allowed to fetch straw and fagots from the stable. The fact being obvious to the Sioux, he was told to go and fetch them, two of the Indians going out into the night to see him do it; one entering the stable with him, the second standing at the door on guard. Quick as thought, his knife was in the side of the red man near him; a second later a slug was in the brain of the one outside. The firing brought out all the yelping band; but Jesse, swift as an antelope, leaped into a creek, got under some trees and stones, in a place which he knew very well, and lay there under cover, still as the dead, while the Sioux, infuriated by their sudden loss, kept up for hours around his hiding-place their wild and horrible yep, yep. The night was intensely cold; he had no shoes; no coat: worse than all else, the snow began to fall, so that he could not stir without leaving traces of his feet along the ground. Happily for him, snow slobbers and numbs an Indian's feet as quickly as it chills a Yengee's. He could hear the Sioux crying out against the cold; after a few hours he found that his enemies were turning their faces eastward. Slowly, the noise of feet and voices bore away; the Indians taking the path towards Sage Creek; and when the air was a little still, Jesse stole from his covert, and ran for his life to the home-station at Sulphur Springs, where he arrived at daybreak, and obtained from his comrades of the road the welcome relief of food and fire.

This brave boy has come back to Pine Grove; a fact which I mention with regret, since the Indians are again menacing the road; and if they come down in strength, Jesse will be marked in their score of vengeance as one of the first to fall.

CHAPTER XIV.

BITTER CREEK.

THE Camp of Peaks, composing the Sierra Madre, having their crown and centre in Fremont's Peak, three hundred feet above the height of Monte Rosa, shed from their snowy sides three water-lines: on the eastern side, towards the Mississippi and the Pacific Ocean; on the western side towards the Columbia River and the Pacific Ocean; on the southern side towards the Colorado River and the Gulf of California. Southwestward of this Peak rises the Wasatch chain, shutting out from these systems of rain-flow the depression known as the Valley of Utah and the Great Salt Lake. Between the two great mountain chains of the Sierra Madre and the Wasatch lies the Bitter Creek country, one of the most sterile spots on the surface of this earth.

This wild Sahara, measuring it from Sulphur Springs to Green River, is one hundred and thirty-five miles in width. It is a region of sand and stones, without a tree, without a shrub, without a spring of fresh water. Bones of elk and antelope, of horse and bullock, strew the ground. Here and there, more thickly than elsewhere, you come upon a human grave; each of which has a story known to the mountaineers. This stone is the memorial of five stock-men who were murdered by the Sioux. Yon pole marks the resting-place of a young emigrant girl, who died on her way to the

Promised Land. That tree is the gallows of a wretch, who was hung by his companions in a drunken brawl. The whole track is marked by skeletons and tragedies; and visible nature is in sternest harmony with the work of man. A little wild sage grows here and there, scattered in lonely bunches in the midst of a weak and stunted grass. The sun-flower all but disappears, attaining, where it grows at all, no more than the size of a common daisy. The hills are low, and of a dirty yellow tint. A fine white film of soda spots the landscape, here in broad fields, there in bright patches, which the unused eye mistakes for frost and snow. When the creek, which lends its bitter name to the valley, is full of water, as in early summer, while the ice is melting, the taste of that water, though nauseous, may be borne; but when the creek runs dry, in the later summer and the fall, it is utterly abominable to man and beast; rank poison, which inflames the bowels and corrupts the blood. Yet men must drink it, or they die of thirst; cattle must drink it, or they will die of thirst. The soil is very heavy, the road is very bad. A train can hardly cross this Bitter Creek country under a week, and many of the emigrant parties have to endure its stern privations ten or twelve days. Oxen cannot pull through the heavy sand, when from scanty food and poisonous drink their strength has begun to fail. Some fall by the way, and cannot be induced to rise; some simply stagger, and refuse to tug their chains. The goad curls round their backs in vain; there is nothing for a teamster to do but draw the yoke and let the poor creatures drop into the rear, where the wolves and ravens put an end to their miseries. The path is strewn with skeletons of ox and mule. Again and again we meet with trains in the Bitter Creek country, in which a third of the oxen are in hospital; that is to say, have been relieved from their labor, thrown on the flank to graze, or left behind on the chance of their recovery, perhaps in care of a lad. When many animals of a stock fall sick, the strain put on the healthy becomes severe, and the caravan, unable to go forward, may have to camp for a week of rest in most unhealthy ground.

Lying between the two great ridges of the Rocky Mountains, the Bitter Creek country, a valley about the average height of Mons Pilatus above the sea, is, of course, intensely cold. The saying of the herdsmen is, that winter ends with July, and begins with August. Many of the mules and oxen die of frost, especially in the fall, when the burning sun of noon is suddenly exchanged for the icy winds of midnight. Frost comes upon the cattle unawares, with a soft, seductive sense of comfort, so that they seem to bend their knees and close their eyes in perfect health; yet, when the morning dawns, it is seen that they will never rise again from their bed of sleep. It is much the same with men; who often lie down in their rugs and skins on the ground, a little numb, perhaps, in the feet; not miserably so, their toes being only just touched with the chill of ice; yet the more knowing hands among them feel that they will never find life and use in those feet again. I heard of one train captain, who, being careful of his men and teams, had put them up for the night, near Black Buttes, in a time of trouble with the Sioux; and who, being well clothed and mounted, had undertaken, in relief of another, to act as their sentinel and guard. All night he sat his pony in the cold; shivering a little, dozing a little; but on the rustling of a leaf, awake, alert, and watchful. When daylight came, and the camp began to stir, he shouted to one of his drivers, and would have drawn his foot from the leather rest, which serves the mountaineer instead of a stirrup; but his leg was stiff and would not obey his will. In his surprise, he tried to raise the other leg, but the muscles once more refused to answer. When he was lifted down from the saddle, his legs were found to have been frozen to the knee; and after three days' agony he expired.

Nothing is more usual than to see men on the prairies and in the mountains who have lost either toes or fingers, bitten away by frost.

Hardly less trying to the mountaineers than frost and snow, are the sudden storms which rage and howl through these lofty plains. On my return from Salt Lake City across the Bitter Creek, a storm of snow, of sleet and hail, swept down upon us, right in our front, hitting us in the face like shot, and soaking us suddenly to the skin. At first we met it bravely, keeping our horses to the fore, and making a little progress, even in the teeth of this riotous squall. But the horses soon gave in. Terrified by the roaring wind, chilled by the smiting hail, they stood stone-still; dogged, stolid, passive, utterly indifferent to the driver's voice and the driver's whip. Taught by his long experience, the driver knew when the brutes must have their way; he suddenly wheeled round, as though he was about to return, and setting the wagon to the fore, put his team under its lee, with their hind-quarters only exposed to the pelting storm. In this position we remained three hours, until the swirl and tumult had gone by; after which we got down from the wagon, shook ourselves dry in the cold night air, and with the help of a little cognac and tobacco (taken as a medicine) we resumed our journey.

A train of emigrants, which had to draw up near us, and await the tempest's passage, was not so lucky in arrangement as ourselves. The men had stopped their caravan as soon as the mules and horses had refused to move; but instead of bracing their frightened animals closer to the wagons, they had loosened their bands and suffered them to face the elements as they pleased. Some of them could not stand this freedom from the trace and curb. For a moment they stood still; they sniffed the air; they shook with panic; then, turning their faces from the wind, they pawed the wet ground, bent down their heads and went off madly into space; a regular stampede, in the course of which many of the poor creatures would be sure to drop down dead from terror and exhaustion. We could not see the end of our neighbors' troubles, for the night came down between us and their camp, and on the instant slackening of the wind, we wheeled the wagon round, and trotted on our way. The emigrants would have to wait for dawn, to commence their search for the wandering mules and horses; some they would find in the nearer creeks, where they happened to first shelter from the driving storm; others they would have to follow over ridge and gully, many a long mile. Once in motion, with the hail and wind beating heavily on their backs, horses will never stop; will climb over mountains, rush into rivers, break through underwood, until the violence of nature has spent itself out. Then they will stand and shiver, perhaps droop and die.

Bullocks, like mules and horses, suffer from these storm-frights, and the experienced teamster of the plains will yoke them together, and lash them to the wagons whenever he sees the sign of a tempest coming on. Herding in a corral, hearing the voices of their drivers, they are less alarmed than when, loose and alone, they break into a stampede; yet even in a corral, with the song of the teamster in their ears, they shake and moan, lie down on the earth and cry, and not unfrequently die of fright.

In the midst of these terrors and confusions in a train—when the horses are either strayed or sick, when the boss is busy with his stock, when the teamsters are exhausted by fatigue and hunger—the road-agents generally fall on the corral and find it an easy prey.

Road-agent is the name applied in the mountains to a ruffian who has given up honest work in the store, in the mine, in the ranch, for the perils and profits of the highway. Many ruined traders, broken gamblers, unsuccessful diggers, take to the road, plundering trains of their goods, robbing emigrants of their mules, and sometimes venturing to attack the mail. They are all well armed; some of them are certain shots. No fear of man, and no respect for woman, restrain these plunderers from committing the most atrocious crimes. Their hands are raised against every one who may be expected to have a dollar in his purse. Every law which they can break, they have already broken; every outrage which they can effect, they have probably already effected; so that their dregs of life are already due to justice; and nothing they can do will add to the load of guilt which they already bear. These plunderers, who roam about the tracks in bands of three or five, of ten or twenty, sometimes of thirty or forty, are far more terrible to the merchant and the emigrant than either Sioux or Ute. The Sioux is but a savage, whom the white man has a chance of daunting by his pride, of deceiving by his craft; but his brother on the road, himself perhaps a trader, a train-man in his happier days, can see through every wile, and measure with a glance both his weakness and his strength.

Many men known to have been road-agents, suspected of being still connected with the bands, are at large; this man keeping a grog-shop, that man living in a ranch, the other man driving the mail. In this free western country you cannot ask many questions as to character. A steady wrist, a quick eye, a prompt invention, are of more importance in a servant than the very best testimonials from his recent place. Life is too rough for the nicer rules to come into play. I saw a fellow in Denver whose name is as well known in Colorado as that of Dick Turpin in Yorkshire. He is said to have murdered half a dozen men; he is free to come and go, to buy and sell; no one molests him; fear of his companions, and of men who live by crimes like his, being strong enough to daunt, for a time, even the Vigilance Committee and their daring Sheriff. On my return through the Bitter Creek country, I had the honor of riding in the mountain wagon with an old road-agent, who laughed and joked over his exploits, caring not a jot for either sheriff or judge. One of his stories ran as follows. He and a wretch like himself, being out on the road, had been rather lucky, and having got a thousand dollars in greenbacks in their pouch, they were making for Denver City, where they hoped to enjoy their plunder, when they saw in the distance five mounted men, whom my companion said he knew at once to be part of a gang in which he had formerly served on terms of share and share. "We are lost now," he said to his companion in crime; "these men will rob us of our greenbacks, possibly shoot us into the bargain, so as not to leave a witness of their deed alive."

"We shall see," replied his more crafty friend. "I know them, and have been out with them; we must get over them as broken-down wretches."

Smearing themselves with dirt, dragging a long face, and looking hungry and miserable, they met the five horsemen with the cry, "Give us five dollars, captain; we are broken down and trying to get on to Denver, where we'll find some friends; give us five dollars!" This cry of distress went straight to the highwayman's heart. He tossed my companion the greenbacks, telling him to be mum, and then dashed on in front of his more suspicious comrades.

Not long ago, a party of these road-agents robbed the imperial mail, with circumstances of unusual harshness, even in the mountains. The story of the crime is in everybody's mouth as that of the Portliff Canyon murder; and is here told mainly from the murderer's confession to Sheriff Wilson.

Frank Williams, a man of bad character, but a good whip, a good shot, an experienced mountaineer, got employment as a driver on the Overland route. On one of this man's visits to Salt Lake he made the acquaintance of one Parker of Atchison, a trader who had been doing business in the Mormon city, and was about to return with his gains to the River town. M'Causland of Virginia, and two other merchants, having with them a large sum of money in gold dust, were proposing to go back with Parker in the mail, for their mutual safety. These names and facts Parker told Frank Williams as they drank together, at the same time asking his advice in the matter as a driver and a friend. Under Frank Williams' suggestion the four men took their places in the stage; they were the only passengers that day; and they made a prosperous journey until they arrived in Portliff Canyon, where Parker found Frank, who had gone back from Salt Lake City to his accustomed drive.

In that canyon they were murdered. In a narrow gorge of the pass, Frank let his whip fall to the ground; he stopped the coach, and ran backwards to pick it up; when a volley of shot came rattling into the mail, and three of the men inside of it fell dead. Eight fellows in masks rushed up to the mail, pulled out the dead and dying, and seized upon their boxes with the gold dust and the greenbacks. Parker was hurt, though not to his death; and on seeing Williams come back, pistol in hand, he cried out to his friend to spare his life. "I am only hipped; help me, Frank, and I shall do!" Frank put the pistol to his friend's head and blew his brains into the air; not daring to allow one witness of his crime to remain alive. He then drove into the station, where he reported that the mail had been robbed, the passengers killed. Two men went out with him to find the dead bodies, and a search was made from Denver to Salt Lake for the assassins. No suspicion fell upon Frank, until a few weeks after the robbery and murder, when news was brought to Sheriff Wilson by a thief, that Frank Williams had left his place on the mail-line, and was spending his money rather freely in the Gentile grog-shops of Salt Lake. Bob instantly took steps to have him watched in those dens; but while he was setting his spies in motion, Williams suddenly appeared in the streets of Denver, close to that cotton-tree on which the Sheriff looks down from his auctioneer's throne. Before he had been a day in Denver, he had bought for himself and his boon-companions seven new suits of clothes, had hired a brothel, and treated nearly every ruffian in the town to drink.

One evening he was seized by Wilson, who conducted him to a midnight sitting of the Vigilance Committee. What took place in that sitting is unknown; the names of those who were present can be only guessed; but it was evident to every one next day that Frank Williams had been found guilty of some atrocious crime. Men who got up early that morning had seen his body dangling from a buggy-pole in Main Street.

CHAPTER XV.

DESCENT OF THE MOUNTAINS.

After passing Fort Bridger, the descent becomes quick, abrupt, and verdant. The track is still rough, stony, unmade; here running over round crests, there cutting into deep canyons, anon toiling through troughs of sand; but on the whole we go dropping down from the high plateau of the Sierras, where Nature is dry and sterile, seemingly unfit for the occupation of man, into deep ravines and narrow dales, in which the wild sage gives place to tall, rank grass. A little scrub begins to show itself in the clefts and hollows; dwarf-oak and maple now putting on their autumnal garb of pink and gold. Stunted pines and cedars become a feature in the landscape; a noise of water babbles up from the glens; long serpentine fringes of balsam and willow show the courses of the descending creeks. We rattle, in the fading light, through Muddy Creek, and roll, in the early darkness, past Quaking Asp, — startled, as we come round the ledge of a sharp hill, to see before us a mighty flame, as though the valley in our front, the hill-side on our flank, were all on fire. It is a Mormon camp. About a hundred wagons, corralled, in the usual way, for defence against Utes and Snakes, are halted in a dark valley, where rocks and crests pile high into the heavens, shutting out the stars. In front of each wagon burns a huge fire; men and women, boys and girls, are gathered round these fires; some eating their supper, some singing brisk songs, others again dancing; oxen, mules, horses, stand about in happy confusion of group and color; dogs sleep round the fires or bark at the mail; and through all this wild, unexpected scene, clash the cymbals, horns, and trumpets of a band. Though we are still high up in the mountains, we feel, as it were, already on the borders of the Salt Lake Eden, that home of the Latter-Day Saints, to which the weaver is called from Manchester, the peasant from Llandudno, the cobbler from Whitechapel.

An hour later we drop into Bear River Station, kept by acting-bishop Myers, an English member of the Mormon Church; a dignitary who has hitherto limited his rights over the weaker sex to the wedding of two wives. One wife lives with him at Bear River; one hired help, a young English woman on a visit (and I fear in some little peril of the heart), with two or three men, his servants, make up this bishop's flock and household. The wife is a lady; simple, elegant, bewitching; who, while we rinse the dust from our throats and dash cold water about our heads and faces, hastily and daintily sets herself to cook our food. Tired and hungry as we are, this Myers appears to us the very model of a working bishop for a working world. At Oxford he would count for little, in the House of Lords for nothing. His words are not choice, his intonation is not good and musical; he hardly (I will not answer for it) knows a Greek particle by sight; but he seems to know very well how a good man should receive the hungry and weary who are cast down at his door on a frosty night. After poking up the stove, heaping wood upon the fire, chopping up a side of mutton (it is the first fresh meat we have seen for days), he runs out of doors to haul water from the well, and puts straw into our coach that our feet may be kept warm in the coming frost. From him we get genuine tea, good bread, even butter; not sage tea, hot dough, and a pinch of salt. The chops are delicious; and the bishop's elegant wife and her ladylike friend, by the grace and courtesy with which they serve the table, turn a common mountain meal into a banquet.

We leave Bear River with respect for one phase of the working episcopacy founded by Brigham Young.

In the night we pass by Hanging Rock and roll down Echo Canyon; a ravine of rocks and nooks, surprising, lovely, fantastic, when they are seen under the light of luminous autumn stars. Early morning brings us to Weber River, where we break our fasts on hot-bake and leather; early day to Coalville, the first Mormon village on our road; a settlement built of wooden sheds, in the midst of rude gardens and patches of corn-fields, hardly redeemed from that wild waste of nature in the midst of which a few Utes and Bannocks hunted the elk and scalped each other not a score of years since. Coal is found here; also a little water, a little wood. We glance with quick eyes into the houses, some of which stand in groups and rows, as we learn from our driver that those wooden cottages which have two or more doors, are the houses of elders who have married two or more wives. We think of the arid sweeps through which we have just come; of our six days' journey among rocky passes and mountain slopes; and gaze with wonder on the courage, industry, fanaticism, which could have been induced, by any teaching, by any promise, to attack this desolate valley, with a view to making out of it a habitation fit for man. But here is Coalville; a town in the hills, at least the beginning of a town; placed in a gorge where engineers and explorers had declared it utterly impossible for either man or beast to live. Patches of corn run down to the little creek. Oxen graze on the hill-sides. Dogs guard the farmhouses. Hogs grub into the soil; chickens hop among the sheaves; and horses stand in the court-yards. Rosy children, with their blue eyes and flaxen curls telling of their pure English blood, play before the gates and tumble in the straw. Girls of nine or ten years are milking cows; boys of the same age are driving teams; women are cooking, washing; men are digging potatoes, gathering in fruit, chopping and sawing planks. Every man seems busy, every place prosperous, though the ravine was but yesterday a desert of dust and stones. From among the green shrubs a neat little chapel peeps out.

Lower down the valleys the scene expands, and herds of cattle dot the wide sweeps of grass. We pass Kimball's Hotel—a station of the Overland Mail—kept by one of Heber Kimball's sons; a man of some wealth, living out here in the lonely hills, with his sheep, his cattle, and his three wives; professing the Mormon creed, though he is said to have been drummed out of the society of Salt Lake for tipsiness and rioting in the public streets. Sharp justice, as we hear, is meted out by the Saints upon offenders; no claims of blood, however high or near, being suffered to protect a criminal from the sentence of his church.

At Mountain Dell, the house of Bishop Hardy, a man having eight wives, three of whom live with him in this mountain shed, we see a little Ute Indian, who has been reclaimed from his tribe, made into a faithful Mormon and a good boy; a shrewd lad, who seems to know the difference between dining off wolf and off mutton, and who hates the red-skins, his brethren in the war-paint, with all his soul. From one of the bishop's wives we learn that he was bought, as a papoose, from his father for a few dollars; that he is a sharp fellow, and works very well when he is made to do so; that he is lazy by nature, and apt to lie much in the sun; that he is slow at books and learning, but takes easily to horses, and drives a team very well. In fact, he is capable of being raised into a white man's servant, and trained, at much cost and care, to fetch in wood and water for the white man's use.

The Mormons have a peculiar view about the red men, whom they regard as a branch of the Hebrew people, who migrated from Palestine to North America in their days of power and righteousness, while they yet held the priesthood in their hands. When, through the sin of disobedience they lost their priesthood, they lost, along with that sacred office, their white color, their bright intelligence, their noble physiognomy. According to the Mormons, some rags and tatters of their early faith—of their ancient institutions—still remain to these remnants of Israel; their belief in one Great Spirit; their division into tribes; their plurality of wives. But the curse of God is upon them and upon their seed. They came of a sacred race,—but a sacred race now lying under the stern reproof of Heaven. "In time—in God's own time," said Young to me, in a subsequent conversation, "they will be recalled into a state of grace: they will then cease to do evil and learn to do good; they will settle down in cities; they will become white in color; and they will act as a nation of priests."

The change will, indeed, be great that transforms a Pawnee and a Ute into the likeness of Aaron and of Joshua.

Before the war broke out, and slavery was banished as an institution from the American soil, the Saints had passed a territorial law permitting the purchase of boys and girls from the Indians, with a view to their being baptized into the church and taught useful trades. Ute and Snake are only too ready to sell their infants; and many young red-skins, bought under that law, are still to be found in these valleys. Of course they are now free as the whites, and far more lazy, treacherous, and wicked.

The bishop's wife, having had her eyes opened by many trials, has come to have little faith in the government plan for reclaiming Utes and Bannocks. She sees that a curse is on them, and on their seed; she hopes that when the time shall come for that curse to be removed, the red man will be capable of thrift, of labor, of salvation; but that removal, she owns to herself, must be the work of God, not that of man.

A long steep canyon, nine or ten miles in length,—with fringe of verdure and beck of water running through it; the verdure feeding cattle, the water working mills,—opens a way from Mountain Dell into the Salt Lake Basin, which we come upon suddenly, and by a sort of surprise, on turning a projecting mountain ledge.

The scene now in front of us, from whatever point of view it may be taken, is one of the half-dozen pure and perfect landscapes which the earth can show. No wonder that the poor emigrant from a Liverpool cellar, from a Blackwall slum, exalted as his vision must be, with religious fervor, and by sharp privation looks down upon it as a terrestrial Paradise.

Lying at the foot of these snowy ranges of the Wasatch mountains, spreads the great plain, far away into the unseen vistas of the north; the whole expanse of valley filled with a golden haze of surprising richness, the effect of a tropical sunshine streaming over fields sown thick with sun-flowers, like an English field with buttercups, and over multitudinous lakelets, pools, and streams: to the left soar into the clouds and curl round the Great Salt Lake a chain of mountains, which the Indians call Oquirrh. In our front lies the sparkling city, the New Jerusalem, in its bowers of trees; beyond that city flows the Jordan, bearing the fresh waters of Utah through the plains into Salt Lake, which darkens and cools the great valley, with its amplitudes of blue. From the lake itself, which is a hundred miles broad, a hundred and fifty miles long, spring two islands, purple and mountainous; Antelope Island (now called Church Island) and Stansbury Island; while, on either side, and beyond the blue waters of the lake itself, run chains of irregular and picturesque heights, the barren sierras of Utah and Nevada.

The air is soft and sweet; southern in its odor, northern in its freshness. Cool winds come down from the Wasatch peaks; in which drifts of snow and frozen pools lie all through the summer months. So clear is the atmosphere that Black Rock on the Salt Lake, twenty-five miles distant, seems but a few hundred yards in our front, and crests which stands sixty miles apart, appear to our sight as though they were peaks of a single range.

Lower down in the valley the golden haze steeps everything in its own delicious light. The city appears to be one vast park or garden, in which you count innumerable masses of dark green trees, with a white kiosk, a chapel, a court-house, sprinkled about it here and there. Above it, on a bank of higher land, is the camp; a cluster of white tents and shanties; from which a Gentile government watches suspiciously the doings of men in this city of the Saints. But the camp itself adds picture to the scene; a bar of color to the landscape of yellow, white, and green.

CHAPTER XVI.

THE NEW JERUSALEM.

A DREAM of the night, helped by a rush of water from the hill-side, (not larger than the Xenil, which gave life to Granada, and changed the barren vega into a garden,) fixed the site of the New Jerusalem. Brigham Young tells me, that when coming over the mountains, in search of a new home for his people, he saw, in a vision of the night, an angel standing on a conical hill, pointing to a spot of ground on which the new Temple must be built. Coming down into this basin of Salt Lake, he first sought for the cone which he had seen in his dream; and when he had found it, he noticed a stream of fresh hill-water flowing at its base, which he called the City Creek. Elder

George Smith, and a few of the pioneers, led this creek through and through a patch of likely soil, into which they then stuck potatoes; and having planted these bulbs, they took a few steps northward, marked out the Temple site, and drew a great square line about it. The square block, ten acres in extent, is the heart of the city, the Mormon holy place, the harem of this new Jerusalem of the West.

The site of the new city was laid between the two great lakes, Utah Lake and Salt Lake,— like the town of Interlachen between Brienz and Thun,—though the distances are here much greater, the two inland seas of Utah being real seas when compared against the two charming lakelets in the Bernese Alps. A river now called the Jordan flows from Utah into Salt Lake; but it skirts the town only, and lying low down in the valley, is useless, as yet, for irrigation. Young has a plan for constructing a canal from Utah Lake to the city, by way of the lower benches of the Wasatch chain; a plan which will cost much money, and fertilize enormous sweeps of barren soil. If Salt Lake City is left to extend itself in peace, the canal will soon be dug; and the bench, now covered with stones, with sand, and a little wild sage, will be changed into vineyards and gardens.

The city, which covers, we are told, three thousand acres of land, between the mountains and the river, is laid out in blocks of ten acres each. Each block is divided into lots of one acre and a quarter; this quantity of land being considered enough for an ordinary cottage and garden.

As yet, the Temple is unbuilt; the foundations are well laid, of massive granite; and the work is of a kind that bids fair to last; but the Temple block is covered with temporary buildings and erections — the old tabernacle, the great bowery, the new tabernacle, the temple foundations. A high wall encloses these edifices; a poor wall, without art, without strength; more like a mud wall than the great work which surrounds the temple platform on Moriah. When the works are finished, the enclosure will be trimmed and planted, so as to offer shady walks and a garden of flowers.

The Temple block gives form to the whole city. From each side of it starts a street, a hundred feet in width, going out on the level plain, and in straight lines into space. Streets of the same width, and parallel to these, run north and south, east and west; each planted with locust and ailantus trees, cooled by two running streams of water from the hill-side. These streets go up north, towards the bench, and nothing but the lack of people prevents them from travelling onward, south and west, to the lakes, which they already reach on paper, and in the imagination of the more fervid saints.

Main Street runs along the Temple front; a street of offices, of residences, and of trade. Originally, it was meant for a street of the highest rank, and bore the name of East Temple Street; upon it stood, besides the Temple itself, the Council house, the Tithing office, the dwellings of Young, Kimball, Wells, the three chief officers of the Mormon church. It was once amply watered and nobly planted; but commerce has invaded the precincts of the modern temple, as it invaded those of the old; and the power of Brigham Young has broken and retreated before that of the money-dealers and the venders of meat and raiment. Banks, stores, offices, hotels,—all the conveniences of modern life,—are springing up in Main Street; trees have in many parts been cut down, for the sake of loading and unloading goods; the trim little gardens, full of peach-trees and apple-trees, bowering the adobe cottages in their midst, have given way to shop-fronts and to hucksters' stalls. In the business portion, Main Street is wide, dusty, unpaved, unbuilt; a street showing the three stages through which every American city has to pass: the log-shanty, the adobe cot (in places where clay and fuel can be easily obtained, this stage is one of brick), and the stone house. Many of the best houses are still of wood; more are of adobe, the sun-dried bricks once used in Babylonia and in Egypt, and still used everywhere in Mexico and California; a few are of red stone, and even granite. The Temple is being built of granite from a neighboring hill. The Council house is of red stone; as are many of the great magazines, such as Godbe's, Jennings', Gilbert's, Clawson's; magazines in which you find everything for sale, as in a Turkish bazaar, from candles and champagne, down to gold dust, cotton prints, tea, pen-knives, canned meats, and mouse-traps. The smaller shops, the ice-cream houses, the saddlers, the barbers, the restaurants, the hotels, and all the better class of dwellings, are of sun-dried bricks; a good material in this dry and sunny climate; bright to the eye, cosy in winter, cool in summer; though such houses are apt to crumble away in a shower of rain. A few shanties, remnants of the first emigration, still remain in sight. Lower down, towards the south, where the street runs off into infinite space, the locust and ailantus trees reappear.

In its busy, central portion, nothing hints the difference between Main Street in Salt Lake City, and the chief thoroughfare, say, of Kansas, Leavenworth, and Denver, except the absence of grog-shops, lager-beer saloons, and bars. The hotels have no bars; the streets have no betting-houses, no gaming-tables, no brothels, no drinking-places. In my hotel — "The Salt Lake"— kept by Col. Little, one of the Mormon elders, I cannot buy a glass of beer, a flask of wine. No house is now open for the sale of drink (though the Gentiles swear they will have one open in a few weeks); and the table of the hotel is served at morning, noon, and night, with tea. In this absence of public solicitation to sip either claret-cobbler, whisky-bourbon, Tom and Jerry, mint-julep, eye-opener, fix-up, or any other Yankee deception in the shape of liquor—the city is certainly very much unlike Leavenworth, and the River towns where every third house in a street appears to be a drinking den. Going past the business quarter, we return to the first ideas of Young in planting his new home; the familiar lines of acacias grow by the becks; the cottages stand back from the road-side, twenty or thirty feet; the peach-trees, apple-trees, and vines, tricked out with roses and sun-flowers, smother up the roofs.

Right and left from Main Street, crossing it, parallel to it, lie a multitude of streets, each like its fellow; a hard, dusty road, with tiny becks, and rows of locust, cotton-wood, and philarea, and the building-land laid down in blocks. In each block stands a cottage, in the midst of fruit-trees. Some of these houses are of goodly appearance as to size and style, and would let for high rentals in the Isle of Wight. Others are mere cots of four or five rooms, in which the polygamous families, should they ever quarrel, would find it difficult to form a ring and fight. In some of these orchards you see two, three houses; pretty Swiss cottages, like many in St. John's Wood, as to gable, roof, and paint: these are the dwellings of different wives. "Whose houses are these?" we ask a lad in East Temple Street, pointing to some pretty-looking villas. "They belong," said he, "to Brother Kimball's family." Here, on the bench, in the highest part of the city, is Elder Hiram Clawson's garden; a lovely garden, red with delicious peaches, plums, and apples, on which, through the kindness of his youngest wife, we have been hospitably fed during our sojourn with the Saints; a large house stands in front, in which live his first and second wives with their nurseries of twenty children. But what is yon dainty white bower in the corner, with its little gate and its smother of roses and creepers? That is the house of the youngest wife, Alice, a daughter of Brigham Young. She has a nest of her own, apart from the other women, — a nest in which she lives with her four little boys, and where she is supposed to have as much of her own way with her lord, as the daughter of a Sultan enjoys in the harem of a Pasha. Elder Naisbit, one of the Mormon poets, an English convert to the faith as it is in Joseph, lives with his two wives and their brood of young children, on the high ground opposite to Elder Clawson, in a very pretty mansion, something like a cottage on the Under Cliff. Much of the city is only green glade and orchard waiting for the people who are yet to come and fill it with the pride of life.

In First South Street stand the Theatre and the City Hall, both fine structures, and for Western America remarkable in style.

The City Hall is used as head-quarters of police, and as a court of justice. The Mormon police are swift and silent, with their eyes in every corner, their grip on every rogue. No fact, however slight, appears to escape their notice. A Gentile friend of mine, going through the dark streets at night towards the theatre, spoke to a Mormon lady of his acquaintance whom he overtook; next day a gentleman called at his hotel, and warned him not to speak with a Mormon woman in the dark streets unless her father should be with her. In the winter months there are usually seven or eight hundred miners in Salt Lake City, young Norse gods of the Denver stamp; every man with a bowie-knife in his belt, a revolver in his hand, clamoring for beer and whisky, for gaming-tables and lewd women, comforts which are strictly denied to them by these Saints. The police have all these violent spirits to repress; that they hold them in decent order with so little bloodshed is the wonder of every western governor and judge. William Gilpin, governor elect of Colorado, and Robert Wilson, sheriff of Denver and justice of the peace, have nothing but praise to give these stern and secret, but most able and effective ministers of police.

With this court of justice we have scarcely made acquaintance. A few nights ago we met the judge, who kindly asked us to come and see his court; but while we were chatting in his ante-room, before the cases were called, some one whispered in his ear that we were members of the English bar, on which he slipped out of sight, and adjourned his court. This judge, when he is not sitting on the bench, is engaged in vending drugs across a counter in Main Street; and as we know where to find him in his store, we sometimes drop in for soda-water and a cigar; but we have not yet been able to fix a time for seeing his method of administering justice at Salt Lake.

The city has two sulphur-springs, over which Brigham Young has built wooden shanties. One bath is free. The water is refreshing and relaxing, the heat 92°.

No beggar is seen in the streets; scarcely ever a tipsy man; and the drunken fellow, when you see one, is always either a miner or a soldier—of course a Gentile. No one seems poor. The people are quiet and civil, far more so than is usual in these western parts. From the presence of trees, of water, and of cattle, the streets have a pastoral character, seen in no other city of the mountains and the plains. Here, standing under the green locust-trees, is an ox come home for the night; yonder is a cow at the gate being milked by a child. Light mountain-wagons stand about, and the sun-burnt emigrants, who have just come in from the prairies, thankful for shade and water, sit under the acacias, and dabble their feet in the running creeks.

More than all other streets, perhaps, Main Street, as the business quarter, offers picture after picture to an artist's eye; most of all when an emigrant-train is coming in from the plains. Such a scene is before me now; for the train which we passed in the gorge above Bear River, has just arrived, with sixty wagons, four hundred bullocks, six hundred men, women, and children, all English and Welsh. The wagons fill the street: some of the cattle are lying down in the hot sun; the men are eager and excited, having finished their long journey across the sea, across the States, across the prairies, across the mountains; the women and little folks are scorched and wan; dirt, fatigue, privation, give them a wild, unearthly look; and you would hardly recognize in this picturesque and ragged group the sober Monmouth farmer, the clean Woolwich artisan, the smart London smith. Mule-teams are being unloaded at the stores. Miners from Montana and Idaho, in huge boots and belts, are loafing about. A gang of Snake Indians, with their long hair, their scant drapery, and their proud reserve, are cheapening the dirtiest and cheapest lots. Yon fellow in the broad sombrero, dashing up the dust with his wiry little horse, is a New Mexican; here comes a heavy Californian swell; and there, in the blue uniform, go two officers from the camp.

The air is wonderfully pure and bright. Rain seldom falls in the valley, though storms occur in the mountains almost daily; a cloud coming up in the western hills, rolling along the crests, and threatening the city with a deluge; but when breaking into wind and showers, it seems to run along the hill-tops into the Wasatch chain, and sail away eastward into the snowy range.

CHAPTER XVII.

THE MORMON THEATRE.

THE play-house has an office and a service in this Mormon city, higher than the churches would allow to it in London, Paris, and New York. Brigham Young is an original in many ways; he is the high-priest of what claims to be a new dispensation; yet he has got his theatre into perfect order, before he has raised his Temple foundations above the ground.

That the drama had a religious origin, and that the stage has been called a school of manners, every one is aware. Young feels inclined to go back upon all first principles; in family life to those of Abraham, in social life to those of Thespis. Priests invented both the ancient and the modern stages; and if experience shows as strongly in Salt Lake City as in New York, that people love to be light and merry—to laugh and glow—why should their teachers neglect the thousand opportunities offered by a play, of getting them to laugh in the right places, to glow at the proper things? Why should Young not preach moralities from the stage? Why should he not train his actors and his actresses to be models of good conduct, of correct pronunciation, and of taste in dress? Why should he not try to reconcile religious feeling with pleasure?

Brigham Young may be either right or wrong in his ideas of the uses to which a playhouse may be turned in a city where they have no high schools and colleges as yet; but he is bent on trying his experiment to an issue; for this purpose he has built a model theatre, and he is now making an effort to train a model company.

Outside, his theatre is a rough Doric edifice, in which the architect has contrived to produce a certain effect by very simple means; inside, it is light and airy, having no curtains and no boxes, save two in the proscenium, with light columns to divide the tiers, and having no other decoration than pure white paint and gold. The pit, rising sharply from the orchestra, so that every one seated on its benches can see and hear to advantage, is the choicest part of the house. All these benches are let to families; and here the principal elders and bishops may be seen every play-night, surrounded by their wives and children, laughing and clapping like boys at a pantomime. Yon rocking-chair, in the centre of the pit, is Young's own seat; his place of pleasure, in the midst of his Saints. When he chooses to occupy his private box, one of his wives, perhaps Eliza the Poetess, Harriet the Pale, or Amelia the Magnificent, rocks herself in his chair while laughing at the play. Round about that chair, as the place of honor, cluster the benches of those who claim to stand nearest to their prophet: of Heber Kimball, first councillor; of Daniel Wells, second councillor and general-in-chief; of George A. Smith, apostle and historian of the church; of George Q. Cannon, apostle; of Edward Hunter, presiding bishop; of Elder Stenhouse, editor of the "Daily Telegraph;" and of a host of less brilliant Mormon lights.

In the sides of the proscenium nestle two private boxes: one is reserved for the Prophet, when he pleases to be alone, or wishes to have a gossip with some friend; the other is given up to the girls who have to play during the night, but who are not engaged in the immediate business of the piece. As a rule, every one's pleasure is considered in this model playhouse; and I can answer, on the part of Miss Adams, Miss Alexander, and other young artists, that this appropriation to their sole use of a private box, into which they can run at all times, in any dress, without being seen, is considered by them as a very great comfort.

Through the quick eye and careful hand of his manager, Hiram Clawson, the President may be congratulated on having made his playhouse into something coming near to that which he conceives a playhouse should be. Everything in front of the footlights is in keeping; peace and order reign in the midst of fun and frolic. Neither within the doors nor about them, do you find the riot of our own Lyceum and Drury Lane; no loose women, no pickpockets, no ragged boys and girls, no drunken and blaspheming men. As a Mormon never drinks spirits, and rarely smokes tobacco, the only dissipation in which you find these hundreds of hearty creatures indulging their appetites, is that of sucking a peach. Short plays are in vogue in this theatre, just as short sermons are the rule in yon tabernacle. The curtain, which rises at eight, comes down about half-past ten; and as the Mormon fashion is for people to sup before going out, they retire to rest the moment they get home, never suffering their amusements to infringe on the labors of the coming day. Your bell rings for breakfast at six o'clock.

But the chief beauties of this model playhouse lie behind the scenes; in the ample space, the perfect light, the scrupulous cleanliness of every part. I am pretty well acquainted with green-rooms and side wings in Europe; but I have never seen, not in Italian and Austrian theatres, so many delicate arrangements for the privacy and comfort of ladies and gentlemen as at Salt Lake. The green-room is a real drawing-room. The scene-painters have their proper studios; the dressers and decorators have immense magazines. Every lady, however small her part in the play, has a dressing-room to herself.

Young understands that the true work of reform in a playhouse must begin behind the scenes; that you must elevate the actor before you can purify the stage. To this end, he not only builds dressing-rooms and a private box for the ladies who have to act, but he places his daughters on the stage as an example and encouragement to others. Three of these young sultanas, Alice, Emily, and Zina, are on the stage. With Alice, the youngest wife of Elder Clawson, I have had the honor to make an acquaintance, which might be called a friendship, and from her lips I have learned a good deal as to her father's ideas about stage reform. "I am not myself very fond of playing," she said to me one day as we sat at dinner, — not in these words, perhaps, but to this effect, — "but my father desires that my sisters and myself should act sometimes, as he does not think it right to ask any poor man's child to do anything which his own children would object to do." Her dislike to playing, as she afterwards told me, arose from a feeling that Nature had given her no abilities for acting well; she was fond of going to see a good piece, and seldom omitted being present when she had not to play. Brigham Young has to create, as well as to reform, the stage of Salt Lake City; and the chief trouble of a manager who is seven hundred miles from the next theatre, must always be with his artists. Talent for the work does not grow in every field, like a sunflower and a peach-tree; it must be sought for in nooks and corners; now in a shoe-shop, anon in a dairy, then in a counting-house; but wherever the talent may be found, Young cannot think of asking any young girl to do a thing which it is supposed that a daughter of his own would scorn.

In New York, in St. Louis, in Chicago, nobody would assert that the stage is a school of virtue, that acting is a profession which a sober man would like his daughter to adopt. Young does not blind himself to the fact that in claiming the theatre as a school of morals, he has to fight against a social judgment. An odor of vice, as of a poisonous weed, infects the air of a playhouse everywhere; though nowhere less offensively than in American towns. Against this evil, much of it the consequence of bad traditions, he offers up, as it were, a part of himself—his children; the only persons in Salt Lake City who could really do this cleansing work. In this way, Alice and Zina may be regarded as two priestly virgins who have been placed on the public stage to purify it by their presence from an ancient but unnecessary stain.

Young, and his agent Clawson, are bestowing much care upon the education of Miss Adams, a young lady who has everything to learn except the art of being lovely; also upon that of Miss Alexander, a girl who, besides being pretty and piquant, has genuine ability for her work. A story, which shows that Young has a feeling for humor, has been told me, of which Miss Alexander is the heroine. A starring actor from San Francisco fell into desperate love for her, and went up to the President's house for leave to address her. "Ha! my good fellow," said the Prophet; "I have seen you play 'Hamlet' very well, and 'Julius Cæsar' pretty well, but you must not aspire to Alexander!"

We saw Brigham Young for the first time in his private box. A large head, broad, fair face, with blue eyes, light-brown hair, good nose and merry mouth; a man plainly dressed, in black coat and pantaloons, white waistcoat and cravat, gold studs and sleeve-links, English in build and looks,—but English of the middle class and of a provincial town: such was the Mormon prophet, pope, and king, as we first saw him in the theatre among his people. A lady, one of his wives, whom we afterwards came to know as Amelia, sat with him in the box; she, too, was dressed in a quiet English style; and now and then she eyed the audience from behind her curtain, through an opera-glass, as English ladies are apt to do at home. She was pretty, and appeared to us then rather pensive and poetical.

The pit was almost filled with girls; on many benches sat a dozen damsels in a row; children of Kimball, Cannon, Smith, and Wells; in some places twenty or thirty girls were grouped together. Young, as he told me himself, has forty-eight living children, some of whom are grown up and married; and, since he sets the fashion of attending this theatre among his people, it is only right that he should encourage

BRIGHAM YOUNG.

his children to appear, both before the foot-lights and behind them. Alice is the young lady married to Clawson. Zina, whom we have seen play Mrs. Musket in the farce of "My Husband's Ghost," is a lady-like girl, tall, full in figure, moon-faced (as the Orientals say), not much of an artist. Emily we have also seen; Elder Clawson is said to be courting her. I am told that the flame is mutual; and that Emily is not unlikely to be gathered home to her sister Alice. Gentile rumor—fond of toying with the domestic secrets of the President's family—says that Alice is not happy with her lord; but this is one of those Gentile rumors which I can almost swear is false. One day last week I had the pleasure of taking Sister Alice down to dinner, of talking with her for a long evening, and of seeing and romping with her four brave boys. A brighter, merrier woman I have rarely seen; and I noted, as a peculiarity in her, not common in either eastern or western America, that she always addressed her husband by his baptismal name of Hiram. American ladies almost everywhere speak to their husbands as Mr. Jones and Mr. Smith, not as William and George. The perils of a double alliance with the Mormon pope are said to be very great; envy among the Elders, collision with the Gentiles, jealousy at Camp Douglas, hostility in Washington; but Elder Clawson is said to be ready to take his chance with Sister Emily, as he has done with Alice, answering, as the Mormons put it, Washington theories by Deseret facts.

The first piece we saw was Charles the Twelfth. Where Adam Brock warns his daughter, Eudigo, against military sparks, the whole pit of young ladies crackled off into girlish laughter; the reference being taken to Camp Douglas and the United States officers stationed there, many of whom were in the house, and heartily enjoyed the fun. This play happens to be full of allusions to soldiers and their amours, and every word of these allusions was appropriated and applied by the Saints to their local politics. The interference of these United States officers and soldiers with the Mormon women is a very sore point with the Saints, some of their wives having, it is said, been seduced and carried off. Young spoke to me with indignation of such proceedings, though he did not name the offenders as connected with the camp. "They cause us trouble," he said; "they intrude into our affairs, and even into our families; we cannot stand such things; and when they are guilty, we make them bite the dust." I thought of all that I had ever heard about Porter Rockwell and his Danite band; but I only smiled and waited for the President to go on. He quickly added, "I never had any trouble of this sort in my own family."

When Charles the Twelfth referred to the amours of his officers, it was good fun to see the Prophet rolling back in his chair, convulsed with merriment, while the more staid Amelia eyed the audience through her opera-glass.

CHAPTER XVIII.

THE TEMPLE.

WHAT the Theatre is to the social life of this people, the Temple is to its religious life. One symbolizes the enjoyment of the present world, the other typifies the glories of a world to come. The playhouse has been raised and opened because its service is concerned with the things which cannot wait; the Temple is proceeding slowly, block being piled on block with the care and leisure of a work designed to last forever

These Mormons profess to have so much religion in their blood and bone, that they can easily dispense, on occasion, with religious forms. A few days ago, I happened to hear the first discourse of Brigham Young to a band of emigrants, the practical character of which would have taken me by surprise, but that my previous intercourse with him had in some degree prepared me for it.

"Brothers and sisters in the Lord Jesus Christ," he said, in substance, "you have been chosen from the world by God, and sent through His grace into this valley of the mountains, to help in building up His kingdom. You are faint and weary from your march. Rest, then, for a day, for a second day, should you need it; then rise up and see how you will live. Don't bother yourselves about your religious duties; you have been chosen for this work, and God will take care of you in it. Be of good cheer. Look about this valley into which you have been called. Your first duty is to learn how to grow a cabbage, and along with this cabbage an onion, a tomato, a sweet potato; then how to feed a pig, to build a house, to plant a garden, to rear cattle, and to bake bread; in one word, your first duty is to live. The next duty—for those who, being Danes, French, and Swiss, cannot speak it now—is to learn English; the language of God, the language of the Book of Mormon, the language of these Latter Days. These things you must do first; the rest will be added to you in proper seasons. God bless you; and the peace of our Lord Jesus Christ be with you."

The Temple is not forgotten; in fact, no people on the earth devote more money to their religious edifices and services than the Mormons. A tenth of all produce—often much more—is cheerfully given up to the church; but the first thought of a convert, the first counsel of an elder, is always that the Saint shall look upon labor, labor of the hand and brain, and most of all labor of the hand, as the appointed sacrifice through which, by God's own law, a man shall be purged from sin and shall attain everlasting peace. All the passions which another sect throws into polemics, the Mormons put into work. They do not shun discussion by the tongue; in fact, they are shrewd of wit, prompt in quotation; but they prefer that their chief controversies with the world should be conducted by the spade.

Hence they thrive where no other men could live. Those engineers who reported that a hundred settlers could never find sustenance in these valleys, were not so much in the wrong as many people, wise after Young's success, suppose. Even Bridger, the old Wasatch trapper, when he offered to give a thousand dollars for every ear of corn to be raised in this valley, was not such a fool as his words may now seem to make him. Those critics only spoke of what might have been expected from ordinary men, impelled by ordinary motives; and nothing on earth is surer than that ordinary men would have perished in these regions. The soil is so dry, so barren, that with all his passion for work, a Mormon can only cultivate four acres of land, while a Gentile on the Missouri and the Kansas rivers can easily cultivate forty acres. Take away the Mormon impetus, and in two years this city of Salt Lake would come to depend, as Denver does, on Indiana and Ohio for its supplies of food.

Who, then, are these working Saints engaged in building this Temple?

Thirty-six years ago, there were six Mormons in America; none in England, none in the rest of Europe; and to-day (1866) they have twenty thousand Saints in Salt Lake city; four thousand each in Ogden, Provo, and Logan; in the whole of their stations in these valleys, (one hundred and six settlements, properly organized by them, and ruled by bishops and elders,) a hundred and fifty thousand souls; in other parts of the United States, about eight or ten thousand; in England and its dependencies, about fifteen thousand; in the rest of Europe, ten thousand; in Asia and the South Sea Islands, about twenty thousand; in all not less, perhaps, than two hundred thousand followers of the gospel preached by Joseph Smith. All these converts have been gathered into this Temple in thirty years.

This power of growth—a power developed in the midst of persecution—is one of the strangest facts in the story of this strange people. In half the span of our life they have risen from nothing into a vast and vital church. Islam, preaching the Unity of God with fire and sword, swept onward with a slower march than these American Saints; for in little more than thirty years they have won a nation from the Christian church; they have occupied a territory larger than Spain; they have built a capital in the desert, which is already more populous than Valladolid; they have drilled an army which I have reason to believe is more than twenty thousand strong; they have raised a priesthood, counting in its ranks many hundreds of working prophets, presidents, bishops, councillors, and elders; they have established a law, a theology, a social science of their own, profoundly hostile to all reigning colleges and creeds.

Counting them man by man, the Saints are already strong; but the returns which are made on paper (so frequently beyond the mark in both churches and armies) stand in their case far below their actual strength, whether we weigh them in the case of either temporal or spiritual power. Other men may be counted by heads; these men must be counted by heads and hearts; for every saint is at once a priest and a soldier; the whole Mormon population being trained alike to controversies of the spirit and of the flesh. Every male adult has a thought in his brain, a revolver in his belt, a rifle in his hand. In every house we find arms: in the Prophet's chamber, in the newspaper office, in the emigrants' shed, in the bath-house, in the common parlor, in the ordinary sleeping-room. On our first arrival at Salt Lake City, the hotel, kept by Colonel Little, a leading Mormon, was full of guests, and a small dog-hole, without a chair, a table, a wardrobe, and with only one camp-bed in it, was offered us by a hasty negro for our quarters. Letters of introduction, instantly delivered, brought friends to our help; but the place was so crammed with visitors that no room could be made or got, and my friend was obliged to accept Colonel Little's hospitalities at his private house. There he found one of the Colonel's wives reading to her group of pretty girls a book in favor of polygamy; and on being shown into a bedroom for the night (a bedroom belonging to one of Colonel Little's sons), he was startled on finding a loaded pistol under his pillow, two Colt's revolvers loaded and capped, slung on the wall; in a corner of the room two Ballard rifles. Young Little, whose room my friend was occupying for the night, is a lad of seventeen.

At first these Saints were a pacific race, warring with the sword of faith only; but when the Gentile spoiler came down upon them, using steel and lead against what they called truth, and when it appeared that the law, appealed to in their stress of mind and body, could give them no help, they girt upon their loins a more carnal weapon. They bought swords and guns, formed themselves into bands; fell steadily to drill, and in a few months they had become more formidable in Iowa and Illinois than their weak numbers could have made them. If they were not strong enough to found a new empire on the Mississippi in defiance of public opinion, they were powerful enough to disturb the adjoining States; and when the Mexican war broke out, to send a brilliant corps to the seat of war. From that day to our own, the martial exercises of the Saints have known no pause. Drill may now be considered as a part of the Mormon ritual; a Saint being as much bound to appear on parade as he is in the tabernacle. It is scarcely a figure of speech to say that every male adult of Deseret—as the Mormons call Utah—holds himself equally ready to start on a mission and to take the field. It is their boast, and I believe not a vain one, that in fifteen minutes they can rally three thousand rifles, each rifle backed by a revolver, around their City Hall. Once, on a false alarm being raised, this body of men was actually under arms.

These Temple builders call themselves Saints, accept the Bible as true, baptize their converts in the name of Christ; but they are not a Christian people, and no church in the world could hold communion with them in their present state. In truth, they approach much nearer both in creed, in morals, and in government, to the Utes and Shoshones than to any Anglo-Saxon church. Young gets a meaning from the Bible which no one else ever found there. It has been often said that the Saints pretend to have a new translation of the Bible; a rendering made by the Holy Spirit; but Brigham Young tells me that this statement is untrue. He claims to understand the Scriptures by a purer light than we Gentiles now possess, and to have the hidden meaning of certain portions of them cleared by Divine revelation; but he takes our Bible as it stands in the authorized English version. "King James' Bible," he said to me with emphasis, "is my Bible; I know of none other." In fact, he seems to regard that version as in some sort divine, and the very language in which it is couched as in some sort sacred. "The English tongue," he said, "is a holy form of speech; the best, the softest, and the strongest language in the world." I think he considers it the language of God and of heaven. "It is holy," he said, "for it is the speech in which the angels wrote the Book of Mormon, the speech in which God has given his last revelation to man." When a friend of mine went into a Salt Lake City book-store, and asked for the Mormon book of faith, the man behind the counter handed him an English Bible. "We have no better book," he said; "all that we believe you will find in those pages." This is what they always say; but it is no less true that they find a thousand facts and doctrines in their Bible which we have never found in ours: a new history of the creation, of the fall, of the atonement, of the future life. In fact, they have made for themselves a new heaven and a new earth.

A Mohammedan mosque stands nearer to a Christian church than this Mormon temple stands. Islam broke down idols, Mormonism sets them up. Smith and Young have peopled their strange heaven with gods of their own making; and the Almighty is in their eyes but a President of Heaven, a chief among spiritual peers, occupying a throne like that of the Roman Jove. In short, this temple is nothing less than the altar of a new people; a people having a new law, a new morality, a new priesthood, a new industry, a new canon, and a new God.

CHAPTER XIX.

THE TWO SEERS.

Nothing is more easy than to laugh at these votaries. They are low people; scum of the earth, dregs of great cities, mire of the roadside, ooze of the river-bank and the ditch. Their prophet was Joe Smith; and that story of his about the gold plates, about the Urim and Thummim, about the Egyptian mummy, about the Spalding manuscript novel, about the sword of Laban, and the angelic visitors, about the Mormon bank, the paper money, and the spiritual wife — may be so told by a man of comic vein as to excite shouts of laughter in a Gentile room. Perhaps the weakest side of the new church is that of the Prophet's actual life, as the strongest side is that of his actual death. Had Smith lived long enough for the facts of his career to become known, many persons think that among a people keenly alive to humor, he would have found no lasting dupes.

Look, say these persons, into that oily, perky face, and say whether you can dream of anything divine lying hid behind it? Smith, having the true instinct of a sectarian, and knowing that the seeds of the Church were sown in the blood of her martyrs, put himself day by day into the paths of the persecutor. No man is popular until he has been abused — no man is thought a saint until he has been calumniated — no man is ranked among the prophets until he has been stoned to death. "Persecution," said Brigham, "is our portion; if we are right, the world will be against us; but the world will not prevail against the elect of God." Smith felt in his heart this truth of truths; he sought for oppression as the sign of his calling, and his enemies in the States indulged him in the dearest wish of his soul.

Thirty-nine times he was cited into courts of law. It is strong evidence of his craft that he contrived to be so often accused without being once condemned. Every charge made against him put new heart into his church. Still the growth of his sect was slow; slow, compared against that of George Fox, that of John Wesley, even that of Ann Lee. Round Smith's own person there was always bickering and division; many of the Saints declaring that their seer was robbing the common till. Rigdon, his partner in the fraud of palming off Spalding's romance as a translation from the golden plates, quitted and exposed him. Other men followed this example; and though many new converts were being made at a distance among people who knew not Joseph in the flesh, the sect could hardly have been kept together, had it not pleased the western rowdies to make Smith a martyr. A gang of ruffians, taking the law into their hands, broke into his prison at Carthage, and shot him down like a dog.

A crime, for which no excuse could be found, infused new spirit into his friends, and opened to his missionaries the ears of thousands. After the murder had been committed, justice was too slow to seize, too weak to punish his assassins; a fact which seemed to carry the appeal of blood from earth to heaven.

When it became known that Smith was dead—that he had been slain for his opinions—his faults were instantly swept aside; the remembrance of his craft, his greed, his sensuality, his ignorance, his ambition, was buried in his secret grave; and the unsought glory of a martyr's death was counted to him by his people, and by many who had not till then become his people, as of higher virtue than would have been the merit of a saintly and heroic life.

It is a story as old as time. Smith—living at Nauvoo, squabbling with his apostles about debts and duns, wrangling with his wife Emma about spiritual wives, subject to constant accusations of theft and drunkenness—was certainly not a man whom the American people had any cause to fear; but his assassination in the jail at Carthage raised this alleged debtor and drunkard, this alleged thief and fornicator, into the rank of saints. Men who could hardly have endured his presence in the flesh proclaimed him, now that he was gone, as a true successor of Moses and of Christ.

Under a new leader, Brigham Young, — a man of lowly birth, of keen humor, of unerring good sense,— the sect emerged from its condition of internal strife; putting on a more decent garb, closing up its broken ranks, laboring with a new zeal, extending its missionary work. Finding that through recent troubles his position on the Mississippi had become untenable, Young advised his followers to yield their prize, to quit the world in which they had found no peace, and set up their tabernacles in one of those distant wilds in the far West, which were then trodden by no feet of men, except those of a few Red Indian tribes, Utes, Pawkees, Shoshones, in what was called the American desert, and was considered by everybody as No-man's land. It was a bold device. Beyond the western prairies, beyond the Rocky Mountains, lay a howling wilderness of salt and stones, a property which no white man had yet been greedy enough to claim. Some pope, in the middle ages, had bestowed it on the crown of Spain, from which it had fallen, as a paper waste, to the Mexican Republic; but neither Spaniard nor Mexican had ever gone up north into the land to possess it. In the centre of this howling wilderness lay a Dead Sea, not less terrible than Bahr Lout, the Sea of Lot. One-fourth of its water was known to be solid salt. The creeks which run into it were said to be putrid; the wells around it were known to be bitter; and the shores for many miles were crusted white with saleratus. These shores were like nothing else on earth, except the Syrian Ghor, and they were more forbidding than the Syrian Ghor in this particular, that the waters of Salt Lake are dull, impure, and the water lines studded with ditches and pools, intolerable to the nostrils of living men. To crown its repulsive features, this desert of salt, of stones, and of putrid creeks, was shut off from the world, eastward by the Rocky Mountains, westward by the Sierra Nevada, ranges of alps high as the chain of Mont Blanc, and covered with eternal ice and snow.

The red men who roamed over this country in search of roots and insects, were known to be the most savage and degraded tribes of their savage and degraded race. A herd of bison, a flight of gulls, a swarm of locusts, peopled the plain with a fitful life. In spring, when a little verdure rose upon the ground, a little wild sage, a few dwarf sunflowers, the locusts sprang from the earth and stript the few green plants of every leaf and twig. No forests could be seen; the grass, where it grew, appeared to be rank and thin. Only the wild sage and the dwarf sunflower seemed to find food in the soil, plants which are useless to man, and were then thought to be poisonous to his beast.

Trappers, who had looked down on the Salt Valley from peaks and passes in the Wasatch Mountains, pictured it as a region without life, without a green slope, even without streams and springs. The wells were said to be salt, as the fields were salt. Finding no wood, and scarcely any fresh water in that region, these explorers had set their seal upon this great American desert as a waste unfit for the dwelling, incapable of the sustenance, of civilized men. But Young thought otherwise. He knew that where the Saint had struck his spade into the ground — at Kirtland in Ohio, at Independence in Missouri, at Nauvoo in Illinois — he had been always blessed with a plentiful crop; and the new Mormon seer had faith in the same strong sinews, in the same rough hands, in the same keen will, being able to draw harvests of grain from the desolate valley of Salt Lake

A carpenter by trade, Young knew how to fell trees, to shape logs, to build carts and trucks, to stake out ground, to erect temporary sheds. The Saints whom he would have to lead were inured to labor and privation; being chiefly New England artisans and Western farmers, men who could turn their hands to any trade, who could face any difficulty, execute any work. An equal number of either English or French converts would have perished in the attempt to move across the plains and the mountains; but the native American is a man of all trades — a banker, a butcher, a carpenter, a clerk, a teamster, a statesman, anything at a pinch, everything in its turn — a man rich in resources and ingenuities, so that a baker can build you a bridge, a preacher can catch you a wild horse, a lawyer can bake you hot cakes. Young knew that in crossing the great plains and in climbing the great ranges, which are loosely clubbed together under the name of Rocky Mountains, the privations of his people would be sharp; but to his practical eye these sufferings of the flesh appeared to be such as brave men could be trained by example to bear and not die. Food and seed might be carried in their light wagons, and a little malt whisky would correct the alkali in the bitter creeks. In his band of disciples every man was master of some craft; every woman was either a dairymaid, a baker, a seamstress, a laundress; nay, the children could be turned to account in the desert roads, for every American girl can milk a cow, every American boy can drive a team.

A party of pioneers (many of whom are still alive in Salt Lake Valley) having been sent forward to explore and report, the word to move on westward was at length given by Young, and in every family of Nauvoo preparations were made for a journey, unmatched in history since the days when Moses led the Israelites out of Egypt. The Saints broke up their cheery homes. They gathered, in their haste, a little food, a few roots and seeds, a dozen kegs of spirits. Then they yoked their mules, their oxen, to the country wagons. Those who were too poor to buy wagons and oxen, made for themselves trucks and wheelbarrows. Pressed upon by their foes, they marched away from Nauvoo, even while the winter was yet hard upon them, crossing the Mississippi on the ice, and started on a journey of fifteen hundred miles, through a country without a road, without a bridge, without a village, without an inn, without wells, cattle, pastures, and cultivated land. As Elder John Taylor told me, they left everything behind; their corn-fields, their gardens, their pretty houses, with the books, carpets, pianos, everything which they contained. The distance to be conquered by these emigrants was equal to that from London to Lemberg, six times that from Cairo to Jerusalem. Their route lay through a prairie peopled by Pawnees, Shoshones, wolves and bears; it was broken by rapid rivers, barred by a series of mountain chains; and the haven to be reached, after all their toils and dangers, was the shore of a Dead Sea, lying in a sterile valley; a land watered with brine, and pastures sown with salt.

CHAPTER XX.

FLIGHT FROM BONDAGE.

THE tale of that journey of the Saints, as we hear it from the lips of Young, of Wells, of Taylor, and of other old men who made it, is a story to wring and yet nerve the hearts of all generous men. When these Mormons were driven by violence from the roofs which they had built, the fields which they had tilled, the days were short and snow lay thick upon the ground. Everything, save a little food for the way-side, a few corn-seeds and potato-roots for the coming year, had to be abandoned to their armed and riotous enemies; the homes which they had made, the temple they had just finished, the graves they had recently dug. Frost bit their little ones in the hands and feet. Hunger and thirst tormented both young and aged. Long plains of sand, into which the wagon-wheels sank to the axle-trees, separated the scanty supplies of water. Wells there were none. Mirage often mocked them with its promises; and even when they came to creeks and streams, they often found them bitter to the taste, and dangerous to the health. The days were short and cold, and the absence of any other shelter from the frost than the bit of canvas roof made the nights of winter terrible to all. Horses sickened by the way. Disease broke out among the cows and sheep, so that milk ran short, and the supplies of mutton were dressed and cooked in fear. Some of the poor, the aged, and the ailing, had then to be left behind; with them a guard of young men who could ill be spared.

Nor was loss of a part of their youth and strength the whole of their calamity in this opening stage of their emigration. Just at the hour when every male arm was most precious to these exiles, the Mexican war broke out; and a government, which had never been strong enough to do them right, came down to them for help in arms and men. Young answered the appeal of his country like a patriot; five hundred youths, the flower of his migrating bands, stepped out before him, and with the blessing of their chief upon their heads, they mustered themselves into the invading corps.

Weakened by the departure of this living force, the Mormons crossed the Missouri River in a ferry made by themselves, entering on the great wilderness, the features of which they laid down on a map, making a rough road, and throwing light bridges over streams, as they went on; collecting grass and herbs for their own use; sowing corn for those who were to come later in the year; raising temporary sheds in which their little ones might sleep; and digging caves in the earth as a refuge from the winter snow. Their food was scarce, their water bad, and such wild game as they could find in the plains—the elk, the antelope, the buffalo—poisoned their blood. Nearly all the malt whisky which they had brought from Nauvoo to correct the bad water, had been seized on the road, and the kegs staved in, by agents of government, on pretence of its being meant for the red-skins, to whom it was unlawful for the whites to sell any ardent spirits. Four kegs only had been saved; saved by Brigham Young himself. An elder, who was present in the boat, and who told me the anecdote, says it is the only time ne ever remembered to have seen the Prophet in a rage. Four kegs were on board the Ferry, when the officer seized them and began to knock in the staves; in that spirit lay the lives of the people; and when Brigham saw the man raise his mallet, he drew his pistol, levelled it at his head, and cried, "Stay your hand! If you touch that keg, you die, by the living God!" The man jumped off the ferry and troubled them no more.

In our own journey across the plains, though the time was August, the weather fine, the passage swift, we suffered keenly from the want of fresh food and of good water. My companion sickened from bile into dysentery; no meat, no drink, would lie in his stomach; nothing but the cognac in our flasks. The water almost killed him. His sun-burnt face grew chalky-white; his limbs hung feeble and relaxed; his strong physique so drooped that a man at one of the ranches, after looking at him for a moment with a curious eye, came up to me and said, "You will feel very lonely when he is left behind." My own attack came later, and in another form. The skin of my hands peeled off, as if it had been either frayed or scraped with a knife; boils came out upon my back; a pock started on my under eyelid; my fingers had the appearance of scorbutic eruptions.

These two diseases, Taylor told me, ravaged the camp of emigrants. Many sickened of dysentery, still more suffered from scurvy.

Some of the Saints fell back in the face of these terrible trials. More fainted by the wayside, and were mournfully laid in their desert graves. Every day there came a funeral, every night there was fresh mourning in the camp. The waste of life is always very great in the emigrant trains: even now, when the roads are made and the stations are provisioned with vegetable food. Of the train which I saw come in.

six had perished on the plains. A young lady told me that eighty had died in the train by which she had arrived; forty would perhaps be an average loss in the mountains and the plains. But no subsequent train has ever suffered like the first. "The waste of life was great," said Brigham Young, as he told the dreadful tale. Yet the brave, unbroken body of male and female Saints toiled along the frozen way. When their hearts were very low, a band of music struck up some lively air, in which the people joined and forgot their woes. By day they sang hymns, at night they danced round the watch-fires. Gloom, asperity, asceticism, they banished from their camps and from their thoughts. Among the few treasures which they had carried with them from Nauvoo was a printing-press; and a sheet of news, printed and published by the wayside, carried words of good counsel into every part of the camp.

After crossing the sands and creeks which have since become known to civilized men on the maps and charts as Nebraska and Dakota, they arrived at the foot of the first great range of those high and broken chains of alps which are commonly grouped together under the name of Rocky Mountains; over these high barriers there was yet no path; and the defiles leading through them were buried in drifts of snow. How the Saints toiled up those mountain-sides, dragging with them oxen and carts, foraging for food, baking their bread and cooking their meat, without help and without guides, it brings tears into the eyes of aged men to tell. The young and bold went forward in advance; driving away the bears and wolves; stoning the rattle-snakes; chasing the elk and the wild deer; making a path for the women and the old men. At length, when they had reached the summit of the pass, they gazed upon a series of arid and leafless plains, of dry river-beds, of verdureless hill-sides, of alkaline bottoms; pools of bitter water, narrow canyons and gorges, abrupt and steep. Day by day, week after week, they toiled over these bleak sierras, through these forbidding valleys. Food was running out; wild game became scarce; the Utes and Snakes were unfriendly; at the end of their journey, should they ever reach it, lay the dry Salt Desert, in which they had consented to come and dwell!

Yet they were not disheartened by these hostile aspects of the country; they had not expected a verdant paradise; they knew that the land had never been seized, because it had not been considered worth taking from the Indian tribes; they expected to find here nothing beyond peace and freedom, a place in which they could take their chance with Nature, and to which they could invite the Saints, their brethren, to a country of their own. Descending the passes with beating hearts and clanging trumpets, they entered on their lonely inheritance; marched upon this slope above the Jordan, near the conical hill on which Brigham had seen the angel in his sleep; laid down the plan of a new city; explored the canyons and water-courses into the hills; and in a few days found, to their sudden joy, not only springs of fresh water, but woody nooks and grassy mounds and slopes.

Not an hour was lost. "The first duty of a Saint when he comes to this valley," said Brigham Young to me, "is to learn how to grow a vegetable; after which he must learn how to rear pigs and fowls, to irrigate his land, and to build up his house. The rest will come in time." Ruled from the first by this practical genius, every man fell to his work. Deseret—country of the Bee—was announced as the

Promised Land and future home of the Saints. It was to them as an unknown, unappropriated soil, and they hoped to found upon it an independent State.

CHAPTER XXI.

SETTLEMENT IN UTAH.

SOON the aspects of this desert valley began to change under their cunning hands; creeks from the hills being coaxed into new paths; fields being cleared and sown; homesteads rising from the ground; sheep and cattle beginning to dot the hills; salt-pits and saw-mills being established; fruit-trees being planted, and orchards taught to bloom and bear. Roads were laid out and made. When the Mormon herdsmen entered the hill ravines, they found pine and cotton-wood, elder, birch, and box: materials precious for the building of their new homes. A new Jerusalem sprang from the ground; a temple was commenced; a newspaper was published. Walnut and other hard woods were planted in favorable spots. The red-skins who had long been the dread of all scouts and trappers in the far west, were won by courtesies and gifts; and in a few months they appeared to have been changed from enemies of the white men into allies. "We found it cheaper," said Colonel Little, "to feed the Indians than to fight them;" and this policy of feeding the Utes and Snakes has been pursued by Young, with two or three brief intervals of misunderstanding, from the day of his first settlement in the valley. For two or three trying years, the Saints of Salt Lake had to wage war against locusts and crickets, those plagues of the older Canaan; but by help of gulls from the lakes, and of their own devices in trapping and pounding the insects, the Mormons contrived to preserve their crops of corn and fruit. A year went by, and the Mormons had not perished in the waste. On the contrary, they had begun to grow, and even to make money. Year after year they have increased in numbers and in wealth, until their merchants are known in London and New York, and their city has become a wonder of the earth.

What are the secrets of this surprising growth of the new society out in these western deserts?

"Look around you," said Young to me, "if you want to know what kind of people we are. Nineteen years ago this valley was a desert, growing nothing but the wild sage and the dwarf sunflower; we who came into it brought nothing with us but a few oxen and wagons, and a bag of seeds and roots; the people who came after us, many of them weavers and artisans, brought nothing, not a cent, not even skill and usage of the soil; and when you look from this balcony, you can see what we have made of it."

How, above all other settlers in the waste lands of western America, have the Saints achieved this work?

Is it an answer to say that these Saints are dupes and fanatics? Nothing is easier than to laugh at Joe Smith and his church; but what then? The great facts remain. Young and his people are at Utah; a church of two hundred thousand souls; an army of twenty thousand rifles. You may smile at Joseph's gift of tongues; his discovery of Urim and Thummim (which he supposed to have been a pair of spectacles!); his sword of Laban; his prose works of Abraham; his Egyptian papyrus; his Mormon paper money; his thirty-nine trials. You may prove, with a swift and biting irony, that the weakest side of this new faith is the actual life of its founder; but will your wit disperse this camp of fanatics? Will your irony change the Utes and Shoshones into enemies of these Saints? Will your arguments arrest those bands of missionaries which are employed in preaching, in a hundred places and to thousands of willing ears, the gospel as it was in Joseph? The hour has gone by, as Americans feel, for treating this Church in sport.

In England, though our soil is said to be the nursery of the Saints, we have not yet learned to think of Mormonism otherwise than as one of our many humors; as a rash that comes out from time to time in our social body; a sign, perhaps, of our occasional lack of health; no one among us has learned to regard it as the symptom of a disease which may be lying at the seat of life. Has Convocation ever given up a day to the Book of Mormon? Has a bishop ever visited the Saints in Commercial Road? Two or three ministers may have fired off pamphlets against them; but have any of these reverend fathers been to see them in their London homes? Rare, indeed, has been this holy strife even on the part of private men. But our brethren in America can hardly affect to treat the Saints in this easy style. The new Church is visible among them; for good and evil it is in their system; not a humor to be cast out like a rash upon the skin. Up to this time our own Saints have been taught to regard England as Egypt, and their old dwelling-place as exile from a brighter home. America is to them Canaan, Salt

Lake City a New Jerusalem. I do not say that this is good for us, though it has an appearance of being good, since it relieves us of a painful duty, and removes from the midst of our cities a cause of shame. The poor, the aged, the feeble, among the Saints, may be left behind in our streets, to die, as they think and say, in the house of bondage; but the rich, the young, the zealous, are bound by their faith to go forward and possess themselves of the Promised Land. With the younger Saints, especially with the female Saints, a change of air is always recommended on a change of creed. Thousands emigrate, though it is also true that thousands remain behind. In London, Liverpool, Glasgow, and in other cities, the other Saints have schools and chapels, books and journals, of which Oxford knows little, and Mayfair less. Not being a political sect, never asking for any right, never urging any wrong; content with doing their work in peace; they escape notice from the press, and engage the thoughts of society as little as the Moravians and the Plymouth Brethren. In London society you may hear in any one week more speculation about Prince and Home, the Abode of Love and the Spiritual Spheres, than you will hear about Young and Deseret in six months. The Saints are not in society; but in Boston, Washington, and New York, these Mormons are a fearful portent, threatening to become a formidable power. Already they have put jurists into session and armies into motion. Colfax, the Speaker, has been to confer with Young; and committees of Congress are sitting on the affairs of Utah. The day appears to be drawing nigh when the problems which these Mormons put before the world may have to be considered by practical men, not in colleges and chapels only, not in senates and in courts of law only, but in the camp and in the battle-field.

That question of how these Mormons are to be dealt with by the American people, is one of the strangest riddles of an age which has bridged the ocean, put a girdle of lightnings round the earth, and tamed to its service the fiery steeds of the sun. A true reply may be far to seek; for we have not yet resolved, finally, how far thought is free from the control of law; and to what extent toleration of creeds implies toleration of the conduct which springs from creeds. One step in advance towards such a reply must be an attempt to find what Mormonism is, and by what means it has grown. It cannot be put aside as either unmixed foolishness or unalloyed vice. Strange as the new sectarians may seem to us, they must have in their keeping some grain of truth. They live and thrive, and men who live by their own labor, thrive by their own enterprise, cannot be altogether mad. Their streets are clean, their houses bright, their gardens fruitful. Peace reigns in their cities. Harlots and drunkards are unknown among them. They keep open more common schools than any other sect in the United States. But being what they are, believing what they do, their merits are perhaps more trying to our patience than their crimes. It is thought that many persons in the United States would be able to endure them a little better if they would only behave themselves a good deal worse.

What have these Saints achieved?

In the midst of a free people, they have founded a despotic power. In a land which repudiates state religions, they have placed their church above human laws. Among a society of Anglo-Saxons, they have introduced some of the ideas, many of the practices, of Red Indian tribes, of the Utes, Shoshones, and Snakes. In the nineteenth century after Christ, they have revived the social habits which were common in Syria nineteen hundred years before his birth.

Hints for their system of government may have been found nearer home than Hauran, in less respectable quarters than the Bible. The Shoshone wigwam could have supplied the Saints with a nearer model of a plural household than the Patriarch's tent; but this fact, if it were true, would hardly be confessed by Kimball and Young. As they state their case, Abraham is their perfect man; who forsook his home, his kindred, and his country, for the sake of God. Sarah is their perfect woman; because she called her husband lord, and gave her handmaid Hagar into his bosom for a wife. Everything that Abraham did, they pronounce it right for them to do; all gospels and commandments of the Church, all laws and institutes of man, being void and of no effect when quoted against the practices of that Arab sheikh. Putting under their feet both the laws of science and the lessons of history, they preach the duty of going back, in the spirit and in the name, to that priestly and paternal form of government which existed in Syria four thousand years ago; casting from them, as so much waste, the things which all other white men have learned to regard as the most precious conquests of time and thought — personal freedom, family life, change of rulers, right of speech, concurrence in laws, equality before the judge, liberty of writing and voting. They cast aside these conquests of time and thought in favor of Asiatic obedience to a man without birth, without education, whom they have chosen to regard as God's own vicar on the earth. No Pope in Rome, no Czar in Moscow, no Caliph in Bagdad, ever exercised such power as the Mormons have conferred on Young. "I am one of those men," said to me Elder Stenhouse—perhaps the man of highest culture whom we saw at Salt Lake City—"who think that Brother Brigham ought to do everything; he has made this church, and he ought to have his way in everything." Many others said the same thing, in nearly the same words. No one would dispute Young's will. "A man had better go to hell at once," said Stenhouse, "if he cannot meet Brigham's eye." In a caste of Hindoos, in a family of Kirghis, in a tribe of Bedouins, such an act of prostration would have seemed to me strange; in free America, among the countrymen of Sydney and Washington, coming from the lips of a writer who could make jokes and quote the last poem, and who is enough American to carry two revolvers in his pockets, it was more than strange. It was a sign.

CHAPTER XXII.

WORK AND FAITH.

Joseph Smith, a poor lad, born in Sharon, Windsor County, Vermont, the son of unlettered parents, had been crazed by one of those revivals which Elder Frederick, the Shaker preacher at Mount Lebanon, regards as the providential season of religious life. This untaught boy had begun to work upon the passions which he felt in play around him; announcing, like many others, but with more insistence than his fellows, that in his trances of body, he had received angelic visitors, that he had spoken with God face to face, that he had been chosen to plant a new Church on earth; a Church of America, the new Canaan, chosen from the beginnings of time to be the home of a new creed and the seat of a new empire. Men who had come to hear him had gone away converted; he had told them that a new priesthood had been chosen, that God had planted His kingdom once again; they had left him convinced, and gone away from his presence carrying these glad tidings into thousands of Christian homes. No force had been used, none could have been used in that early stage of their career; for the Saints had then no weapon save the word; they toiled in a pacific vineyard, and made their conquests in the face of vigilant foes. A fair hearing for their gospel, an open field for their preachers, were all they had asked, and more than what they had received. They sent no Khaled to the nations, with his offer of either conversion, slavery, or death; not because such a line of policy would have been contrary to the genius of their creed; but simply because, in a free state, and under a secular law, they had found no means for carrying out their plans. From the day of their dawn an Arab spirit had been strong upon them. Should a time ever come, when they can cut their withes and buckle on their swords, they may be found fierce as Gideon, ruthless as Omar; but in the past they have been obliged to occupy the ground of a suffering rather than that of a militant Church. Everything done by them as yet, has been effected by word of mouth, by what they describe as the power of truth.

How have these settlers in the wilderness done the things we see?

Simply, answers Young, by the power of work and

faith; by doing what they profess, by believing what they say.

Nearly all the forces which are found most powerful to sway men's minds in our lay societies, — genius, reputation, office, birth, and riches, — have been wanting to these Saints. No man of the stamp of Luther, Calvin, Wesley, has appeared among them. In intellect, Joseph was below contempt. Brigham is a man of keen good sense. Pratt is a dreamer. Kimball is unlettered. Wells, Cannon, Taylor, Hooper, — the brightest men among them, — have shown no worldly gifts, no scholarship, eloquence, poetry, and logic, to account for such sudden and sustained success as they have met with in every land.

The bee has been chosen by the Saints as an emblem of Deseret, though nature has all but denied that insect to this dry and flowerless land. Young's house is called the Beehive; in it no drone ever finds a place; for the Prophet's wives are bound to support themselves by needle-craft, teaching, spinning, dyeing yarn, and preserving fruit. Every woman in Salt Lake has her portion of work, each according to her gifts, every one steadfastly believing that labor is noble and holy; a sacrifice meet for man to make, and for God to accept. Ladies make gloves and fans, dry peaches and figs, cut patterns, prepare seeds, weave linen and knit hose. Lucy and Emiline, sometimes called the lights of Brigham's harem, are said to be prodigies of skill in the embroidery of flowers. Some of Emiline's needlework is certainly fine, and Susan's potted peaches are beyond compare. On men fall the heavier toils of the field, the ditch, and the hill-side, where they break the ground, dam up the river, fell the maple and the dwarf-oak, pasture the cattle, and catch the wild horse. But the sexes take each their share of a common task: rearing houses, planting gardens, starting workshops, digging mines; each with a strain of energy and passion never found on the eastern slopes of this Wasatch chain.

The ministry is unprofessional and unpaid. Every Saint being a priest, no man in the church is suffered to accept a cent for his service, even though his time, his faculties, his life itself, should be spent in doing what his brethren regard as the work of God. Duty to the church comes first; duty to the family, to the individual, comes next; but with such an interval as puts collision and confusion utterly out of question.

Prophets, presidents, bishops, elders, all pursue their avocations in the city and on the soil; sell ribbons, grow peaches, build mills, cut timber, keep ranches, herd cattle, drive trains. One day, we met a venerable man, with a small basket on his arm, covered with a snow-white napkin; his appearance struck us; and we learned that he was Joseph Young, elder brother of Brigham, and President of the Seventy. He was taking his basket of peaches to market for sale.

An apostle holds the plough, a patriarch drives a team. In a city where work is considered holy, the brightest dignitary gains in popular repute by engaging in labor and in trade. These Saints have not one idle gentleman in their church. Brigham Young is a mill-owner, cotton-planter, farmer; Heber Kimball is a mill-owner, grazier, manufacturer of linseed oil; George Smith is a farmer and miller; Orson Pratt is a teacher of mathematics; Orson Hyde is a farmer; John Taylor, formerly a wood-turner, is now a mill-owner; Wilford Woodruff is a farmer and grazier; George Cannon is a printer and editor. These men are the foremost lights in the church, and they are all men of laborious, secular habits. Young, Kimball, Taylor, are now rich men; the twelve apostles are said to be mostly poor; but whether they are rich or poor, these Mormon elders live on what they can earn by the labor of their hands and brains, taking nothing, it is said, for their loftier services in the church.

The unpaid functions of a bishop are extremely numerous; for a Mormon prelate has to look, not merely to the spiritual welfare of his flock, but to their worldly interest and wellbeing; to see that their farms are cultivated, their houses clean, their children taught, their cattle lodged. Last Sunday, after service at the Tabernacle, Brigham Young sent for us to the raised dias on which he and the dignitaries had been seated, to see a private meeting of the bishops, and to hear what kind of work these reverend fathers had met to do. We rather wondered what our friends at Bishopsthorpe and Wells would think of such a scene. The old men gathered in a ring; and Edward Hunter, their presiding bishop, questioned each and all, as to the work going on in his ward, the building, painting, draining, gardening; also as to what this man needed, and that man needed, in the way of help. An emigrant train had just come in, and the bishops had to put six hundred persons in the way of growing their cabbages and building their homes. One bishop said he could take five bricklayers, another two carpenters, a third a tinman, a fourth seven or eight farm-servants, and so on through the whole bench. In a few minutes I saw that two hundred of these poor emigrants had been placed in the way of earning their daily bread. "This," said Young, with a sly little smile, "is one of the labors of our bishops." I confess, I could not see much harm in it.

CHAPTER XXIII.

MISSIONARY LABOR.

The spirit of the Mormon church may best be read in the missionary labors of these Saints. It is their boast, that when they go out to convert the Gentiles, they carry with them no purse, no scrip; that they go forth, naked and alone, to do the Lord's work in the Lord's way; trusting in no arm of flesh, in no power of gold; taking no thought of what they shall eat and where they shall lie down; but putting their lives and fortunes wholly in the hands of God.

The way in which an elder may be called to such missionary work has, in this age of dollars, an air of primitive romance. Young (say) is walking down Main Street; he sees a young fellow driving a team, galloping a horse, riding in a cart; a thought comes into his prophetic mind; and, calling that young elder to his side, he tells him that the Lord has chosen him to go forth and preach, mentioning, perhaps, the period and the place; the time may be for one year, for three years, for ten years; the locality may be in Liverpool, in Damascus, in Delhi, in Pekin. Asking only a few hours' time to put his house in order, to take leave of his friends, to kiss his wives and children, that young elder, chosen from the street, will start on his errand of grace.

I have talked with a dozen of such missionaries; young men who have been called from the ranch, from the saw-mill, from the peach-garden, at a moment's notice, to depart without purse or scrip, to go forth, naked and alone, into the ends of the earth. Elder

Stenhouse had been sent to labor in France and Switzerland, Elder Riter in Austria, Elder Naisbit in England, Elder Dewey in India and Ceylon. Their method was the same.

Without money and without food, the missionary starts on his journey; hiring himself as a driver, a guard, a carpenter, to some train of merchandise going either towards the river or towards the sea, as the case may be. If his sphere is Europe, the young elder works as a laborer to New York, where he hires himself out either as a clerk, or as a mechanic, according to his gifts, until he can save his passage-money; if this course is inconvenient to him, either as to his person or his mission, he agrees with some skipper to serve before the mast, on which he will take his place humbly with the poor sailors, to whom, as the ship heaves onward, he finds many opportunities for preaching the glad tidings of a Mormon's rest in the Valley of the Mountains. He is not a man of books. "We have no colleges here," said Young, "to train our young men to be fools; we just take a fellow from the hills, who has been felling wood, killing bears, and catching wild colts; we send him out on a mission, and he comes back to us a man." Arrived in Europe, without a penny, without a home, the missionary finds, if he can, a lodging in the house of some local saint. If he cannot find such lodging, he sleeps on a bench, on a stone step, under a tree, among the litter of a dock. "I landed in Southampton," said Elder Stenhouse, when relating his many victories of the spirit, "without a farthing in my purse, and I sold the boots from my feet to buy a plank from which I could preach." Elder Dewey told me he had travelled from Salt Lake to San Francisco, from San Francisco to Ceylon, from Ceylon to Poonah, toiling, preaching, begging, never fearing for the flesh, but confiding everywhere and always in the protection of God; laboring among California miners, among Chinese sailors, among Cingalese farmers, among Bombay teamsters and muleteers, seldom wanting for a shelter, never wanting for a meal. Such is the spirit of the young Mormon elder. Sometimes he is helped forward by a Saint, oftentimes by a stranger and a Gentile; at the worst, he gets employment as a tailor, as a carpenter, as a dock-yard laborer. Living on crusts of bread, sleeping beneath lowly roofs, he toils and preaches from town to town, ardent in the doing of his daily task; patient, abstinent, obscure; courting no notice, rousing no debates; living the poor man's life; offering himself everywhere as the poor man's friend. When his task is done, he will preach his way back from the scene of his labor to his pleasant home, to his thriving farm, to his busy mill, in the valley of the Great Salt Lake.

In this Mormon city, where every man is an elder, almost every man is a priest. Any Saint, therefore, may be called to these missionary toils; and no Eastern slave obeys his master with such swift alacrity as that which is shown by the Saint who is called by Young to start for a distant land.

The glad tidings which men like Dewey and Stenhouse scatter among deck-passengers, dock-men, street-porters, farm-servants, and their fellows, are of a kind which the desolate and the discontented long to hear. They pronounce against the world and the world's ways. They declare the need for a great change; they promise the poor man merrier times and a brighter home. They offer the starving bread, the houseless roofs, the naked clothes. To the craftsman they promise mills, to the peasant farms. The heaven of which they tell is not placed by them wholly beyond the grave; earth itself is, in their opinion, a part of heaven; and as the earth and all that is in it are the Lord's, they announce that these riches of the earth are the true inheritance of His saints. The rich, they say, have corrupted the faith of Christ, and the churches of the rich are engaged in the devil's work. They represent Joseph as a pastor of the poor. They suggest that ignorance is a saving virtue, and that lowly people are the favorites of God.

Other churches besides that of the Saints hold some of these gospels; but the Mormon preacher is seen to act as though he believed them to be true. Show the young missionary a beggar, an outcast, a thief,—one who is in despair and ready to perish,—and he will act as though he considered himself chosen of God to save that miserable wretch. With men who appear in fine clothes, who dwell in great houses, who dine off silver plate, he has no concern. His task lies in Five Points, not in Madison Square; in Seven Dials, not in Park Lane. The rich, the learned, the polite, have their own creeds and rituals, beyond his power to either mend or mar. They have no need of him, and he never seeks them in their pride. What could he say to them? Would they listen to his promise of a brighter day? Would they care for his paradise of farms and pastures? Passing these worldlings by, as men to whom he has not been sent, the Saint goes lower in the scale of life; seeking out those victims of the world for whom no one but himself appears to care. In the wants and cravings of the poor he finds an opening for his message. But he does not praise the lowly for being poor; he does not lead them to infer that a state of pauperism is a state of grace; his doctrine is, that riches are good things; and he holds out a promise, which he can back by a thousand examples, that the Saints will become rich by the toil of their hands and by the blessing of God. To men hungering after lands and houses, the prosperity which he can truly describe as existing in Deseret, and which he warmly invites them to come and share, is a great and potential fact.

Care of the poor is written down strongly in the Mormon code of sacred duties. A bishop's main function is to see that no man in his ward, in his county, is in want of food and raiment; when he finds that a poor family is in need, he goes to his more prosperous neighbor, and in the Lord's name demands from him a sack of wheat, a can of tea, a loaf of sugar, a blanket, a bed; knowing that his requisition will be promptly met. The whole earth is the Lord's, and must be rendered up to Him. Elder Jennings, the richest merchant in Salt Lake City, told me of many such requisitions being made upon himself; in bad times, they may come upon him twice or thrice a day. In case of need, the bishop goes up to the Tithing office and obtains the succor of which his parishioner stands in need; for the wants of the poor take precedence of the wants of the church; but the appeal from personal benevolence to the public fund has seldom to be made. For if a Saint has any kind of store, he must share it with his fellow; if he has bread, he must feed the hungry; if he has raiment, he must clothe the naked. No excuse avails him for neglect of this great duty. The command to sell what we have, and give the money to the poor, is to most of us an empty rule; but the Mormon, like the Arab and the Jew, whose spirit he has had breathed into him, knows nothing of such pious fictions. "Feed my flock," is to him an injunction that admits of no denial, and of no delay.

A special fund is raised for the relief of necessitous Saints; and Young himself, the servant of all, discharges in person the troublesome duties of this trust. I went with Bishop Hunter, a good and merry old man, full of work and humor, to the emigrants' corral, to see the rank and file of the new English arrivals; six hundred people from the Welsh hills and from the Midland shires; men, women, and children; all poor and uncomely, weary, dirty, freckled with the sun, scorbutic from privation; when I was struck by the tender tones of his voice, the wisdom of his counsel, the fatherly solicitude of his manner in dealing with these poor people. Some of the women were ill and querulous; they wanted butter, they wanted tea; they wanted many things not to be got in the corral. Hunter sent for a doctor from the city, and gave orders for tea and butter on the Tithing office. Never shall I forget the yearning thankfulness of expression which beamed from some of these sufferers' eyes. The poor creatures felt that in this aged bishop they had found a wise and watchful friend.

Yet the Saints, as a rule, are not poor in the sense in which the Irish are poor; not needy as a race, a body, and a church; indeed, for a new society, starting with nothing, and having its fortunes to make by labor, they are rich. Utah is sprinkled with farms and gardens; the hill-sides are pictured with flocks and herds; and the capital city, the New Jerusalem, is finely laid out and nobly built. Every man labors with his hand and brain; the people are frugal; their fields cost them nothing; and the wealth created by their industry is great. To multiply flocks and herds, to lay up corn and wheat, is with them to obey the commands of God.

CHAPTER XXIV.

MORMON LIGHT.

Fully to comprehend these Saints, you must look beyond the beauty of their city, the prosperity of their farms, the activity of their workshops, the extent of their villages, into the spiritual sources of their strength.

Joseph taught his disciples a doctrine by no means new; that in every religion there is a germ of good, and perhaps a germ of evil; and he proposed by divine assistance (and the aid of Rigdon, Young, and Pratt), to extract the grain of good out of every old creed, and add it to the church which he was founding for his people. He took much from Mohammed, more from Paul, most of all from Abraham; but in his free handling of religious notions, he had no scruple about borrowing from the Hindoos, from the Tartars, from the Mohawks. The doctrinal notes of his church may be numbered and explained: —

1. God is a person, with the form and flesh of man.

2. Man is a part of the substance of God, and will himself become a god.

3. Man is not created by God, but existed from all eternity, and will exist to all eternity.

4. Man is not born in sin, and is not accountable for offences other than his own.

5. The earth is a colony of embodied spirits, one of many such settlements in space.

6. God is President of the Immortals, having under him four orders of beings: (1), Gods — that is to say, immortal beings, possessed of a perfect organization

of soul and body; being the final state of men who have lived on earth in perfect obedience to the law; (2), Angels — immortal beings, who have lived on earth in imperfect obedience to the law; (3), Men — immortal beings, in whom a living soul is united with a human body; (4), Spirits — immortal beings, still waiting to receive their tabernacle of flesh.

7. Man, being one of the race of gods, becomes eligible, by means of marriage, for a celestial throne; his household of wives and children being his kingdom, not on earth only, but in heaven.

8. The Kingdom of God has been again founded on the earth; the time has come for the Saints to take possession of their own; but by virtue, not by violence; by industry, not by force.

Joseph would appear to have got nearly all these doctrines from Rigdon and Pratt. Pratt — the leading scholar of the Mormon Church — too much of a scholar for Young to comprehend and tolerate, has laid down, in various books and lectures, a cosmogony of heaven and earth, which Young has strictly warned us not to receive as truth. Once, if not more than once, Pratt's writings have been formally condemned by the First Presidency and by the Twelve; though he still continues to hold rank as an apostle. "But for me," said Brigham, smiling, "he would have been thrust out of the church long ago." When we put the doctrine of spirit and matter inculcated by Pratt before the President for his opinion, he said, impatiently, "We know nothing about it; it may be all true, it may be all false; we have no light as to those things yet." What has been stated above in the numbered paragraphs is official doctrine taught in the Mormon schools, from the catechism written by Elder Jacques, and formally adopted by Young.

These propositions would seem to have been drawn by the Saints from the oldest and newest mythologies under heaven.

The Mormon God appears to be the same in nature and shape as Homer's Zeus. Their Angels are not unlike the beni-elohim of St. Paul; not angels and spirits in the old English sense, but rather bodiless and unseen beings, as of fine air and invisible flame. Their Men, as beings which are uncreated, indestructible, are the creations of Pythagoras; and as beings born without sin, accountable only for their own evil deeds, are the fancies of Swedenborg.

Some confusion has arisen, in Utah and elsewhere, as to the Mormon doctrine of angels — a confusion caused by the reveries and speculations of Orson Pratt. Young had been good enough to teach us the true and official belief of his church on this curious subject. Angels, he says, are imperfect beings, incapable of rising into the higher grade of gods, to whom they are now, and will be forever, the messengers, ministers, and servants. They are immortal beings who have passed through the stage of spirits in space, and of men on earth, but who have not fulfilled the law of life, not spent their strength in perfect obedience to the will of God. Hence they have been arrested in their growth towards the higher state. On my asking in what they had failed to observe the law, Young answered, "In not living the patriarchal life — in not marrying many wives, like Abraham and Jacob, David and Solomon; like all those men who are called in Scripture the friends of God." In fact, according to Young, angels are the souls of bachelors and monogamists, beings incapable of issue, unblessed with female companions, unfitted to reign and rule in the celestial spheres. In the next world, my friend and myself —

he being unmarried as yet — and I having only one wife — may only aspire to the rank of bachelor angels, while Young and Kimball are to sit, surrounded by their queens, on celestial thrones!

These notes of the faith, as it is held in Salt Lake City — as it is taught in our own midst — in the Welsh mountains, in the Midland shires, among the Mersey dockmen, in the Whitechapel slums — mystical though they read in the main, exert a mighty spell over the imagination and a mighty power upon the actual life of their people. Nothing is useless in the Mormon system; Nanak himself was not more practical in his reforms than Young. Faith is their principle of action; what they believe they do; and those who would comprehend the position taken up by these Saints on earth — defended by twenty thousand rifles — must try to understand what they think of heaven.

Like the Moslems, the Mormons are a praying people. Religion being their life, every action of the day, whether social or commercial, is considered by them in reference to what may be conceived as the will of God. Hence, they have little respect for policy, caution, compromise; they seem to live without fear; they take no account of the morrow; but trust for safety, succor, and success, to Heaven, and to Heaven alone. Refer, in speaking with them, to the Chicago platform; one of the planks of which is the suppression of polygamy by force, and they only smile at your worldly wisdom, and tell you they are living the divine life, and that God will know how to protect His own. Hint to them that Young is mortal, and will one day need a successor; again they smile at your want of understanding, saying they have nothing to do with such things; that God is wise and strong, capable of raising up servants to guide His church. Their whole dependence seems to be on God. It is right to add — as a point within my knowledge — that they also take good care to keep their powder dry.

Confidence in the divine power to help and save them is not so much the effect of weakness and humility, as of strength and pride. Young puts man much higher in the scale of being than any Christian priest has ever done; higher, perhaps, than any Moslem mollah; though the Koran makes the angels dwelling in Paradise servants of the faithful who are gathered to their rest. Bab in Persia, Nanak in the Punjab, go beyond Mohammed; teaching their scholars that man is part of the personality of God; but Young describes man as an uncreated, indestructible portion of the Highest; a being with the faculty of raising an order of immortal and unbodied spirits into the exalted rank of gods. How much a high belief in man's rights and powers, as a son of God, and a special favorite of Heaven, can steady the soul in danger, and nerve the arm in battle, was seen in every conflict of the Jews, and is written in every history of the Sikhs.

The secular notes of the Mormon Society may be gathered into three large groups: — (1) Those which define its relations to man as a member and as a stranger; (2) Those which define the method and the principle of its government; (3) Those which define the condition of its family life.

CHAPTER XXV.

SECULAR NOTES.

THE first group of secular notes embraces two leading ideas.

1. The new church, established in Utah, though it is called the Church of America, is free, and (with one passing exception) open to all the world; to men of every race, clime, creed, and color; taking into its bosom the Jew from New York, the Buddhist from San Francisco, the Parsee from Calcutta, the Wesleyan from Liverpool, the Moslem from Cairo, the Cheyenne from Smoky Hill River.

The one passing exception is the Negro. "The Negro," Brigham said to me this morning, "is a descendant of Cain, the first murderer, and his darkness is a curse put on his skin by God." Only one Negro has ever yet been admitted into brotherhood with the Saints: the act of Joseph, done at Nauvoo. Until God shall have removed this curse, Young will have none of these Cainites in his church.

2. The new church not only receives all comers, but tolerates all dissenters; asking no questions, putting no test, demanding no sacrifice. Thus, a man of any other creed may be enrolled among the Saints without losing his identity; without breaking his idols, without rooting up his faith, without shedding his habits; in a word, without that spiritual change which Christians understand as being born to a new life. The convert to Mormonism accepts a new truth, in addition to the truths which he may have held beforetime. Joseph is proposed to him as a reconciler, not as a separator;

the Saints insisting that there is some good in every form of religion, and that no sect on earth enjoys a monopoly in the love of God.

Let us look into these two leading ideas, not in their dogmatical, but in their political aspects:

The Church is free and open. In its first appeals, a new creed has commonly been proposed to a particular race, its ritual adapted to a special zone. We see in history so many examples of such appeals succeeding on the spot, and failing everywhere beyond it, that students are apt to deny the possibility of a common faith, and to treat religion as an affair of climate and of race. The law of Moses made few converts beyond the Hebrew tribes. Confucius finds no followers out of China. The Great Spirit only reigns in the American woods. The Guebres have never carried their worship out of Persia and India. Dagon was a local god, the symbol of a people fond of the sea. Thor is a denizen of the frozen North. Brahma is only known to Hindoos, who make no converts; and so strictly is this law of living apart, for themselves only, fixed in the Hindoo's habits of thought, that a man of one caste can never pass into another; a Brahman born must remain a Brahman; a Sudra born must remain a Sudra all his life. Buddhism has, in some respects, the character of a universal church, having drawn to itself many tribes and nations, and become the chief religion of the world, if the mere number of its temples and congregations could confer that rank; yet, among the four hundred of millions of men who worship Buddha, there is no instance of a people having ever been converted to the faith in whom the reception of his creed had not been prepared by a natural inclination towards the Oriental belief in transmigration of souls; so that Buddhism itself, however widely it may be diffused throughout the earth, is but the religion of a particular race. Islam is the creed of Arabia and the Arabs. When carried eastward to the Ganges, westward to the Guadalquiver, it was borne forward on the points of a myriad lances, not received by the people of India and of Spain on its merits as a saving faith; and, being neither a natural growth nor a free adoption in those countries, it wore itself out in Spain, while in Persia and India it has rooted itself chiefly among men of Semitic race. Nanak in the Punjab, Bab in Persia, may be said to have founded sects on a wider plan than most other religious leaders: for the Sikhs and Babees are both missionary churches, taking their own from among Moslem, Buddhist, and Hindoo flocks; yet the notion of having one free and open church, which should make the brown man and the white man, the black man and the red man, brothers and equals, has scarcely ever yet dawned upon these fiery advocates of faith.

Thus, nearly all our creeds have either some open or some latent reference to condition. An ancient legend says that the Arabian prophet told his followers they would prevail in arms and plant the true faith wherever the palms bore fruit; a legend which has been almost verified in fact for a thousand years; but Mohammed never dreamt of offering his half-tropical system of social life to the white barbarians of the North; to hungry hunters beyond the Euxine, to frozen woodsmen of the Helvetic Alps. His rule of rejecting wine and pork, wise enough on the Nile and on the Jordan, would have been wasteful of nature on the Danube and the Elbe. His code was written for the palm-bearing zones, and within those zones it has always thriven. No Babee is found settled out of Persia, no Sikh out of Upper India; in each case a man finds his religious rites adapted to the country in which he dwells.

Christianity itself, though nobler in spirit, tougher in framework, than any of these geographical creeds, has yet very much the appearance of being mainly the religion of the Gothic race. Although our creed sprang up in Palestine, and flourished for some years in Egypt and Syria, it never took hold of the Semitic mind, never rooted itself in the Semitic soil. No Arab tribe has been finally won to the cross, just as no Gothic tribe has finally been gained to the Crescent. The half Oriental churches which remain in Africa and Asia—the Abyssinian, the Coptic, the Armenian—have no connection with the great Arabian family of man. In fact, no branch of the Christian society has ever yet clearly put forth the pretension of offering itself to all nations as a free and open church; we pride ourselves on being local and exclusive—Greeks, Latins, Anglicans, Lutherans—rather than branches of one living, universal church. The largest Christian community on earth defines its catholicity as Roman and Apostolic, instead of aiming to include the world and owning no founder except Jesus Christ.

How much power is lost by the existence of this parish spirit in our churches, a statesman feels the instant that some object, common to the whole Christian society, comes into view; such as that question of the Holy Sepulchre which, only a dozen years ago, drove the Russ and Frank into fraternal strife.

The new church is tolerant of differences in belief and habits of life.—Laymen like More and Locke have written most eloquently on the policy of tolerating all kinds of opinion; but no large branch of the Christian Church has ever yet entered on the practice of their liberal views. On no better ground than a difference of opinion as to points which only the highest intellects can master, Greek, Roman, Lutheran, Dutch, Genevan, are at deadly feud; mocking each other's rites, impugning each other's motives, condemning each other's actions; saying evil things, doing evil works to their brethren, with a bitterness of hate increasing with the narrowness of their dividing lines. To wit, the prelates of Rome and England go on damning each other from fast to feast with a ferocity which they would shrink from displaying towards an Imam in Egypt, a Gosain in Bengal, a prophet at Salt Lake. We make watch-words and warn-words to prevent people from coming near us who might otherwise share in our gospel of love and peace. With as little ruth as the Gileadite swordsmen felt towards the flying bands on the Jordan, we slay all brethren who either can not or will not pronounce our shibboleth.

As our Founder left it, the Church was loving and merciful; as men have made it, it is hard and cruel as a Hindoo caste. A Brahman does not stand aloof from a Sudra with fiercer pride than a Greek Christian shows towards a Copt. Even at the cradle and at the the tomb of Christ, we fight for our parish creeds, until the very Bedouins, who have to part the quarrelling disciples, blush for shame. Is it better in London, Rome, and Moscow, than in Bethlehem and Zion? Do the hundred Hindoo sects revile each other in a darker spirit than our own congregations? Who will say it? A worshipper of Vishna may live in the same convent as a worshipper of Ṣiva, and the two Hindoo hermits will dwell in their narrow den in peace. How would it fare in the same shed with a Calvinist and a Catholic? Chaitanya taught the fine truth that faith abolishes and replaces caste; so that Brahman, Kshatrya, Vaisya, and Sudra, whatever their rank and state may be on earth, are equals and brothers in the sight of God. Some Christians preach the same; but where is the national church that has adopted this beneficent truth? Why, a Greek will not allow that a Latin can be saved from hell, and every Armenian monk believes that his Coptic rival will be burnt in everlasting fire. Our churches, even on our parish greens, are worn and torn by internal feuds. Of all races on the earth, the Anglo-Saxon is, in matter of thought and speech, the most liberal, the most tolerant; yet we have had our lurid Smithfield fires, and our list of martyrs lengthens into a mighty host. Within the existing pale we have a High Church faction fighting a Low Church faction, much as Hanafees strive against Malikees in the orthodox Arab mosque. Some writers see a spiritual good in this wide separation of sect from sect; but the political results of it are not to be concealed; and these results are, in England strife, in Europe bloodshed, in Palestine the occupation of our Holy Places by the Turk. A tolerant Church would save society from enormous waste of power.

CHAPTER XXVI.

HIGH POLITICS.

THE second group of secular notes — those notes which define the method and the principle of Mormon government — ascend into the highest region of politics. Three points may be mentioned as of supreme importance for the understanding of this peculiar people.

(1.) The new church assumes that God is in personal contact with his Saints; guiding them now, as He did in past times, as He will do in future times, by a revelation of his will through a chosen seer; not in their great affairs only, their battles, famines, and migrations, but also in their rural and domestic troubles, such as the planting of fields, the building of a store, and the sealing of a wife.

(2.) The new church asserts that true worship is true enjoyment; a blessing from on high, bountifully given by a father to his children; not a tribute levied by a prince, not a penance exacted by a priest; but a light and innocent play, a gladness in the spirit and in the flesh; a sense of duty being done, of service accepted, and of life refreshed.

(3.) In the new church work is honorable, the recovery of barren places noble, the production of corn and oil, of fruit and flowers, of gum and spices, of herbs and trees, a saving act; the whole earth being regarded by the Saints as a waste to be redeemed by labor into the future heaven.

These notes deserve a close attention from those who would comprehend the political growth of the Mormon Church.

The new church is divinely ruled.—The notion of God being always present among his people, making known his wishes from day to day, through one selected and unfailing channel, though it may appear to reverential persons very profane, is one that must strike a ruler and a thinker, bent on governing men through their hopes and fears, as offering him a vast reserve of strength. Upon a certain class of minds, it is known that the mere sense of distance serves to dim all light, to deaden all fear; so that, with persons having such minds, the authority of right and truth is apt to grow faint, in exact proportion to the remoteness of their vouchers. For men of this feeble stamp, everything must be new and near. To them old edicts are of doubtful force; to them ancient traditions are out of date. Indeed, for every one save the highly trained, to whom Euclid is the same as De Morgan, laws have a tendency to become obsolete. A church that takes a particular year as its point of departure, and stands to it forever, must always reckon on coming into conflict with this weakness of the human heart. To say that a thing is a long way off, that it happened a long time ago, is to express a kind of moral despair. Men wish to get nearer to the sources; if the grace could be given to them, they would like to see God face to face. Moses cannot speak for them; Sinai is but a name. They never felt the waves of Galilee stilled beneath them. They were not standing in the Gentile court when the Temple vail was rent in twain.

To men of this class, clamorous for a sign, Jerusalem answered by a succession of prophets, who brought the Jewish heaven down to earth, and served it to the people with their daily bread; Rome answers now, as she answered of old, with her mystery of the actual Presence of God in the bread and wine. Rome and

Jerusalem found in such means a defence against feeble spirits; but cities of a wider culture—London, Boston, Amsterdam, Geneva—have no resources against such craving of the spirit, excepting the critical opinions of their learned men. But this critical learning does not always answer. A faith which has to find its support in logic and in history, will always appear to some devout and unreasoning minds as a secular sort of canon, resting on man when it should only lean on God. Religious doubt is more exacting, and more illogical, than philosophical doubt. Perhaps the peril arising from its presence in any society is greatest in the freest and most educated states; religious doubt being one of the products of civilization quicker in its physical than in its moral growth. As the mind may be clouded with excess of light, it may also become morbid from excess of health. Freedom starts inquiries to which replies are not yet ready, and the philosopher's difficulty makes the impostor's opportunity. When men ask for a sign and receive a date, what marvel if they should turn away? Souls which are groping in the dark do not ask you for controversy, for history, for logic; they want a living gospel, an instant revelation, a personal God.

Here the Saint steps in to supply all wants. When Young, with a peculiar emphasis, says, "This I know," his followers take his voice for that of God. Their eyes dilate, their faces brighten, at his word; new hope, fresh courage, shoot into their hearts. Accepting the counsel, the encouragement, as divine, life begins for them, as it were, anew. It would be simple blindness in our pastors not to see that in our own age, and in the most liberal nations, many weak souls, from lack of true imaginative insight, are falling from a faith which they cannot any longer grasp as they might an actual fact; on one side turning into Rationalism, on the other side into Romanism—here becoming Spiritualists, there inquiring about the Mormons. To the frail who are crying out for guidance, the Reasoners say, Come to us and be cured of creeds; the Saints say, Come to God and be saved from hell.

The service of God is the enjoyment of life.—On its social side, the Mormon church may be regarded as gay, its ritual as festive. All that the elder creeds have nursed in the way of gloom, austerity, bewilderment, despair, is banished from the New Jerusalem. No one fears being damned; no one troubles his soul about fate, free-will, election, and prevenient grace. A Mormon lives in an atmosphere of trust; for in his eyes, heaven lies around him in his glowing lake, in his smiling fields, in his snowy alps. To him, the advent of the Saints was the Second Coming, and the founding of their church a beginning of the reign of God. He feels no dread, he takes no trouble, on account of the future. What is, will be; to-morrow like to-day, the next year like the past one; heaven a continuation of the earth; where to each man will be meted out glory and power according to the fulness of his obedience in the present life. The earth, he says, is a Paradise made for enjoyment. If it were possible to think that Young and Pratt had ever read the Hindoo sages, we should imagine that they had borrowed this part of their system from the disciples of Vallabracha, the prophet of pleasure, the expounder of delight.

From whatever source this idea of a festal service may have come, Euphrosyne reigns in Utah. Young might be described as Minister of Mirth; having built a great theatre, in which his daughters play comedies and interludes; having built a social hall, in which the young of both sexes dance and sing; and having set the example of balls and music-parties both in the open air and under private roofs. Concerts and operas are constantly being given. Water-parties, picnics, all the contrivances for innocent amusement, have his hearty sanction. Care is bestowed on the ripening of grapes, on the culture of peaches, on the cooking of food; so that an epicure may chance to find in the New Jerusalem dainties which he would sigh for in vain at Washington and New York. When dining in the houses of apostles, we are always struck with the abundance of sweets and fruits, with the choiceness of their quality, and the daintiness of their preparation. A stranger who sees the Theatre crowded and the Temple unbuilt, might run away with the notion that Young is less of a Saint than his people pretend to think. It would be a mistake; such as we make in Bombay, when we infer that the Maharajahs have no religion, because in some of their services they clothe themselves in purple and begin with a feast.

The new church regards work as noble.—That work is noble is a very old phrase, known to the Jews, held by the Essenes, sanctioned by St. Paul. It was a legend among monks in the middle ages; and it lies at the root of all English, French, and American systems for reforming and regenerating society. But the principle that manual labor is good in itself, and for its own sake, a blessing from heaven, a solace to the heart, a privilege, an endowment to the spirit, a service, an act of obedience, has never been taken as her fundamental social truth by any church. Handwork may have been called useful; it has nowhere been treated by the law as noble. In our old world, the names of prince and gentleman are given to those who write and think, not to those who plough and trench, who throw in the seed and gather up the sheaves. By noble labor, we mean the work of judges, statesmen, orators, priests; no one in Europe would think of saying that to plant a tree, to dig a drain, to build a house, to mow a field, would be noble toil. The Hindoo puts his laborers into the two lowest castes; if they are husbandmen, into the third caste; if artisans, into the fourth; their estate being in either case far less honorable than that of a warrior, that of a priest. A Sudra's soul and body counts for less than one hair from a Brahman's head; for among the Hindoos, work is regarded as a curse, never as a blessing, and the free laborer of Bengal ranks but one degree higher than a pariah and a slave. Now and then the Hebrews had glimpses of a better law:—"Seest thou a man skilful in his work, he shall stand before kings;" the theory of God and Nature; and from this Hebrew source, not from any dreams of Owen, Fourier, and St. Simon, the Saints have borrowed their idea, translating it, not into language only, but into extensive pastures and smiling farms. With them, to do any piece of work is a righteous act; to be a toiling and producing man is to be in a state of grace.

What need is there to dwell on the political value of such a note?

CHAPTER XXVII.

MARRIAGE IN UTAH.

But the most singular, the most powerful, of these three groups of secular notes, even when we study them from a political point of view only, is that which defines the conditions of family life, particularly in what it has to say of marriage. Marriage lies at the root of society, and the method of dealing with it marks the spirit of every religious system.

Now the New American church puts marriage into the very front of man's duties on earth. Neither man nor woman, says Young, can work out the will of God alone; that is to say, all human beings have a function to discharge on earth—the function of providing tabernacles of the flesh for immortal spirits now waiting to be born—which cannot be discharged except through that union of the sexes implied in marriage. To evade that function is, according to Young, to evade the most sacred of man's obligations. It is to commit sin. An unwedded man is, in Mormon belief, an imperfect creature; like a bird without wings, a body without soul. Nature is dual; to complete his organization, a man must marry a wife. Love, says Young, is the yearning for a higher state of existence; and the passions, properly understood, are the feeders of our spiritual life.

Looking to this dogma of the duty of wedlock solely as a source of political power, we should have to allow it very great weight. What waste it saves! In many religious bodies marriage is simply tolerated, as the lesser form of two dark evils. Those Essenes from whom we derive so much, allowed it only to the weak, and on account of weakness; they thought it better for a good man to refrain from marriage; and in the higher grades of their society the relation of wife and husband was unknown. Many orders among the Hindoos practise celibacy. The Greeks had their Vestal virgins, the Egyptians their anchorites, the Syrians their ascetics. In the Pagan Olympus, abstinence was a virtue, praised, if not practised, by the gods. Hestia and Artemis were honored above all the denizens of heaven, because they rose beyond the reach of love; nay, the idea of marriage being a kind of corruption had so far sunk into the Pagan mind as to crop out everywhere in the common speech. To be unloved was to be unspotted; to be single was to be pure. In all Pagan poetry the title of virgin is held to be higher than that of mother, nobler than that of wife. Among Christian communities marriage is a theme of endless disputation; one church calling it a sacrament, another calling it a contract; all churches considering it optional; few regarding it as meritorious; many denouncing it as a compromise with the devil. The Greek church encourages celibacy in a class; the Latin prohibits marriage to its priests. The Gothic church may be said to stand neutral; but no church in the world has ever yet come to insist on the duty of marriage as necessary to the living of a true Christian life.

On the contrary, every religious body which has dealt with the topic at all — Greek, Armenian, Coptic, Latin, Abyssinian — declares by facts, no less than by words, that any union of the sexes in the bands of wedlock is hostile to the highest conception of a Christian life. Hence the monastic houses; hence the celibacy of priests;. institutions which infect the mind of society, arresting the growth of many household virtues, poisoning some of the sources of domestic life. A wifeless priest is a standing protest against wedded love; for if it be true that the human affections are a snare, leading men away from God, it is surely a good man's duty to crush them out. A snare is a snare, a sin a sin, to be avoided equally by the layman and the priest.

Young has turned the face of his church another way. With him marriage is a duty and a privilege; and the elders, being considered examples to the people in all good works, are enjoined to marry. A priest and elder must be a husband; even among the humbler flock, it is held to be a disgrace, the sign of an unregenerated heart, for a young man to be found leading a single life.

But the Saints have pushed the doctrine a step farther; for instead of denying to their popes and priests the consolation of woman's love, they encourage them to indulge in a plurality of wives; and among their higher clergy,—the Prophet, the apostles, and the bishops,—this indulgence is next to universal. Not to be a pluralist is not to be a good Mormon. My friend, Captain Hooper, though he is known to be rich, zealous, insinuating,—an admirable representative of Utah in Congress,—has never been able to rise high in the church, on account of his repugnance to taking another wife. "We look on Hooper," the Apostle Taylor said to me yesterday at dinner, "as only half a Mormon;" at which every one laughed in a sly, peculiar way. When the merriment, in which the young ladies joined, had died down, I said to Hooper, "Here 's a great chance for you next season. Pick out six of the prettiest girls in Salt Lake City;

marry them in a batch; carry them to Washington; and open your season in December with a ball!" "Well," said Hooper, "I think that would take for a time; but then I am growing to be an old fellow."

Young, who is fond of Hooper, proud of his talents, and conscious of his services, is said to be urging him strongly to marry one more wife at least, so as to cast in his lot finally, whether for good or evil, with the polygamous church. If Hooper yields, it will be from a sentiment of duty and fidelity towards his chief.

Every priest of the higher grades in Salt Lake Valley has a plural household; the number of his mates varying with the wealth and character of the elder. No apostle has less than three wives.

Of the marriages of Brigham Young, Heber Kimball, and Daniel Wells, the three members of what is here called the First Presidency, no accounts are kept in the public office. It is the fashion of every pious old lady in this community, who may have lost her husband by death, to implore the bishop of her ward to take measures for getting her sealed to one of these three Presidents. Young is, of course, the favorite of such widows; and it is said that he never makes a journey from the Beehive without being called upon to indulge one of these poor creatures in her wish. Hence, a great many women hold the nominal rank of his wife whom he has scarcely ever seen, and with whom he has never held the relations of a husband, as we in Europe should understand the term. The actual wives of Brigham Young, the women who live in his houses—in the Beehive, in the Lion House, in the White Cottage—who are the mothers of his children, are twelve, or about twelve, in number. The queen of all is the first wife, Mary Ann Angell, an aged lady, whose five children—

three sons, two daughters—are now grown up. She lives in the White Cottage, the first house ever built in Salt Lake Valley. Joseph and Brigham, her eldest sons, chiefs of their race, are already renowned in missionary labors. Sister Alice, her eldest daughter, is my friend—on the stage. The most famous, perhaps, of these ladies is Eliza Snow, the poetess, a lady universally respected for her fine character, universally applauded for her fine talents. About fifty years old, with silver hair, dark eyes, and noble aspect—simple in attire, calm, lady-like, rather cold—Eliza is the exact reverse to any imaginary light of the harem. I am led to believe that she is not a wife to Young in the sense of our canon; she is always called Miss Eliza; in fact, the Mormon rite of sealing a woman to a man implies other relations than our Gentile rite of marriage; and it is only by a wide perversion of terms that the female Saints who may be sealed to a man are called his wives. Sister Eliza lives in the Lion House, in a pretty room, on the second floor, overlooking the Oquirrh mountains, the Valley, the River Jordan, and the Salt Lake; a poet's prospect, in which form and color, sky and land and water, melt and fuse into a glory without end. Young's less distinguished partners are: Sister Lucy, by whom he has eight children; Sister Clara, by whom he has three children; Sister Zina, a poetess and teacher (formerly the wife of Dr. Jacobs), by whom he has three children; Sister Amelia, an old servant of Joseph, by whom he has four children; Sister Eliza (2), an English girl (the only Englishwoman in the Prophet's house), by whom he is said to have four or five children; Sister Margaret, by whom he has three or four children; Sister Emeline, often called the favorite, by whom he has eight children. Young himself tells me, that he has never had, and never will have, a favorite in his house; since desires and preferences of the flesh have no part in the family arrangements of the Saints.

The Apostles have fewer blessings than the Presidents; but the Twelve are all pluralists. The following figures are supplied to me by George A. Smith, cousin of the Prophet Joseph, and Historian of the Church,—

Orson Hyde, first apostle, has four wives;
Orson Pratt, second apostle, has four wives;
John Taylor, third apostle, has seven wives;
Wilford Woodruff, fourth apostle, has three wives,
George A. Smith, fifth apostle, has five wives;
Amasa Lyman, sixth apostle, has five wives;
Ezra Benson, seventh apostle, has four wives;
Charles Rich, eighth apostle, has seven wives;
Lorenzo Snow, ninth apostle, has four wives;
Erastus Snow, tenth apostle, has three wives;
Franklin Richards, eleventh apostle, has four wives;
George Q. Cannon, twelfth apostle, has three wives.

With the exception of John Taylor, the apostles are considered poor men; and in Salt Lake it is held dishonest for a man to take a new wife unless he can maintain his family in comfort, as regards lodging, food, and clothes. Some of the rich merchants are encouraged by Young to add wife on wife. A bold and pushing elder said to me last night, in answer to some banter, "I shall certainly marry again soon; the fact, is, I mean to rise in this church; and you have seen enough to know that no man has a chance in our society unless he has a big household. To have any weight here, you must be known as the husband of three women."

CHAPTER XXVIII.

POLYGAMOUS SOCIETY.

On the political strength which this fashion of plurality lends to the Saints of Salt Lake City, a few words may be said. Two questions present themselves, — In the first place, has the promise of a plurality of wives proved to be a good bribe, inducing men of a certain class to join the Mormon Church? And, in the second place, has the practice of plurality shown itself to be a means by which, when converts have been won, they can be made to multiply in numbers far beyond the ordinary rate?

To the first query, only one answer can be truly given. Name the motive as you please; call it, with the Saints, desire of the spirit; call it, with the Gentiles, desire of the flesh; the fact will remain — that a license for making love to many women, for sealing them as wives, for gathering them into secluded harems, has acted in the past, and is acting in the present, as a powerful and seductive bribe.

Young and Pratt declare that the carnal appetites have no immediate share in their own selection of brides; that this business of selection is the work of Heaven; that the act of sealing is a religious rite; and that a wife for eternity, the queen and partner of a celestial throne, can be given to a man by none but God. Young told me, with a laughing eye, that they would put their wives in evidence of what they say; many of these ladies being old, plain, uneducated, ill-mannered; though others, as my eyes inform me, are young, fresh, delicate, and charming. But, who can doubt that Young, with his keen sense of power, and his mastery of all the springs of action, is well aware of the political uses to be made of this great appeal of beauty to the carnal man? If taking a fresh wife once a year be an act of obedience, it serves the Saints very much like a call of pleasure. Yet, who shall say they are insincere? Young told me that in the early days of their strange institution, he was much opposed to plural households, and I am confident that he speaks the truth. Among the Mormon presidents and apostles, we have not seen one face on which liar and hypocrite were written. Though we daily meet with fanatics, we have not seen a single man whom we can call a rogue. Their faith is not our faith—their practice is not our practice. What then? Among the Hindoos many sects indulge in rites which English people call licentious; some, indeed, being so abominable, that a man who sees them for the first time is apt to call for the police. Could the Ras Mandala be performed in London? Would the Kanchulayas be allowed to celebrate their worship in New York? Yet there are men and women, living under the sceptre of Victoria, who in perfect faith, if not in perfect innocency, imitate the amorous sports of Krishna, choosing the partners of their delirious worship by the lottery of the vest.

Young may believe in what he says, and in what he does (for I think him, in the sphere of his knowledge and his customs, an honest man); but some of his followers are accused of taking pains to preach a plurality of wives, as one of the rewards of conversion to his church; and I know that they are fond of quoting the promise made by Nathan to David, that he should wed and enjoy the wives of his enemy Saul. That this gospel of indulgence is found by the Saints to be most alluring in Gentile lands, their missionaries would certainly not deny. It may be that either the flesh is weak or the spirit strong; but the Welsh peasant, the London tailor, the Lancashire weaver, is found to pore with a rapt eye and a burning pulse over the pictures painted by missionaries of that Paradise near Salt Lake, in which a man is free to do all things that his arm can compass, to have as many houses as he can build, as many wives as he can feed and govern. An unregenerate man is told that a harem may be not only lawfully kept, but easily gained,— the female heart being opened by a special providence to the truth as it lies in Young,— that there are plenty of beautiful girls at Salt Lake; and that a Saint is invited and enjoined to live up to the perfect law. Few elders, it is said, come back to Utah from a journey without bringing a new favorite, won from among the Gentiles to his fold. One of Young's wives was a married lady in New York, who fell in love with the Prophet and fled with him from her husband's house. It is one of the pleasantries of Utah, that Kimball never lets a missionary go forth on a journey without giving him injunctions to bring back young lambs. It is noted, as a rule, that the high dignitaries of the church have been blessed by heaven with the prettiest women; one of those recompenses of a virtuous life which Helvetius conceived as desirable, but which no society has ever yet had the wit and daring to adopt.

To the second query two answers may be returned. In a fixed society, like that of Turkey, of Syria, of Egypt, the existence of polygamy would have no great influence on the powers of increase. Once, indeed, men thought otherwise. Writers, like Montesquieu, seeing that polygamy prevailed in many parts of the

East, imagined that in these regions the females must be far in excess of the males, and that the appropriation of several women to one man was a rule of nature, made from the earliest times, by way of correcting a freak of birth. Travellers, like Niebuhr, finding his Arab sheikhs with harems, hinted that polygamy arose from the circumstance that Arab women grow old and barren while their husbands are still young and hale. These delusions have long since gone the way of all error.

Now, we can happily say, in the light of science, that even in Egypt and Arabia the males and females are born in about equal numbers; the males being a little in excess of the females. We see, then, that Nature has put the human family on the earth in pairs; rejecting by her own large mandate all those monstrous and irregular growths apart from the conjugal relations established by herself between male and female; whether those growths have taken the shape either of polygamy or of polyandry, either many wives to one husband, or many husbands to one wife. The true law of nature, therefore, is, that one male and one female shall make their home together; and in the old country, where the sexes are equal, where the manners are uniform, and where the religion is common, any departure from this true law will rather weaken than increase the multiplying power of the country as a whole. So far the answer seems to go one way. The question, however, is, not as to the growth of a whole nation; but as to that of a particular family, of a particular community, of a mere sect within the boundaries of that nation. Even in Arabia, it is clear that if a particular sheikh could invent some means of getting from other tribes a great many of their women, until he had enough females in his power to give three wives to every male adult in his camp, the tribe of that sheikh would increase in numbers faster than their neighbors who had only one wife apiece. This is something like the case in America with the Saints. Their own society could not give them the plurality of wives which they announce as the social law of all coming time. But granted that, by either good or evil means, they could get the women into their church, it is idle to deny that the possession of such a treasure gives them enormous powers of increase. One man may be the father of a hundred children; one woman can hardly be the mother of a score. We know that Jair and Hillel must have been polygamists, the moment we hear that the first had thirty sons and the second had forty sons.

It is not an easy thing to count the number of children in the different households at Salt Lake. The census papers cannot be quoted, since they were made up, the Apostle Taylor tells me, mainly by guessing on the part of a Gentile officer, who would not go about and count. In this city a moslem jealousy appears to guard such facts as would be public property in London and New York. Young tells us he has forty-eight children now alive. Kimball has, perhaps, an equal number. Every house seems full; wherever we see a woman, she is nursing; and in every house we enter two or three infants in arms are shown to us. This valley is, indeed, the true baby land. For a man to have twenty boys and girls in his house is a common fact. A merchant with whom we were dining yesterday, could not tell us the number of his children until he had consulted a book then lying on his desk. One of his wives, a nice English lady, with the usual baby at her breast, smiled sweet reproof on his ignorance; but the fact was so; and it was only after counting and consulting that he could give us the exact return of his descendants. This patriarch is thirty-three years old.

It was by means of polygamy that Israel increased in a few generations so as to confound all sense of numbers; and no one can mistake the tendency among these American Saints. Young has more children than Jair; Pratt than Hillel; Kimball than Ibzan. This rate of growth may not be kept up for a hundred years; in time it must slacken of itself for want of supplies; but for the present moment it exists:—not the least ominous of those facts which a statesman of the New America has to face.

CHAPTER XXIX.

THE DOCTRINE OF PLURALITIES.

When the Saints were engaged in seizing, as they say, for their own use, all that was found to be fair and fruitful in other creeds, they would appear to have added to the relations of husband and wife, as these have been fixed by the codes of all civilized States, whether Christian, Moslem, Jewish, or Hindoo, some highly dramatic details. Not only have the Saints adopted polygamy into their church, but they have borrowed it under its oldest and most savage form.

Taken by itself, apart from surrounding schools of thought, the mere fact of a new church having brought itself to allow plurality of wives among its members, would not need to startle us very much, since many of us are familiar with such a system in legend and in history, even though we may be strangers to it by actual sight and sound. Abraham and David practised it. Neither Moses nor Paul forbade it; and Mohammed, while purifying it of the grosser Oriental features, sanctioned it by his deeds. Polygamy enters into the poetry of Cordova, the romance of Bagdad. The enterprising Parsee, the learned Brahman, the fiery Rajpoot, all embrace it. Even in the Christian Church, opinions are divided as to whether it is wrong in itself, or only a trouble in the social body. Many of the early converts, both in Syria and in Egypt, were polygamists; and the questions which have recently disturbed Colenso and the Kaffir chief had arisen in primitive times, when the policy of admitting men having several wives into fellowship was affirmed by fathers of the church. Nor would the appearance of polygamy in these plains of Salt Lake be a novel and surprising fact, since everything that we know of Ute and Shoshone compels us to believe that plurality has always been the domestic law of these valleys. The sides of these sierras are wild and bare; a poor country and a hard life induce polygamy; and all the tribes of red men which seek a scanty subsistence in these glens and plains practise the nomadic custom of stealing and selling squaws. A big chief prides himself on having plenty of wives; and the white men, who have come to live among these Utes, Cheyennes, Arappahoes, and Kiowas, whether they began as trappers, guides, interpreters, or hunters, have almost always fallen into the Indian way of living. The dozen pale-faces, known to be dwelling with Indian tribes at this moment — hunting buffalo, cutting scalps — are all polygamists; often with larger harems than the biggest native chiefs.

But the Saints have not simply revived polygamy

in Utah; they have returned to that form of domestic life in both its unlimited and its incestuous forms. In their search for the foundations of a new society, they have gone back to the times when Abram was called out of Hauran; undoing the work of all subsequent reformers; setting aside not only all that Mohammed, but all that Moses had done for the better regulation of our family life. Moses forbade a man to take a wife of his own flesh and blood. Mohammed restrained his followers to a harem of three or four wives; a moderation at which Young and Kimball, who appeal from Moses to Abraham, only laugh. Who, they ask, married his half-sister Sarai? — the man of God. Hence the Saints of Utah have set up a claim to marry their own half-sisters, without being able to plead for this practice either the Arab custom or the Arab need. They find no objection, either in nature or in revelation, to the custom of breeding in and in; a subject on which we one day had a curious talk with Young and the Twelve. Young denied that degeneracy springs from marriage between men and women who may be near in blood.

The Saints go much beyond Abram; and I, for one, am inclined to think that they have found their type of domestic life in the Indian's wigwam rather than in the Patriarch's tent. Like the Ute, a Mormon may have as many wives as he can feed; like the Mandan, he may marry three or four sisters, an aunt and her niece, a mother and her child. Perhaps it would not be too much to say that in the Mormon code there is no such crime as incest, and that a man is practically free to woo and wed any woman who may take his eye.

We have had a very strange conversation with Young about the Mormon doctrine of incest. I asked him whether it was a common thing among the Saints to marry mother and daughter; and, if so, on what authority they acted, since that kind of union was not sanctioned either by the command to Moses or by the "revelation" to Smith. When he hung back from admitting that such a thing occurred at all, I named a case in one of the city wards, of which we had obtained some private knowledge. Apostle Cannon said that in such cases the first marriage would be only a form; that the elder female would be understood as being a mother to her husband and his younger bride; on which I named my example: and in which an elder of the church had married an English woman, a widow, with a daughter then of twelve; in which the woman had borne four children to this husband; and in which this husband had married her daughter when she came of age.

Young said it was not a common thing at Salt Lake.

"But it does occur?"

"Yes," said Young, "it occurs sometimes?"

"On what ground is such a practice justified by the church?"

After a short pause, he said, with a faint and wheedling smile: "This is a part of the question of incest. We have no sure light on it yet. I cannot tell you what the church holds to be the actual truth; I can tell you my own opinion; but you must not publish it—you must not tell it—lest I should be misunderstood and blamed." He then made to us a communication on the nature of incest, as he thinks of this offence and judges it; but what he then said I am not at liberty to print.

As to the facts which came under my own eyes, I am free to speak. Incest, in the sense in which we use the word,—marriage within the prohibited degrees,—is not regarded as a crime in the Mormon church. It is known that in some of these saintly harems, the female occupants stand to their lords in closer relationship of blood than the American law permits. It is a daily event in Salt Lake City for a man to wed two sisters, a brother's widow, and even a mother and daughter. A saint named Wall has married his half-sister, pleading the example of Sarai and Abraham, which Young, after some consideration, allowed to be a precedent for his flock. In one household in Utah may be seen the spectacle of three women, who stand towards each other in the relation of child, mother, and grand-dame, living in one man's harem as his wives! I asked the President, whether, with his new lights on the virtue of breeding in and in, he saw any objection to the marriage of brother and sister. Speaking for himself, not for the church, he said he saw none at all. What follows I give in the actual words of the speakers: —

D. "Does that sort of marriage ever take place?"

Young. "Never."

D. "Is it prohibited by the church?"

Young. "No; it is prohibited by prejudice."

Kimball. "Public opinion won't allow it."

Young. "I would not do it myself, nor suffer any one else, when I could help it."

D. "Then you don't prohibit, and you don't practise it?"

Young. "My prejudices prevent me."

This remnant of an old feeling brought from the Gentile world, and this alone, would seem to prevent the Saints from rushing into the higher forms of incest. How long will these Gentile sentiments remain in force?

"You will find here," said Elder Stenhouse to me, talking on another subject, "polygamists of the third generation; when these boys and girls grow up, and marry, you will have in these valleys the true feeling of patriarchal life. The old world is about us yet; and we are always thinking of what people may say in the Scottish hills and the Midland shires."

A revival of polygamy, which would have been singular in either Persia or Afghanistan, sprang up slowly, and by a sort of secret growth. It began with Rigdon and his theory of the spiritual wife, which he is said to have borrowed from the Vermont Methodists. At first, this theory was no more than a mystical speculation; having reference, less to the world and its duties, than to heaven and its thrones. We know that it was preached by Rigdon, that it was denounced by Joseph, that it crept into favor with the elders, that it gave rise to much scandal in the Church, and that it was finally superseded by a more practical and useful creed.

The spirit evoked by that fanatic in the infant church could not be laid; sealing women went on; the first in the new Prophet's household, afterwards in the harems of Kimball, Pratt, and Hyde, whose marriages, only half secret, put an end to the mystical restraints involved in the theory of spiritual husbands and spiritual wives. They were polygamous, but polygamous without disguise. Years afterwards, Young produced a paper, which he said was a true copy of a revelation made to Joseph at Nauvoo, commanding him, after the manner of Abraham, of Jacob, and of David, to receive into his bosom as many wives as should be given unto him of God. This paper was not in Joseph's handwriting, nor in that of Emma, his wife. Young declares that it was written down from the Prophet's lips by a male disciple; adding, with a true touch of nature, that when Emma had first heard it read, she had seized the paper and flung it on the fire.

Young tells me that he was himself opposed to the doctrine, and that he preached against it, foreseeing what trouble it would bring upon the Church. He says that he shed many bitter tears over the sacred writing; and that only on his being convinced by Joseph that the command to marry more wives was a true revelation, he submitted his prejudices and his passions to the will of God. He is very emphatic on this point. "Without this revelation on polygamy," he said to us, "we should have lived our religious life, but not so perfectly as we do now. God directed men, through Joseph, to take more wives. This is what we most firmly believe." As he spoke, he appealed to the apostles who were sitting round us, every one of whom bowed and acquiesced in these words.

For years, the Saints admit that nothing had come of this revelation; that was kept a secret from the world; two things having to be seen before such a dogma could be openly proclaimed in the Church; (first) how it would be received by the great masses of the Saints at home and abroad; and (second) how it would be regarded by the American courts of law. To ascertain how it would be welcomed by the Saints, sermons were preached and poetry was composed. Female missionaries called on the people to repent of their sins, and to return to the principles of patriarchal life. Every Sarai was encouraged to bring forth her Hagar. A religious glow ran through the Mormon Society, and the whole body of Saints declared for publishing the command from God to Joseph in favor of taking to his bosom a plurality of wives.

Two thousand elders came together in the New Jerusalem, and after hearing a discourse from Orson

Pratt, and a speech from Brigham Young, they received and adopted the revelation, (August 29, 1852); a remarkable date in the history of their church, one of the saddest epochs in that of the Saxon race.

Nearly all those elders were of English blood; a few only were Germans, Gauls, and Danes; nineteen in every twenty, at least, were either English or American born. That day the red men and the white men made with each other an unwritten covenant, for the Shoshone had at length found a brother in the Pale-face, and the Pawnee saw the morals of his wigwam carried into the Saxon's ranch.

But the new dogma from Heaven was announced by Young as a special and personal, rather than a common and indiscriminate, property of the Saints. The power to take many wives was given to them as a grace, not as a right. Plurality was permitted to a few, not enjoined upon the many. In the eyes of Young, it was regarded, not as a privilege of the earth, but as a gift of heaven; a peculiar blessing from the Father to some of His most favored sons.

The Prophet seems to have noted from the first, that in this passionate and robust society, full of young life and young ideas, his power of giving women to his elders and apostles would be of higher moment to him, as a governing force, than even his power of blessing the earth and unlocking the gates of heaven. Such an authority has made him the master of every house in Utah. No Pope, no Caliph, no Gosain, ever exercised this power of gratifying every heart that lusted after beauty; but when it came into Young's hands, through the march of ideas and events, he held it in his grip, as a faculty inseparable from his person and his rank. A saint may wed one woman without seeking leave from his Prophet; that privilege may be considered one of his rights as a man; but beyond this limit he can never go, except by permission of his spiritual chief. In every case of taking a second wife, a special warrant is required from heaven, which Young alone has the right to ask. If Young says yea, the marriage may take place; if he says nay, there is no appeal from his spoken word. In the Mormon church polygamy is not a right of man, but a gift of God.

CHAPTER XXX.

THE GREAT SCHISM.

THIS dogma of a plurality of wives has not come into the church without fierce disputes and a violent schism.

George A. Smith, cousin of Joseph, and Historian of the Mormon Church, tells me from the papers in his office, that about five hundred bishops and elders live in polygamy in the Salt Lake valleys; these five hundred elders having, as he believes, on the average, about four wives each, and probably fifteen children; so that this very peculiar institution has come, in fourteen years, to affect the lives and fortunes, more or less, of ten thousand persons. This number, large though it seems, is but a twentieth part of the following claimed by Young. Assuming, then, that these five hundred pluralists are all of the same opinion;—in the first place, as to the divine will having been truly manifested to Joseph; in the second place, as to that manifestation having been faithfully recorded; and in the third place, as to that record having been loyally preserved,—there must still be room for a very large difference of opinion. The great body of male Saints must always be content with a single wife; Young himself admits so much. Only the rich, the steadfast, the complaisant, can be indulged in the luxury of a harem even now, when the thing is fresh and the number of female converts is large enough to supply the want. As nature itself is fighting against this dogma, the humble Saint cannot hope to enjoy in the future any of the advantages which he is now denied. Many, even among the wealthy, hesitate, like Captain Hooper, to commit themselves forever to a doubtful rule of family order, and to a certain collision with the United States. Some protest in words, and some recede from the Church, without, however, renouncing the authority of Joseph Smith.

The existence of a second Mormon Church—of a great schismatic body, is not denied by Young, who of course considers it the devil's work. Vast bodies of the Saints have left the Church on account of polygamy; twenty thousand, I am told, have done so, in California alone. Many of these non-pluralist Saints exist in Missouri and in Illinois. Even among those who fondly cling to their Church at Salt Lake City, it is apparent to me that nineteen in twenty have no interest, and not much faith, in polygamy. The belief that their founder Joseph never lived in this objectionable state is widely spread.

Prophets, bishops, elders, all the great leaders of the faith, assert that for months before his death at Carthage, the founder of Mormonism had indulged himself though in secret, with a household of many wives. Of course they do not call his sealing to himself these women an indulgence; they say he took to himself such females only as were given to him of God. But they claim him as a pluralist. Now, if this assertion could be proved, the trouble would be ended, since anything that Joseph practised would be held a virtue, a necessity, by his flock. On the other side, a pluralist clergy is bound to maintain the truth of this hypothesis. For if Joseph were not a polygamist, he could hardly, they would reason, have been a faithful Mormon and a saint of God; since it is the present belief of their body that a man with only one wife will become a bachelor angel, a mere messenger and servant to the patriarchal gods. So, without producing much evidence of the fact, the elders have stoutly asserted that Joseph had secretly taken to himself a multitude of women, three or four of whom they point out to you, as still living at Salt Lake in the family of Brigham Young.

Still, no proof has ever yet been adduced to show that Joseph either lived as a polygamist or dictated the revelation in favor of a plurality of wives. That he did not openly live with more than one woman is admitted by all — or by nearly all; and so far as his early and undoubted writings are concerned, nothing can be clearer than that his feelings were opposed to the doctrines and practices which have since his death become the high notes of his church. In the Book of Mormon he makes God Himself say that He delights in the chastity of women, and that the harems of David and Solomon are abominations in His sight. Elder Godbe, to whom I pointed out this passage, informed me that the bishops explain away this view of polygamy, as being uttered by God at a time when He was angry with His people, on account of their sins, and as not expressing His permanent will on the subject of a holy life.

The question of fact is open like the question of inference. Joseph, it is well known, set his face against Rigdon's theory of the spiritual wife; and it is equally well known that he neither published the revelations which bear his name, nor spoke of such a document as being in his hands.

Emma, Joseph's wife and secretary, the partner of all his toils, of all his glories, coolly, firmly, permanently denies that her husband ever had any other wife than herself. She declares the story to be false, the revelation a fraud. She denounces polygamy as the invention of Young and Pratt—a work of the devil—brought in by them for the destruction of God's new church. On account of this doctrine, she has separated herself from the Saints of Utah, and has taken up her dwelling with what she calls a remnant of the true church at Nauvoo.

The four sons of Joseph—Joseph, William, Alexander, David—all deny and denounce what they call Young's imposture of plurality. These sons of Joseph are now grown men; and their personal interests are so clearly identified with the success of their father's church, to the members of which their fellowship would be precious, that nothing less than a personal conviction of the truth of what they say can be honestly considered as having turned them against Brigham Young.

As it is, these sons of the original seer have formed a great schism in the church. Under the name of Josephites, a band of Mormons are now gathering round these sons of the prophet, strong enough to beard the lion in his den. Alexander Smith has been at Salt Lake while I have been here, and has been suffered to preach against polygamy in Independence Hall.

Young appears to me very sore on account of these young men, whom he would gladly receive into his family, and adopt as his sons, if they would only let him. David he regards with a peculiar grace and favor. "Before that child was born," he said to me one day, when the conversation turned on these young men, "Joseph told me that he would be a son; that his name must be David; that he would grow up to be the guide and ruler of this church." I asked Young whether he thought this prophecy would come to pass. "Yea," he answered; "in the Lord's own time, David will be called to this work." I asked him whether David was not just now considered to be out of the church.

"He will be called and reconciled," said Young, "the moment he feels a desire to be led aright."

This schism on account of polygamy—led, as it is, by the Prophet's widow and her sons—is a serious fact for the church, even in the judgment of those bishops and elders who in minor affairs would seem to take no heed for the morrow. Young is alive to it; for in reading the Chicago platform, he can see how easily the Gentile world might reconcile itself to the Prophet's sons in Nauvoo, while waging war upon himself and the supporters of polygamy in Utah.

The chief—almost the sole—evidence that we have found in Salt Lake City in favor of Joseph having had several wives in the flesh is an assertion made by Young.

I was pointing out to him the loss of moral force to which his people must be always subject while the testimony on that cardinal point of practice is incomplete. If Joseph were sealed to many women, there must be records, witnesses, of the fact; where are those records and those witnesses?

"I," said Young, vehemently, "am the witness. I myself sealed dozens of women to Joseph."

I asked him whether Emma was aware of it. He said he guessed she was; but he could not say. In answer to another question, he admitted that Joseph had no issue by any of these wives who were sealed to him in dozens.

From two other sources we have obtained particles of evidence confirming Young's assertion. Two witnesses, living far apart, unknown to each other, have told us they were intimate with women who assert that they had been sealed to Joseph at Nauvoo. Young assures me that several old ladies, now living under his roof, are widows of Joseph; and that all the apostles know them, and reverence them as such. Three of these ladies I have seen in the Tabernacle. I have learned that some of these women have borne children to the second Prophet, though they bore none to the first.

My own impression (after testing all the evidence to be gathered from friend and foe) is, that these old ladies, though they may have been sealed to Joseph for eternity, were not his wives in the sense in which Emma, like the rest of women, would use the word wife. I think they were his spiritual queens and companions, chosen after the method of the Wesleyan Perfectionists; with a view, not to pleasures of the flesh, but to the glories of another world. Young may be technically right in the dispute; but the Prophet's sons are, in my opinion, legally and morally in the right. It is my firm conviction, that if the practice of plurality should become a permanent conquest of this American church, the Saints will not owe it to Joseph Smith, but to Brigham Young.

CHAPTER XXXI.

SEALING.

Much confusion comes upon us from the use of this word sealing in the English sense of marriage. Sealing may mean marriage; it may also mean something else. A woman can be sealed to a man without becoming his wife, as we have found in the case of Joseph's supposed widows; also in the instance of Eliza Snow, the poetess, who, in spite of being sealed to Young, is called Miss Snow, and regarded by her people as a spinster. Consummation, necessary in wedlock, is not necessary in sealing. Marriage is secular; sealing is both secular and celestial.

A strange peculiarity which the Saints have intruded into the finer relations of husband and wife is that of continuity. Their right of sealing man and woman to each other may be for either time or eternity; that is to say, the man may take the woman as his wife either for this world only, as we all do in the Christian church, or for this world during life and the next world after death. The Ute has some inkling of the ideas on which these Saints proceed, since he dreams that in the hunting-grounds beyond the sunset he will be accompanied by his faithful dog and his favorite squaw. The Mosaic Arab, when the thought of a resurrection dawned upon his mind, peopled his heaven with the men and women whom he had known on earth, and among the rights which he carried forward into the brighter land, was that of claiming the society of his mortal wife. The Moslem Arab, though he has learned from a later poetry to adorn his paradise with angelic houris, still fancies that a faithful warrior who prays for such a blessing will be allowed to associate in heaven with the humble partner of his cares on earth. It is only in our higher, holier heaven that these human joys and troubles are unknown, that there is no giving and taking in marriage, that the spirits of the just become as the angels of God.

Upon the actual relations of husband and wife, Ute and Arab theories of reunion after death in the old bonds of wedlock have no effect beyond that of exciting a good and loving woman to strive with a warmer zeal to satisfy the affections of her lord, so as to ensure her place by his side in the celestial wigwam, in a paradisiacal tent. But among the Saints of Salt Lake the notion of a marriage for time being a contract, not only different in duration, but also in nature, from the sealing for eternity, has led to very strange and wholly practical results. A Mormon elder preaches the doctrine that a woman who has been sealed to one husband for time may be sealed to another for eternity. This sealing must be done on earth, and it may be done in the lifetime of her earlier lord. In some degree, it is a gift to the woman of a second choice; for among these Saints the female enjoys nearly the same power of selecting her celestial bridegroom as the male enjoys of selecting his mortal bride.

Of course, the question is always coming forward as to what rights over her person on earth this sealing of a woman's soul for eternity confers. May the celestial rite be performed without the knowledge and consent of the husband for time? Can it be completed without invasion of his conjugal claims? Is it clear that any man would suffer his wife to be sealed to another if he were told of the fact, since an engagement for eternity must be of more solemn nature and more binding force than the minor contract for time? It is not probable that the intimacies of a man and woman who are linked to each other in the higher bond would be more close and secret than the intimacies of earth.

Some Saints deny that it is a common thing in Utah for a woman to be sealed to one man for earth and another man for heaven. It may not be common; but it occurs in more than one family; it gives occasion for some strife; and the humbler Saint has less protection against abuse of such an order than he would like to enjoy. Young is here the lord of all. If the Prophet says to an elder, "Take her," the woman will be taken, whether for good or evil. Often, I am told, these second and superior nuptials are made in secret, in the recesses of the endowment-house, with the help of two or three confidential chiefs. No notice of them is given; it is doubtful whether any record of them is kept. What man, then, with a pretty wife, can feel sure that her virtue will not be tempted by his elders into forming that strange, indefinite relation for another world with a husband of superior rank in the church? The office of priest, of prophet, of seer, has in every country a peculiar charm for women; what curates are in London, abbés in Paris, mollahs in Cairo, gosains in Benares, these elders and apostles are in Utah; with the added grace of a personal power to advance their female votaries to the highest of celestial thrones. Except the guru of Bombay, no priest on earth has so large a power of acting on every weakness of the female heart as a Mormon bishop at Salt Lake. Who shall assure the humbler Saint that priests possessing so much power in heaven and on earth will never, in these secret sealings for eternity, violate his right, outrage his honor, as a married man?

Another familiarity, not less strange, which the Mormons have introduced into these delicate relations of husband and wife, is that of sealing a living person to the dead.

The marriage for time is an affair of earth, and must be contracted between a living man and a living woman; but the marriage for eternity, being an affair of heaven, may be contracted, say these Saints, with either the living or the dead; provided always that it be a real engagement of the persons, sanctioned by the Prophet, and solemnized in the proper form. In any case it must be a genuine union; a true marriage, in the canonical sense, and according to the written law; not a Platonic rite, an attachment of souls, which would bind the two parties together in a mystical bond only. There comes the rub. How can a woman be united in this carnal conjunction to a man in his grave? By the machinery of substitution, say the Saints.

Substitution! Can there be such a thing in marriage as either one man, or one woman, standing in the place of another? Young has declared it. The Hebrews had a glimmering sense of some such dogma, when they bade the younger brother perform a brother's part; and are not all the Saints one family in the sight of God? Among the Hebrews, this rule of taking a brother's widow to wife was an exception to general laws; and in the Arab legislation of Mohammed, it was put away as a remnant of polyandry, a thing abominable and unclean. No settled people has ever gone back to that rule of a pastoral tribe. But Young, who has no fear of science, deals in audacious originality with this and with every other question of female right. A woman may choose her own bridegroom of the skies, but, like the man who would take a second wife, the woman who desires to marry a dead husband, can do it in no other way than on Young's intercession and by his consent. Say, that a girl of erratic fancy takes into her head the notion that she would like to become one of the heavenly queens of a departed saint; nothing easier, should her freak of imagination jump with the Prophet's humor. Young is her only judge, his yea or nay her measure of right and wrong. By a religious act, he can seal her to the dead man, whom she has chosen to be her own lord and king in heaven; by the same act he can give her a substitute on earth from among his elders and apostles; should her beauty tempt his eye, he may accept for himself the office of proxy for her departed saint.

In the Tabernacle I have been shown two ladies who are sealed to Young by proxy as the wives of Joseph; the Prophet himself tells me there are many more; and of these two I can testify that their relations to him are the same as those of any other mortal wives. They are the mothers of children who bear his name. Two of the young ladies whom we saw on the stage, Sister Zina and Sister Emily, are daughters of women who profess to be Joseph's widows. About the story of all these ladies there is an atmosphere of doubt, of mystery, which we can hardly pierce. Two of them live under Brigham's roof; a third lives in a cottage before his gate; a fourth is said to live with her daughter at Cotton Wood Canyon.

My own impression is, that while some of the old ladies may have been sealed to the Prophet as his spiritual wives only, these younger women elected him to be their lord and king years after his death.

Joseph is the favorite bridegroom of the skies. Perhaps it is in nature, that if women are allowed to choose their spouses, they should select the occupants of thrones; certain it is that many Mormon ladies yearn towards the bosom of Joseph, not poetically, as their Christian sisters speak of lying in the bosom of Abraham, but potentially, as the Hindoo votary of Krishna languishes for her darling god. Young, it is said, keeps all such converts to himself; the dead Prophet's dignity being so high that none save his successor in the temple is considered worthy to be his substitute in the harem. Beauties whom Joseph never saw in the flesh, who were infants and Gentiles when the riots of Carthage took place, are now sealed to him for eternity, and are bearing children in his name.

Except the yearning of Hindoo women towards their darling idol, there is perhaps no madness of the earth so strange as this erotic passion of the female Saints for the dead. A lady of New York was smitten by an uncontrollable desire to become a wife to the murdered Prophet. She made her way to Salt Lake, threw herself at Brigham's feet, and prayed with genuine fervor to be sealed to him in Joseph's name. Young did not want her; his harem was full; his time was occupied: he put her off with words; he sent her away; but the ardor of her passion was too hot, to damp, too strong to stem. She took him by assault, and he at length gave way; after sealing her to Joseph for eternity, he accepted towards her the office of substitute in time, and carried her to his house.

On the other side, the Mormons affect to have such power over spirits as to be able to seal the dead to the living. Elder Stenhouse tells me that he has one dead wife, who was sealed to him, by her own entreaty, after her death. He had known this young lady very well; he describes her as beautiful and charming; she had captivated his fancy; and in due time, had she lived, he might have proposed to make her his wife. While he was absent from Salt Lake City on a mission, she fell sick and died; on her death-bed she expressed an ardent wish to be sealed to him for eternity, that she might share the glories of his celestial throne. Young made no objection to her suit; and on Stenhouse's return from Europe to Salt Lake the rite was performed, in the presence of Brigham and others, his first wife standing proxy for the dead girl, both at the altar and afterwards. He counts the lost beauty as one of his wives; believing that she will reign with him in heaven.

CHAPTER XXXII.

WOMAN AT SALT LAKE.

And what, as regards the woman herself, is the visible issue of this strange experiment in social and family life?

During our fifteen days' residence among the Saints, we have had as many opportunities afforded us for forming a judgment on this question as has ever been given to Gentile travellers. We have seen the President and some of the apostles daily; we have been received into many Mormon houses, and introduced to nearly all the leading Saints; we have dined at their tables; we have chatted with their wives; we have romped and played with their children. The feelings which we have gained as to the effect of Mormon life on the character and position of woman, are the growth of care, of study, and experience; and our friends at Salt Lake, we hope, while they will differ from our views, will not refuse to credit us with candor and good faith.

If you listen to the elders only, you would fancy that the idea of a plurality of wives excites in the female breast the wildest fanaticism. They tell you that a Mormon preacher, dwelling on the examples of Sarai and of Rachel, finds his most willing listeners on the female benches. They say that a ladies' club was formed at Nauvoo to foster polygamy, and to make it the fashion; that mothers preach it to their daughters; that poetesses praise it. They ask you to believe that the first wife, being head of the harem, takes upon herself to seek out and court he prettiest girls; only too proud and happy when she can bring a new Hagar, a new Billah to her husband's arms.

This male version of the facts is certainly supported by such female writers as Belinda Pratt.

In my opinion, Mormonism is not a religion for woman. I will not say that it degrades her, for the term degradation is open to abuse; but it certainly lowers her, according to our Gentile ideas, in the social scale. In fact, woman is not in society here at all. The long blank walls, the embowered cottages, the empty windows, doorways, and verandas, all suggest to an English eye something of the jealousy, the seclusion, the subordination of a Moslem harem, rather than the gayety and freedom of a Christian home. Men rarely see each other at home, still more rarely in the company of their wives. Seclusion seems to be a fashion wherever polygamy is the law. Now, by itself, and apart from all doctrines and moralities, the habit of secluding women from society must tend to dim their sight and dull their hearing; for if conversation quickens men, it still more quickens women;

and we can roundly say, after experience in many households at Salt Lake, that these Mormon ladies have lost the practice and the power of taking part even in such light talk as animates a dinner-table and a drawing-room. We have met with only one exception to this rule, that of a lady who had been upon the stage. In some houses, the wives of our hosts, with babies in their arms, ran about the rooms, fetching in champagne, drawing corks, carrying cake and fruit, lighting matches, iceing water, while the men were lolling in chairs, putting their feet out of window, smoking cigars, and tossing off beakers of wine. (N. B.—Abstinence from wine and tobacco is recommended by Young and taught in the Mormon schools; but we found cigars in many houses, and wine in all except in the hotels!) The ladies, as a rule, are plainly, not to say poorly, dressed; with no bright colors, no gay flounces and furbelows. They are very quiet and subdued in manner, with what appeared to us an unnatural calm; as if all dash, all sportiveness, all life, had been preached out of them. They seldom smiled, except with a wan and wearied look; and though they are all of English race, we have never heard them laugh with the bright merriment of our English girls.

They know very little, and feel an interest in very few things. I assume that they are all great at nursing, and I know that many of them are clever at drying and preserving fruit. But they are habitually shy and reserved, as though they were afraid lest your bold opinion on a sunset, on a watercourse, or a mountain-range, should be considered by their lords as a dangerous intrusion on the sanctities of domestic life. While you are in the house, they are brought into the public room as children are with us; they come in for a moment, curtsy and shake hands; then drop out again, as though they felt themselves in company rather out of place. I have never seen this sort of shyness among grown women, except in a Syrian tent. Anything like the ease and bearing of an English lady is not to be found in Salt Lake, even among the households of the rich. Here, no woman reigns. Here, no woman hints by her manner that she is mistress of her own house. She does not always sit at table; and when she occupies a place beside her lord, it is not at the head, but on one of the lower seats. In fact, her life does not seem to lie in the parlor and the dining-room, so much as in the nursery, the kitchen, the laundry, and the fruit-shed.

The grace, the play, the freedom of a young English lady, are quite unknown to her Mormon sister. Only when the subject of a plurality of wives has been under consideration between host and guest, have I ever seen a Mormon lady's face grow bright, and then it was to look a sentiment, to hint an opinion, the reverse of those maintained by Belinda Pratt.

I am convinced that the practice of marrying a plurality of wives is not popular with the female Saints. Besides what I have seen and heard from Mormon wives, themselves living in polygamous families, I have talked, alone and freely, with eight or nine different girls, all of whom have lived at Salt Lake for two or three years. They are undoubted Mormons, who have made many sacrifices for their religion; but after seeing the family life of their fellow-Saints, they have one and all become firmly hostile to polygamy. Two or three of these girls are pretty, and might have been married in a month. They have been courted very much, and one of them has received no less than seven offers. Some of her lovers are old and rich, some young and poor, with their fortunes still to seek. The old fellows have already got their houses full of wives, and she will not fall into the train as either a fifth or a fifteenth spouse; the young men being true Saints, will not promise to confine themselves for ever to their earliest vows, and so she refuses to wed any of them. All these girls prefer to remain single,—to live a life of labor and dependence—as servants, chambermaids, milliners, charwomen,—to a life of comparative ease and leisure in the harem of a Mormon bishop.

It is a common belief, gathered in a great measure from the famous letter on plurality by Belinda Pratt, that the Mormon Sarai is willing to seek out, and eager to bestow, any number of Hagars on her lord. More than one Saint has told me that this is true, as a rule, though he admits there may be exceptions in so far as the Mormon Sarai falls short of her high calling. My experience lies among the exceptions solely. Some wives may be good enough to undertake this office. I have never found one who would own it, even in the presence of her husband, and when the occasion might have been held to warrant a little feminine fibbing. Every lady to whom I have put this question flushed into denial, though with that caged and broken courage which seems to characterize every Mormon wife. "Court a new wife for him!" said one lady; "no woman could do that; and no woman would submit to be courted by a woman."

The process of taking either a second or a sixteenth wife is the same in all cases. "I will tell you," said a Mormon elder, "how we do these things in our order. For example, I have two wives living, and one wife dead. I am thinking of taking another, as I can well afford the expense, and a man is not much respected in the church who has less than three wives.

Well, I fix my mind on a young lady, and consider within myself whether it is the will of God that I should seek her. If I feel, in my own heart, that it would be right to try, I speak to my bishop, who advises and approves, as he shall see fit; on which I go to the President, who will consider whether I am a good man and a worthy husband, capable of ruling my little household, keeping peace among my wives, bringing up my children in the fear of God; and if I am found worthy, in his sight, of the blessing, I shall obtain permission to go on with the chase. Then I lay the whole matter of my desire, my permission and my choice, before my first wife, as head of my house, and take her counsel as to the young lady's habits, character, and accomplishments. Perhaps I may speak with my second wife; perhaps not; since it is not so much her business as it is that of my first wife; besides which, my first wife is older in years, has seen more of life, and is much more of a friend to me than the second. An objection on the first wife's part would have great weight with me; I should not care much for what the second either said or thought. Supposing all to go well, I should next have a talk with the young lady's father; and if he consented to my suit, I should then address the young lady herself."

"But before you take all these pains to get her," I asked, "would you not have tried to be sure of your ground with the lady herself? Would you not have courted her and won her good will before taking all these persons into your trust?"

"No," answered the elder; "I should think that wrong. In our society we are strict. I should have seen the girl, in the theatre, in the tabernacle, in the social hall; I should have talked with her, danced with her, walked about with her, and in these ways ascertained her merits and guessed her inclinations; but I should not have made love to her, in your sense of the word, got up an understanding with her, and entered into a private and personal engagement of the affections. These affairs are not of earth, but of heaven, and with us they must follow the order of God's kingdom and church."

This elder's two wives live in separate houses, and seldom see each other. While we have been at Salt Lake, a child of the second wife has fallen sick; there has been much trouble in the house; and we have heard the first wife, at whose cottage we were dining, say she would go and pay the second wife a visit. The elder would not hear of such a thing; and he was certainly right, as the sickness was supposed to be diphtheria, and she had a brood of little folks playing about her knees. Still the manner of her proposal told us that she was not in the habit of daily intercourse with her sister-wife.

It is an open question in Utah whether it is better for a plural household to be gathered under one roof or not. Young sets the example of unity, so far at least as his actual wives and children are concerned. A few old ladies, who have been sealed to him for heaven, whether in his own name or in that of Joseph, dwell in cottages apart; but the dozen women, who share his couch, who are the mothers of his children, live in one block close to another, dine at one table, and join in the family prayers. Taylor, the apostle, keeps his families in separate cottages and orchards; two of his wives only live in his principal house; the rest have tenements of their own. Every man is free to arrange his household as he likes; so long as he avoids contention, and promotes the public peace.

"How will you arrange your visits, when you have won and sealed your new wife?" I asked my friendly and communicative elder; "shall you adopt the Oriental custom of equal justice and attention to the ladies laid down by Moses and by Mohammed?"

"By heaven, sir," he answered, with a flush of scorn, "no man shall tell me what to do, except ——" giving the initials of his name.

"You mean you will do as you like?"

"That 's just *it.*"

And such, I believe, is the universal habit of thought in this city and this church. Man is king, and woman has no rights. She has, in fact, no recognized place in creation, other than that of a servant and companion of her lord. Man is master, woman is slave. I cannot wonder that girls who remember their English homes should shrink from marriage in this strange community, even though they have accepted the doctrine of Young, that plurality is the law of heaven and of God. "I believe it 's right," said to me a rosy English damsel, who has been three years in Utah, "and I think it is good for those who like it; but it is not good for me, and I will not have it."

"But if Young should command you?"

"He won't!" said the girl with the toss of her golden curls; "and if he were to do so, I would not. A girl can please herself whether she marries or not; and I, for one, will never go into a house where there is another wife."

"Do the wives dislike it?"

"Some don't, most do. They take it for their religion; I can't say any woman likes it. Some women live very comfortably together; not many; most have their tiffs and quarrels, though their husbands may never know of them. No woman likes to see a new wife come into the house."

A Saint would tell you that such a damsel as my rosy friend is only half a Mormon yet; he would probably ask you to reject such evidence as trumpery and temporary; and plead that you can have no fair means of judging such an institution as polygamy, until you are able to study its effects in the fourth and fifth generation.

Meanwhile, the judgment which we have formed about it from what we have seen and heard may be expressed in a few words. It finds a new place for woman, which is not the place she occupies in the society of England and the United States. It transfers her from the drawing-room to the kitchen, and when it finds her in the nursery it locks her in it. We may call such a change a degradation; the Mormons call it a reformation. We do not say that any of these Mormon ladies have been worse in their moralities and their spiritualities by the change; probably they have not; but in everything that concerns their grace, order, rank, and representation in society, they are unquestionably lowered, according to our standards. Male Saints declare that in this city women have become more domestic, wifely, motherly, than they are among the Gentiles; and that what they have lost in show, in brilliancy, in accomplishment, they have gained in virtue and in service. To me, the very best women appear to be little more than domestic drudges, never rising into the rank of real friends and companions of their lords. Taylor's daughters waited on us at table; two pretty, elegant, English-looking girls. We should have preferred standing behind their chairs and helping them to dainties of fowl and cake; but the Mormon, like the

Moslem, keeps a heavy hand on his female folks. Women at Salt Lake are made to keep their place. A girl must address her father as "Sir," and she would hardly presume to sit down in his presence until she had received his orders.

"Women," said Young to me, "will be more easily saved than men. They have not sense enough to go far wrong. Men have more knowledge and more power; therefore they can go more quickly and more certainly to hell."

The Mormon creed appears to be that woman is not worth damnation.

In the Mormon heaven, men, on account of their sins, may stop short in the stage of angels; but women, whatever their offences, are all to become the wives of gods.

CHAPTER XXXIII.

THE REPUBLICAN PLATFORM.

"We mean to put that business of the Mormons through," says a New England politician; "we have done a bigger job than that in the South; and we shall now fix up things in Salt Lake City."

"Do you mean by force?" asks an English traveller.

"Well, that is one of our planks. The Republican Platform pledges us to crush those Saints."

This conversation, passing across the hospitable board of a renowned publicist in Philadelphia, draws towards itself from all sides the criticism of a distinguished company of lawyers and politicians; most of them members of Congress; all of them soldiers of the Republican phalanx.

"Do you hold," says the English guest,—"you as a writer and thinker,—your party as the representatives of American thought and might,—that in a country where speech is free and tolerance wide, it would be *right* to employ force against ideas,—to throw horse and foot into a dogmatic quarrel,—to set about promoting morality with bayonets and bowie-knives?"

"It is one of our planks," says a young member of Congress, "to put down those Mormons, who, besides, being infidels, are also Conservatives and Copperheads."

"Young is certainly a Democrat," adds an Able Editor from Massachusetts, himself a traveller in the Mormon land; "we have no right to burn his block on account of his politics; nor, indeed, on account of his religion; we have no power to meddle with any man's faith; but we have made a law against plurality of wives, and we have the power to make our laws respected everywhere in this Republic?"

"By force?"

"By force, if we are driven by disloyal citizens to the use of force."

"You mean, then, that in any case you will use force—passively, if they submit; actively, if they resist?"

"That's our notion," replies our candid host. "The government must crush them. That is our big job; and next year we must put it through."

"You hold it right, then, to combat such an evil as polygamy with shot and shell?"

"We have freed four million negroes with shot and shell?" replies a sober Pennsylvanian judge.

"Pardon me, is that a full statement of the case?

That you have crushed a movement of secession by means of military force is true; but is it not also true that, five or six years ago, every one acknowledged that slavery was a legal and moral question, which, while peace and order reigned in the slave-states, ought not to be treated otherwise than on legal and moral grounds?"

"Yes, that is so. We had no right over the negroes until their masters went into rebellion. I admit that the declaration of war gave us our only standing."

"In fact, you confess that you had no right over the blacks until you had gained, through the rebellion, a complete authority over the whites who held them in bondage?"

"Certainly so."

"If, then, the planters had been quiet; keeping to the law as it then stood; never attempting to spread themselves by force, as they tried to do in Kansas; you would have been compelled, by your sense of right, to leave them to time and reason, to the exhaustion of their lands, to the depopulation of their States, to the growth of sound economical knowledge,—in short, to the moral forces which excite and sustain all social growths?"

"Perhaps so," answers the Able Editor. "The Saints have not yet given us such a chance. They are very honest, sober, industrious people, who mind their own business mainly, as men will have to do who try to live in yon barren plains. They are useful in their way, too; linking our Atlantic states with the Pacific states; and feeding the mining population of Idaho, Montana, and Nevada. We have no ground of complaint, none that a politician would prefer against them beyond their plural households; but New England is very sore just now about them; for everybody in this country has got into the habit of calling them the spawn of our New England conventicles, simply because Joseph Smith, Brigham Young, Heber Kimball, all the chief lights of their church, happen to be New England men."

"When New England," adds a representative from Ohio, with a laugh, "goes mad on any point, you will find that she contrives in this Republic to have her way."

"When her way is just and open — sanctioned by moral principle and by human experience — it is well that she should have her way. But will Harvard and Cambridge support an attack by military power on religious bodies because they have adopted the model of Abraham and David? You have in those western plains and mountains a hundred tribes of red-men who practise polygamy; would you think it right for your missionary society to withdraw from among them the teacher and his Bible, and for General Grant to send out in their stead the soldier and his sword? You have in those western territories a hundred thousand yellow men who also practise polygamy; would you hold it just to sink their ships, to burn their ranches, to drive them from your soil, with sword and fire?"

"Their case is different to that of the Saints," rejoins the Able Editor; "these red-skins and yellow-skins are savages; one race may die out, the other may go back to Asia; but Young and Kimball are our own people, knowing the law and the Gospel; and whatever they may do with the Gospel, they must obey the law."

"Of course, everybody must obey the law; but how? Those Saints, I hear, have no objection to your law when administered by judge and jury, only to your law when administered by colonels and subalterns."

"In other words," says the Pennsylvanian judge,

"they have no objection to our law when they are left to carry it out themselves."

"We must put them down," cries the young member of Congress.

"Have you not tried that policy of putting them down twice already? You found them twelve thousand strong at Independence, in Missouri; not liking their tenets (though they had no polygamy among them then), you crushed and scattered them into thirty thousand at Nauvoo; where you again took arms against religious passion, slew their Prophet, plundered their city, drove them into the desert, and generally dispersed and destroyed them into one hundred and twenty-seven thousand in Deseret! You know that some such law of growth through persecution has been detected in every land and in every church. It is a proverb. In Salt Lake City, I heard Brigham Young tell his departing missionaries, they were not to suggest the beauty of their mountain home, but to dwell on the idea of persecution, and to call the poor into a persecuted church. Men fly into a persecuted church, like moths into a flame. If you want to make all the western country Mormon, you must send an army of a hundred thousand troops to the Rocky Mountains."

"But we can hardly leave these pluralists alone."

"Why not — so far at least as regards bayonets and bowie-knives? Have you no faith in the power of truth? Have you no confidence in being right? Nay, are you sure that you have nothing to learn from them? Have not the men who thrive where nobody else can live, given ample evidence that, even though their doctrines may be strange and their morals false, the principles on which they till the soil and raise their crops, are singularly sound?"

"I admit," says the Able Editor, "they are good farmers."

"Good is a poor term, to express the marvel they have wrought. In Illinois, they changed a swamp into a garden. In Utah, they have made the desert green with pastures and tawny with maize and corn. Of what is Brigham Young most fond? Of his harem, his temple, his theatre, his office, his wealth? He may pride himself on these things in their measure; but the fact of his life which he dwelt upon most, and with the noblest enthusiasm, is the raising of a crop of ninety-three and a half bushels of wheat from one single acre of land. The Saints have grown rich with a celerity that seems magical even in the United States. Beginning life at the lowest stage, recruited only from among the poor, spoiled of their goods and driven from their farms, compelled to expend millions of dollars in a perilous exodus, and finally located on a soil from which the red-skin and the bison had all but retired in despair, they have yet contrived to exist, to extend their operations, to increase their stores. The hills and valleys round Salt Lake are everywhere smiling with wheat and rye. A city has been built; great roads have been made; mills have been erected; canals have been dug; forests have been felled. A depot has been formed in the wilderness from which the miners from Montana and Nevada can be fed. A chain of communication from St. Louis to San Francisco has been laid. Are the Republican majority prepared to undo the progress of twenty years in order to curb an obnoxious doctrine? Are they sure that the attempt being made, it would succeed? What facts in the past history of these Saints permit you to infer that persecution, however sharp, would diminish their number, their audacity, and their zeal?"

"Then you see no way of crushing them?"

"Crushing them! No; none. I see no way of dealing with any moral and religious question except by moral means employed in a religious spirit. Why not put your trust in truth, in logic, in history? Why not open good roads to Salt Lake? Why not encourage railway communication; and bring the practical intellect and noble feeling of New England to bear upon the household of many wives? Why not meet their sermons by sermons; try their science by science; encounter their books with books? Have you no missionaries equal to Elder Stenhouse and Elder Dewey? You must expect that while you act on the Saints, the Saints will re-act upon you. It will be for you a trial of strength; but the weapons will be legitimate and the conclusions will be blessed. Can you not trust the right side and the just cause, to come out victoriously from such a struggle?"

"Well," says the judge, "while we are divided in opinion, perhaps, as to the use of physical force, we are all in favor of moral force. Massachusetts is our providence; but, after all, we must have one law in this Republic. Union is our motto, equality our creed. Boston and Salt Lake City must be got to shake hands, as Boston and Charleston have already done. If you can persuade Brigham to lie down with Bowles, I am willing to see it. . . . . And now pass the wine."

CHAPTER XXXIV.

UNCLE SAM'S ESTATE.

In climbing the slopes of yon rivers from New York to Toledo; in running down the Mississippi Valley from Toledo to St. Louis; in mounting the Prairies from St. Louis to Virginia Dale; in crossing the Sierras from Virginia Dale to the Great Salt Lake; in winding through the Wasatch chain, the Bitter-creek country, and the Plains from Salt Lake City to Omaha; in descending the Missouri from the middle waters to its mouth; in traversing the table-lands of Indiana and Ohio; in threading the mountain-passes of Pennsylvania; in piercing the forests, following the streams, lounging in the cities of Virginia; in pacing these streets of Washington, mixing with these people in the gardens of the White House, and under the dome of the Capitol, a man will find himself growing free of many great facts. He will be in daily contact with the newest forms of life, with a world in the earlier stages of its growth, with a society everywhere young in genius, enterprise, and virtue; but probably no other fact will strike his imagination with so large a force as the size of what is here called, in the idiom of the people, Uncle Sam's Estate.

"Sir," said to me a Minnesota farmer, "the curse of this country is that we have too much land;" a phrase which I have heard again and again; among the iron-masters of Pittsburg, among the tobacco-planters of Richmond, among the cotton-spinners of Worcester. Indeed, this wail against the land is common among men who, having mines, plantations, mills, and farms, would like to have large supplies of labor at lower rates of wages than the market yields. There have been times in which a similar cry was raised in England, by the Norfolk farmers, by the Manchester spinners, by the Newcastle coalmen. Those who want to get labor on the lowest terms must always be in favor of restricting the productive acreage of land. But whether a Minnesota farmer, a Pennsylvania miner, or a Massachusetts cotton-spinner, may like it or dislike it, nobody can dispute the fact that the first impression stamped on a traveler's eye and brain in this great country is that of stupendous size.

During the Civil War, when the Trent affair was waxing warm between the two main branches of our race—a brother's quarrel, in which there was some right and a little wrong on both sides—a New York publisher put out a map of the United States and Territories, stretching from the Atlantic Ocean to the Pacific Ocean, from the line of the great lakes to the gulfs of Mexico and California; on the margin of which map there was an outline of England drawn to scale. Perhaps it had not been designed by the draughtsman to rebuke our pride; still, it made us look very small on paper; and if we had been a people piquing ourselves on the possession of "much dirt" in the Home County called England, that map might have cut us to the quick. Space is not one of our island points. In three or four hours we hurry from sea to sea, from Liverpool to Hull, from the Severn to the Thames; in the lapse between breakfast and dinner we wing our way from London to York, from Manchester to Norwich, from Oxford to Penzance. It is the common joke of New York, that a Yankee in London dares not leave his hotel after dark lest he should slip off the foreland and be drowned in the sea.

The Republic owns within her two ocean frontiers more than three million square miles of land; a fourth part of a million square miles of water, either salt or fresh; a range of Alps, a range of Pyrenees, a range of Apennines; forests by the side of which the Schwarzwald and the Ardennes would be German toys; rivers exceeding the Danube and the Rhine, as much as these rivers exceed the Mersey and the Clyde.

Under the crystal roof in Hyde Park, when the nations had come together in 1851, each bringing what it found to be its best and rarest to a common testing place, America was for many weeks of May and June represented by one great article—a vast, unoccupied space. An eagle spread its wings over an empty kingdom, while the neighboring states of Belgium, Holland, Prussia, and France were crowded like swarms of bees in their summer hives. Some persons smiled, with a mocking lip, at that paper bird, brooding in silence above a mighty waste; but I for one never came from the thronging courts of Europe into that large allotment of space and light, without feeling that our cousins of the West had hit, though it may have been by chance, on a very happy expression of their virgin wealth. In Hyde Park, as at home, they showed that they had room enough and to spare.

Yes: the Republic is a big country. In England, we have no lines of sufficient length, no areas of sufficient width, to convey a just idea of its size. Our longest line is that running from Land's End to Berwick,—a line which is some miles shorter than the distance from Washington to Lexington. Our broadest valley is that of the Thames,—the whole of which would lie hidden from sight in a corner of the Sierra Madre. The State of Oregon is bigger than England; California is about the size of Spain; Texas would be larger than France if France had won the frontier of the German Rhine. If the United States were parted into equal lots, they would make fifty-two kingdoms as large as England, fourteen empires as large as France. Even the grander figure of Europe,—the seat of our great powers, and of many lesser powers,—a continent which we used to call the world, and fight to maintain in delicate balance of parts,—fails us when we come to measure in its lines such amplitudes as those of the United States. To wit; from Eastport to Brownsville is farther than from London to Tuat, in the Great Sahara; from Washington to Astoria is farther than from Brussels to Kars; from New York to San Francisco is farther than from Paris to Bagdad. Such measures seem to carry us away from the sphere of fact into the realms of magic and romance.

Again, take the length of rivers as a measurement of size. A steamboat can go ninety miles up the Thames; two hundred miles up the Seine; five hundred and fifty miles up the Rhine. In America, the Thames would be a creek, the Seine a brook, the Rhine a local stream, soon lost in a mightier flood. Some of these great rivers, like the Kansas and the Platte, flowing through boundless plains, are nowhere deep enough for steamers, though they are sometimes miles in width; yet the navigable length of many of these streams is a wearisome surprise. The Mississippi is five times longer than the Rhine; the Missouri is three times longer than the Danube; the Columbia is four times longer than the Scheldt. From the sea to Fort Snelling, the Mississippi is plowed by steamers a distance of two thousand one hundred and thirty-one miles; yet she is but the second river in the United States.

Glancing at a map of America, we see to the north a group of lakes. Now, our English notion of a lake is likely to have been derived from Coniston, Killarney, Lomond, Leman, and Garda. But these sheets of water give us no true hint of what Huron and Superior are like, scarcely indeed of what Erie and Ontario are like. Coniston, Killarney, Lomond, Leman, and Garda, put together, would not cover a tenth part of the surface occupied by the smallest of the five American lakes. All the waters lying in Swiss, Italian, English, Irish, Scotch, and German lakes, might be poured into Michigan without making a perceptible addition to its flood. Yorkshire might be sunk out of sight in Erie; Ontario drowns as much land as would make two duchies equal in area to Schleswig and Holstein. Denmark proper could be washed by the waves of Huron. Many of the minor lakes of America would be counted as inland seas elsewhere; to wit, Salt Lake, in Utah, has a surface of two thousand square miles; while that of Geneva has only three hundred and thirty; that of Como, only ninety; that of Killarney, only eight. A kingdom like Saxony, a principality like Parma, a duchy like Coburg, if thrown in one heap into Lake Superior, might add an island to its beauty, but would be no more conspicuous in its vast expanse than one of those pretty green islets which adorn Loch Lomond.

Mountain masses are not considered by some as the strongest points of American scenery; yet you find masses in this country which defy all measurement by such puny chains as the Pyrenees, the Apennines, and the Savoy Alps. The Alleghanies, ranging in height between Helvellyn and Pilatus, run through a district equal in extent to the country lying between Ostend and Jaroslaw. The Wasatch chain, though the name is hardly known in Europe, has a larger bulk and grandeur than the Julian Alps. The Sierra Madre, commonly called the Rocky Mountains, ranging in stature from a little below Snowdon to a trifle above Mont Blanc, extend from Mexico, through the Republic into British America, a distance almost equal to that dividing London from Delhi.

No doubt, then, can be felt as to the size of this Anglo-Saxon estate. America is a big country; and size, as we know in other things, becomes, in the long run, a measure of political power.

Leaving out of view all rivers, all lakes, there remain in the United States about one thousand nine hundred and twenty-six million acres; nearly all of them productive land; forest, prairie, down, alluvial bottom; all lying in the temperate zone; healthy in climate, rich in wood, in coal, in oil, in iron; a landed estate that could give to each head of five million families a lot of three hundred and eighty-five acres.

CHAPTER XXXV.

THE FOUR RACES.

On this fine estate of land and water dwells a strange variety of races. No society in Europe can pretend to such wide contrasts in the type, in the color, as are here observable; for while in France, in Germany, in England, we are all white men, deriving our blood and lineage from a common Aryan stock, and having in our habits, languages, and creeds, a certain bond of brotherhood, our friends in these United States, in addition to such pale varieties as the Saxon and Celt, the Swabian and Gaul, have also the Sioux, and Negro, and the Tartar; nations and tribes, not few in number, not guests of a moment, here to-day and gone to-morrow; but crowding hosts of men and women, who have the rights which come of either being born on the soil or of being settled on it for life. White men, black men, red men, yellow men; they are citizens of this country, paying its taxes, feeding on its produce, obeying its laws.

In England we are apt to boast of having fused into one strong amalgam men of the most hostile qualities of blood; blending into a perfect unit the steadfast Saxon, the volatile Celt, the splendid Norman, and the frugal Pict; but our faint distinctions of race and race fade wholly out of sight when they are put alongside of the fierce antagonism seen on this American soil. In the Old World we have separate classes, where in this new country they have opposite nations; we have

THE FOUR RACES.

slight variation in the quality, where they have radical difference in the type. To a negro in Georgia, to a Pawnee in Dakota, to a Chinese in Montana, a white man is just a white man; no more, no less; the Gaul, the Dane, the Spaniard, the Saxon, being, in his simple eyes, brethren of one family, members of one church. Our subtler distinctions of race and race are wholly invisible in this stranger's eyes.

In the western country you may sit down at dinner in some miner's house with a dozen guests, who shall not be matched, in contrasting types and colors, even in a Cairene bazaar, an Aleppo gateway, a Stamboul mosque. On either side of you may sit—a Polish Jew, an Italian count, a Choctaw chief, a Mexican rancher, a Confederate soldier (there called a "whitewashed reb"), a Mormon bishop, a Sandwich Island sailor, a Parsee merchant, a Boston bagman, a Missouri boss. A negro may cook your meat, a Chinese draw your cork, while the daughters of your host--bright girls, dainty, well dressed—may serve the dishes and pour out your wine; the whole company being drawn into these western regions by the rage for gold, and melting toward each other, more like guests who dine in a New York hotel than like strangers who come either to trade in an Egyptian bazaar, to lodge in a Syrian khan, or pray in a Turkish mosque. You may find, too, under one roof as many creeds as colors. Your host may be a Universalist; one of that soft American sect which holds that nobody on earth will ever be damned, though the generous and illogical fellow can hardly open his lips without calling on one of his guests to be so. The Mormon will put his trust in Joseph, as a natural seer and revelator; the Chinese will worship Buddha, of whom he knows nothing but the name; the Jew will pray to Jehovah, of whom he cannot be said to know much more. The Choctaw chief may invoke the Big Father, whom white men call for him the Great Spirit. Sam—all negroes there are Sams—may be a Methodist; an Episcopalian Methodist, mind you; Sam and his sable brethren hating everything that is low. The Italian count is an infidel; the Mexican a Catholic. Your whitewashed reb repudiating all religions, gives his mind to cocktails. The Missourian is a Come-outer, a member of one of those new churches of America which profess to have brought God nearer to the earth. That the Parsee holds a private opinion about the sun we may fairly guess; Queen Emma's countryman is a Pagan; while the Boston bagman, now a Calvinist, damning the company to future miseries of fire and brimstone, was once a Communist of the school of Noyes.

White men, black men, red men, yellow men—all these chief types and colors of the human race—have been drawn into company on this western soil, this middle continent, lying between China and the Archipelago on one side, Africa and Europe on the other, where they crowd and contest the ground under a common flag.

The White Man, caring for neither frost nor fire, so long as he can win good food for his mouth, fit clothing for his limbs, appears to be the master in every zone; able to endure all climates, to undertake all labors, to overcome all trials; casting-nets into the Bay of Fundy, cradling gold in the Sacramento Valleys, raising dates and lemons in Florida, trapping beavers in Oregon, raising herds of kine in Texas, spinning thread in Massachusetts, clearing woods in Kansas, smelting iron in Pennsylvania, talking buncombe in Columbia, writing leaders in New York. He is the man of plastic genius, of enduring character; equally at home among the palm-trees and the pines; in every latitude the guide, the employer, and the king of all.

The Black Man, a true child of the tropics, to whom warmth is like the breath of life, flees from those bleak fields of the North, in which the white man repairs his fiber and renews his blood; preferring the swamps and savannas of the South, where, among palms, cotton-plants, and sugar-canes, he finds the rich colors in which his eye delights, the sunny heats in which his blood expands. Freedom would not tempt him to go northward into frost and fog. Even now, when Massachusetts and Connecticut tempt him by the offer of good wages, easy work, and sympathizing people, he will not go to them. He only just endures New York; the most hardy of his race will hardly stay in Saratoga and Niagara beyond the summer months. Since the South has been made free for Sam to live in, he has turned his back on the cold and friendly North, in search of a brighter home. Sitting in the rice-field, by the canebrake, under the mulberry-trees of his darling Alabama, with his kerchief round his head, his banjo on his knee, he is joyous as a bird, singing his endless and foolish roundelay, and feeling the sunshine burn upon his face. The negro is but a local fact in the country; having his proper home in a corner—the most sunny corner—of the United States.

The Red Man, once a hunter of the Alleghanies, not less than of the prairies and the Rocky Mountains, has been driven by the pale-face, he and his squaw, his elk, his buffalo, and his antelope, into the far western country; into the waste and desolate lands lying westward of the Mississippi and Missouri. The exceptions hardly break the rule. A band of picturesque peddlers may be found at Niagara; Red Jackets, Cherokee chiefs, and Mohawks; selling bows and canes, and generally sponging on those youths and damsels who roam about the Falls in search of opportunities to flirt. A colony, hardly of a better sort, may be found at Oneida Creek, in Madison County; the few sowing maize, growing fruit, and singing psalms; the many starving on the soil, cutting down the oak and maple, alienating the best acres, pining after their brethren who have thrown the white man's gift in his face, and gone away with their weapons and their war-paint. Red Jacket at the Falls, Bill Beechtree at Oneida Creek—the first selling beaded work to girls, the second twisting hickory canes for boys—are the last representatives of mighty nations, hunters and warriors, who at one time owned the broad lands from the Susquehanna to Lake Erie. Red Jacket will not settle; Bill Beechtree is incapable of work. The red-skin will not dig, and to beg he is not ashamed. Hence, he has been pushed away from his place, driven out by the spade, and kept at bay by the smoke of chimney fires. A wild man of the plain and forest, he makes his home with the wolf, the rattlesnake, the buffalo, and the elk. When the wild beast flies, the wild man follows. The Alleghany slopes, on which, only seventy years ago, he chased the elk and scalped the white woman, will hear his war-whoop, see his war-dance, feel his scalping-knife, no more. In the western country he is still a figure in the landscape. From the Missouri to the Colorado he is master of all the open plains; the forts which the white men have built to protect their road to San Francisco, like the Turkish block-houses built along the Syrian tracks, being mainly of use as a hint of their great reserve of power. The red men find it hard to lay down a tomahawk, to take up a hoe; some thousands only of them have yet done so; some hundreds only have learned from the whites to drink gin and bitters, to lodge in frame-houses, to tear up the soil, to forget the chase, the war-dance, and the Great Spirit.

The Yellow Man, generally a Chinese, a Malay, sometimes a Dyak, has been drawn into the Pacific states from Asia, and from the Eastern Archipelago, by the hot demand for labor; any kind of which comes to him as a boon. From digging in the mine to cooking an omelette and ironing a shirt, he is equal to everything by which dollars can be gained. Of these yellow people there are now sixty thousand in California, Utah, and Montana; they come and go; but many more of them come than go. As yet these harmless crowds are weak and useful. Hop Chang keeps a laundry; Chi Hi goes out as cook; Cum Thing is a maid-of-all-work. They are in no man's way, and they labor for a crust of bread; carrying the hod when Mike has run away to the diggings, and scrubbing the floor when Biddy has made some wretch the happiest of his sex. Supple and patient, these yellow men, though far from strong, are eager for any kind of work; but they prefer the employments of women to those of men; delighting in an engagement to wash clothes, to nurse babies, and to wait on guests. They make very good butlers and chamber-maids. Loo Sing, a jolly old girl in pig-tail, washes your shirts, starching and ironing them very neatly, except that you cannot persuade him to refrain from spitting on your cuffs and fronts. To him spitting on linen is the same as damping it with drops of water; and the habits of his life prevent him, even though you should catch him by the pig-tail, and rub his tiny bit of nose on the burning iron, from seeing that it is not the same to you. To-day, those yellow men are sixty thousand weak; in a few years they may be six hundred thousand strong.

They will ask for votes; they will hold the balance of parties. In some districts they will make a majority; selecting the judges, forming the juries, interpreting the laws. Those yellow men are Buddhists, professing polygamy, practicing infanticide. Next year is not more sure to come in its own season than a great society of Asiatics to dwell on the Pacific slopes. A Buddhist church, fronting the Buddhist churches in China and Ceylon, will rise in California, Oregon, and Nevada. More than all, a war of labor will commence between the races which feed on beef and the races which thrive on rice; one of those wars in which the victory is not necessarily with the strong.

White man, black man, red man, yellow man, each has a custom of his own to follow, a genius of his own to prove, a conscience of his own to respect; custom which is not of kin, genius which is largely different, and conscience which is fiercely hostile. These four great types might be represented to the eye by four of my friends: H. W. Longfellow, poet, Boston; Eli Brown, waiter, Richmond; Spotted Dog, savage, Rocky Mountains; and Loo Sing, Laundry boy, Nevada. Under what circumstances will they blend into a common stock?

CHAPTER XXXVI.

SEX AND SEX.

NEXT, perhaps, after its huge size, and its varied races, the fact which is apt to strike a stranger most in the United States, is the disproportion almost everywhere to be noted between sex and sex.

To such a dinner as we have imagined taking place in the western country, no woman will have sat down; not because there are no ladies in the house, but because these ladies have something else to do than dine with guests. Your host may have been a married man, pluming himself with very good right, on his winsome wife, his bevy of sparkling girls; but his wife and her daughters, instead of occupying seats at the board, will have to stand behind the chairs, handing round the dishes, pouring out the tea, aiding Loo Sing to uncork the wine. Females are few in yonder western towns; you may spend day after day without falling in sight of a pretty face. At the wayside inn, when you call for the chamber-maid, either Sam puts in his woolly head, or Chi Hi pops in his shaven crown. Hardly any help can be hired in those wastes; Molly runs away with a miner; Biddy gets married to a merchant; and when guests ride in from the track, the fair creatures who live on the spot, the joy of some husband's home, of some father's eyes, have no choice beyond either sending these guests on their way, hungry, unrested, or cooking them a dinner and putting it on the board. At Salt Lake, in the houses of Mormon apostles and of wealthy merchants, we were always served by the young ladies, often by extremely delicate and lovely girls.

At first this novelty is rather hard to bear; not by the ladies so much as by their guests. To see a woman who has just been quoting Keats and playing Gounod, standing up behind your seat, uncorking catawba, whipping away plates, and handing you the sauce, is trying to the nerves, especially when you are young and passably polite. In time you get used to it, as you do to the sight of a scalping-knife, to the sound of a war-whoop; but what can a lady at the mines, on the prairies, on the lonely farmsteads, do when a guest drops in? Help she has none, excepting Sam and Loo Sing. In that district of many males and few females, every girl is a lady, almost every woman is a wife. Men may be hired at a fair day's wages, to do any kind of male labor; to cook your food, to groom your horse, to trim your garden, to cut your wood; but women to do female work, to make the beds, to serve at table, to nurse the bairns; no, not for the income of a bishop, can you get them. Biddy can do better. Girls who are young and pretty have a lottery full of prizes ready to their hand; even those who may be old and plain can have husbands when they please. Everywhere west of the Mississippi there is a brisk demand for women; and what girl of spirit would let herself out for hire when the church door is open, and the bridal bells are ready? Who would accept the position. of a woman's help when she has only to say the word, and become a man's help-mate?

Your hostess on the Plains may have been well born, well educated, well dressed; both she herself and her bevy of girls may be such as would be considered magnetic in Fifth Avenue, attractive in May Fair. They may speak French very well; and when some of you selfish fellows gathered under their window to smoke and chat, they will have charmed your ears with the most brilliant passages from Faust. Now, to hear Sibyl's serenade in the shadow of the Rocky Mountains is a treat on which you may not have counted; but the fact remains that only one hour earlier in the day the contralto has been acting as your cook. Once before in my life the same sort of thing has occurred to me; in Morocco, where a dark-eyed Judith, daughter of a Jew in whose house I was lodging for the night, first fried my supper of fowls and tomatoes, and then lulled me to sleep by the notes of her guitar as she sat on the door-step.

This comedy of the sexes may be found in action, not only out yonder in Colorado and the western prairies, but here in the shadow of the Capitol, in every State of the Union, almost in every city of each State. After all the havoc of war,—of which this disparity between males and females was an active, though an unseen, cause,—the evidence of inequality meets you at every turn; in the ball-rooms at Washington, in the streets of New York, in the chapels of Boston, at the dinner-tables of Richmond, as well as among the frame sheds of Omaha, in the plantations of Atlanta, in the miners' huts near Denver, in the theater of Salt Lake City. The cry is everywhere for girls; girls—more girls! In a hundred voices you hear the echoes of a common want; the ladies cannot find servants, the dancers cannot get partners, the young men cannot win wives. I was at a ball on the Missouri River where half the men had to sit down, though the girls obligingly danced every set.

Compared against the society of Paris and of London, that of America seems to be all awry. Go into the Madeleine,—it is full of ladies; go into St. James's

Palace,—it is full of ladies. Every house in England has excess of daughters, about whom mothers have their little dreams, not always unmixed with a little fear. When Blanche is thirty, and still unsettled, her very father must begin to doubt of her ever going out into life. An old adage says that a girl at twenty says to herself, Who will suit me? at thirty, Whom shall I suit? Here in America it is not the woman, but the man, who is a drug in the matrimonial market. No Yankee girl is bound, like a Scottish lassie, like an Irish kerne, to serve in another woman's house for bread. Her face is her fortune and her lips a prize; her love more precious than her labor; her two bright orbs of more value than even her nimble hands. War may have thinned, to her disadvantage, the rank and file of lovers, but the losses of male life by shot and shell, by fever and ague, by waste and privation, have been more than replaced to her from Europe; and the disproportions of sex and sex, noted before the war broke out, are said to be greater since its close. The lists are crowded with bachelors wanting wives; the price of young men is ruling down, and only the handsome, well-doing fellows have a chance of going off!

This sketch is no effort of a fancy, looking for extremes and loving the grotesque. When the census was compiled (in 1860), the white males were found to be in excess of the white females, by seven hundred and thirty thousand souls. Such a fact has no fellow in Europe, except in the Papal States, where society is made by exceptional forces, governed by exceptional rules. In every other Christian country,—in France, England, Germany, Spain,—the females are in large excess of the males. In France there are two hundred thousand women more than men; in England three hundred and sixty-five thousand. The unusual rule here noticed in America is not confined to any district, any sea-board, any zone. Out of fifty-two organized States and Territories, only eight exhibit the ordinary rule of European countries. Eight old settlements are supplied with women; that is to say, Maryland, Massachusetts, New Hampshire, New Jersey, New York, North Carolina, Rhode Island, Columbia; while the other fifty-four settlements, purchases, and conquests, from the Atlantic Ocean to the Pacific Ocean, lack this element of a stable, orderly, and virtuous state,—a wife for every young man of a proper age to marry. In some of the western regions, the disparity is such as strikes the moralist with awe: in California there are three men to every woman; in Washington, four men to every woman; in Nevada, eight men to every woman; in Colorado, twenty men to every woman.

This disparity between sex and sex is not wholly caused, as will be thought, by the large immigration of single men. It is so in degree, no doubt, since far more males arrive by ship at Boston and New York than females; but if all the new-comers were sent back, if no fresh male was allowed to land in New York unless he brought with him a female companion, a sister, a wife, still a large percentage of the people would have to go down into their graves unmarried. More males are born than females. Casting off the German and Irish quota, there would still be four men in the hundred in this great Republic for whom nature has sent no female mates. Immigration only comes to the help of nature; Europe sending in hosts of bachelors to fight for the few women, who would otherwise be insufficient for the native men. In the whole mass of whites, the disproportion is five in the hundred; so that one man in every twenty males born in the

United States can never expect to have a wife of his own.

What is hardly less strange than this large displacement of the sexes among the white population, is the fact that it is not explained and corrected by any excess in the inferior types. There are more yellow men than yellow women, more red braves than red squaws. Only the negroes are of nearly equal number; a slight excess being counted on the female side.

Very few Tartars and Chinese have brought their wives and daughters with them into this country. On their first coming over they expected to get rich in a year, and return to sip tea and grow oranges in their native land. Many of those who are now settled in California and Montana, are sending for their mates, who may come or not; having mostly, perhaps, been married again in the absence of their lords. The present rate is eighteen yellow men to one yellow woman.

As yet, the red-skins have been counted in groups and patches only; in the more settled districts of Michigan, Minnesota, California, and New Mexico; but in all these districts, though the influences are here unusually favorable to female life, males are found in excess of females, in the proportion of five to four.

Think what this large excess of men over women entails, in the way of trial, on American society—think what a state that country must be in which counts up in its fields, in its cities, seven hundred and thirty thousand unmarried men!

Bear in mind that these crowds of prosperous fellows are not bachelors by choice, selfish dogs, woman-haters, men useless to themselves and to the world in which they live. They are average young men, busy and pushing; fellows who would rather fall into love than into sin; who would be fond of their wives and proud of their children if society would only provide them with lawful mates. What are they now? An army of monks without the defense of a religious vow. These seven hundred and thirty thousand bachelors have never promised to be chaste; many of them, it may be feared, regard the tenth commandment as little more than a paper law. You say to them in effect, "You are not to pluck these flowers, not to trample on these borders, if you please." Suppose that they will not please? How is the unwedded youth to be hindered from coveting his neighbor's wife? You know what Naples is, what Munich is. You have seen the condition of Liverpool, Cadiz, Antwerp, Livorno; of every city, of every port, in which there is a floating population of single men; but in which of these cities do you find any approach to New York, in the show of open and triumphant vice?

Men who know New York far worse than myself, assure me that in depth and darkness of iniquity, neither Paris in its private haunts, nor London in its open streets, can hold a candle to it. Paris may be subtler, London may be grosser, in its vices; but for largeness of depravity, for domineering insolence of sin, for rowdy callousness to censure, they tell me the Atlantic City finds no rival on the earth.

Do all these evils come with the anchoring ship, and stream from the quays into the city? No one will say so. The quays of New York are like the quays of any other port. They are the haunts of drabs and thieves; they are covered with grogshops and stews; but the men who land on those quays are not viler in taste than those who land in Southampton, in Hamburg, in Genoa. What, then, makes the Empire City a cesspool by the side of which European ports seem almost pure? My answer is, mainly the disparity of sex and sex.

New York is a great capital; rich and pleasant, gay and luxurious; a city of freedom, a city of pleasure, to which men come from every part of the Union; this man for trade, that for counsel, a third for relaxation, a fourth for adventure. It is a place for the idle man, as well as for the busy man. Crowds flock to its hotels, to its theaters, to its gaming-houses; and we need no angel from heaven to tell us what kind of company will amuse an unmarried man having dollars in his purse.

On the other side, this demand for mates who can never be supplied, not in one place only, but in every place alike, affects the female mind with a variety of plagues; driving your sister into a thousand restless agitations about her rights and powers; into debating woman's era in history, woman's place in creation, woman's mission in the family; into public hysteria, into table-rapping, into anti-wedlock societies, into theories about free love, natural marriage, and artistic maternity; into anti-offspring resolutions, into sectarian polygamy, into free trade of the affections, into community of wives. Some part of this wild disturbance of the female mind, it may be urged, is due to the freedom and prosperity which women find in America as compared against what they enjoy in Europe; but this freedom, this prosperity, are in some degree, at least, the consequences of that disparity in numbers which makes the hand of every young girl in the United States a positive prize.

CHAPTER XXXVII.

LADIES.

"THE American lady has not made an American home," says sly old Mayo; a truth which I should hardly have found out, had I not met with it in an American author. Ladies, it is true, are very much at home in hotels; but I have only to remember certain streets in Boston, Philadelphia, Richmond, and New York—indeed, in Denver, Salt Lake City, and St. Louis—to feel that America has homes as bright as any to be found in Middlesex and Kent. "What do you say, now, to our ladies?" said to me a bluff Yankee, as we sat last night under the veranda, here in the hotel at Saratoga. "Charming," of course I answered, "pale, delicate, bewitching; dashing, too, and radiant." "Hoo!" cried he, putting up his hands; "they are just not worth a d——. They can't walk, they can't ride, they can't nurse." "Ah, you have no wife," said I, in a soothing tone. "A wife!" he shouted; "I should kill her." "With kindness?" "Ugh!" he answered; "with a poker. Look at these chits here, dawdling by the fountain. What are they doing now? what have they done all day? Fed and dressed. They have changed their clothes three times, and had their hair washed, combed, and curled three times. That is their life. Have they been out for a walk, for a ride? Have they read a book? have they sewn a seam? Not a bit of it. How do your ladies spend their time? They put on good boots, they tuck up their skirts, and hark away through the country lanes. I was in Hampshire once; my host was a duke; his wife was out before breakfast, with clogs on her feet and roses on her cheeks; she rode to the hunt, she walked to the copse; a ditch would not frighten her, a hedge would not turn her back. Why, our women, poor, pale——." "Come," I said, "they are very lovely." "Ugh!" said the saucy fellow, "they have no bone, no fibre, no juice; they have only nerves; but what can you expect? They eat pearlash for bread; they drink ice-water for wine; they wear tight stays, thin shoes, and barrel skirts. Such things are not fit to live, and, thank God, in a hundred years not one of their descendants will be left alive."

When looking at these sweet New England girls, as they go trooping past my window, I cannot help feeling that with this delicate pallor, winsome and poetic as it looks to an artist in female beauty, there must be lack of vital power. My saucy friend had got an inkling of the truth. Would that these dainty cousins of ours were a trifle more robust! I could forgive them for a little rose-blush on the cheek; at present you can hardly speak to them without fearing lest they should vanish from before your face.

Woman, in her time, has been called upon to endure a great deal of definition. In prose and in verse she has been called an angel, a harpy, a saint, an ogress, a guardian, a fate; she has been likened to a rose and a palm, to the nightshade and the upas; she has been painted as a dove and a gazelle, a magpie and a fox. Poetry has made her a fawn, a nightingale, a swan; while satire has represented her as a jay, a serpent, and a cat. By way of coming to a middle term, a wit described her as a good idea—spoiled! Wit, poetry, satire, only exhaust their terms; for how can a phrase describe an infinite variety?

A lady, as a single type, would, perhaps, be easier to define than woman; she would certainly be easier to express by an example. Asked to produce a perfect woman, I might hesitate long, comparing strength and weakness, merit and frailty, so as to get them in the most subtle relations to each other; asked to produce a perfect lady, I should point to Miss Stars at Washington, Mrs. Bars of Boston, and to many more. Not that perfect ladies are more common than perfect women; they are far less common; but we seize the type more easily, and we know in what soils to expect their growth. A typical woman is a triumph of Nature; a typical lady is a triumph of Art.

Among the higher classes in America, the traditions of English beauty have not declined; the oval face, the delicate lip, the transparent nostril, the pearl-like flesh, the tiny hand, which mark in May Fair the lady of high descent, may be seen in all the best houses of Virginia and Massachusetts. The proudest London belle, the fairest Lancashire witch, would find in Boston and in Richmond rivals in grace and beauty whom she could not feign to despise. Birth is one cause, no doubt, though training and prosperity have come in aid of birth. In some of our older colonies, the people drew their blood from the very heart of England in her most heroic time and mood, when men who were born of gentle mothers flung themselves into the great adventure for establishing New States. The bands who came out under Raleigh's patent, under Brewster's guidance, were made up of soldiers, preachers, courtiers, gentlemen; some coming hither to seek a fortune, others to find an asylum; and though crowds of less noble emigrants followed after them—farmers, craftsmen, menials, moss-troopers, even criminals—the leaven was not wholly lost. The family names remained. Even now this older race of settlers keeps its force in some degree intact, making the women lovely, the men gallant and enduring, in the fashion of their ancient types. This higher range of female beauty, which is chiefly to be found in the older cities and in families of gentle race, is thoroughly English in its style; reminding the stranger of a gallery of portraits in a country house; here of Holbein and Lely, there of Gainsborough and Reynolds. Leslie, I think, brought some of his sweetest English faces from the United States.

In many of the younger cities of the Union, there is also a great deal of beauty, backed by a good deal of wit and accomplishment; but the beauty of these younger cities (at least that sample of it which I see here in Saratoga, and that which I saw a little while ago at Lebanon springs) is less like the art of Gainsborough and of Reynolds than that of Guido and of Greuse. Much Flemish blood is in it. The skin is fairer, the eye bluer, the expression bolder, than they are in the English type. New York beauty has more dash and color; Boston beauty more sparkle and delicacy. Some men would prefer the more open and audacious loveliness of New York, with the Rubens-like rosiness and fullness of the flesh; but an English eye will find more charm in the soft and shy expression of the elder type. In New York, the living is more splendid, the dressing more costly, the furnishing more lavish, than in New England; but the effect of this magnificence, as an educating agent, is found to be rather upon the eye than upon the soul. May I illustrate my meaning by example? In Fifth Avenue you may find a mansion which has cost more money to build than Bridgewater House in London, and in which the wines and viands served to a guest may be as good as any put on an English board, but an American would be the first to feel how wide an interval separated these two houses. One house belongs to wealth; the other, to poetry. One boasts of having marble columns and gilded walls; the other, of possessing Raphael paintings and Shakspeare quartos. In Fifth Avenue there is a palace; in Cleveland Row there is a shrine.

Some of this difference is what I find (or fancy) between the beauties of Boston and Richmond and those of Washington and New York. Of course, I am not speaking of shoddy queens and petroleum empresses; these ladies make a class apart, who, even when they chance to live in Fifth Avenue, have no other relation to it than that of being there, like the hickories and limes. I speak of the real ladies of New York, women who would be accounted ladies in Hyde Park, when I say that, as a rule, they have a style and bearing, a dash, a frankness, a confidence, not to be seen among their sisters of either New England or Old England. "I was very bad upon him; but I got over it in time, and then let him off," said a young and pretty woman of New York to a friend of mine, speaking of her love affairs, in the secrecy of a friendship which had lasted two long days. By *him*, she meant a swain whom she, in the wisdom of sixteen summers, had chosen from the crowd—one whom, if the whim had only held her a trifle longer, she might have made her husband by lawful rites. The girl was not a brazen minx, such as a man may sometimes see in a train, in a river boat, playing with big words and putting on saucy airs, but a sweet and elegant girl, a lady from brow to instep, with a fine carriage, a low voice, a cultured mind; a piece of feminine grace, such as a man would like to have in a sister and strive to compass in a wife. Her oddity consisted, first, in the thing which she said; next, in her choice of words; in other phrase, it lay in the difference between an English girl's and an American girl's habits of thought with regard to the relations of men and women. "I was bad upon him, but I let him off," expresses, in very plain Saxon words, an idea which would hardly have entered into an English girl's mind, and, even if it had so entered, would never have found that dry and passionless escape from her lips.

In that phrase lay hidden, like a pass-word in a common saying, the cardinal secrets of American life: the scarcity of women in the matrimonial market, and the power of choosing and rejecting which that scarcity confers on a young and pretty girl.

CHAPTER XXXVIII.

SQUATTER WOMEN.

The fruits of this excess of males over females in the American market are not confined to young damsels who flirt and pout in Saratoga, in Newport, and at the Falls; they come in equal harvests to the peasant girls of Omaha, St. Joseph, and Leavenworth. In the western country, the excess of males is greater than it is in the eastern, with advantages to match on the part of our fairer sex.

Among the many points of difference between life in

the Old World and life in the New, none comes more vividly to the eye than the daily contrast between the gait, dress, speech, and occupations of females in the lower ranks. If Fifth Avenue is a paradise for women, so, each in its own degree, is the mill, the ranch, the oil-spring, the rice-field, and the farm-yard.

I am old enough to recall with a smile my boylike indignation when I first saw females laboring in the open country; not with the men, their fathers and sweethearts, as they might do for a day of haymaking in my own Yorkshire; but alone on the hillsides, in gangs and parties, gaunt and wasted things, ill-clad, ill-fed, pallid with toil, and scorched by the sun. This trial happened to me in beautiful Burgundy, on the slopes of sweet Tonnerre, to which I had gone in the heyday of youth, full of dreams and pastorals. Good old Josephine, poor little Fan, how my heart used to ache for you, as you trotted off in the early day, in your old flap hats, your thin calico skirts, and thick wooden clogs, with the rakes and hoes in your hands, the jar of fresh water on your heads, the basket of brown bread and onions on your arms, leaving that lazy old Jean, who called one of you wife, the other of you daughter, asleep in his crib! How my fingers used to twitch and claw the air when, later in the day, the rascal would come out into the street, shake himself into good humor, gabble about the news, play his game of dominoes at the estaminet door, and enjoy his pipe of tobacco on the steps of St. Pierre! Since that boyish day, I have seen the feminine serfs at their field-work in many parts of the earth; the Celt in Connaught, the Iberian in Valentia, the Pawnee in Colorado, the Fellaheen in Egypt, the Valack in the Carpathian mountains, the Walloon in Flanders, the Negress in Kentucky; but I have never yet been able to look down on this grinding and defacing toil without flushing veins. After so much waste, it was rather comical to find Loo Sing making beds and Hop Chang washing clothes.

In my own country, the peasant girl is not everything that poets and artists paint her. In spite of our Mayday games, our harvest-homes, and many other country pastimes, relics of an older and a merrier age, the English peasant girl is a little loutish, not a little dull. As a rule, she is not very tidy in her person, not very neat in her dress, not very quick with her fingers, not very gainly on her feet. The American girl of the same rank in life is in every respect, save one, her superior.

It may come from living in a softer climate, from feeding on a different diet, from inheriting a purer blood; but from whatever cause it springs, there can be no dispute about the fact, that in Lancashire and Devonshire, indeed, in every English shire, you find among the peasant women a degree of personal beauty nowhere to be matched, as a general rule, and on a scale for comparison, in the United States. Many American girls are comely, many more are smart; but among the lower grades of women, there is no such wide and plentiful crop of rustic loveliness as an artist finds in England; the bright eyes, the curly locks, the rosy complexions, everywhere laughing you into pleasant thoughts among our Devonshire lanes and Lancashire streets. But then comes the balance of accounts. With her gifts of nature, our English rustic must close her book, in presence of her keen and natty American sister.

A few weeks ago, I rode out with a friend to see Cyrus Smith, a peasant farmer, living in the neighborhood of Omaha. Omaha is a new city, built on the

Missouri; a place that has sprung into life in a dozen years; and is growing up like a city in a fairy tale. Yesterday it had a hundred settlers, to-day it has a thousand, to-morrow it may have ten thousand. Twenty years ago, the Omaha Indians lodged under its willows, and the king of that tribe was buried on horseback, by the adjacent bank. Now, it is a city, with a railway line, a capital, a court-house, streets, banks, omnibuses, hotels. What Chicago is, Omaha threatens to become.

Cyrus Smith is a small squatter, living near a tiny creek, in a log-hut, on a patch of forest land, which he has wrung from nature by the toil of his hand, the sweat of his brow. The shed is not big, the plot of land is not wide. Within a narrow compass, everything needful in the way of growing stuff and rearing stock, for a family of young children, must be done; cows must be stalled, pigs littered, poultry fed. There is no wealth to spare in Smith's ranch; the fare is hard, the living is only from hand to mouth; yet on the face of affairs, there is no black sign of poverty, of meanness, such as you would see about an Irish hovel, a Breton cabin, a Valack den. Walk up this garden way, through these natty little beds of fruit-trees, herbs, and flowers. This path might lead to a gentleman's villa; for the road is wide and swept, and neither sink nor cesspool, as in Europe, offends the eye. Things appear to have fallen into their proper places. The shed, if rough, is strong and snug; a rose, a japonica, a Virginia creeper, climbing round the door. Inside, the house is so scrupulously clean, that you might eat your lunch as comfortably off its bare planks as you could from the shining tiles of a Dutch floor. The shelves are many, the pots and pans are bright. Something like an air of gentle life is about you; as though a family of position, suddenly thrown upon its own resources, had camped out in the prairie, halting for a season on its march. In the little parlor, there is a vase of flowers, a print, a bust of Washington. You see at one glance that there is a bright and wholesome woman in this house.

Annie Smith is the type of a class of women found in America—and in some parts of England—but nowhere else. In station she is little above a peasant; in feeling she is little below a lady. She has a thousand tasks to perform: to light her fires, to wash and dress her children, to scrub her floor, to feed her pigs and fowls, to milk her cows, to fetch in herbs and fruits, to dress and cook the dinners, to scour and polish her pails and pans, to churn her butter and press her cheese, to make and mend the clothes; but she laughs and sings through these daily toils with such a gay humor, such a perfect taste, such an easy compliance, that her work seems like pleasure and her care like pastime. She is neatly dressed; beyond, as an Englishman might think, her station in life, were it not that she wears her clothes with a perfect grace. Her hands feel soft as though they were cased all day in kid. Her manner is easy, her countenance bright. Her idiom, being that of her class, amuses a stranger by its unconscious sauciness of tone. But her voice is sweet and low, as becomes her sex, when her sex is at its best. Oddities of expression you will hear from her lips, profanities never. Dirt is her enemy; and her sense of decency keeps the whole homestead clean. She rises with the sun, oftentimes before the sun; her beds are spotless, her curtains and hangings like falling snow. A Sicilian crib, with sheets unwashed for a year, is a thing beyond her imagination to conceive. No herding with the kine, no sleeping in the stable, so common in France, in Italy, in Spain, is ever allowed to her son, to her servant, by Annie Smith. A Kentish barn in hop-time, a Caithness bothy in hay-time, would appear in her eyes to be the abomination of abominations. Her chicks, her pigs, her cattle, are all penned up in their roosts, their styles, their sheds. A Munster peasant puts his pig under the bed, a Navarrese muleteer yokes his team in the house, an Epirote herdsman feeds his goats in the ingle, and an Egyptian fellah takes his donkey into his room. But these dirty and indecent habits of the poor people in our lazy Old World are not only unknown but incomprehensible to American women of the grade of Annie Smith.

Another thing about her takes the eye; the quality of her everyday attire. In England, our female rustics, from the habit of going to church on Sundays, have caught the custom of dressing themselves in better clothes on one day of the week than on the other six days. They have, in fact, their Sunday gowns, compared with which their ordinary wear is nothing but mops and rags. In these respects their sisters in Italy and France resemble them; the contadina having her festa boddice, the paysanne her saint's-day cap. The Suffolk farmer's wife, whom you see coming out of church to-day, her face bright with soap, her bonnet gay with ribbon, has no objection to be seen by you again to-morrow, grimy with dirt, and arrayed in patches. Not so in America; where Annie thinks it would be in bad taste for her to dress gaudily one day, and shabbily six days. True economy, she says, makes her dress herself cleanly and nattily, even when the materials of her gown are poor. One good suit is cheaper than two suits, though one of them may be coarse in texture and mean in make. Good dressing is a habit of the mind, not a question of the purse.

Any woman with a needle in her hand may be tidily dressed.

All round Smith's holding near Omaha lies a colony of bachelors; four men out of five in this territory being without a wife. Annie feels some influence from the common fact; her house is a pleasant center for the young; and as bachelors are apt to grow untidy in their ranches, she finds it pleasant fun to suggest without words the blessings which accrue to a man who is lucky enough to procure a wife.

How sad to think that every man who may deserve it cannot win the prize!

CHAPTER XXXIX.

FEMININE POLITICS.

If all that I hear from the female politicians of these New England States—particularly from those of beautiful Burlington—be true, the great reform coming forward in the United States is a moral and social change; a reform of thought even more than of society; a change in the relations of man to woman, which is not unlikely to write the story of its progress on every aspect of domestic life.

Compared with such a revolution, all other issues of right and wrong—bases of representation, negro suffrage, reconstruction, State rights, repudiation, and the like—are but the topics of a day, trifles of the vestry, accidents of time and place, in two words, parish politics. Domestic reform, when it comes at all, must be wide in scope, grave in principle. The question now on trial in the United States is said by these female advocates of Equal Rights to be, in effect, neither more nor less than this: Shall our family life be governed in the future of our race by Christian law or by Pagan law?

We have had an old saying among us, that "a clever woman can make any man she pleases propose to marry her;" and this London phrase, I am told, has been very much the New York fact.

In the face of our surplus million of spinsters, the saying is a pleasantry, as you may see at any crush-room, kettle-drum, and croquet party. Who does not know a hundred clever women, among the brightest of their sex, who are dropping down the stream, unbidden to the church upon its banks? If that saying about a clever woman being able to marry whom she pleased, were true, should we always hear it with a smile? Who would risk meeting those clever women? "Come now, and bring the lady that owns you," were Lady Morgan's coquetting words to a friend whom she was coaxing to drop in upon one of her morning concerts. Yet the brilliant Irish lady wrote, that in all ages, in all climates, women have behaved like saints, and been treated like serfs. It is not a female saying, that a woman can marry any one she likes.

"Woman and her Master" gave a voice to that cry of the female heart, which has led London into founding a Ladies' College in a side street, a Ladies' Club over a pastry-cook's shop; which has helped New York into calling congresses of maids and matrons on love, marriage, divorce, with the kindred topics of natural selection, artistic maternity, and the mediatorial privilege of the sex.

It must be owned, that as yet our own female politicians have made but puny efforts to free themselves from the bonds of law. With us, Reform has to wait on times and seasons. In English society, the masculine mind still bears the bell, and the most daring of her sex cannot hope, when she lays her hand on our forms and canons, to have the laughter on her side. She knows it will be against her. Not so her American sister; come what may, the Vermont heroine, the New Hampshire reformer, has no dread of being baffled by a sneer. Mary Cragin may renounce her marriage vows, Anna Dickenson may mount the platform, Mary Walker may put on pantalettes. What do they care for men's jests and gibes? Young girls being now in brisk demand, women are free from all fear of misadventure and neglect, even though they should presume to look the great question of their destinies in the face. Prudence of the trading sort having no part in what these ladies may say and do, they are free to think of what is right in fact, of what is sound in law; to come together in public, to teach and preach, to defy the world, and to hold a parliament of their own. Why should they not? If men may meet in public to discuss affairs, why may not women? Are parish politics more important to a people than domestic politics?

No man with eyes and heart will say that everything in relation to our home affairs has yet been placed on a perfect footing—that justice everywhere reigns by the side of love—that behind the closed door, the curtained window, all the relations of husband and wife, of parent and child, are tempered and ennobled by a Christian spirit. If this cannot be said, with even a show of truth, then we have failed as yet to plant on our hearths the religion of love. And if we have failed in our attempt after a Christian life, why may not the reasons of our failure be asked in a public place, in presence of those whom it concerns? But whether men may think it right or wrong to put such queries, American damsels have begun to think, to write, and to vote upon them. Domestic life is said to be woman's sphere; domestic reform, then, is feminine work. Some of these Vermont politicians have got far beyond writing and voting on domestic love. Oneida Creek and Salt Lake City—communities founded by Vermont men—are practical replies to the one great question of our day,—What shall be done to reform the abuses of our social and domestic life?

All the ladies who have entered these lists in favor of their sex—who have begun to preach and write on woman's place in the household, on equality of male and female, on free trade in love, on slavery in marriage, on the right of divorce, on sexual resurrection—whether they lift up their voices with a Margaret Fuller at Brook Farm, a Mary Cragin at Oneida Creek, an Antoinette Doolittle at Mount Lebanon, a Belinda Pratt in Salt Lake City, an Eliza Farnham of New York—have gone back, in these debates, to the very first of First Principles: the absence of all guiding light, of all settled law, even of all safe tradition on the subject of domestic life, compelling them, in search of evidence, to question books, to waylay facts, to criticise codes. These ladies have entered on their task with spirit. No sphere has been too high, no abyss has been too deep, for their prying eyes. They have soared to Olympus, they have plunged into Hades, in search of examples of the actual working of a law of love. They have turned to Syria and to Egypt, to Athens and to Rome; they have appealed to nature and to art, to poetry and to science; they have disputed the story of Eve, denied the wisdom of Lycurgus, invaded the seclusion of Sarah's tent. From every country they have sought an argument, a warning, a reproof. They have gone down to the threshing-floor with Ruth, they have read the story of Aspasia, they have dwelt on the fate of Lucretia, they have invoked the spirit of Jane Grey. In every land they have found a model and a moral; and though the model may vary with woman's height, and color, and education, the moral is said to be everywhere the same. Until the new era—which their newest prophetess, Eliza Farnham, has been good enough to describe as Woman's Era—dawned upon the sex in America, they have found that the female had been treated by the male, sometimes as a toy, often as a victim, generally as a chattel, always as a slave. Where, they ask, in glancing through the story of our race, can a woman's eye find anything to admire? Let her pass into an Arab harem, into a Hindoo zenana, into a Kaffir krall, into a New York hotel, into a Pawnee wigwam, into a Mayfair house, and what will she find in these female cages? Equality of the sexes, freedom of the affections? Nowhere. East and west, north and south, she will find little more than government by the strong. As regards higher principles of order, she will see alike in the Christian house and in the heathen cave, the same confusion of ideas, the same difference of laws—the greatest confusion, the wildest divergence, being found, it is alleged by some, in the United States.

In no country under heaven, say these female reformers of domestic life, is the woman held equal to the man. An Arab is allowed to marry four wives; a Jew gives daily thanks that he was born a man; a Persian doubts, in spite of the Koran, whether his concubine has any soul. Baron and feme, the lord and his woman, are the rough old English names of husband and wife. In America, in the midst of liberty and light, the station of woman has hardly been improved—if she measures the improvements by Christian lengths. At Onondaga, in New York, the principal people have petitioned the legislature in favor of abolishing all the laws against seduction. Even in Boston, in Philadelphia, in New York, the most refined, the most wealthy societies of America, her position, say these female politicians, is little better than it is among the Perfectionists and Mormons, even when she has given herself to the man of her choice. See what she has to yield! She must give up to him her name; she must cease to be a citizen; she must transfer to him her house and land; she must sink herself in her new lord. What more does the negress yield on being sold as a slave? In legal jargon, the married lady becomes a feme covert; a creature to be treated as an infant, who can hardly do either right or wrong; a change which, while shielding her on one side, robs her on the other of all her natural rights. No court, no canon, no society, does the woman justice. What is a wedding-ring but a badge? What is a harem but a prison? What is a house but a cage? Why should man have the court, the camp, the grove, while woman has only love? Why should not girls aspire to shine in the senate, to minister in the church? Why may not Elizabeth Stanton represent New York in Congress? Why should not Olympia Brown have the charge of souls at Weymouth? Must women be condemned forever to suckle fools and chronicle small beer? Such ladies as Lucy Stone and Mary Walker put these queries to the world, while an army of wives and maidens waits for its reply.

The very names which the two sexes use toward each other in wedlock imply, it is alleged, the relations of lord and slave. Husband means master; wife means servant. In many parts of America, as in England north of the Trent, a woman of the lower classes never speaks of her husband otherwise than as her "master;" and a husband of the same parts, in the same class, would never talk of his wife except as his "woman;" when he would let you see that he pets her, as his "little woman." Are these relations, ask indignant Eliza Farnham, persuasive Caroline Dall, to be the lasting bases of the married state in a free, a pacific, and a religious land?

No other topic ever did, no other topic ever will, excite in the human breast so keen a curiosity as the relations of man to woman, of woman to man; two bright and plastic beings, unlike in form, in genius, and in office; yet linked by nature in the strongest bonds; fated, as the case may be, to make each other either supremely wretched or supremely blest. Society is the fruit of these relations. Law is but a name for the order in which they exist. Poetry is their audible voice. All epics, tragedies, and stories rest upon them, as the fountains of our nobler and our finer passions. From these relations spring our highest love and our sternest hate. Minor dramas play themselves out. Simpler problems get themselves solved. To wit: the rules which govern the relations of man with man—whether as prince and subject, priest and laic, father and son, creditor and debtor, master and slave—are found to have been obeying for ages a certain law of growth, which has been softening them, until the old, harsh spirit of pagan law has been all but wholly cast out of our daily life. Is it the same with those rules which govern the more delicate relations of man with woman? In no very large degree.

Is it not a sad, surprising fact, that in the nineteenth century of gospel light, the laws under which women are compelled to live in wedlock should be worse in America than they are in Asia? In Turkey, marriage makes a bond woman free; in the United States (if we believe these champions of Equal Rights), it turns a free woman into a slave. In the East, polygamy is dying out; the only quarter in which it is being revived is the West.

Is it true that our domestic affections lie beyond the sphere of law? Men like John H. Noyes, women like Harriet Holton, say so boldly; and at Wallingford and Oneida Creek, the sexes have deposed all human codes and agreed to live with each other by the light of grace. But this opinion, with the practice which depends upon it, is the fancy of a small, though an active and seducing school. The world thinks otherwise; for the world believes in a law of God, even though it may have ceased to confide in a law of man.

CHAPTER XL.

HUSBANDS AND WIVES.

About the main facts which lie at the root of this feminine discontent with existing rules, there is hardly any debate among men of sense. All who have eyes to see, admit them. When you enter upon a study of that nameless science, so often in our thoughts, which may be called the Comparative Anatomy of Domestic Life, you are certainly met on the threshold of inquiry by the astounding fact, that the rights of woman in wedlock would seem to have had scarcely any connection with the scheme of Christian progress. All other rights appear to increase with time. The subject wins concessions from his prince; the layman rises to the level of his priest; the child obtains protection against his sire; the debtor secures some justice from his creditor; the slave is freed from his owner; but hardly any change in her condition, hardly any improvement in her standing, comes to the wedded wife. As a mere chattel, a damsel may be safe; as a wedded wife, the mistress of a home, the law takes hardly any note of her existence; even after all the changes wrought by a dozen years of reform, the law may be described as almost blind to her sufferings, deaf and dumb to her appeals.

When you compare the relations of man with man, and of man with woman, in Asia and America, you are struck at every turn by unsuspected contrasts. Whether you look on man as a citizen, as a laic, as a son, as a debtor, as a servant, you find him better placed before the law in America than in Asia. Could a fellah in Damascus dare to say in a rich man's presence, "I am as good as you?" Could the ryot of Lucknow answer to his lord, "Go to, my vote is as good as yours, and I will not serve you?" Would not such an offender be dispatched to the gateway and punished with twenty stripes? But is there any such difference between Damascus and Boston, between Lucknow and Philadelphia, in respect of the relation of man with woman? Not at all. The contrast lies another way; for in Turkey, in Persia, in Egypt, in Mohammedan India, the privileges of married women stand on a surer footing as to justice than they do in Massachusetts, Pennsylvania, and New York. If you doubt this fact, take down from your shelves the Hidayah, that legal code which an English lawyer has to administer in our Indian courts, and your doubts will pass away into quaint surprise. On opening the Hidayah, you will find that the harem life, which many of those who have never seen it are content to picture as a drama of poisons, bowstrings, slaves, and eunuchs, is guarded and secured, so far as the females go, by a host of wise and compassionate rules, which are not to be broken with impunity by the stronger sex. Many persons here in Boston imagine that a harem is a jail, an Oriental wife a slave; though a very slight acquaintance with Mohammedan law would show them that an English wife is far worse off as a woman than any of her swarthy sisters of Egypt and Bengal.

In one short chapter of a dozen pages, Blackstone set down in his Commentaries all that he could find in our books about the legal relations of an English husband to the woman whom he makes his wife. In the Hidayah (Arabic Commentaries) the chapters which contain the rules defining the relations of a Moslem husband to his Moslem wife, are long enough to fill a volume. A New England advocate of Equal Rights for the two sexes, would describe our English code—and after it the American code—as making a free woman into a serf by the machinery of a civil contract and a solemn right; in some respects as worse than into a serf, since, by the mere act of marriage, it cancels all the rights to which she may have been born, takes away her family name, disposes of her goods and lands, and gives her person into the power of a man who may squander her fortune and break her heart. How far would such a description by the New England advocate be unfair? Who does not know that such cases may be occurring in any town? We need not look for examples in the divorce courts:—they meet us in these streets, they cry aloud to us from these balconies. Our common law gives up the wife so thoroughly into her husband's power, that a woman, who comes to the altar young, confiding, beautiful, and rich, may be compelled by brutal treatment, for which the law can give her no redress, to quit it, after a dozen years, an outraged woman with a ruined fortune and a wasted frame. One course, and one only, can save her from the risk of these evils:—a settlement made on her account with the law before she has entered on the fatal right.

Nothing so gross and cruel towards a young and loving girl could happen in either Turkey, Persia, or Mohammedan India. In a Moslem country, every right which a female, whether rich or poor, enjoys by her birth, remains with her, a sacred property, to her death. No man can take it from her. After she has passed from her father's house into her husband's home, she is still a citizen, a proprietor, a human being. She can sue her debtors, and recover her own in the open courts. All the privileges which belong to her as a woman and as a wife are secured to her, not by the courtesies that come and go, but by actual text in the book of law. A Moslem marriage is a civil act, needing no mollah, asking no sacred phrase. Made before a judge, it may also be unmade before a judge. But the Eastern contract is in this respect more logical than the Western contract, that it gives to the man no power upon the woman's person beyond what the law defines, and none whatever upon her lands and goods. A Persian, a Turkish bride, being married to a man of her own rank and creed, retains in the new household which she enters to become the soul, her separate existence as her father's child. A New England bride, on being married to a man of her own rank and creed, becomes lost in him. A Turkish wife is an independent and responsible person, knowing what is right and wrong, and with the same faculty of receiving and devising property which she held in her spinster days. What is hers is not her lord's. She may sue her debtor, without the concurrence of her nearest friend. She may receive a pension, sign a bond, execute a trust. Compared against her Asiatic sister, what a helpless being an American lady seems!

The very first lesson, then, to be drawn from this study of the Comparative Anatomy of Domestic Life, is that rules of law are not beyond some sort of fair and equal application, even in the midst of those secrecies which feed, and those sanctities which guard, the love of husband and wife. Such rules of law are found in Asia. They exist in Cairo, in Bagdad, in Delhi, in a hundred cities of the East. Our own magistrates have to take account of them in India; where the most intricate questions of domestic right,

—questions relating to dowry, to divorce, to preference, to maintenance, to conjugal fidelity, are brought before the courts, and require to be considered and decided on principles utterly unknown in Westminster Hall. In dealing with such cases between man and woman, we have to lay aside our Statutes at large, our civil law and common law; to forget our jargon of baron and feme, covert and sole. The Suras of Mohammed supply us with the principles, the Commentaries of Abu Yusuf with the details, of a practicable Moslem code. Who, then, in the face of our large Indian experience, will be bold enough to say, that law cannot be made to reach the innermost recesses of a household? In Delhi, in Lucknow, in Madras, not to speak of Cairo, of Damascus, of Jerusalem, law penetrates to the nursery and to the bridal chamber. Of course, there may be secret tyrannies in Asia, as there may be in America; violence of the strong against the weak may be fierce as the passion, subtle as the genius, of an Oriental race; but the excesses of a Moslem husband find no sanction either in the silence or in the provisions of his actual code. If he does wrong, he does it as wrong, and with the fear of punishment in his heart. When a man commits an abuse of the harem, however trifling, he knows that for the victim of his temper there is a swift and sure appeal to an impartial judge.

But how, it may be asked, does a married woman come to have a higher security against oppression in an Asiatic city than in American cities? Surely it cannot be because those Asiatic cities are Moslem in creed, while these American cities are Christian? Nothing in our Gospel makes a Christian wife a slave; and in its sweet tenderness to woman, the Gospel stands high above the Koran, high above every other book. Why, then, is the law of Christendom so harsh to wedded women, while that of Islam appears to be so mild?

This question goes deep down into the roots of things, and a full answer to it would supply the motto for that revolution which the female politicians declare to be coming upon American social life.

CHAPTER XLI.

DOMESTIC LAW.

When the New England seeker after better things than she can find just now in a woman's lot, turns aside, with her aching heart, from the wrongs of time towards the promise of a golden age of justice, in she knows not what new cities of Bethlehem, Wallingford, Lebanon, Salt Lake, the sites of her new experiments in living, no man will say that she is troubled without cause. Let her remedy be sought in the right place or in the wrong, the evil is dark and vast; pervading the whole community, and passing in its degrees of shame, from the delicate tortures of the boudoir down to the rough brutalities of the street. Even here in Boston, with all its learning, all its refinement, all its piety, the wrongs of women are so gross, that Caroline Dall confessed to a female audience she could neither lay them bare nor speak of them by their proper names. Yet on all these sufferings of the weaker sex, the American law is silent, the American magistrate is powerless. How, ask the reformers, have these evils grown upon us?

That prior question of how it has come to pass that a Turkish, Persian, Egyptian lady enjoys in marriage a securer state than her paler sister of Boston, Richmond, New Orleans, would open up for us a glimpse of some forgotten truths; since it would start a second question, — How have we Christians come by our marriage laws, and how have the Mohammedan nations come by theirs? The answer is not far away; for the facts are written broadly in our histories, minutely in our statutes. We get our marriage laws from the Pandects; the Moslems get theirs from the Koran. In this difference of origin lies the secret of their difference in tone and spirit. Our laws have a civil and commercial source; theirs have a moral and religious source.

Here, indeed, an inquirer strikes his axe upon the root. Our life is a divided duty: a moral life based on the Gospel, a family life based on the civil law. While our morals have their root in Christianity, our statutes have their root in Paganism. And thus it is, in the main degree at least, that woman's griefs in marriage, and in all the relations of sex and sex, have come upon her, like many other evils in our social body, from the fact of our deriving our morals from one source, the Gospels, our laws from another source, the Pandects.

One of the sorry jests in which we are apt to array our falsehoods, says that our English and American codes of law are founded on the precepts of our faith. Let us try this dogma by a test. A just and pious man, fresh from his study of Holy Writ, shall walk with the Bible in his hand, into the Supreme Court of the United States, and shall then and there try to persuade the presiding judge that the Sermon on the Mount is good American law, binding on every

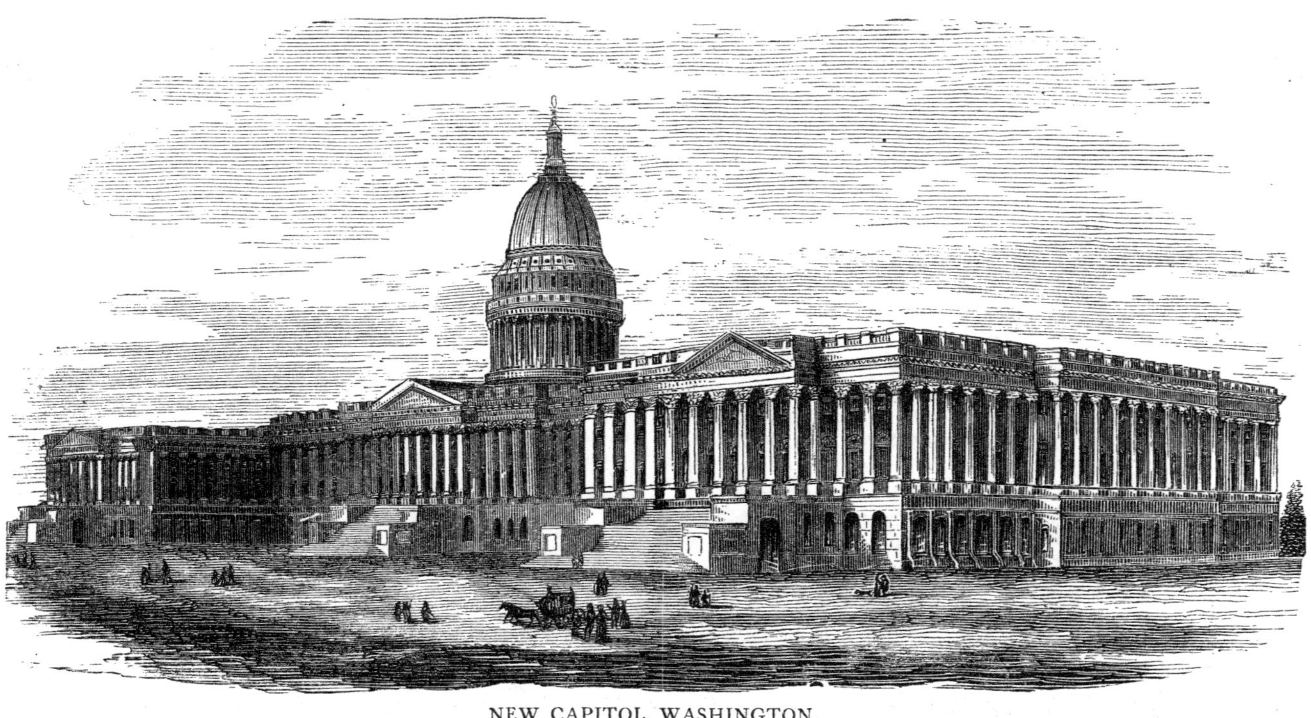

NEW CAPITOL, WASHINGTON.

follower of Christ. Have you any kind of doubt as to what would become of that just and pious man? You know that the judge would pity, the advocate quiz, the audience mock, and the officer seize him. Remove the scene from the Capitol at Washington, to the gateway of Damascus. In the Oriental city, such a man might go before the cadi, Koran in hand, assured that his citations from the holy book would be heard; and if his views of them were sound, that they would govern the verdict to be given. And the reason is plain. An Oriental has not two laws: one for the street, another for the gate; one for his harem, a second for his mosque. His moral life and his civil life have one source, one end, and he finds no war between the teachings of his cadi and his priest. In Boston, in New York, we have a moral code which only on two or three points of moment approaches the edge of our domestic code. What do our judges know of Christ, of Moses, and of Abraham? As lawyers, nothing. These names are not among those which may be quoted in our acts and commentaries. The judges who dispense our law have heard of Justinian, of the civilians; but of the immutable precepts of our faith, the divine foundations of our moral life, they are powerless, as magistrates on the bench, to take any public and judicial note. They must abide by the text, a mixture of the Saxon common law and of the Roman civil law.

A prime result of our laws being Pagan while our morals are Christian, is the fact, so strange and bewildering to an Oriental, that, with us, the practice of virtue is regarded as a private affair, a thing between a man and his Maker only, not, as with the Moslems, between a man and his fellow. Thus, in Boston, in New York, no law compels a man to be chaste, compassionate, dutiful. One of those wits who speak truth in jests and parables, has said that, in our society, a rich, unscrupulous sinner may contrive to break every commandment in the decalogue, without losing his place either at good men's feasts or in ladies' cabinets. If he is great in evasion, pleasant in manner, choice in hospitality, he may run the whole round of offence, from following false gods to coveting his neighbor's wife. His only art is to avoid being seen by the police. Is that parable untrue? What man who drives in Fifth Avenue, who walks on yon common, shuts his eyes on the world so far as to dream that our manners are all alike? You need not be a cynic to see that fashion sits down to its meat and wine, day after day, year after year, with wretches who, in any part of Islam, would be taken before the cadi and beaten on the feet. With two exceptions, perhaps, a sinner may break the ten commandments openly, in these public streets, and no one shall lay hands upon him. While he refrains from killing his foe and robbing his friend, he is safe. What magistrate on the bench would think of asking whether a man accused before him bowed to a false god, put away graven images from his house, abstained from the use of oaths, kept holy the Sabbath day, honored his father and mother, respected the purity of his neighbor's wife, drove out the sin of covetousness from his soul? Not one. And why?

Because the magistrate in his office on the bench is the minister, not of our moral system, but of our civil code.

The truth is, we English and Americans have hardly yet embraced Christianity as a scheme of life. We find our religion at church, and when we have sung our psalms and breathed our prayers, we go back into the streets to be governed for another week by our pagan law. Our courts of justice have no authority to notice moral offences, unless they happen to have been injurious to a fellow-citizen in either his peace or his purse. Mere lack of honor, virtue, reverence, goes on our bench for nothing. A wretch may curse his parents, may profane the Sabbath, may worship stocks and stones, without earning for himself the penalty of a stripe. The same wretch may break his wife's heart, may squander his child's estate, may destroy his friend's happiness, yet he shall escape all punishment of his crimes. Some of the darkest transgressions in the sight of God—the God whose will we obey—are treated by the code under which we live, as of no more moment than the whimsies of a child. Fornication is not condemned. Seduction is treated as a wrong done, not to the girl, who may be its victim, but only to the owner of her service. Adultery is classed with such small injuries as theft; a loss of property rather than of purity and credit; and the man whose name may have been tarnished forever by a seducer, must plead against the destroyer of his peace, not his outraged honor, but the loss of his daughter's service, of his wife's society. In some of the United States, they have gone a little way towards rounding off these lines of separation between Christian morals and the civil code. In New York, a fellow may be lodged in jail for seducing girls; but the legislatures have hardly, as yet, even touched the fringe of a mighty evil. Those Onandago reformers of the law who petitioned in favor of replacing the felon's cell by a bridal wreath—going back to the prosaic plan of considering the act of seduction as an act of marriage—have no remedy to suggest for the still darker outrage of seducing and debauching a married woman. Nor can they find one under a law which treats the crimes of seduction and adultery as a wrong to the man's estate, but not to his moral life.

In all the advancing schools of American thought, this topic is discussed, the evil is admitted, a remedy is sought. At Oneida Creek they have put an end to adultery by abolishing marriage. At Mount Lebanon they have done the same thing by prohibiting love. At Salt Lake, again, they have checked the evil by punishing adultery with death. But these sectional trials leave the law intact, and the courts and legislatures of the Union are continually being vexed by petitions in favor of substituting some higher rule for the one in vogue. Will they ever find such a rule while they cling to the code of Justinian in preference to the word of God?

In a Moslem country, the Prophet's word is law, each line a command, each sura an institute. The Prophet's object being, according to his lights, to promote among his people not only the public peace, but holy living; his precepts were adapted to the regulation of every act of a believer in the harem, in the mosque, in the bazaar. On the other side, our Saviour's word has only obtained in our western society the force of a moral precept, which every one may adopt, and every one may reject, at pleasure.

Again, our pagan statutes seem to have been framed for service only in the public streets. We have a saying that our house is our castle; it is so sometimes, in a wide and wicked sense. No writ runs in it. Law pauses at the threshold; and the crown itself, the majesty of public right, can only break those portals after due solemnities and in the wake of some atrocious crime. In a Moslem harem, no such feudal secrecy is found. Every room in a house is open to the

Koran; every act of the lord must be conformable to rule; and a man's wife, his child, his slave, may cite the Koran against him. In Islam, every one knows the law by heart; the Koran being a text which can never fall out of date. All Moslem jurists must adopt this text, which they are only free to expound within certain limits, and every cadi may go back to the original in his day of doubt. The basis of public justice is the same in every age and in every land. In states like England and America, we have no great body of divine, indisputable law, by which all queries might be answered, all problems might be solved. When a case arises in our courts, which no enactment appears to meet, where do our judges look for guidance? Do they turn to the Gospels. Do they read St. Paul? They never think of such a course. The Gospels make no part of our legal store. If we teach the decalogue in our infant-schools, and preach it in our chapels, we make no use of it in our law courts. Proud, as it would seem, of our Pagan code, which puts so much of our conduct into contrast with our creed, we make a boast of this freedom from restraint, and only on our grand occasions, as it were, admit the presence in our midst of a purer law.

Now it is one of the open facts of our modern societies in London and New York, that a woman's rank in the family is either high or low according to the loyalty with which we follow that Gospel law of love which the courts of justice may, if they please, ignore. A Turk is not permitted by the cadi to set aside *his* Sermon on the Mount as a precept for Sundays, for good women, for men in childhood and old age. Even in the privacy of his harem, an Asiatic is governed by some kind of moral and religious rules; while an American is governed in his home only by legal and commercial precepts, from which every moral and religious feeling may have been utterly divorced. Thus it happens that an Oriental wife, though she may be living in the state of polygamy, has in some capital points a wider freedom in her circle than the most highly cultured lady of New York.

Is that the end of our long endeavor after a Christian life? No religious man or woman thinks so; and at this moment a thousand busy brains and gentle hearts are working on the problem of our passage from this stage of growth into a religion of higher truth. Some of these seekers after better things may be groping in the dark; looking for light where light is not; but in so far as they are seeking honestly and with earnest heed to get into the better way, they deserve our study and respect.

Foremost among these seekers after light, are the Brethren of Mount Lebanon in the State of New York.

CHAPTER XLII.

MOUNT LEBANON.

On a sunny hill-side, three miles south of New Lebanon Springs, (a watering-place in the upper country of the lovely river Hudson, at which idlers from New York and Massachusetts spend the hot weeks of summer, lounging in frame sheds, flirting under chestnuts, driving over broken roads, sipping water from the well,—which a negro has just told me that a horse may drink without doing itself any harm!) stands a group of buildings, prim and yet picturesque; the chief home of a religious body, small in number, singular in dress and in ideas, and only to be found, as yet, in the United States.

This village is Mount Lebanon, the chief home and centre of a celibate people, founded by Ann Lee; known to scoffers as a comic institution unattached, under the name of the Shaker Village; Shaker being a term of mockery and reproach, like most of our religious names; one which the members meekly accept, and of which they are shyly proud. Among the elect they are known as the United Society of Believers in Christ's Second Appearing.

Needing a little rose-water, I asked a friend where the best might be got. "You must apply," he said, "at any of the stores where they sell Shaker scents." Inquiring about the best place for collecting American shrubs and flowers, my companion said, "You must ride over to Mount Lebanon, as no one in either New York or Massachusetts can match the Shakers in producing seeds and plants." My curiosity was piqued. Why should the villagers of Mount Lebanon excel the rest of their countrymen in such an art? Of course, I knew that the Essenes were florists and seedsmen, as well as rearers of bees and growers of herbs and corn: but then those Hebrew anchorites lived in a time when husbandry was contemned as a servile art, unfit to occupy the thoughts, to engage the hands of free men; and they gave themselves up to a life of field labor, not for the profits which it might bring them, but as an exercise of the spirit and a trial of the flesh. In the neighborhood of Mount Lebanon, — a ridge of wooded hills, furrowed with bright dales and glades, and with tiny becks of water running east and south from the Springs, — no man affects to despise farming as a lowly craft, the work of women and slaves; on the contrary, all the best talents of this region are invested in the land; and renown of its kind lies in waiting for the man who shall produce from his acres the finest and most ample crops. "Why, then," I asked my friend, "where all are striving to excel in the art of producing plenty from the soil, should the Shakers of Mount Lebanon be the only seedsmen in the State?" "Guess," said he, after a moment's thought, "it is because they give their minds to it."

This saying about the Shakers giving their minds to the culture of land may be used as a key to unlock nearly all the secrets of Mount Lebanon. As you climb up this green hill-side from the pretty hamlet of New Lebanon, you may see in the clean roads, in the bright swards, in the trim hedges, more than all else, in the fresh meek faces of men and girls, and in the strange sad light of their loving eyes, how much has been done in a few short years towards converting this corner of New York State from a rugged forest, the haunt of Iroquois and Lenni Lenape, into the likeness of an earthly Eden. The rough old nature shows itself near. Yon crests and tops are clothed in their primeval woods, though the oaks and chestnuts are now in their second growth. Rocks crop out, and stones lie about you. Much of the land has never been reclaimed. The paths are all open; and every man with a gun may shoot down game, as freely as he might in the prairies of Nebraska. But the hand of man has been laid on the soil with a tight, though a tender grasp; doing its work of beauty, and calling forth beauty in exchange for love and care. Where can you find an orchard like this young plantation on our left? Where, save in England, do you see such a sward? The trees are greener, the roses pinker, the cottages neater, than on any slope. New Lebanon has almost the face of an English valley, rich with the culture of a thousand years. You see that the men who till these fields, who tend these gardens, who bind these sheaves, who train these vines, who plant these apple-trees, have been drawn into putting their love into the daily task; and you hear with no surprise that these toilers, ploughing and planting in their quaint garb, consider their labor on the soil as a part of their ritual, looking upon the earth as a stained and degraded sphere, which they have been called to redeem from corruption and restore to God.

The plan, the life, the thought of Mount Lebanon are written in its grassy streets. This large stone building on your right—an edifice of stone in a region of sheds and booths—is the granary; a very fine barn, the largest (I am told) in America; a cow-shed, a hay-loft, a store-house, of singular size and happy contrivance; and its presence here, on a high place, in the gateway, so to speak, of the community, is a typical fact.

The Granary is to a Shaker what the Temple was to a Jew.

Beyond the barn, in the green lane, stands North House, the dwelling of Elder Frederick and Elderess Antoinette (in the world they would be called Frederick W. Evans, and Mary Antoinette Doolittle), co-heads of this large family in the Shaker Society. Below their house, among the shrubs and gardens, lies the Visitors' house, in which it has been my fortune to spend, with Frederick and Antoinette, a few summer days. Around these buildings rise the sheds and stores of the family. Next come a host of gardens, in which the Baltimore vine runs joyously up poles and along espaliers; then the church lying a little way back from the road, a regular white frame of wood, plain as a plank, with a boiler roof, a spacious, airy edifice, in which the public service of the society is sung, and danced on Sunday, to the wondering delight, often the indecent laughter of a crowd of idlers from the Springs. Near by stands Church House, of which Elder Daniel and Elderess Polly (in the world Daniel Crossman and Polly Reed) are the co-heads; with the school, the store, at which pretty trumperies are sold to the Gentile belles. Beyond these buildings, higher up the hill, stand South House, East House, and some other houses. In all these dwellings live families of Shakers. Elder Frederick is the public preacher; but every family has its own male, its own female head. One family lives at Canaan, seven miles distant, to which I have made a separate visit; while just beyond the crest of yon hill, in the State of Massachusetts, you find another society — the settlement of Hancock.

No Dutch town has a neater aspect, no Moravian

hamlet a softer hush. The streets are quiet; for here you have no grog-shop, no beer-house, no lock-up, no pound; of the dozen edifices rising about you—work-rooms, barns, tabernacle, stables, kitchens, schools, and dormitories—not one is either foul or noisy; and every building, whatever may be its use, has something of the air of a chapel. The paint is all fresh; the planks are all bright; the windows are all clean. A white sheen is on everything; a happy quiet reigns around. Even in what is seen of the eye and heard of the ear, Mount Lebanon strikes you as a place where it is always Sunday. The walls appear as though they had been built only yesterday; a perfume, as from many unguents, floats down the lane; and the curtains and the window-blinds are of spotless white. Everything in the hamlet looks and smells like household things which have been long laid up in lavender and rose-leaves.

The people are like their village; soft in speech, demure in bearing, gentle in face; a people seeming to be at peace, not only with themselves, but with nature and with heaven. Though the men are oddly attired—in a sort of Arab sack, with a linen collar, and no tie, an under vest buttoned to the throat and falling below the thighs, loose trousers rather short, and broad-brimmed hat, nearly always made of straw,—they are grave in aspect, easy in manner, with no more sense of looking comic in the eyes of strangers than either an English judge on the bench or an Arab sheikh at his prayer. The women are habited in a small muslin cap, a white kerchief wrapped round the chest and shoulders, a sack or skirt dropping in a straight line from the waist to the ankle, white socks and shoes; but apart from a costume neither rich in color nor comely in make, the sisters have an air of sweetness and repose which falls upon the spirit like music shaken out from our village bells. After spending a few days among them, seeing them at their meals and at their prayers, in their private amusements and in their household work, after making the personal acquaintance of a score of men, of a dozen women, I find myself thinking that if any chance were to throw me down, and I were sick in spirit, broken in health, there would be few female faces, next after those of my own wife and kin, that would be pleasanter to see about my bed. Life appears to move on Mount Lebanon in an easy kind of rhythm. Order, temperance, frugality, worship—these are the Shaker things which strike upon your senses first; the peace and innocence of Eden, when contrasted with the wrack and riot of New York. Every one seems busy, every one tranquil. No jerk, no strain, no menace, is observed, for nothing is done, nothing can be done in a Shaker settlement by force. Every one here is free. Those who have come into union came unsought; those who would go out may retire unchecked. No soldiers, no police, no judges, live here; and among the members of a society in which every man stakes his all, appeal to the courts of law is a thing unknown. Unlike the Syrian Lebanon, she has no Druse, no Maronite, no Ansayri, no Turk, within her frontier; peace reigns in her councils, in her tabernacles, in her fields. Look at these cheery urchins, in their broad straw hats and with their dropping sash, as they leap and gambol on the turf, laughing, pulling at each other, filling this green hill-road with the melodies only to be heard when happy children are at play. Their hearts are evidently light. Look at these little blue-eyed girls (those two with the curly heads are children of a bad mother, who eloped last year with a neighbor, when their father was away in the field with Grant), very shy, and sweet, and clean, and comely are they in their new attire; if ever you saw little girls like angels, surely these are such.

Yet, is it not strange to us that young men and young women should be found living in this beautiful place, in the midst of peace and plenty, without thoughts of love? And is it not sad to reflect that those merry boys and girls, whose voices come in peals of laughter down the lane, will never, if they stay in this community, have little ones of their own to play on the village sward?

The Shaker is a monk, the Shakeress a nun. They have nothing to say to this world; yet their church, so often described as a moral craze, a religious comedy, a ritual of high jinks, at best a church of St. Vitus, not of St. Paul, will be seen, when we come to understand it, to have some singular attractions. The magnetic power which it is exercising on American thought would, of itself, compel us, even though we should be found unwilling hearers, to sit out the comedy and try to comprehend the plot.

CHAPTER XLIII.

A SHAKER HOUSE.

During the days which I have been spending at North House, the guest of Frederick and Antoinette, I have had every opportunity given to me of seeing and judging for myself the virtues and failings of the Shaker brethren. I have been eating their food, lodging in their chambers, driving in their carriages, talking with their elders, strolling over their orchards; I have been with them of a morning in the field, at noon by the table, at night in their meeting-rooms; watching them at their work, at their play, at their prayers; in short, living their life, and trying to comprehend the spirit which inspires it.

My room is painfully bright and clean. No Haarlem vrouw ever scraped her floor into such perfect neatness as my floor; nor could the wood, of which it is made, be matched in purity except in the heart of an uncut forest pine. A bed stands in the corner, with sheets and pillows of spotless white. A table on which lie an English Bible, some few Shaker tracts, an inkstand, a paper-knife; four cane chairs, arranged in angles; a piece of carpet by the bed-side; a spittoon in one corner, complete the furniture. A closet on one side of the room contains a second bed, a wash-stand, a jug of water, towels; and the whole apartment is light and airy, even for a frame house. The Shakers, who have no doctors among them, and smile at our Gentile ailments—headaches, fevers, colds, and what not—take a close and scientific care of their ventilation. Every building on Mount Lebanon—farm, granary, mill, and dwelling—is provided with shafts, fans, flappers, drafts, and vents. The stairway is built as a funnel, the vane as an exhauster. Stoves of a special pattern warm the rooms in winter, with an adjustment delicate enough to keep the temperature for weeks within one degree of warmth. Fresh air is the Shaker medicine. "We have only had one case of fever in thirty-six years," says Antoinette: "and we are very much ashamed of ourselves for having had it; it was wholly our fault."

North House, the dwelling of Elder Frederick's family, has the same whiteness and brightness, the same order, the same articles in every room. Antoinette led me over it yesterday, from the fruit-cellars to the roof, showing me the kitchens, the ladies' chambers, the laundries, the meeting-rooms, and the stoves. My friend William Haywood (civil engineer to the City of London) and his wife, were with me; the engineer was no less smitten by surprise at the singular beauty and perfect success which the Shakers have attained in the art of ventilation, than the lady was charmed by the sweetness, purity, and brightness of the corridors and rooms. Males and females dwell apart as to their rooms, though they eat at a common table, and lodge under a common roof. "How do you treat a man who comes into union with his wife and children — that sometimes happens?" Antoinette smiled, "Oh, yes! that happens pretty often; they fall into the order of brother and sister— and make very pretty Shakers." "But," said the lady, "they see each other?" "That is so," answered Antoinette; "they live in the same family; they become brother and sister. They do not cease to be man and woman; in forsaking each other, they only cease to be husband and wife." Some of these ladies who live under

Frederick's roof in North House, have husbands (as the world would call them) living close beside their rooms; but they would hold it to be a weakness, perhaps a sin, to feel any personal happiness in each other's company. They live for God alone. The love that is in their hearts — so far as it is capable of bearing bounteous fruit — ought to be shed on each of the Saints alike, without preference on account of either quality or sex.

Is it always so? After this morning's early meal, Antoinette, who had come into my room, where Frederick and some of the Elders had already dropt in for a social chat in answer to some of my wondering worldly questions, told me, in the presence of four or five men, that she felt towards Frederick, her co-ruler of the house, a special and peculiar love, not as towards the man, and in the Gentile way, as she had heard of the world's doings in such matters, but as towards the child of grace and agent of the heavenly Father. She told me, also, that she had sweet and tender passages of love with many who were gone away out of sight — the beings whom we should call the dead — and that these passages of the spirit were of the same kind as those which she enjoyed with Frederick. The functions which these two persons exercise in the family, as male and female chiefs, give them the privilege of this close relation, — this wedlock of the soul, if I may use that phrase to express a sympathy which, not being of the world, has no worldly words to represent it.

The ladies usually sleep in pairs, two in a room; the men have separate rooms. One bed is made to slide beneath another, so that when the chamber is arranged for the day-time, there is ample space and a sense of air. Nothing in these apartments hints that the people who occupy them seek after an ascetic life. All the ladies have looking-glasses in their rooms, though they are sometimes told, in love, to guard their hearts against the abuse to which these vanities might lead. "Females," says Frederick in his homely humor, "need to be steadied, some." The dress of these ladies, though the rule is strict as to shape, is not confined to either a single color. On some of the pegs hang dresses of blue cotton, lawn stuff, white muslin; and even at church a good many of the ladies appear in lilac gowns, a color which becomes them well. "We leave the individual taste rather free," says Frederick; "we find out by trial what is best; and when we have found a good thing, either in a dress or in anything else, we stick to it."

These Shakers dine in silence. Brothers and sisters sit in a common room, at tables ranged in a line, a few feet apart. They eat at six in the morning, at noon, at six in the evening; following in this respect a rule which is all but uniform in America, especially in the western parts of this continent from the Mississippi River to the Pacific Ocean. They rally to the sound of a bell; file into the eating-room in a single line, women going up to one end of the room, men to the other; when they drop on their knees, for a short and silent prayer; sit down, and eat, helping each other to the food. Not a word is spoken, unless a brother need some help from a brother, a sister from a sister. A whisper serves. No one gossips with her neighbor; for every one is busy with her own affairs. Even the help that any one may need is given and taken without thanks; such forms of courtesy and politeness not being considered necessary in a family of saints. Elder Frederick sits at the end, not at the head, of one table. Elderess Antoinette at the other end.

The food, though it is very good of its kind, and very well cooked, is simple; being wholly, or almost wholly, produce of the earth; tomatoes, roast apples, peaches, potatoes, squash, hominy, boiled corn, and the like. The grapes are excellent, reminding me of those of Bethlehem; and the eggs, hard eggs, boiled eggs, scrambled eggs, are delicious. The drink is water, milk, and tea. Then we have pies, tarts, candies, dried fruits and syrups. For my own part, being a Gentile and a sinner, I have been indulged in cutlets, chickens, and home-made wine. "Good food and sweet air," says Frederick, "are our only medicines." The rosy flesh of his people, a tint but rarely seen in the United States, appears to answer very well for his assertion, that in such a place no other physic is required. These people say, they want no Cherokee medicines, no plantation bitters, no Bourbon cocktails, none of the thousand tonics by which the dyspeptic children of New York whip up their flagging appetites, and cleanse their impure blood. Frederick has a fierce antipathy to doctors. "Is it not strange," says he, "that you wise people of the world keep a set of men, who lie in wait for you until by some mistake of habit you fall sick, and who then come in, and poison you with drugs?" How can I reply to him, except by a little laugh?

No words being spoken during meals, about twenty minutes serves them amply for repast. One minute more, and the table is swept bare of dishes; the plates, the knives and forks, the napkins, the glass, are cleaned and polished, every article is returned to its proper place, and the sweet, soft sense of order is restored.

A man has little inducement to dally with the cheery wine; and as no cigar has ever been allowed to profane the precincts of North House, I rise after a cup of black coffee, and, joining a knot of Brethren, stroll into the fields.

Dropping with Frederick into the schools, the barns, the workshops, I have learned that the Shaker estate on and around Mount Lebanon consists of nearly ten thousand acres of the best woodland and lowland in the State of New York. For a long time, as lots fell into the market, the family has been buying land; but they have now got as much as they can cultivate; more, indeed, than they can cultivate by their own forces; and for some years past they have been compelled, by the extent of their family estates, to hire laborers from among the world's people in the villages about. As they are never angry, never peevish, never unjust (I have heard this said elsewhere, by men who hate their principles and traduce their worship), Gentile laborers come to them very freely, and remain as long as they are allowed to stay. These smiths in the forge by the roadway are World's people; that lad in the cart is a cottager's son; those fellows making hay in the meadow are Gentiles working on the Shaker lands. These laborers have come to Mount Lebanon to live and learn. They get a very fine schooling, and are paid for being at school. No other farming in America reaches the perfection that is here attained; and a clever young lad can hardly pass a season among these fields and farms without picking up good habits and useful hints.

But the chiefs of Mount Lebanon can see that this system of mixed labor, this throwing of the saint and sinner into a common society, for the sake of gain, is foreign to the genius of their order. Such a system, if it were to grow upon them, would be hostile to their first conception of celestial industry; it would, in fact, by the operation of a natural law, degenerate into a feudal and commercial business, in which the Saints would be the bankers and proprietors, the sinners would be the laborers and serfs. That is not an end for which they have denied themselves so much. Even their wish to do good among the Gentiles must not lead them into what is wrong; and they are now considering whether it may not be wiser for them to part with all their surplus lands.

I need not say that any estate which has been for a few years under Shaker ploughs and spades will sell in the market at what would otherwise be considered as a fancy price.

Climbing up the hill-road from the pretty valley of New Lebanon, I notice the fine rows of apple-trees growing in the hedges, after the English fashion in some counties. Elder Frederick, himself of English birth, is pleased to hear me speak of the old country. "Aye," says he; "this green lane, and these fruit-trees, carry me back to my old home." Americans of the higher class, when they are grave and tender, always speak of England by the name of Home. The trees in this lane are planted with care and skill; but I notice, not without curiosity, that in the midst of so much order, one apple-tree stands a little from the line. "How do you prevent the passers-by — the lane being a public highway — from snatching at the fruit and injuring your trees?" The Elder smiles; if the flush of light in his soft blue eyes can be called a smile. "Look at yon tree," says he, "a little in front of the rest; that is our sentinel; it bears a large, sweet apple, which ripens a fortnight before the others; and it is easy for every one to reach. Those who want an apple pluck one from its boughs, and leave the other trees untouched." Is it always true, that the children of this world are wiser in their generation than the children of light?

Every man among the brethren has a trade; some of them have two, even three or four trades. No one may be an idler, not even under the pretence of study, thought, and contemplation. Every one must take his part in the family business; it may be farming, building, gardening, smith-work, painting; every one must follow his occupation, however high his rank and calling in the church. Frederick is a gardener and an architect. We have been out this afternoon seeing an orchard of apple-trees which he has planted, the great barn which he has built, and I have good grounds for concluding that this orchard, this barn, are the finest works of their kind in the United States. The Shakers believe in variety of labor, for variety of occupation is a source of pleasure, and pleasure is the portion meted out by an indulgent Father to his Saints.

The ladies at Mount Lebanon—all these sisters are ladies in speech, in manner, in garb—have no outdoor work to perform; some are employed in the kitchen, some in waiting on others (duties which they take in turn, a month for each course), some in weaving cloth, some in preserving fruit, some in distilling essences, some in making fans and knick-knacks. Maple syrup is an article for which they have a good demand; they make rose-water, cherry-water, peach-water; they sew, they sing, they teach children, and teach them very well. Their school is said to be one of the best for a good general education in New York State.

CHAPTER XLIV.

SHAKER UNION.

VERY little study of the work of the followers of Ann Lee will serve to show that Shakerism, as an actual fact in the domestic life of America (whatever we may think about its origin), is far from being a mere folly, to be seen on a Sunday morning with a party of ladies, a diversion between the early dinner and the afternoon drive, to be wondered at, laughed over, and then forgotten as a thing of no serious consequence to the world. Mount Lebanon is the centre of a system which has a distinct genius, a strong organization, a perfect life of its own, through which it would appear to be helping to shape and guide, in no slight and unseen measure, the spiritual career of the United States.

In many of their ideas the Shakers would appear to be followers of the Essenes, and in the higher regions of emotion they seem to be wielding the same sort of power as that Hebrew society of bee-masters and seedsmen.

Their church is based on these grand ideas: — The kingdom of heaven has come; Christ has actually appeared on earth; the personal rule of God has been restored. In the wake of these ideas, dependent upon them follow many more: — the old law is abolished; the command to multiply has ceased; Adam's sin has been atoned; the intercourse of heaven and earth has been restored; the curse is taken away from labor; the earth, and all that is on it, will be redeemed; angels and spirits have become, as of old, the familiars and ministers of men.

Only the elect, it is said, are aware of these mighty changes having taken place on the earth; for the many are blind and deaf, as they were of old, knowing not the Lord when He calls them into union. A few are chosen by the grace of God, and in the hearts of His own elected ones He reigns and works. On being called by Him, men die to the world, forgetting in their new and heavenly stage of existence its rivalries, and pleasures, and its passions. In the firm belief of these people, the call which they obey is not to a mere change of life, but to a new life of the soul, in which the world has no share. Birth and marriage are at an end; death itself has become to them only a change of dress, a shedding of the visible robe of flesh for an invisible glory of the spirit.

These fundamental ideas control the Shaker policy, inward and outward.

Thus, no man can be born into their body, as no member of their church can marry. In union, as they say it is in heaven, the sexes must dwell apart; love must be celibate, in spirit and in fact, shedding its worldly and unregenerate relations with the flesh. Most of those who come into union at Mount Lebanon are young men and girls, such as in Italy and Spain would go into monasteries and convents; but when married people enter, they must agree in future to live apart, in chastity and obedience, pure from all fancies and desires of their olden life. Again, no man may be drawn by lures of the world into union with their body, since the elected ones are strictly forbidden to make use of any lure, any argument, with the Gentile. God, it is said, in His own time, in His own way, will draw to Himself the men whom He has made His own. The Shaker union being considered by them as the heavenly kingdom, they are to have no part in the task of peopling it with Saints; for the children of grace can be called into His rest by none but God. Heaven must be sought of man; she will never again go forth to seek; her day of missionary work being past.

If the community of Saints gives much to a member, it demands much as the price of his fellowship. When a man is led upwards of the spirit into a yearning after peace, he must offer at the gates of Mount Lebanon everything which a man of the world would prize: his wealth, his ease, his glory, his affections; for what is earth to heaven, and what is man in the sight of God? Before an applicant can be received into this society, he must throw his possessions into a common fund; he must consent to labor with his hands for the general good; he must forget all ranks and titles of the world; he must abandon his house and kin, his books and friends; he must tear himself away from his wife and child. On these high terms, and on no other, can a Gentile enter into the Shakers' rest.

Yet thousands of persons enter into union. Mount Lebanon is but one of eighteen Shaker societies, which are scattered throughout these United States. Besides New Lebanon, there are two other settlements in New York State, namely: Water Vliet, in Albany county (the original Shaker society), and Groveland, in Livingston county. There are four villages in Massachusetts: Hancock (the birthplace of Lucy Wright) and Tyringham in Berkshire county, Harvey and Shirley in Middlesex county; two in New Hampshire: Enfield in Grafton county, Canterbury in Merrimac county; two in Maine: Alfred in York county, New Gloucester in Cumberland county; one village in Connecticut: Enfield in Hartford county (the birthplace of Meacham, the Shaker Moses); four villages in Ohio:

White Water in Hamilton county, Water Vliet in Montgomery county, Union village in Warren county, and North Union in Cuyahoga county; two in Kentucky: Pleasant Hill in Mercer county, and South Union in Logan county. In spite of their hard life,—what may seem to us their very hard life,—the Shakers increase in number; the census of 1860 reporting them as more than six thousand strong.

Of course, when they are measured against the thirty millions of Christian people living in the United States, some six or seven thousand celibate Shakers may appear of but small account; and this would be the truth, if the strength of spiritual and moral forces could be told in figures, like that of a herd of cattle and a kiln of bricks. But if numbers are much, they are far from being all. One man with ideas may be worth a Parliament, an army,—nay, a whole nation without them. The Shakers may not be scholars and men of genius. In appearance they are often very simple; but they are men with ideas, men capable of sacrifice. Unlike the mass of mankind, who live to make money, the Shakers soar above the level of all common vices and temptations, and from the height of their unselfish virtue, offer to the worn and wearied spirit a gift of peace and a place of rest.

No one can look into the heart of American society without seeing that these Shaker unions have a power upon men beyond that of mere numbers. If a poll-tax were decreed, they might pay less into the exchequer than the Seceders, the Second Adventists, the Schwenkfelders, and the Jews; but their influence on the course of American thought is out of all comparison with that of such minor sects. The Shakers have a genius, á faith, an organization; which are not only strange, but seductive; which have been tried in the fire of persecution, and which are hostile to society as it stands. A Shaker village is not only a new church, but a new nation. These people, who have just been out with me in the fields and lanes, know nothing of New York, of the United States. They are not Americans; and have no part in the politics and quarrels so often raging around them. They vote for no President; they hold no meetings; they want nothing from the White House. The right to think, vote, speak, and travel, is to them but an idle dream; they live with angels, and are more familiar (as they tell me) with the dead than with the living. Sister Mary, who was sitting in my room not an hour ago, close to my hand, and leaning on this Bible, which then lay open at the Canticles, told me that the room was full of spirits; of beings as palpable, as audible to her, as my own figure and my own voice. The dreamy look, the wandering eye, the rapt expression, would have alarmed me for her state of health; only that I know with what sweet decorum she conducts her life, and with what subtile fingers she makes damson tarts. Frederick has the same beliefs; if you like the word better, the same illusions. What need can such a people have for votings and palavers? God is their only right; obedience to His will their only freedom.

That such a community should be able to exist in the United States, is a sign; that it should have seized upon men's affections, that it should have become popular and prosperous, growing without effort, conquering without conflict, drawing towards itself many pure, unselfish persons from the adjoining towns and states, is little less than a judgment on our churches. And such, in truth, the Shakers call it.

On entering into union with the believers, then, a convert must withdraw himself from the world; paying off all debts, discharging all bonds and trusts, renouncing all contracts, cancelling all wills and settlements, giving up all friends and kinsmen, as though he were parted from them by the grave. Indeed, the call which he receives from God is to be accepted as a proof that his past life as a sinful creature is at an end:—in final words, the flesh is deposed and the world put away.

On being received into the union, he no longer regards the earth as a spoil to be won, but as a pledge to be redeemed. By man it fell, by man it may be restored. Every one chosen of the Father has the privilege of aiding in this redemption; not only by the toil of his hands, by the contrivance of his brain, but by the sympathy of his soul; covering the world with verdure, filling the air with perfume, storing the granary with fruit.

The spirit in which he puts his hand out is a new one to him. Hitherto, the earth has been his servant; now it is his partner, bound to him by celestial ties. He looks at the face of nature with a lover's eyes, and the great passions of his heart, directed from his money, from his wife, now turn upon the garden and the field. But he understands that labor alone is not enough; he knows that the laborer must be worthy of his task, that this fanaticism must be guided by angelic wisdom. According to Shaker theories, the earth has been accursed and darkened by human passions, and must be redeemed into beauty by human love. Man makes the landscape smile and frown; the plant you train will grow into your likeness; and if you would have a lovely garden, you should live a lovely life. Such at least is the Shakers' thought.

My Gentile brother, if we were to flout this notion

as a crazy dream, the fact would still remain, and we should have to account for it as we might, that these Shakers get more out of the earth by love, than we get by our craft. This fact is not a thing to be disputed and denied; the evidence is found in a hundred Broadway stores and London shops. If we deny that the earth will answer love by love, we are bound to explain the beauty and fertility of Mount Lebanon in some other way.

This morning I have spent an hour with Frederick in the new orchard, listening to the story of how he planted it, as to a tale by some Arabian poet. "A tree has its wants and wishes," said the Elder; "and a man should study them as a teacher watches a child, to see what he can do. If you love the plant, and take heed of what it likes, you will be well repaid by it. I don't know if a tree ever comes to know you; and I think it may; but I am sure it feels when you care for it and tend it; as a child does, as a woman does. Now, when we planted this orchard, we first got the very best cuttings in our reach; we then built a house for every plant to live in, that is to say, we dug a deep hole for each; we drained it well; we laid down tiles and rubble, and then filled in a bed of suitable manure and mould; we put the plant into its nest gently, and pressed up the earth about it, and protected the infant tree by this metal fence." "You take a world of pains," I said. "Ah, Brother Hepworth," he rejoined, "thee sees we love our garden."

Thus, when a Shaker is put upon the soil, to beautify it by his tilth, the difference between his husbandry and that of a Gentile farmer, who is thinking solely of his profits, is likely to be great. While the Gentile is watching for his returns, the Shaker is intent upon his service. One tries for large profits, the other strives for good work. Is it strange that a celibate man, who puts his soul into the soil — who gives to it all the affection which he would otherwise have lavished on wife and child — should excel a mere trading rival in the production of fruits and flowers?

CHAPTER XLV.

MOTHER ANN.

SITTING with Elder Frederick, who has been taking much pains to make me understand his intricate and difficult code of morals, I have heard how these seedsmen and florists of Mount Lebanon have been made what they are in skill, in gentleness, in temperance — in all the virtues which they display — through loyal obedience to the lessons taught them by Ann Lee; a female saint, who is only known to her followers by the august and holy name of Mother. She may be spoken of as Mother Ann.

As a distinct and sacred people, the Shakers have this peculiar boast among American churches — that, while they are wholly of the New World in thought, in feeling, and in platform, having no life beyond these great waters, they draw the original germ of their existence from the old paternal soil. If they are called to an American paradise, the messenger of heaven who called them into rest was a female English seer.

About a hundred years ago, a poor woman, living at Bolton-on-the-Moors, a bleak and grimy town, in the most stony part of South Lancashire, announced that she had received a call from heaven to go about the streets of her native town and testify for the truth. Her name was Jane; her husband, James Wardlaw, a tailor, with gifts of speech, had become her first convert and expositor. These poor people had previously belonged to the Society of Friends; in which they had been forward in bearing testimony against oaths, against war, against formality in worship. Living in a hard and rocky district, in the midst of a coarse and brutal population, Jane had seen about her, from her youth upwards, a careless church, a Papist gentry, a drunken and fanatical crowd. Going out into the market-place, she had declared to these people, that the end of all things was at hand, that Christ was about to reign, that His second appearance would be in a woman's form, as had been long ago prefigured in the Psalms. Jane had never said that she herself was the female Christ; but she had acted as though she believed that all the powers of earth and heaven had been given into her hands; receiving converts in His name, confessing and remitting sins, holding communication with unseen spirits. It was assumed by her own people that she was filled with the Holy Ghost; and whatsoever thing she affirmed, in the power of her attendant spirits, had been received by her followers as the voice of God. But her reign had not been long.

Among the early converts of this female witness had been a girl named Ann Lee, daughter of a poor blacksmith; a girl of parts, though she had never been taught to read and write. Born in Toad Lane (now Todd Street), Manchester, a lane of ale-houses and smithies, Ann had been brought up, first in a cotton mill, next in a public kitchen; a wild creature from her birth, a prey to hysteria and convulsions; violent in her conduct, ambitious of notice, and devoured by the lust of power. Like many girls of her class, she had been married while she was yet a child; married to a neighboring lad, a smith of the name of Stanley; a man poorer even than herself. To this man she had borne four infants, all of whom had died in their tender years; and these losses of the young mother may have touched her mind with a morbid repugnance to the offices and duties attending on a woman's share in our common conjugal life. Joining the sect of Jane Wardlaw, Ann also had begun to sally forth into the streets and witness for the truth; lecturing the blacksmiths of Toad Lane, the weavers of New Cross, on the things to come, until the prosy old parish constable had seized her as a nuisance, and the magistrate had sent her to jail as a disturber of the public peace. While she was lying in prison — Old Bailey prison, on the Irwell — she said a light had shone upon her, and the Lord Jesus had stood before her in the cell, and become one with her in form and spirit. Jane Wardlaw had never yet pretended to have wrestled with so high a power; and when Ann Lee came out of prison, the little church of six or seven persons to whom she told her story, had raised her to the rank of Mother, in place of their foundress, the tailor's wife.

A feminine church had been now openly proclaimed in Manchester and Bolton, with Mother Ann as that queen who was described by David, as that Bride of the Lamb who was seen in the Apocalypse by John. Christ, it was now proclaimed, had come again; not in His pomp and power, as the world expected Him, but in the flesh of a factory girl, who could neither read nor write.

As the rough lads and lasses of her native town had only laughed at this pretence of a female church, Ann had received a second revelation from heaven, commanding her to shake the dust of Toad Lane from her feet, to gather up the sheep of her tiny fold, and to seek for them, and for herself, a home in the Promised Land. The spirits who waited upon her, angels and ministers, had drawn her thoughts to America, as the hope of free men and the seat of God's future church. Five males (William Lee, James Whittaker, John Hocknell, Richard Hocknell, James Shepherd), and two females (Mary Partington and Nancy Lee) had been minded to cast in their lot with her; and although the master of the ship in which they sailed from Liverpool had threatened, on the voyage out, to pitch them all into the sea for what he called their indecent conduct, Ann, with her husband Stanley, and her seven disciples, had landed safely in the bay of New York.

The only one of this little band who had felt no true faith in Mother Ann was her husband; but in spite of his want of grace, she had proceeded, on their reaching the Promised Land, to put her gospel of abstinence into force; insisting on the need for living a holy life, and separating herself, a Bride of the Lamb, from her husband's side. Her fixed idea had been, that she and her people should make eternal war against the flesh. By lust man fell from heaven; by abstinence from carnal thoughts he might hope to regain his celestial rank. No form of earthly love could be tolerated in the Redeemer's kingdom. Men called into grace must live as the angels live; among whom there is neither marrying nor giving in marriage. Every member, therefore, of her church had been compelled to renounce his yearning after love; the wives consenting to dwell in a house apart from their husbands, the husbands in a house apart from their wives. They had put to themselves this question: If all men, born into the world, are born in sin, and made the heirs of death in the world to come, how can the Saint, when raised from his fallen nature, dare to augment this empire of sin and death?

It would have been hard for Stanley to answer that question from Mother Ann's point of view, otherwise than as she answered it; but her husband, though he could not give his reasons, had felt that, as a married man, he was being badly used. He was no mystic; and when his wife had put her self-denying ordinance into force against him, he had taken up (I am grieved to write it) with another woman of New York. Mother Ann had left him, and had left New York City, going up the Hudson River as far as Albany, then a small frontier town, facing the great wilderness towards the west. Even there her people had found the world too much with them. Pushing out into the back-woods, to a spot then known to the red-skins as Niskenna, they had built log shanties, and taken up their abode in the green waste, founding the township now so famous as Water Vliet, the original Shaker settlement in New York.

For three years and six months these strangers had waited in their lonely huts, clearing the forest, tilling the soil, rearing bees and fowls, and waiting for a sign from heaven. They had made no efforts to convert the Gentiles. They had fled from, rather than sought, the society of men. They had preached no sermons, printed no books, written no letters, announced no gospel. Desolation could hardly have been more complete than they found on the Hudson River at Niskenna. But this nest of seven believers in Mother Ann's divine commission, being comforted by angels of the night, had waited and watched for the promised coming in of the Saints. At length their faith in her promises had been crowned by wonders. A religious revival which had broken out in Albany, spread into the villages of Hancock and New Lebanon, where it had caught up, in its electrical vortices, many substantial sinners, including, among other well-to-do people, Joseph Meacham and Lucy Wright. Joseph and Lucy, with some of their neighbors who had heard of the coming of Ann Lee, had gone over the hills to Niskenna, as a deputation from the revivalist camp (Spring of 1780), and after seeing her way of life, hearing her words of peace, and being told of the appearance to her in the Manchester jail, they had embraced her creed, admitted her right, and become her first disciples on the American soil. Meacham had been adopted by Ann as her eldest son; and the Mother had then declared that, after her time, the power would be given unto him from God to put the kingdom of heaven into perfect order. The result of this visit of Lucy and Joseph to Mother Ann had been the foundation of the Shaker societies in Hancock and Mount Lebanon.

Ann had now fallen into trouble, the inheritance of seers and prophets from of old. The War of Independence being at that time brisk, and the people ardent in the cause, the farmers and woodmen of New York had taken up the notion that these Shakers, who raised their voices against war as the devil's work, had come into the land as enemies, perhaps as spies; a charge which the gentry of Albany told Ann and her disciples they must rebut by taking the colonial oaths. But how were they to take the colonial oaths, seeing that their principles forbade them to swear at all? First, Meacham and the men, afterwards Ann and the women, had been thrown into jail, where they had been visited by many people, and become a topic of discourse throughout New York. Instead of calming men's minds and putting Ann down, the gentry of Albany soon found that they had been the means of spreading the fame of this strange prophetess through their colony, into both the English and American camps. What could they do with a prisoner who told them she was the female Christ? They had thought her crazy, and they had fancied, she being an English-born woman, that it would be well to send her with a pass into the British lines. With that end in view, she had been sent down the river, but the plan could not be carried into effect on account of the war; and, in the meantime, she had been lodged for security in Poughkeepsie jail, where she held a little court of her own among her attendant spirits, and left behind her in that town, when she quitted it, memories and influences which have taken shapes in the Spiritualist theories of a later time.

Set free by Governor Clinton (December, 1780), Ann had come out of prison a famous woman; and after three months had been spent by her at Water Vliet, in the midst of her male and female elders, she started on a tour of exhibition, visiting Harvard in Massachusetts, and many other places in the New England colonies, increasing the number of her disciples, and providing the materials for her future model societies. Her work had been long and toilsome; not without profit to her in many ways; but after twenty-eight months had been spent in these travels, she had returned to Water Vliet, near the Hudson River, in September, 1783, wasted in vigor, though she seemed to have become sublimed in spirit. One winter and one summer more she had held on to her task, but in the fall of 1784, she had gathered her disciples round her, given them a promise and a blessing, and after yielding up the visible keys of her kingdom to Joseph and Lucy, as her successors in the male and female headships of the kingdom of God, she had passed away from their sight.

According to the doctrines now held by the Shaker church, Mother Ann did not die, as mortal men and women die; she became changed to the world, transfigured and transformed, made invisible to the flesh through excess of light. From what I have heard and read, it seems to me probable that some of Ann's people were amazed at her disappearance—an event on which they had not counted; nor could they reconcile it with her story of that second advent in the Manchester jail, where their Lord had taken flesh in a woman's form. Their faith appears to have been sorely tried; but Joseph Meacham and Lucy Wright—the divinely appointed king and queen of the new kingdom—had proved themselves equal to the moment. With the corpse of Ann before them, they had stoutly affirmed that she was not dead. The queen foretold by David could never die; the Bride whom John had seen in his vision could never sink into the grave. The Queen had been covered with robes of light; the Bride had passed into the secret chamber. Ann had withdrawn herself for a little while from the world, which had no part in her; but she would live and reign forever amongst her own true children of the resurrection. The dust before them was nothing but a worn-out garment which the Mother had cast away.

Joseph and Lucy had caused this dust to be lifted up, and put away in a field, not in any sacred place, in any consecrated ground, where it might rest in peace for the final rising; but in a common field, where it might soon be lost and forgotten, where in time the plough would go through it, causing it to mingle with the earth from which it had been drawn. A Shaker expects no further rising of the dead. In his conviction, the dead are now risen, and are even now rising. To be called into grace, is the same as being raised from the dead into a new life. Frederick and Antoinette believe that they have passed through the shadow, that they will die no more, that when their season comes they will only be withdrawn, like Mother Ann, from the world. They are living now, they are firmly convinced, in the Resurrection Order.

CHAPTER XLVI.

RESURRECTION ORDER.

When Joseph Meacham and Lucy Wright had put the dust of Mother Ann away, telling her people that she had only changed her raiment, being clothed in her celestial robes as Bride of the Lamb, all difficulties appear to have been conquered, and the faith of the wavering to have been made strong. The doctrine was seductive and bewitching. Ann was still living in their midst; in dreams, in ecstasies, they could see her, they could hear her voice. The change which had come upon her would one day come upon them. How glorious for the saints to think that Death is but a change in the costume of life; that the dissolving soul dies only to the flesh; that the glory to which the elect attain conceals them from the world, but leaves them visible to eyes, audible to ears, which have been purified and exalted by the gift of grace!

To this dogma of the existence of a world of spirits —unseen by us, visible to them—the disciples of Mother Ann most strictly hold. In this respect, they agree with the Spiritualists; indeed, they pride themselves on having foretold the advent of this spiritual disturbance in the American mind. Frederick tells me (from his angels), that the reign of this spiritualistic frenzy is only in its opening phase; it will sweep through Europe, through the world, as it is sweeping now through America; it is a real phenomenon, based on facts, and representing an actual, though an unseen force. Some of its professors, he admits, are cheats and rogues; but that is in the nature of spirit-movements, seeing that you have evil angels as well as good angels. Man is not the only deceiver. If men are false, is there not one who is the father of lies? When the higher and nether world shall have come yet nearer to the earth—in the riper days of the Resurrection—both good and evil spirits may be expected to have greater power on earth.

Antoinette, who has just been sitting in my room, asserts that she talks with spirits more freely and confidingly than she does with me; yet I cannot see that Antoinette is crazy on any other point, and she certainly makes neat and sensible speeches. This room, in which I am writing—the guest-chamber of North House—which seems to me empty and still, is to her full of seraphim and cherubim, who keep on singing and haranguing the livelong day. Mother Ann is here present; Lucy and Joseph are present; all the brethren who have passed out of human sight are present—to her. You have only to watch Antoinette for a moment, when you are not yourself engaging her attention, to see, by her hushed face, by her rapt eye, by her wandering manner, that she believes herself in another presence, more revered, more august, than anything of earth. Yes; those whom we Gentiles call the dead are with her; and by this ethereal process of belief, the brethren of Mount Lebanon have conquered death and put an end to the grave.

This morning, when Antoinette first came into my room, I thought she was very grave and sweet; in her hand she held a paper, as though she had brought it in to show me; and on my inquiring what it was about she laid it on my table, saying it was a song which she had heard in the night, sung by angelic choirs. My eyes ran towards it; and from her way of speaking I could see that she meant to give it me as a parting token. "Sign it, Sister Antoinette," I said, "and let me have it." She wrote her name on the margin of this song; from a perusal of which the reader will see that either the copyist mistook some of the seraphic words, or else that the angels are not particular as to syntax and rhyme.

Let us ascend the heavenly scale,
  In purity be rising;
In deeds of charity and love
  Let not our souls be wanting.

On the immortal hills of truth
  Are flowers eternal blooming;
I long to breathe that fragrant air,
To join my voice with angels there,
  So sweetly they are singing.

I do not understand Antoinette to say that this hymn was made by the seraphs expressly for me. She is too simple to indulge in jests; and I could not hurt her mind by any lay remark. Perhaps it may be as well to add that all the chants and marches used by the Shakers in their services are learnt in dreams and reveries. None of their sacred poetry is very good, according to our secular canons, though some of it has a lilt, a fire, that would make effective verse if it had only been managed with a little more art. I have rarely heard a finer effect, of its kind, in music than that produced in the frame church on Mount Lebanon by four or five hundred Shakers, men and women, marching to this chant:

To the bright Elysian fields,
In the Spirit-land I go!
Leaving all inferior joys,
All pleasures below.

For my spirit reaches upward,
To that celestial land,
Where, by the power of truth and love,
The Saints as sisters stand.

The murmuring of the waters,
From the troubled sea of time,
Can never reach the peaceful shores
Of that pure, that happy clime,
Where angels the banners of love gently wave,
And where saints do triumph over death and the grave!

If we may judge by the rules established in this lower world, your angels make much better tunes than rhymes. The Shakers' marches are often very fine.

To Joseph Meacham, Mother Ann's first adopted son on the American soil, and to Lucy, her daughter and successor in the female sphere, the government of this Church descended by divine appointment; and their rule, which is beyond appeal, was made more easy to them by the promise of their departed founder. "The time will come," Mother Ann had said, "when the Church will be gathered into order;

but not until after my decease. Joseph Meacham is my first-born son in America; he will gather the Church into order; but I shall not live to see it." And with this promise on her lips she had passed out of mortal sight.

As yet, the believers in Mother Ann being the second incarnation of Christ, had been scattered through the world, living in it bodily for the greater part, though they were not of it in the spirit. Joseph and Lucy had drawn these believers apart into settlements: to Water Vliet and Mount Lebanon in New York, to Harvard and Shirley in Massachusetts, to Enfield in Connecticut, to Canterbury in New Hampshire, to Union Village and White Water in Ohio, to Pleasant Hill and South Union in Kentucky. Under their rule, a covenant had been written down and accepted by the brethren. The divine government had been confirmed: elders and deacons, female as well as male, had been appointed; celibacy had been confirmed as binding on the Saints, and community of goods had been introduced among them. When Joseph had also passed out of sight in 1796, he had bequeathed an undivided power to Lucy, who then became the leader, representing Mother Ann, and for five-and-twenty years governing these Shaker societies with the powers of a female Pope. When her time had also come, she named her successor; for who, unless the chosen, shall have the right to choose? But she had named an Elderess, not a Mother; and since her day the title of Mother has been abandoned, no female saint having sprung up among them worthy to bear so august a name. The present female leader of the Society is Betsy Bates; she is simply called Elderess Betsy; she represents the Mother only in the body, for Ann is thought to be herself present among her children in the spirit. The chief elder and successor to Joseph is Daniel Boler, who may be regarded as the Shaker bishop; but the active power of the Society (as I fancy) lies with Elder Frederick, the official preacher and expositor of Shaker doctrine. If the Shaker communities should undergo any change in our day, through the coming in of other lights, I fancy that the change will have to be brought about through him. Frederick is a man of ideas, and men of ideas are dangerous persons in a Society which affects to have adopted its final form. Boler represents the divine principle, Frederick the art and government of the world.

The Family at North House contains two orders of members, (1) Probationers, (2) Covenanters. The first are men and women who have come in for a time, to see how they like it, and whether it likes them. Men in this early stage of the celestial trial retain their private fortunes, and maintain some slight relation to the Gentile world. Men of the second stage may be said, in effect, to have taken the vow of chastity, and to have cast in their lot for good and evil with the brethren. The chiefs have very little trouble, Frederick tells me, with the novices, for any one may go out when he pleases, taking all that he brought in away with him. A poor fellow who puts in nothing, is generally sent away, if he desires to leave, with a hundred dollars in his purse. The rich men give less trouble than the poor, being generally persons of higher culture and of more earnest spirit. One of my female friends in the community, Sister Jane, came in as a child with her father, Abel Knight, one of the first citizens of Philadelphia. She is young, pretty, educated, rich; but she has given up the world and its delights; and if ever I saw a happy-looking damsel, it is Sister Jane.

As regards their notions of the duty of living a celibate life, there is (as Elder Frederick tells me) a great mistake abroad. They do not hold that a celibate life is right in every place and in every society, at all times; they know, that if the rule of absolute self-denial were commonly adopted, the world would be unpeopled in a hundred years; but they say that marriage is a state of temptation to many (as wine-drinking is a state of temptation to many), and they consider that for a male and female priesthood, such as they hold themselves to be as respects the world, this temptation is to be put away. That claim of being a sort of priesthood of the Saints, appointed to serve God and to redeem the world from sin, runs through the whole of their institutions. To this end, indeed, they have passed through death and the resurrection into a state of grace. To this end they have adopted the rule of absolute submission of their own will to the will of God. "We admit," says Frederick, "two orders in the world — one of Generation, one of Resurrection." They claim to stand in the Resurrection order; to them, therefore, the love which leads men into marriage is not allowed. We Gentiles stand in the Generation order, therefore the love which ends in marriage is still for a time allowed. "Generation," says Frederick, "is a great foe to Regeneration, and we give up what is called our manhood as a sacrifice for the world."

"You mean to say, then, that in fact you are offering yourselves as an atonement?" He paused a moment; his blue eyes closed, and when he opened them again, slowly, as if waking from a trance, he smiled.

"The Order of the Resurrection," he added, "is

celibate, spiritual; in it there is no marriage; only love and peace."

In their social economy, as in their moral sentiment, these Shakers follow the ancient Essenes. They drink no wine, they eat no pork. They live upon the land, and shun the society of towns. They cultivate the virtues of sobriety, prudence, meekness. They take no oaths, they deprecate law, they avoid contention, they repudiate war. They affect to hold communion with the dead. They believe in angels and in spirits, not as a theological dogma, but as a practical human fact.

One circumstance which gives to the Shaker society an importance in the Union far beyond its rivals (Tunkers, Moravians, Mennonites, Schwenkfelders), is the fact of its being much devoted to the work of education. Every Shaker settlement is a school; a centre from which ideas are circulated right and left, into every corner of the land. Men who would laugh at the pretensions of Mother Ann, if they stood alone, can hardly help being touched, if not seduced, in spirit, by avowals like these now following:—

The church of the future is an American Church.

The old law is abolished, the new dispensation begun.

Intercourse between heaven and earth is restored.

God is king and governor.

The sin of Adam is atoned, and man made free of all errors except his own.

Every human being will be saved.

The earth is heaven, now soiled and stained, but ready to be brightened by love and labor into its primeval state.

These propositions, which display the genius of Shakerism so far as it pretends to be a social and political power, at war with the principles and practices of a republican government, are apt to fascinate many men who would object to a celibate life, to a female priest, to a community of goods. With more or less of clearness in avowal, these principles will be found in the creed of every new American church.

CHAPTER XLVII.

SPIRITUAL CYCLES.

AND how, we begin to ask, so soon as we have left the witcheries of Mount Lebanon behind us, and begun to look on the matter with a purely secular eye, are these eighteen settlements of Shakers recruited? In Rome, in Seville, convents may be fed from the lay society in which the laws of increase hold their natural sway; but in Enfield, at Mount Lebanon, in Groveland, no lay community of Shakers stands outside the church, from which the losses by death can be repaired. The whole church being celibate, the losses by death are fixed and final; so many to the year; the whole generation in thirty years. Calls, fresh calls, must be made under pain of extinction; but how are men called from a busy world, from a prosperous society, into a life of labor, chastity, confinement, and obedience? In Italy and Spain, it is found an uneasy task to persuade young men to renounce the affections, even for an indolent service. Nature is strong, and a life without love appears to many of us worse than a tomb. One great branch of the Christian Church, the

Latin, has adopted celibacy in principle, making it the rule for its clergy of all ranks, and fostering the practice in its lay societies; but her success in this particular branch of her policy has hardly equalled her efforts; and in no country of Europe, even in Sicily and Andalusia, has she found willing recruits, except when she has taken them from the world at an early age, and exercised upon them her most potent spells. The Greek, the Armenian, the Lutheran, the Anglican churches, have ceased to fight against nature, though they are all inclined, perhaps, to assign some merit to a virgin life, and to desire a celibate condition for a section of their priests. In all these churches there is something like a balance of advantages in what is given and what is withheld. The position of a priest, of a monk, is one of high respect in the sight of men. The service to which he is called is noble and popular; one conferring rank and power, the right to stand among the highest, to be exempted from labor, to be protected from violence, to be free of great houses, and to find a welcome at good men's feasts. The Shaker has none of these dignities, none of these pleasures to expect in return for his pledge of chastity; in their stead, he has before him a daily task, coarse fare, and an ugly dress.

Under a missionary like Khaled, we can imagine converts being made to the Shaker Church; a man who offered you a choice of either Shakerism or death, might be expected to bring proselytes to the fold; but then, these believers have no Khaleds among them; they employ no sword, they exercise no fascination of the tongue and pen. Where then do they find recruits? Is the keen New Englander anxious to give up his will, his freedom, and his intellect, in exchange for a fixed belief, a daily drill, and a peasant's toil? Is the rich

New Yorker bent on stripping himself of his costly mansion, his splendid equipage, in favor of a coarse habit, a rood of land, and a narrow cell? Is the smart Kentuckyian ready to forswear his rank, his office, his ambition, for a life of daily labor, abstinence, and care?

"No," said Elder Frederick, in one of my parting conversations, "not in ordinary times. In God's own time he must and will; being then divinely touched and rapt, and acting in the spirit of a wisdom higher than the world. It is chiefly in our spiritual cycles that the elect are called."

When the seasons come and go at their usual pace, when the air is still and the minds of men are tranquil, the rich New Yorker, the smart Kentuckyian, would no more dream of coming into union, than of going to live in a Pawnee wigwam or a negro shed. But in the day of spiritual wrath, when the vials are being opened on the land, when sinners run staggering up and down, when the colleges are mute, and the churches of the world stricken dumb, then heaven itself comes forward into line, and, working through her unseen forces, draws to herself the rich, the daring, and the worldly spirit, as easily as a little child. In the hands of God, we are only as the potter's clay. The strong will bends, the proud heart breaks, in His frown. It has been in the midst of these moral and spiritual commotions, that all the new creeds, all the new societies, of America have either risen or gathered strength; not the poor Tunkers, the aggressive Mormons, the celibate Shakers only; but the powerful Methodists, the prosperous Baptists, the rigid Presbyterians, the fervent Universalists. The Episcopal Church, and the Roman Church, may stand aloof; the educated and refining intellect of these elder branches of the Christian society holding that the teachings of Christ and His chosen apostles were final, that the age of miracle is past, and that the gospels are complete. The members of these great conservative churches may ask no day of an especial grace; they may doubt the origin, the efforts, and the fruits of these periodical awakenings of the spirit. They may choose to walk in the old paths, to avoid novelties and eccentricities, to keep their flocks from excitements and illusions. But the younger rivals for dominion, acting, as they say, in the apostolic missionary spirit, have been prompt to seize upon all occasions of drawing souls into the Church. All the new sects and societies of America have wrought, and not without success, in this great field of conversion; the Shakers in a spirit less eager and more confident than the rest. Other sects regard a revival as a movement in the mind inviting them to labor for the good of souls; the Shakers look upon it as a Spiritual Cycle—the end of an epoch—the birth of a new society. Only in the fervor of a revival, says Elder Frederick, can the elect be drawn to God:—that is to say, in a Gentile phrase, drawn into a Shaker settlement. Mount Lebanon sprang from a revival; Enfield sprang from a revival; in fact, the Shakers declare that every large revival being the accomplishment of a Spiritual Cycle, must end in the foundation of a fresh Shaker union.

Thus, it would appear that this wild and weird phenomenon in the religious kingdom, which some of our Gentile clergy deem an accident, an illusion, answering to no law of life, is to the Shakers the effect of a special providence. Angels are employed upon the work. In the Shaker economy a revival has, therefore, a place, a function, and a power. It is their time of vintage; when the shoots, which they have not planted, bring them grapes, when the presses, which they have not filled, yield them oil. They reckon on these periodical revivals as the husbandman reckons on the spring and fall; waiting for the increase which their spiritual cycles bring them, just as the farmers expect their hay-time and their harvest-home.

When the last Ulster revival broke out, I happened to be in Derry; and, having watched the course of that spiritual hurricane from Derry to Belfast, I am able to say that, excepting the scenery and the manners, a revival in Ulster is very much the same thing as a spiritual cycle in Ohio and Indiana.

In this country, the religious passion breaks out, like a fever, in the hottest places and in the wildest parts; commonly on the frontiers of civilized states; always in a sect of extreme opinions, generally among the Ranters, the Tunkers, the Seventh-day Baptists, the Come-outers, and the Methodists.

Methodism, the large religion of America, if we may count the church by heads, was itself the offspring of a kind of revival. John Wesley had tried America, and failed; Whitfield had followed him, and succeeded; the time being more propitious to his work. The early preachers had won their way, as the revivalist preachers still carry on the fight; lodging roughly and faring coarsely; tramping up muddy ridges, sleeping on leaves and deer-skins, tenting among wolves and beavers; suffering from the red men, from the mean whites, from the besotted negroes; forcing their way into jails, gin-shops, and hells; searching out poverty, misery, and crime. The revivalist is a fanatic, if you like the word; he speaks from his hot blood, not from his cool head; his talk is a spasm, his eloquence a shriek; but while philosophers may smile and magistrates may frown at his ravings, the swarthy miner, the lusty backwoodsman, the sturdy farmer and carter, confess to the power of his discourse. He does the rough work of the spirit which no other man could do. Trench would be tame, Stanley inaudible, in the prairie; Wilberforce would faint, and Noel would die, of a year on the forest skirt.

Yet a camp-meeting, such as I have twice seen in the wilds of Ohio and Indiana, is a subject full of interest; not without touches, in its humor and its earnestness, to unlock the fountains of our smiles and tears. The hour may be five in the afternoon of a windless October day; when myriads of yellow flowers and red mosses light up the sward, when the leaves of the oak and the plane are deepening into brown, when the maples gleam with crimson, and the hickory drips with gold. Among the roots and boles of ancient trees, amidst buzzing insects and whirring birds, rise a multitude of booths and tents, with an aspect strange, yet homely: for while this camp of religious zealots is utterly unlike the lodgments of an Arab tribe, of an Indian nation, of any true pastoral people on the earth, it has features which recall to your eye and ear the laughters and sounds of an English fair and an Irish wake. Epsom on a Derby day is not so unlike a revival camp in the woods as many think. Carts and wagons are unhorsed; the animals tethered to the ground, or straying in search of grass. In a dozen large booths men are eating, drinking, smoking, praying. Some fellows are playing games; some lolling on the turf; others are lighting fires; many are cooking food. Those lads are cutting pines, these girls are getting water from the stream. In the centre of the camp, a pale rivivalist marabout, standing on the stump of a tree, is screeching and roaring to a wild, hot throng of listeners, most of them farmers and farmers' wives, from the settlements far and near; a sprinkling of negroes, in their dirty finery of shawl and petticoat; a few red men in their paint and feathers:—all equally ablaze with the orator himself, fierce partners in his zeal and feeders of his fire. His periods are broken by shouts and sobs; his gestures are answered by yells and groans. Without let, without pause, in his discourse, he goes tearing on, belching forth a hurricane of words and screams; while the men sit around him, white and still, writhing and livid, their lips all pressed, their hands all knotted, with the panic and despair of sin; and the women rush wildly about the camp, tossing up their arms, groaning out their confessions, casting themselves downward on the earth, swooning into sudden hysterics, straining at the eyes and foaming at the mouth; the staid Indian looking with contempt on these miseries of the white man's squaw, and the negroes breaking forth into sobs, and cries, and convulsive raptures of "Glory! glory, Alleluja!"

Many visitors fall sick, and some die in the camp. In the agonies of this strife against the power of sin and the fear of death (I am told by men who have often watched these spiritual tempests) the passions seem to be all unloosed, and to go astray without let or guide. "I like to hear of a revival," said to me a lawyer of Indianapolis; "it brings on a crop of cases." In the revivalist camp men quarrel, and fight, and make love to their neighbors' wives. A Methodist preacher of twenty-five years' experience, first in New England, then on the frontiers, afterwards on the battle-fields of Virginia, said to me, "Religious passion include all other passions; you cannot excite one without stirring up the others. In our Church we know the evil, and we have to guard against it as we may. The young men who get up revivals are always objects of suspicion to their elders; many go wrong, I would say one in twenty at the least; more, far more than that number bring scandal on the Church by their thoughtless behavior in the revivalist camps."

In a week, in a month, perhaps, the fire of religious zeal may begin to flicker and lie down. Quarrels break out, and bowie-knives are drawn. The cynical laugh, the indifferent drive away. Horses are now put up; wagons are laden with baggage and women; the publican strikes his tent; and the riff-raff goes in search of another field. One by one the brawlers are knocked off, until the marabout himself, disgusted with his hearers, ceases to give tongue. Then the last horse is saddled, the last cart is on the road, and nothing appears to have been left of that singular camp but a few burnt logs, a desecrated wood, and two or three freshly-made graves.

And is that all? The Shaker says, No. In the frenzies of that camp-meeting he detects a moral order, a spiritual beauty, utterly unseen by secular eyes. To him, a revival is God's own method of calling His children to Himself. Without a revival, there can be no resurrection on a large and inclusive scale: — and no revival, it is said by him, is ever quite wasted to the human race. Some soul is always drawn by it into the peace of heaven.

Frederick told me that every great spiritual revival which has agitated America since his Church was planted, has led to a new society being founded on the principles of Mother Ann. The eighteen unions represent eighteen revivals. According to Elder Frederick, who is watching with a keen and pitying eye the vagaries of the new spiritualist movements in America, a nineteenth revival is now at hand, from the action of which he expects a considerable extension of his Church.

CHAPTER XLVIII.

SPIRITUALISM.

During the past month of August, a crowd of Spiritualists has been holding conference in this picturesque port and peculiar city of Providence, Rhode Island.

The disciples came in troups from the east and the west; some being delegates from circles and cities, representing thousands who stayed at home; still more being disciples who scorned either to admit any rule or to express any one's opinions save their own. Eighteen States and Territories were represented on the platform by accredited members; more than half of them, it seems, by ladies. A first convention of Spiritualists, on a scale sufficiently vast to be called national, was held two years ago at Chicago; a second was held one year ago at Philadelphia; but in those two meetings, regarded by the zealous as experimental, the delegates came together less by choice than chance. Convenience of men and women, not moral significance, had ruled the selection of a place of meeting; but when a platform had been voted in Chicago, and a great appeal to the public had been made in Philadelphia, moral considerations came into play. The scene of the third National Convention of Spiritualists was fixed in this city, on account of the peculiar fame of Providence as a camp of heretics and reformers, — the refuge of Roger Williams, the home of religious toleration, the city of "What Cheer?"

Quiet observers of the scene were struck with the wild and intellectual appearance of this cloud of witnesses. Their eyes, I am told, were preternaturally bright; their faces preternaturally pale. Many of them practised imposition of hands. Nearly all of the men wore long hair; nearly all the women were closely cropped.

Pratt's Hall in Broad Street was engaged for the sittings: a capacious chamber, though not too large for the crowd of angels and of mortals who came pressing in. Yes, angels and mortals. Elderess Antoinette is not more certain that she sees and hears the dead than are all these hirsute men. In Broad Street, angels stood in the doorway, spectres flitted about the room. Their presence was admitted, their sympathy assumed, and their counsel sought. A dozen times the speakers addressed their words, not only to delegates present in the flesh, but to heavenly messengers who had come to them in the spirit.

L. K. Joslin, a leader in the local circles, welcomed the delegates to this city of refuge, in their character of heretics and infidels. "To-day," he said, addressing his mortal hearers, "the Spiritualists of the United States are the Great Heretics; and, *as such*, the Spiritualists of Providence greet you with their welcome, believing that you are infidel to the old heresies that cursed rather than blessed our whole humanity." These words appear to have been official; also what followed them, in reference to the celestial portion of his audience. "But not unto you alone," he said, with a solemn emphasis, "do we look for counsel, for inspiration, and the diviner harmonies. The congregation is greater than the seeming. There are others at the doors. Those of other ages, who were the morning lights to the world, fearless, true, and martyred in the earth-life for their devotion to the truth—the cherished wise and good of the long-ago, and the loved ones of the near past — they will manifest their interest in, and favor with their presence, the largest body of individuals on this continent who realize their actualized presence and power. And unto them, as unto you, we give the greeting." Loud applause, not hushed and reverent, I am told, responded to this welcome of the heavenly delegates.

John Pierpont, of Washington, an aged preacher (once a student of Yale College — the school of American prophets), in yielding the chair which he had held at Philadelphia, spoke of the term Infidel as applied to himself and his brethren in the spirit. "I am infidel," he exclaimed, "to a great many of the forms of popular religion; because I do not believe in many of the points which are held by a majority of the Christians, nay, even of the Protestant Church." He went on to say, that instead of putting his faith in creeds and canons, he put it in progress, liberty, and spirits.

Ten days after Pierpont's delivery of this speech the old man died; and in less than ten days after his funeral, Mrs. Conant, a Boston medium, who writes spirit messages for half the American public, announced that she had got his soul back again in her drawing-room; a presence visible to her, sensible to some, audible to many. Charles Crowell and J. M. Peebles report that in their presence, Mrs. Conant fell into a spirit-trance, when the soul of John Pierpont passed into her (after the fashion set by Ann Lee), and spoke to them through her lips of that higher world into which he had just been raised. "It was evident," they say, "that some spirit was taking possession of her, for it portrayed its last earthly scene. The departure must have been very easy, for there was no struggle in the demonstration; merely a few short breathings, an earnest and steady gaze, and all was over. An effort was made to speak, and soon this immortal sentence was uttered:—

"'Blessed, thrice blessed, are they who die with a knowledge of the truth.'

"After a slight pause, the spirit resumed:—

"'*Brothers and Sisters*, the problem is now solved with me. And because I live, you shall live also; for the same *divine Father and Mother* that confers immortality upon one soul bestows the gift upon all.'"

Pierpont would not seem to have made much progress in celestial knowledge by the change from flesh to spirit; for while he was on earth he confined his arguments on spirit-rapping and spirit-writing very much to these forms:—"I have seen, and therefore I know; I have felt, and therefore I believe." It would seem to have struck Pierpont's spirit that his communication might be regarded as unsatisfactory to his mortal friends, seeing how warm a curiosity impels many of them to inquire into the mysteries of a higher world; and he spoke to Crowell and Peebles, through Mrs. Conant, in a tone of apology. "I regret," he is reported to have said, "that I cannot portray to you the transcendent beauty of the vision I saw just before I passed to the spirit-world. The glories of this new life are beyond description. Language would fail me should I attempt to describe them." Mortals had heard that language used before John Pierpont died.

When Pierpont left the chair, Newman Weeks, of Vermont, was elected president for the year. Among the vice-presidents were several ladies: Mrs. Sarah Horton of Vermont, Mrs. Deborah Butler of New Jersey, Doctoress Juliette Stillman of Wisconsin.

Warren Chase, of Illinois, one of the male vice-presidents, declares that more than three millions of

Americans, men and women, have already entered into this movement. Three millions is a large figure; no church in these States, not even the Methodist, can sum up half that number of actual members. The Spiritualists count in their ranks some eminent men; shrewd lawyers, gallant soldiers, graceful writers; with not a few persons who can hardly escape the suspicion of being simply rogues and cheats. Still, the fact about them which concerns a student of the New America most is their reported strength in numbers. A society of three million men and women would be formidable in any country; in a republic governed by popular votes, they must wield an enormous force for either good or ill; hence, one is not surprised on finding their leaders boast of having power to control the public judgments of America, not only as to peace and war, dogma and practice, but even on the more delicate questions of social and moral life. A fair and open field is not to be refused when hosts so mighty throw down wager of battle on behalf of what they hold to be true, however strange their faith may seem.

These millions, more or less, of Spiritualists, announce their personal conviction that the old religious gospels are exhausted, that the churches founded on them are dead, that new revelations are required by man. They proclaim that the phenomena, now being produced in a hundred American cities—signs of mysterious origin, rappings by unknown agents, drawings by unseen hands; phenomena which are commonly developed in darkened rooms and under ladies' tables—offer an acceptable ground-plan for a new, a true, and a final faith in things unseen. They have already their progressive lyceums, their catechisms, their newspapers; their male and female prophets, mediums, and clairvoyants; their Sunday services, their festivals, their picnic parties, their camp-meetings; their local societies, their state organizations, their general conferences; in short, all the machinery of our most active, most aggressive societies. Their strength may be put too high by Warren Chase; outsiders cannot count them, since they are not returned in the census as a separate body; but the number of their lyceums, the frequency of their picnics, the circulation of their journals, are facts within the reach of some sort of verification. A man would hardly be wrong in assuming that a tenth part of the population in these New England States, a fifteenth part of the population of New York, Ohio, and Pennsylvania, lie open, more or less, to impressions from what they call the spirit-world.

Some of these zealots urge a most ancient origin for their faith, while others maintain that they are a new people, blessed with an unworn revelation, a growth of the American soil, an exclusive property of the American church. They allude but seldom to the Shakers, from whom they seem to have derived nearly all their canons, with not a few of their practices. They prefer to trace their origin to the visions of Andrew Jackson Davis and the happy audacities of Kate and Caroline Fox. A majority, perhaps, of the National delegates would have resented, as an injury to their country, any attempt to carry back the spiritual movement to an older source than the revelations of their own Poughkeepsie seer.

Poughkeepsie, pronounced Po'keepsie, the Mecca, the Benares, the Jerusalem, of this new church, is a green, though busy and thriving town, lying at the foot of a picturesque bluff on the river Hudson, midway from Albany to New York. Seen from the river, the place is quaint and Swiss-like, with its quay, its rickety exchange. A bend in the stream, there five or six hundred yards in width, landlocks the river, so as to form, as it were, two pretty lakelets; the higher one backed by the Catskill mountains, the lower one by the Hudson highlands. The nearer bank is bare and weird; with rock above and scrub below; but the western shore, a rolling ridge of hill, is bright with sycamore, beech, and oak. Schools, churches, colleges abound in the city; and among persons who have never been touched by unseen fingers, guns, carpets, beer, and cotton, are mentioned as its productions. Among the elect, the chief production of Po'-keepsie is a Seer.

When Mother Ann had been lodged in the jail of this river town, she had gathered a little court of curious people round her, to whom she communicated her strange experiences of the unseen world. Andrew Davis, the poor cobbler, is the spiritual descendant of Ann Lee, the poor factory girl. Davis sees signs and dreams dreams; but his revelations have scarcely gone beyond the hints afforded by Mother Ann. In his trances, he declares that in dying, men only change their garments, that the spirits of the dead are about us everywhere, that sensitive persons can communicate with them. He asserts that medicines are useless and hurtful, and that all diseases may be cured by laying on of hands. He describes a new method of education, in which a sort of dancing with the arms and hands in Shaker fashion is largely introduced. He denounces the Christian Church as an institution of the flesh, the time of which has passed away, and he proposes in its stead a new and everlasting covenant of the spirit.

Such are, in brief, the bases of what Newman

Weeks, Sarah Horton, Deborah Butler, and the associated brethren proclaimed in Pratt's Hall as that new covenant, which is to elevate man from the lowest earth into the highest heaven. Like Elder Frederick, they maintained the dual nature of the Godhead, assuming a female and a male essence—a Motherhood as well as Fatherhood in the Creator—and, like Sister Mary and Elderess Antoinette, they inferred from this duality of God the equal right and privilege of the sex on earth. Indeed, from first to last, the ladies seem to have played the leading parts in Providence, whether in exposition or in expostulation. There was much of both these articles. Miss Susie Johnson said she was tired of talk and wanted to work. "I am ready," cried the young reformer, "to work with any man or woman, or any community, that will show me the first practical step, by virtue of which we shall be laying the foundation of a higher morality, of a stricter integrity, of a better government, and, finally, of a higher destiny for the whole human race. I want to do something, and I want to see others who are ready to work. It is very much easier, I know, to pray for the salvation of mankind than to work for it, and oftentimes you get very much more credit for praying than for working; but it is not that I am after. I am sincerely devoted to the interests of the children of the coming generation."

Mrs. Susie Hutchinson was bolder still in rebuke of her brethren in the spirit. This lady, who represented the Charleston Independent Society of Spiritualists in the Convention, said she had labored for eight years in the cause of Spiritualism, but had always been ashamed of her associates. The official report makes her say: "She had never met a whole-souled, noble Spiritualist yet, but she had hoped that there would be a class of people here who would show themselves worthy of being called men and women. She had hoped that they would pass resolutions that should be active, and not dead letters, going back to the buried past, and that they would find manhood and womanhood coming up to the work of humanity. If there was one single soul in the universe to be shut out from the convention, she wanted to be shut out with them. If there was a single person going to hell, she wanted to go with them; and if there was a work to be done in the lower regions, she would go and help the Eternal Father to do that work."

Not a few of the delegates pretended to the possession of miraculous powers; to the gift of tongues, to spiritual insight, to the art of healing. Nearly all the adepts undertake to cure diseases by imposition (scoffers say by very great imposition) of hands. In a current copy of "The Banner of Light," you may count a score of male and female—mostly female—mediums, who publicly advertise to cure diseases of every kind—for due amount of dollars—by spirit-agencies; a certain virtue being conveyed from the physician to her patient, by a movement of the hands, in imitation of the apostolic rite. These announcements of the healing mediums are often curious and suggestive. Among lesser lights in these circles, Mrs. Eliza Williams, a sister of Andrew Jackson Davis, announces that she will "examine and prescribe for diseases and cure the sick by her healing powers, which have been fully tested." Mrs. S. J. Young advertises herself as a business and medical clairvoyant; Mrs. Spafford as a trance-test medium; Mrs. H. S. Seymour as a business and test-medium. Some of these advertisements are full of mystery to the carnal mind. Mrs. Spencer undertakes to cure chills and fevers by her "positive and negative powders," adding, "for the prevention and cure of cholera this great spiritual medicine should be always kept on hand." Dr. Main, who dates from the Health Institute, requests those persons who may wish to have his opinion, to "enclose a dollar, a postage-stamp, and a lock of hair." Mrs R. Collins "still continues to heal the sick in Pine Street." Madam Gale, clairvoyant and test-medium, "sees spirits and describes absent friends." Mrs. H. B. Gillette, electric, magnetic, healing, and developing medium, "heals both body and mind." But Mrs. Gillette appears to be distanced by Dr. George Emerson, who announces a "new development of spirit-power." This medium is "developed to cure diseases by drawing the disease into himself;" and he advertises that he is ready to perform this miracle of spirit-art by letter, at any distance, for ten dollars. In some respects, however, the ladies make a bolder show of might than anything yet assumed by the rougher sex. Mrs. S. W. Gilbert, describing herself as a Dermapathist, not only offers to cure disease, but to teach the art of curing it—in so many lessons, at so much a lesson!

A tone of stern hostility towards the religious creeds and moral standards of all Christian nations marked the speeches of men and women throughout this Convention; a tone which is hardly softened by a word in the official reports.

Miss Susie Johnson said, she for one would build no more churches, "for they had already too long oppressed and benighted humanity."

Mr. Andrew Foss "thanked God this was not an age of worship, but of investigation."

Dr. H. T. Child said that "Spiritualism has bridged

the gulf between Abraham's bosom and the rich man's hell. Let thanksgiving be added to thanksgiving for every blow that is struck to weaken the superstructure of human law—law which, by the hand of man, punishes man for doing wrong."

Mr. Perry said, "As a Spiritualist, I have yet to learn that we hold anything as sacred; and I am opposed to any resolution that has the word sacred in it."

Mr. Finney said, "The old religion is dying out. We are here to represent this new religion, born of the Union and of the types of humanity in a cosmopolitan geography, the die of which was cast in the forges of Divine Providence."

This was, in fact, the substance of what was said in presence of the assembled delegates, mortal and celestial, at the third National Convention.

These resolutions were adopted, which the Spiritualists consider as of great importance. The first was, to oppose the teaching of Sunday-schools, and to substitute for it that of their own progressive lyceums: the second, to procure the writing of a series of essays on Spiritualism: the third, to discountenance the use of tobacco and strong drinks. A proposal to found a National Spiritual College was ordered to stand over for discussion next year. One resolution, of no immediate importance, showed how broad an action might be taken by these Spiritualists on the political field, if they should gain in strength of numbers and in unity of purpose. It referred to the Labor question, and ran as follows:

"*Resolved*, That the hand of honest labor alone holds the sovereign sceptre of civilization; that its rights are commensurate with its character and importance; and hence, that it should be so fully and completely compensated as to furnish to the toiling millions ample means, times, and opportunities for education, culture, refinement, and pleasure; and that equal labor, whether performed by men or women, should receive equal compensation."

These reformers pay no respect to our Old World notions of political science.

When we essay to judge a system so repugnant to our feelings, so hostile to our institutions as this school of Spiritualism, it is needful—if we would be fair in censure—to remember that, strange as it may seem to on-lookers, it has been embraced by hundreds of learned men and pious women. Such a fact will appear to many the most singular part of the movement; but no one can assert that a theory is simply foolish, beneath the notice of investigators, which has been accepted by man like Judge Edmonds, Dr. Hare, Elder Frederick, and Professor Bush.

CHAPTER XLIX.

FEMALE SEERS.

In this learned, bright, and picturesque city of Boston, the home of Agassiz, Longfellow, Holmes, and Lowell, there has risen up a branch of the female priesthood of America, which puts forward a claim to regulate science, to supersede induction, and to lay down a new method. The women are Female Seers.

These priestesses, who may be called Elizabethans, from the name of their founder and hierophant, Elizabeth Denton, are not, properly speaking, a church; hardly, indeed, a sect; and certainly not a learned society. Perhaps they may be called a school; since they profess to have everything to learn and everything to teach. Like most other branches of the great Spiritualist family, they live in the world, of which they enjoy the pleasures and covet the distinctions with unflagging zest. On Boston Common, they are undistinguishable by outward signs from the world of ordinary people (if, in truth, it can be said that on Boston Common there are any ordinary people). Their mark is that of an inward, intellectual gift; the peculiar power of these Female Seers being the ability to read into the very heart of mill-stones.

Obeying the common law of these new societies, the school of Elizabeth is a female school, with ladies for its prophets and interpreters. Men may become members of the school, may share in its riches, help to propagate its gospels; but no male creature has ever yet dared to assert his possession of its miraculous gifts.

In our new philosophy, superior gifts depend on superior organization. Man, with his coarser grain, his harder fibre, his duller spirit, is unequal to the flights and ecstasies of the nobler sex. In New York idiom, man has been played out, and woman must have her turn.

Anne Cridge began it. Anne Cridge is a sister of William Denton, of Boston, a person of some consequence here—for a man; a student, a geologist, a collector, one who can chop logic and quote authorities in defence of the doings of his school. The new Gospel of the Female Seers came to Anne Cridge and her brother William in this odd manner. Buchanan, a doctor in Cincinnati, had noticed in his practice, that some persons can be purged without pills and doses, simply by being made to hold the cathartic medicine in their hands. It was an act of the imagination; not to be expected from every one, perhaps, but certainly to be found in some, especially in females of delicate genius and of sensitive frame. Why not in Anne Cridge? The delicate genius, the sensitive frame, were hers by nature and not by choice. A trial was made. Now, a fancy that could supply the place of a bolus, should be capable of higher service than purging the body of its viler humors; and with a sly feminine frankness, Anne tried her powers of seeing through obstacles on some of her friends' unopened letters. The gift soon grew upon her. Putting a sealed paper to her temples, she perceived traces upon it, not with her eyes, but with her brain, of the figure of a man writing,—the figure of a man who had written that paper,—so that she could tell his height, his color, and the shape of his eyes. A thought now struck her brother. This image of a man writing must be a sun-picture, which had been thrown upon the paper as upon a lens. He could not himself see it; only his sister Anne could see it; but this defect of vision was a consequence of his grosser qualities of mind. Denton lacked imagination. Still, it was made clear to him that Nature must be in the daily habit of multiplying pictures of herself; that every surface must receive and may retain such pictures; and that you only want a seer capable of reading them, in order to arrive at Nature's innermost secrets. It was a fine idea; Denton thought the beginning of a new era: for if Anne, by pressing a piece of paper against her forehead, could find on it the figure of its writer, with an outline of the room in which it had been folded and sealed, why should she not be able to read the images which must have been pictured on all other surfaces; on flints, on bones, on shells, on metals? Why not? If the images mirrored on all substances by light, are not, as we fancy, transient, but remain upon them, sinking into them, it is simply a question of test—of an agent sensitive enough to perceive and recover these vanishing lines. Such an agent Denton had found in his sister Anne.

Having found his reader of Nature, all the past life of the world would be opened to him, as one great fragment of time is to the Wandering Jew, with the added advantage that he could go further back in time and could read the things which no human eyes had ever seen: to wit, if his theory were true, you would only need to break a piece of rock from the Matterhorn, wrap it in paper, and place it against the reader's brow, in order to learn, as from the pages of a book, the story of the glaciers, from the age when Switzerland and Swabia were fields of ice, through the melting periods, down to the day when forest, lake, town, vineyard, laughed upon the scene; to scratch a flint from the limestone quarries of the White Mountains, and you would find engraved upon it pictures of the primeval forest, of the Indian camp, the red-skins in their paint and feathers, brandishing their spears, and tossing in their war-dance; to pick a bit of lava from a vault in Pompeii, and you would obtain a map of the Italian city, with its houses, gardens, baths and circuses, its games, its festivals, its civic and religious life; to chip a scale from the tower of Seville, and you would instantly restore the old Moorish life of that proud city, with its ensigns and processions, its dusk population, its gleaming crescents and heroic pomp of war; to snatch a bone from a heap of sailors' ballast lying on the quays, and mayhap you would have pictured on this fossil the condition of England thousands of years before Cæsar sailed from the Somme, with portraits of the savages who fished, and fought, and fed goats and sheep on our shores and downs. If the theory were only true, a new light had dawned upon the world; history had obtained a great supplement, science a new basis, art a fresh illustration.

But Anne, the first Female Seer, now found a rival in this art of reading stones in Elizabeth Denton, her brother's wife. It may be that Elizabeth was jealous of Anne passing day after day in her husband's study, even though it were only among books, bones, skins, and ores, gazing with him into the mysteries of life, while she herself was sent out into the nursery and the kitchen. In her eyes, it is probable that in such services to science one woman would seem to be as good as another—in her own case a great deal better. Certain it is, that she one day told her husband that she, too, was a Female Seer, able and willing to look for him into the soul of things. Denton tried her with a pebble, which she instantly read off in a fashion to extinguish the modest pretensions of sister Anne. In the published list of experiments, we are told that a piece of limestone from Kansas, full of small fossil shells, was held by Anne Cridge against her brow, when she read off: "A deep hole here. What shells! small shells; so many. I see water; it looks like a river running along." The next experiment was tried upon Elizabeth: a bit of quartz from Panama being held before her eyes: "I see what looks like a monstrous insect; its body covered with shelly wings, and its head furnished with antennæ nearly a foot long. It stands with its head against a rock. . . . I see an enormous snake coiled up among wild, wiry grass. The vegetation is tropical." "Well done," cried Denton.

Proud of the gifts so suddenly displayed by his

wife, he announced that a new science had been seen, a new interpretation of the past revealed, and opening a fresh page in the great book of nature, he wrote down the word Psychometry, by which he meant the Science of the Soul of things. Of course, being only a male, he cannot show this soul to others; he does not affect to see it for himself. He is privileged through his sister and his wife. But being a man of letters and ideas, he has shaped out the new mystery of the universe in these surprising terms: —

"In the world around us radiant forces are passing from all objects to all objects in their vicinity, and during every moment of the day and night are daguerreotying the appearances of each upon the other; the images thus made not merely resting upon the surface, but sinking into the interior of them; there held with astonishing tenacity, and only waiting for the suitable application to reveal themselves to the inquiring gaze. You cannot, then, enter a room by night or day, but you leave on going out, your portrait behind you. You cannot lift your hand, or wink your eye, or the wind stir a hair of your head, but each movement is infallibly registered for coming ages. The pane of glass in the window, the brick in the wall, and the paving-stone in the street, catch the pictures of all the passers-by, and faithfully preserve them. Not a leaf waves, not an insect crawls, not a ripple moves, but each motion is recorded by a thousand faithful scribes in infallible and indelible scripture."

It is a pity that men are not allowed to see these pictures, to read these histories, of our globe. But the male vision is dull, the male mind prosaic. Only the female sense can peer into these solid depths. It is rather hard upon us; but whose fault is it if man's grosser nature cannot soar to these feminine heights?

Growing by what it feeds on, the mysterious faculty in Elizabeth Denton has left that of Anne Cridge immeasurably behind. She has acquired the gift of looking, not into flints and fossils only, but into the depths of the sea, into the centre of the earth. She can hear the people of past times talk, she can taste the food which saurians and crustaceans scrunched in the pre-diluvian world.

From these Female Seers we have learned that men were once like monkeys; that even then the women were in advance of men; being less hairy and standing more erect than their male companions. It is coming to be always thus, when the story of man's life is told by a properly qualified female saint and seer.

CHAPTER L.

EQUAL RIGHTS.

"ARE you a member of the Society for Promoting Equal Rights, as between the two sexes?" I asked a young married lady of my acquaintance in New York. "Certainly not," she replied with a quick shrug of the shoulders. "Why not?" I ventured to say, pursuing my inquiry. "Oh," she answered, with a sly little laugh, "you see I am very fond of being taken care of." Were it not for this unfortunate weakness on the part of many ladies, the Society for Promoting Equal Rights would soon, I am told, comprise the whole female population of these states, especially of these New England states!

The reform which ladies like Betsey Cowles, Lucy Stone, and Lucretia Mott, would bring about by way of equalizing the rights of sex and sex, would give to woman everything that society allows to men, from pantaloons and latch-keys up to seats in the legislature and pulpits in the church. In assertion of female rights, Harriet Noyes and Mary Walker have taken to pantalettes; Elizabeth Staunton has offered herself as a candidate for the representation of New York; and Olympia Brown has been duly ordained as a minister of the gospel.

When the first Female Congress was called in Ohio, under Presidentess Betsey Cowles, the ladies, after much reading and speaking, adopted twenty-two resolutions, with a preamble echoing the form of the Declaration of Independence: —

"Whereas all men are created equal, and endowed with certain God-given rights, and all just government is derived from the consent of the governed; And whereas the doctrine that man shall pursue his own substantial happiness, is acknowledged by the highest authority to be the great precept of nature; And whereas this doctrine is not local but universal, being dictated by God Himself: Wherefore . . . ."

Then come the resolutions, which take the form of an open declaration, that the ladies of Ohio shall in future consider the laws which, in their opinion, press unfairly on the sex, as of no effect and void.

"1. Resolved: That all laws contrary to these fundamental principles, or in conflict with this great precept of nature, are of no binding obligation.

"2. Resolved: That all laws which exclude women from voting are null and void.

"3. Resolved: That all social, literary, pecuniary, and religious distinctions between man and woman are contrary to nature.

"9. Resolved: That it is unjust and unnatural to

hold a different moral standard for men and for women."

Lydia Pierson put her foot down on what she held to be the true cause of female inferiority: the habit among girls of marrying early in life. Lydia told her audience that, if they wanted to be men they must stay at school until they were twenty-one.

Massachusetts — the true leader in every movement of opinion — now took up the question, and the first National Woman's Rights Convention was held in Worcester, with Paulina Davis, of Rhode Island, Presidentess, and Hannah Darlington, of Pennsylvania, Secretary.

Paulina described the object of that female parliament to be - - an epochal movement, the emancipation of a class, the redemption of half the world, the re-organization of *all* social, political, and industrial interests and institutions. She said, This is the age of peace, and woman is its sign. The Congress voted the following resolutions.

"That every human being of full age, who has to obey the law, and who is taxed to support the government, should have a vote:

"That political rights have nothing to do with sex, and the word 'male' should be struck out of all our state constitutions:

"That the laws of property, as affecting married persons, should be revised, so as to make all the laws equal; the wife to have during life an equal control over the property gained by their mutual toil and sacrifices, to be heir of her husband to the extent that he is her heir, and to be entitled at her death to dispose by will of the same share of the joint property as he is."

Other resolutions declared the right of women to a better education than they now enjoy, to a fair partnership with men in trade and adventure, and to a share in the administration of justice. A male listener said he liked the spirit of this female parliament, since he found they meant by woman's rights the right of every lady to be good for something in life!

One topic of discourse in this Congress was Dress. It would hardly be outstripping facts to say that the husk and shell, so to speak, of every question now being raised for debate in America, as between sex and sex, belongs to the domain of the milliner and the tailor. What are the proper kinds of clothes for a free woman to fold about her limbs? Is the gown a final form of dress? Is the petticoat a badge of shame? Does a man owe nothing to his hat, his coat, his pantaloons, his boots? In short, can a female be considered as equal to a male until she has won the right to wear his garb? Queries such as these have a serious as well as comic side. Feminine science is so far advanced in these countries, that many a topic which would be food for jokes and poesies in London, is treated here as a question of business would be considered in a Broadway store.

Now, dress, if you consider it apart from the rules of Hyde Park and Fifth Avenue, denotes something other than the personal taste of its wearer. Dress is the man; and something more. Dress not only tells you what a man does, but what he is. Watch the tide of life, as it flows and surges through the Broadway, past the Park, the Battery, and the Quays, and you will see that the preacher has one costume, the postman another, the sailor a third; that a man of easy habit clothes himself in a garb which a man of swift and decisive movements could not wear. A flowing garment impedes the owner; a man or woman in skirts cannot run like a fellow in pantaloons.

Helene Marie Weber was one of the first to don coat and trousers, and her assumption of male attire was a cause of loud explosions. Helene, besides being a writer on reform, on female education, and on dress, was a practical farmer, who ploughed land, sowed corn, reared pigs, and went to market with her produce, habited like a man, in boots, breeks, and buttons. Apart from this fancy, she is described as a strictly pious and lady-like person, modest in mien, unassuming in voice. In a letter which she wrote to the Ladies' Congress, she mentions that she had been abused in the English and American papers for wearing trousers; she declares that she has no desire to be an Iphis; that she never affected to be other than a woman, and has never been mistaken for a man except by some hasty stranger. Her common garb she describes as consisting of a coat and pants of black cloth; her evening dress as a dark blue coat with gilt buttons, buff cassimere vest, richly trimmed, with gold buttons, and drab breeches. She adds, with a sweet feminine touch, that all her clothes are made in Paris!

Many of the points to which these ladies lent their countenance were of serious import; others were only noticeable for the comedy to which they gave birth. I have heard that a deputation of ladies in one of these New England towns went up to their minister's house to protest against the commencement of the daily lessons with the words, "Dearly beloved brethren," as implying that the women were either not present or counted for nothing in the congregation. They wished to have their pastor's views on a project for amending the Book of Common Prayer. "Well, I have thought over that matter, ladies," said the preacher; "but I think, on the whole, this text may stand; for you see the brethren always embrace the sisters."

The more serious question discussed in the Equal Rights Association is the position of woman in marriage. "The whole theory of the common law," they say, "in relation to the married woman, is unjust and degrading." What, they ask, are the natural relations of one sex to the other? Is marriage the highest and purest form of those relations? What are the moral effects of marriage upon man and wife? Is marriage a holy state?

Any appeal to the code for guidance on such questions would be idle; for the rule under which we live has no reply to make in matters of moral and religious truth. The Institutes, Pagan alike in origin and in spirit, consider a woman as little more than a chattel; and the relation of husband and wife as only a trifle more advanced than that of a master and his slave. They see no moral beauty in the state of marriage; see nothing in it beyond a partnership in family business, akin to that which exists in a trading firm. No Roman ever dreamt of love being divine, of marriage being a union of two souls; and this Gothic sentiment, so common in our poetry, in our traditions, in our households, finds no food whatever in the civil law. Hence it has come to pass in America, that every sect of social reformers—Moravian, Tunker, Shaker, Perfectionist, Mormon, Spiritualist—has commenced its efforts towards a better life by discarding and denouncing the civil law.

That the state of marriage is the highest, most poetic, most religious stage of the social relations, is denied by few, even in America. It is denied by some. The Moravians and Tunkers treat the institution with a certain shyness; not denying that for carnal persons it is a good and profitable state; but affecting to believe that it is not holy, not conducive to the highest virtue. The Shakers, we have seen, repudiate marriage altogether, as one of those temporal institutions which have done their appointed office on this earth, and have now passed away, so far, at least, as concerns the elected children of grace.

CHAPTER LI.

THE HARMLESS PEOPLE.

THE Tunkers, who say they came into America from a small German village on the Eder, all from one little dorf, owe the name by which they are known, not only here, in Lancaster, Pennsylvania, about which they are largely settled, but in Boston and New York — to a pun. They profess Baptist tenets; and the word "tunker" meaning to dip a crumb into gravy, a sop into wine, they are described by those who use it, in a very poor joke, as dippers and sops. They are also called Tumblers, from one of the abrupt motions which they make in the act of baptism. We English style them Dunkers, by mistake. Among themselves they are known as Brethren; the spirit of their association being that of fraternal love. The name by which they are known in the neighborhood of their villages in Pennsylvania, Ohio, and Indiana, is that of the Harmless People.

Under any and every name, they are a sober, pious, and godly race; leavening with a simple virtue the mighty fermentations going forward on the American soil.

These Tunkers live in little villages and groups of farms, for their common comfort and advantage; but not in separate communities, like the Shakers and Perfectionists. They remain in the world, subject to the law. In some respects, they may be considered as in a state of change, even of decay; for, in these later days, they have begun to take interest on money lent, once strictly forbidden among them; and they have commenced to build chapels and churches instead of confining their religious services, like the ancient Jews, to houses and sheds. In some of these chapels, I am sorry to say, there is even a hint at decoration; but with these slight drawbacks, the Tunkers are true to the practices of their faith, of which these brief particulars may be given.

They are said to believe that all men will be saved; a dogma which is common to almost every new sect in the United States; though some of their body deny that universal salvation is held as a binding article of their creed. They dress in plain clothes, and use none but the simplest forms of address. They swear no oaths. They make no compliments. They will not fight. They wear long beards, and never go to law. In their worship they employ no salaried priest. Males and females are considered equals, and the two sexes are alike eligible for the diaconate. Every man in a congregation is allowed to rise (as in the Jewish synagogue) and expound the text; the man who proves himself ablest to teach and preach is put in the minister's place; but the people pay him in respect, not in dollars, for his service. Like Peter and Paul on their travels, the Tunker apostles may be lodged with their brethren, and even helped on their way with food and gifts; but in theory and practice they accept no fees, even when they happen to be poor and unable to leave for a week, for a month, without loss, their little patches of ground. These unpaid preachers wait upon the sick, comfort the dying, bury the dead. They have also to marry young men and maids; a few, not many, of the more carnal spirits; a duty which is often the most troublesome part of their daily toils.

For the Tunkers, like the Essenes, whom they resemble in many strong points, have peculiar views about the holiness of a single life; holding celibacy in the highest honor; and declaring that very few persons are either gifted or prepared for the married state. They do not refuse to bind any brother and sister who may wish to enter into that bond to each other; but they make no scruple about pointing out to them, in long and earnest discourse, the superior virtues of a single life. The preacher does not say that matrimony is a crime; he only hints a profound dislike to it; treating it as one of those evil things from which he would willingly guard his flock.

When a brother and sister come to him wanting to be made one flesh, he looks down upon them as sinners who ought to be questioned and probed as to their secret thoughts; and, if it may be, delivered by him through grace from a terrible snare. He alarms them by his inquisition, he frightens them by his prophecies. In his words and in his looks he conveys to their minds the idea that in wanting to be married they are going headlong to the devil. It is not easy to say what the object of these Harmless People may be in opposing the tendency of their folks to love and marry; for the Tunkers are shy of publication and explanation; but it is open to conjecture that their motives may be partly physiological, partly religious. A wise man, who could have his way in every city of the world, would put an end to all marriages of deformed and idiotic persons; on the same lines of justification, a Tunker might dissuade from marriage a pair of lovers who could do nothing to improve the race. But some mystic dream, about chastity being a holy state, acceptable as such to God, and meritorious in the eyes of men, has more to do with it, I think, than any consideration they may have for improvements in the Tunker breed.

Of course, the Tunker body is not the first professing Christian Church which has felt it a duty to encourage people to live a single life, though the fact of such encouragement may be considered as having a meaning in that country, where every child is a fortune, which it never can have had in Europe and in Asia, where the separation of a great many monks and anchorites from the reproducing classes may have been justified on economical, if not on moral, grounds.

In the Churches of Jerusalem, Antioch, and Rome, the question of whether celibacy was or was not a holy state, was mooted long and freely, for apostles could be quoted on either side in the dispute, and the teachers, each according to his argument, might cite on this side the example of Peter, on that side the precept of Paul. The sentiment in favor of living a single life did not come from Paul, much less from Christ; it had sprung up among the Essenic farms and villages of Judea; had spread from the hill-side into the city and the schools; had become popular among the Pharisees, as a protest against the flesh and the devil; and, in this sense only, it appears to have been adopted by the ascetic Saul. After his conversion to a new creed, Paul, being a man of mature age, going to and fro in the world on his Master's work, was unlikely to change his habits. The spirit of the Essene was strong in Paul, but in pleading for chastity of the body, as a condition acceptable to God, it should not be hastily assumed that he set up his voice, even by implication, against God's own ordinance of marriage. Those only who have studied the social life of Corinth under Junius Gallio, — a sink of vice, appalling even to men most knowing in the ways of degenerate Greece, — can guess what may have been the apostle's motive for advising his disciples in that city to observe a more ascetic rule than any which they saw in vogue around them; but any man of sense may judge from the sacred text how far a special state of morals, special even among the Greeks, must have driven St. Paul into urging upon the Church of Corinth a true and resolute watchfulness over matters not otherwise recommended by him to the infant church. When he says to them, he would to God they were as he is, he speaks (if I read him rightly) as a chaste man rather than as a single man. How could an apostle of such practical and commanding genius as St. Paul conceive the idea of banishing marriage from the new society? Three reasons forbid it, any one of which would have been strong enough to deter him: (first) because Elohim, the God of his fathers, had instituted marriage for Adam and all his seed; (second) because Paul knew, and said, that if men do not marry, they will do much worse; and (third) because the rule of abstinence, if it could have been enforced by him, would have destroyed in one generation all his converts, and with them, perhaps, the very Church of Christ.

Have we any right to infer from Paul's advice to the Corinthians, that he held the views of Ann Lee, or even of Alexander Mack? Greece was not America; the Syrian Aphrodite is not worshipped in New York. St. Paul had to urge the merits of chastity on a people to whom that word, and all that it expresses, were unknown. His converts had been worshippers of Astarte, and in denouncing their abominations, he used the fiery freedom of a man whose life was pure and stainless. Yet he weighed his words, and in the tempest of his wrath took time to say, when he spoke in his own name only, as a private man, and when he delivered counsel in the name of our Lord. The Greeks understood him. Writing in their idiom, speaking of their manners, both well known to him — child of a Greek city, pupil in a Greek school — his meaning must have been clearer to them than it is to strangers. Hence the Greek church may be taken as a safer guide to the sense of a difficult and contested passage than any other, especially than that of the American Tunker. The Greek church has no doubt about it. By many canons and by constant usage, that church affirms that St. Paul was in favor of wedlock, not in the communicant only, but in the priest.

Unhappily for Christian unity, the Western church took another view of the text. The Pauline and Platonic Fathers wrote in mystical phrases of the superior sanctity of an unmarried life; and long before any law of the church had come to forbid priest and bishop to marry, it had become a fashion among the higher clergy to abstain, and to live, as they phrased it, for the church alone. Strange to say, this fashion took root in Rome, in the midst of a people boasting as their chief glory, of having had for their founder and bishop St. Peter, Prince of the Apostles, a married man.

The adoption of this celibate principle by Rome was the germ of both the great schisms in the Christian society; first, of a parting between East and West, afterwards, in the West itself, of a parting between

North and South. Disputes about dogma may be set aside; disputes about social order may not. A priest can be persuaded to hear reason on such topics as election and foreknowledge, who cannot be induced to admit that marriage is a state of sin. In the sixth and seventh centuries this battle of celibacy had been fiercely fought, the Petrine church being for it, the Pauline church against it; and on this rock of contradictions, the first great Christian society had struck and split. The Council of Tours had suspended for a year all priests and deacons who were then found living with their wives, of whom there were many thousands in Italy, Gaul, and Spain. The Council of Constantinople had declared that priests and deacons ought to live with their wives like laymen, according to the ordinance and custom of the apostles, a canon which they still observe. Not only did the Greek Church separate from that of Rome on this cardinal policy, but the clergy and laity of the West and North — of England, Germany, and France — stood out against it; and the main efforts of the Roman church for five hundred years were given to this domestic question. Ages elapsed before Rome had crushed the opposition to her policy in England, Germany, and France, in which countries married priests were to be found so late as the times of the Black Prince: at length she won her cause; but on the morrow of her triumph the Reformation began.

No man can read the ballads and chronicles from Piers Ploughman's Complaint to Pecock's Repressor, without feeling how much it was beyond the power of a celibate clergy to dwell in peace with a congregation of Gothic race. The cry for a married priesthood rose from every corner of the West and North; and when the clerical reformers took the field against

Rome, the first pledge of their sincerity, given and taken, was to marry wives. All the great men who led the Reformation in their several countries—Luther, Calvin, Cranmer—had to give this pledge of their faith; thus the newly-made Christian societies of North and West, to which America is heir, were founded on the broadest principles of human nature, not on the narrowest criticism of a text.

But Rome, after these great schisms in the church, clings fondly to her ancient order. She looks on woman as a snare. Into the crypt of St. Peter (a married saint) no female is allowed to enter, except on a single day of the year. A lady may not call upon the Pope, except in mourning robes. In the Roman mass no music is permitted for the female voice. But the Italian church is logical in its practice, though it may be wrong in its principle. Where it is considered sinful in a priest to marry, how can you prevent the female being despised?

This question may be put to the American celibate schools: to the Tunkers of Ohio, to the Shakers of New York.

CHAPTER LII.

THE REVOLT OF WOMAN.

ELIZABETH DENTON, founder though she be of a school of Female Seers, is not the highest and boldest of these feminine reformers. One school of writers, a school which is already a church, with its codes and canons, its seers and sects, soars high above local wranglings, into what is said to be a region of yet nobler truths. Rights of Woman! exclaim the party. What is right compared with power? what is usage compared with nature? what is social law compared with celestial fact? A woman's right to love, say these female reformers, is a detail, her claim to labor, a mistake. Neither the first nor the second should be urged on the world's attention. One ought to be assumed, the other must be dropped. Woman's right to love is implied in a yet larger claim, and by the new theory of her life her only relation to labor is to be exempt from it.

These reformers make no feint, they hit straight out. According to them, only meek and weak reformers would think of prating about equal powers and laws. Women, they say, are not the equals of man; they are his superiors. They do not ask from him either chivalry or courtesy; they claim the sovereign rule. In throwing down such a gage, they are well aware how much they surprise and offend their masculine hearers; but they speak to women, and do not expect that men will receive the truth. They have a gospel to deliver, a duty to discharge, a war to conduct; a social war; no more, no less. Up to this time, they allege that women have been held in bondage; but their day has come, their chains are falling off, a deliverer is at hand; a truce, they cry, to compliments, to hypocrisies, to concessions on all sides; the movement now on foot is a Revolt of Woman against Man.

The first principle of this new party is, that of the two sexes Woman is the more perfect being, later in growth, finer in structure, grander in form, lighter in type. The distinctions between the two are wide and deep, one being allied to cherub and seraph, the other to stallion and dog. What man is to the gorilla, woman is to man. Female superiority is not confined to a few degrees of more or less; it is radical, organic, lying in the quality of her brain, in the delicacy of her tissues: a superiority of essence, even more than of grade. If nature works, as it would seem, through an ascending series, woman is the step beyond man in Nature's ascent towards the form of angelic life. And this is true, not only of human beings, but of all beings, from the female mollusk to the New England lady. Man is but the paragon of animals, while woman, by her gifts of soul, belongs to the celestial ranks. He is a lord of the earth, while she is a messenger from heaven.

The sexes, too, according to this female creed, differ in office, as they differ in endowment. Man is here to be a tiller of the soil, while his sister, nursed at the same breast, is meant for a prophetess and seer. One is made coarse and rough, that he may wrestle with the outward world; the other tender and douce, that she may commune with the spiritual spheres. Each sex, then, has a province of its own, in which the whole of its duty lies. Man has to work, woman to love. He labors with the flesh, she with the spirit.

A husband is a grower and getter, his wife is a giver and spender; not in the way of jest and caprice, but by the eternal settlement of law. Man has to toil and save, that woman may dispense and enjoy; the higher intelligence turning his material gifts into use and beauty: as warmth draws wine and oil, color and perfume, from the watered field. One sex is a cultivator, the other a reconciler. He deals with the lower, she with the higher aspects of nature. Man conquers the soil, Woman mediates with God.

The Prophetess of this new church is Eliza Farnham, of Staten Island; the temple is unbuilt, but the faith and the votaries are said to be found in every populous city of the United States.

Five-and-twenty years have elapsed since the Truth of Woman first flashed upon Eliza; then a poor girl, unmarried, unlettered, untravelled, like most of these female seers; having read but little, speaking no tongue save one; yet keen and shrewd, with thoughts in her brain, and words upon her lips. This Truth of Woman came upon her in 1842, the year in which it is said that Joseph Smith received a command from God to restore plurality of wives; came upon her, not by induction, but by intuition; in plainer words, she drew her dogma of superiority, as Smith drew his dogma of plurality, not from any facts in nature, but from the depth and riches of her mind. Like Smith, she either kept the secret to herself, or shared it only with her chosen friends. But women, she confesses, can teach each other fast, and her ideas were spread abroad by an unseen agency. When the Truth came upon her, she was yet a virgin; to prove its power, she married, becoming in turn a wife, a mother, a widow; making money and losing it; toiling with her hands for bread; burying her children as she had buried her husband; wandering from town to town, and from State to State; living upon other people's bounty; getting past the turn of a woman's life; watching the gray hairs start upon her head, the crow's feet pucker at her eyes; and then, with the evening shadows falling sadly on her life, having felt the joys and griefs of womanhood in all its phases, she was ready to begin the war, not secretly, and in other names, but with her principles avowed and her forces in the field.

The Revolt of Woman opened, as it ought to have opened, with an attack on pure Intellect: a faculty which the world, in its folly and injustice, puts above woman's susceptibilities and inspirations. Reason is man's stronghold; a fortress which he has built for himself, and in which he dwells alone. Yes; reason is the basis on which he has planted all those canons, systems, poetries, sciences, mythologies, which he turns with such deadly art against the partner of his life. But when Eliza came to look into this pure Intellect, what did she find? A high power, a divine faculty, a test of nature, an instrument of truth? Nothing of the kind. She saw in Intellect nothing more than a coarse bungler, dealing with nature in a slow, material way, gathering up a few dates and facts, tracing out causes and sequents, catching through harmonies at law. What was man's gift compared against woman's grace? A process against a power. A woman has no need of method. She knows the fact when she sees it, feels the truth when it is unseen. What man with his logic, observation, and procedure, toils up to in a generation, she perceives at once. To him, intellect is a tiresome and uncertain guide; to her, intuition is a swift, unfailing diviner's rod. Has not man, asked Eliza, been using his reason for ages past, without having fallen on the central truth of life—the natural sovereignty of the female sex? Reason may have its uses and duties, of a humble kind; since it may teach a man how to cut down trees, how to build boats, how to snare game, how to reap corn and sow potatoes, how to fence his field and protect his camp; and for these uses it may be kept for a little while; but only in its proper place, as the servant of woman's far higher will.

The reign of Science was announced as over, that of Spiritualism as begun. Science is the offspring of man, Spiritualism of woman. The first is gross and sensual, a thing of the past; the second, pure and holy, a thing of the future. Science doubts, Spiritualism believes; one is of earth, the other is of heaven. Now that the Gospel of Woman is declared, Science has ceased to have a leading part in the discovery of truth; the objective world is about to pass into the subjective, and the superior sex will read for us, by their inner light, the mysteries of heaven and hell.

Eliza had no special theology to teach. She rejected Peter and Paul, Luther and Cranmer; but she had faith in Swedenborg. Peter and Paul had put women under men.

Eliza proudly contended that although her Truth of Woman is new and strange, it admits of proof convincing to the female mind. As to the masculine mind, a thing of lower grade, she was not concerned about its ways. A Virginian never thought of arguing with his slave. The Truth, which she had to preach, did not require man's sanction to make it pass; and she confined her discourse to the superior sex.

Her evidence in favor of the Truth of Woman lay in the following syllogism:—

Life is exalted in proportion to its organic and functional complexity; woman's organism is more complex, and her totality of functions larger, than those of any other being inhabiting our earth; therefore her position in the scale of life is the most exalted—the sovereign one.

That was Eliza's secret. The most complex life is the highest; woman's life is the most complex; ergo, woman's life is the highest. If the premises are sound, the conclusion must be also sound. Eliza felt so sure of her syllogism, that she rested her case upon it. What she claimed for woman is only what Nature gives her—the sovereign place.

It is the same, says Eliza, through all the animal grades. The females have more organs than the male, and organs are the representatives of power. All females have the same organs as males with two magnificent sets of structure which males have not; structures which concern the nourishing of life. She admits that the male is often physically larger than the female, so far as size can be measured by bulk of body, by length of arm, and by width of chest; but in lieu of any argument to be drawn from such a fact in favor of the male, it is urged that he is only bigger in the grosser parts—in bones and sinews—not in nerves and brains. Where the higher functions come into play, woman is in advance of man. Her bust has a nobler contour, her bosom a finer swell. The upper half of her skull is more expansive. All the tissues of her body are softer and more delicate. Her voice is sweeter, her ear quicker. Her veins are of brighter blue, her skin is of purer white, her lips are of deeper red. More than all else, as fixing the grade of woman above that of man, her brain is of higher quality and of quicker growth.

On every side, then, says Eliza, the female bears away the bell. She is aware that an old saying, based on what may be seen in a wood, in a street, in a farm-yard, asserts the superior beauty, no less than the superior size, of the male animal. But she disputes the facts. It is true that nearly all male animals have a grander figure; that nearly all male birds have a brighter plumage than their mates; that in some species the males have special ornaments, such as the lion's mane and the peacock's tail; but these appearances, she contends, deceive the eye, while true beauty is always to be found in the female form. The lioness is nobler than the lion; the pea-hen statelier [illegible] the coc[illegible] The beauty of your dung-hill rooster [illegible] feathers and his voice. Pluck him to the skin, and you will find that he has neither the softness nor the beauty of his female mates. But Eliza will not rest her argument for feminine superiority on birds; for her sex in birds is something of a mystery to her; and for many reasons (chiefly because girls are called nightingales, doves, and wrens) she inclines to the belief that the feminine of our higher order answers to the masculine in birds.

All, therefore, that is best and brightest in the two beings—outward and inward—beauty to the eye, softness to the touch, music to the ear—the heart to love, the brain to guide—are developed in the female on a richer scale. On his side, man has little to recommend him beyond a brutal strength. In short, the picture which Eliza draws of man and woman is very much like that of Caliban and Miranda on their lonely rock.

In support of these views of nature, she appeals to history, poetry, science, and art; citing Cornelia and the Mother of the Gracchi (whom she describes as *two* noticeable Roman wives); cutting up Shakspeare for his low views and slavish pictures of women; pooh-poohing Bacon for his lack of true method and insight; braining Michael Angelo for his absence of all feminine grace. There is novelty in her appeal, and in the illustrations by which she supports it. Eliza declares that Cornelia *and* the Mother of the Gracchi were but "average mothers of a later time;" that Shakspeare says nothing of woman that is to her credit, or to his own. Portia, it is true, is sensible, courageous, brilliant, without vanity; but Eliza knows a hundred American women who are better than she. Imogen is pure and loving; but the man is to be pitied who does not "know a score or two of finer girls." Rosalind, Perdita, Ophelia, Beatrice, are fools, if pretty ones, in whom Eliza can see "little goodness save the emptiness of evil." Pious Cordelia, noble Isabella, how are ye fallen, stars of the morning! Darwin, too, though he is allowed to be excellent in speculation, gets beyond his depth when dealing with structure, missing his chance of falling upon the Truth of Woman. Strange, she thinks, how so good a naturalist as Darwin is, should have treated rudimentary organs in male animals as remains of lost powers, when it is clear to her that they are the germs of new powers. But so it is: Darwin considers the rudimentary mammæ as the ruins of old organs, which once had uses; in other words, that male functions were at some distant period in the past a little nearer to female functions than they stand at present. Eliza, on the contrary, conceives that these mammæ are the germs of new organs, growing with the growth of time; in other words, that male functions will, by progress and development, come into closer resemblance to female functions. Science is wrong, like history, and poetry, and art. But what is science? Just what man knows:—man, who knows nothing; and who is only a grade higher in the scale of being than a chimpanzee! A true science would show you that woman, as a being with no waste organs, no rudimentary powers, stands at the head of all created things.

Milton's Eve — though fairest, wisest, best — is not high enough in the scale for Eliza. Eve is not made first of the twain in Paradise; first, as she ought to be, in virtue of her keener insight, her braver spirit, her larger longings. Nay, the Female Seer grows hot against the Bible for its hard and cruel way of dealing with that story of the Fall; urging that the Scriptures tell the tale as a man was sure to conceive it, to his own advantage, and to woman's loss. She writes it out afresh, and puts the thing in another light.

In this new version of the Fall, Eve is not weak, but strong. She finds Adam in bonds, and she sets him free. He is bound by a bad law to live in a state of darkness and bondage, a mere animal life, without knowing good from evil. She breaks his fetters, and shows him the way to heaven. The consequences of her act are noble; and through her courage Man did not fall, but rise. She did "a great service to humanity," when she plucked the forbidden fruit.

In the details of the Fall, Eliza finds much comfort, when she can read them by her own inward light. Wisdom (in the form of a Serpent) addressed the woman, not the man, who would have cared little for the tree of knowledge. The temptation offered to her was spiritual. She took the forbidden fruit, in the hope of becoming wiser and diviner than she had been. Man followed her. Yes: the ascendancy of woman began in Paradise!

VAN INGEN.SNYDER

CHAPTER LIII.

ONEIDA CREEK.

On the opposite verge of thought to the systems of Mother Ann, of Elizabeth Denton, of Eliza Farnham, stands a body of reformers who call themselves, in their dogmatic aspect, Perfectionists, in their social aspect, Bible Communists. These people aver that they have discovered the only way; and have reduced to practice what their rivals in reform have only reduced into talk. They profess to base their theory of family life on the New Testament, most of all on the teachings of St. Paul.

What these Bible People (as they call themselves) have done in the sphere of life and thought has certainly been attempted in no faltering spirit. They have restored, as they say, the Divine government of the world; they have put the two sexes on an equal footing; they have declared marriage a fraud and property a theft; they have abolished for themselves all human laws; they have formally renounced their allegiance to the United States.

The founder of this school of reform — a school which boasts already of having its prophets, seminaries, periodicals, and communities — its schism, its revivals, its persecutions, its male and female martyrs, — is John Humphrey Noyes: a tall, pale man, with sandy hair and beard, gray, dreamy eyes, good mouth, white temples, and a noble forehead. He is a little like Carlyle; and it is the fashion among his people to say that he closely resembles our Chelsea sage; a fiction which is evidently a pleasant delusion to the Saint himself. He has been in turn a graduate of Dartmouth College in Connecticut, a law clerk at Putney in Vermont, a theological student in Andover, Massachusetts, a preacher at Yale College, New Haven, a seceder from the Congregational Church, an outcast, a heretic, an agitator, a dreamer, an experimentalizer; finally, he is now acknowledged by many people as a sect-founder, a revelator, a prophet, enjoying light from heaven and personal intimacies with God.

I have been spending a few days at Oneida Creek, the chief seat of the three societies founded by Noyes, — Oneida, Wallingford, and Brooklyn, — as the guest of Brother Noyes. I have lived in his family; had a good deal of talk with him; had access to his books and papers, even those of a private nature; had many conversations with the brothers and sisters whom he has gathered into order, both in his presence and apart from him; had leave from him to copy such of the Family papers as I pleased. The account which follows of this extraordinary body of men has been written fresh from their own mouths, and from my own observation, on the spot which it describes.

"You will find," said Horace Greeley, as we parted in New York, "that Oneida Communism is a trade success; the rest you will see and judge for yourself."

From Oneida, a young and busy town on the New York Central Railway, a wide and dusty road, on either side of which, behind a line of frame-houses and their little gardens, the forest is still green and fresh, leads you to Oneida Creek; a part of that Indian reservation which was left by a compassionate legislature to the Oneidas, one of the Six Nations famous in the early history of New York for their honesty, their good faith, and their constant friendship for the whites. Twenty years ago the Creek ran through a virgin soil.

Here and there a log house peeped from beneath the trees, in which some remnants of a great and unhappy tribe of hunters stood, as it were, at bay. The water yielded fish, the forest game. The only clearings had been made by fire; woods either burnt by chance or felled for winter fuel. A patch of maize might be seen on some sunny slope; but the Oneida Indian is a very poor farmer at his best; and the district in which he dwelt with his squaw and his papoose, a tangle of brier and swamp and stones, was unbroken to the use of man. He sold his land to a pale-face, richer than himself, for a sum of money not equal in value to the maple and hickory woods upon it. From this second owner the Perfectionists bought the Creek, with its surrounding woods and open; and in twenty years the surface has been wholly changed. Roads have been cut through the forest; bridges have been built; the Creek has been trained and dammed; mills for slitting planks and for driving wheels have been erected; the bush has been cleared away; a great hall, offices and workshops have been raised; lawns have been laid out, shrubberies planted, and footways gravelled; orchards and vineyards have been reared and fenced; manufactures have been set going — iron-work, satchel-making, fruit-preserving, silk-spinning; and the whole aspect of this wild forest land has been beautified into the likeness of a rich domain in Kent. Few corners in America can compete in loveliness with the swards and gardens lying about the home of the Oneida family, as these things arrest the eyes of a stranger coming upon them from the rough fields even of the settled region of New York.

The home, which stands on a rising knoll commanding some pretty views, is remarkable without and within; for among the laws which the Bible Communists have put behind them are the seven orders of architecture. The builder of this pile is James Hamilton, once a New England farmer, carpenter, what not, as a New Englander is apt to be; a man of sense and tact, not much of a scholar, not at all an orator, but a person of some natural gifts, which fit him to be a ruler and contriver in the midst of inferior men. He is the head of this Oneida family, just as Noyes is the head of all the Perfectionist families; and being master of the house, so to speak, he is also builder of the house; though he claims that everything in it, from the position of a fireplace to the furnishing of a library, is the result of a special sign from heaven. I may add, without offence, that Brother Hamilton was open to new lights, even when they flashed from a Gentile brain; most of all to those of my fellow-traveller, William Haywood, architect and engineer.

In the centre of the pile, approached by a wide passage and a flight of stairs, is the great hall; a chapel, a theatre, a concert room, a casino, a working-place, all in one; being supplied with benches, lounging-chairs, work-tables, a reading-desk, a stage, a gallery, a pianoforte. In this hall the sisters play and sew, the elders preach, the librarian (Brother Pitt) reads the news, the young men and maidens make love—so far as such a Gentile art is allowed to live in this curious place. Near the great hall is the drawing-room, properly the ladies' room; and around this chamber stand the sleeping-apartments of the family and its guests. Beneath this floor, on either side of the wide passage, are the offices, together with a reception room, a library, a place of business. Kitchen, refectory, fruit-cellar, laundry, are in separate buildings. The store is in front of the home, divided from it by a lawn; and farther away, peeping prettily through the green trees, stand the mills, farms, stables, cow-sheds, presses, and general workshops. The estate is about six hundred acres in extent; the Family gathered under one roof number about three hundred. Everything at Oneida Creek suggests taste, repose, and wealth; and the account-books prove that during the past seven or eight years the Family have been making a good deal of money, which they have usefully laid out, either in the erection of new mills, or in draining and enriching the soil.

The men affect no particular garb; though the loose coat, the wide-awake, and peg-top breeches, common in every part of rural America, make up their ordinary wear. They have no dress for Sundays and holidays; having abolished Sundays and holidays along with every other human institution. But they are open to new lights on dress, saying that the last thing has not yet been done in the way of hats and boots. At one of their evening meetings, I heard Brother Pitt, a well-read man, deliver his testimony in favor of peg-tops. The ladies wear a dress which is peculiar, and to my eyes becoming. It may be made of any material and of any color; though brown and blue for out-door wear, white for evening in the meeting-room, are the prevailing tints. Muslin, cotton, and a coarse silk, supply the materials. The hair is cut short, and parted down the centre. No stays, no crinolines, are worn. A tunic falling to the knee, loose trousers of the same material, a vest buttoning high towards the throat, short hanging sleeves, and a straw hat; these simple articles make up a dress in which a plain woman escapes much notice, and a pretty girl looks bewitching. I am told that it is no part of Noyes' design that the young ladies of his family should look bewitching; for such is not his theory of a modest and moral woman's life; but for my own poor self, being only a Gentile and a sinner, I could not help seeing that many of his young disciples have been gifted with rare beauty, and that two of the singing-girls, Alice Ackley and Harriet Worden, have a grace and suppleness of form, as well as loveliness of face and hand, to warm a painter's heart.

So much of the Oneida Community you may see in a few hours, if you simply wander about the place, with Brother Bolls, a gentleman who for twenty-five years has been a Baptist preacher in Massachusetts, and who is now a Perfectionist brother in Oneida, with this special duty of receiving ordinary strangers. You see a fine house, a noble lawn, a green shrubbery, orchards shining with apple-trees, pear-trees, plum-trees, cherry-trees, prolific vineyards, excellent farms, busy workshops, grazing cattle, whizzing mills, and grinding saws,—peace, order, beauty, and material wealth; and these are what the picnic visitors, who come in thousands to stare in wonder, to hear good music, to eat squash and pastry, always see. They are something; signs of life, but not the life itself. The secrets of this strange success, the foundations on which this community rests, the social features which sustain it, are of deeper interest than the fact itself; and these mysteries of the Society are not explained to picnic parties by Brother Bolls.

It is well known that all the Communistic trials which have been made in England, Germany, and America, from Rapp's Harmony, and Owen's New Harmony, down to Cabet's Icaria, have been failures. Men with brains, women with hearts, have often turned from what they deem the evils of competition to what they hope may prove the saving principles of association; but no body of such reformers, with the sole exception of your wifeless followers of Ann Lee, have ever yet been able to work an association in which they held a community of goods. Each failure may have had its own history, its own explanation, showing how near it came to success; but the fact of failure cannot be denied. The Socialists had to quit New Lanark; the Rappists had to sell Harmony; the Icarians have been swept from Nauvoo. Liberty, equality, fraternity, have not hitherto paid their weekly bills; and a society that does not pay its expenses, must, in the long run, go to the wall, even though it should, in other respects, reproduce the image of paradise on the earth. Man may not sit all day under a palm-tree, munching his creel of dates, and feeling at peace with heaven and earth. Want prods him forward; and he has no choice but one of the two evils—either to work or die. Each trial and failure of association puts the principle into peril. See what you come to, laughs the Sadducee, happy in his broad lands, his mansions, gardens, vineyards, when you disturb the order of time, of nature, and of Providence! You come to waste, to beggary, and death. Competition, which is the soul of trade, for ever! and blessed be heaven, which fights on the side of the great capitalists!

If the theory of mutual help, as against that of self-help, be the true principle of social life, as so many men say, so many women feel, why have nearly all the attempts to live by it, and under it, ended in disaster?

"I tell you," said Brother Noyes to me this morning, "they have all failed because they were not founded on Bible truth. Religion is at the root of life; and a safe social theory must always express a religious truth. Now there are four stages in the true organization of a family: (1) Reconciliation with

God; (2) Salvation from sin; (3) Brotherhood of man and woman; (4) Community of labor and of its fruits. Owen, Ripley, Fourier, Cabet, began at the third and fourth stages; they left God out of their tale, and they came to nothing."

Noyes makes no secret of his opinion that he has contrived, by the Divine favor, a new and perfect system of society; that he has already established, by trial, the chief principles of the new domestic order; and that it only remains for the communities of Oneida, Wallingford, and Brooklyn, to work out a few details, in order to its universal adoption in the United States. If the reader cares to hear how this man — who has done so much in America, and of whom so little is known in England — came to think as he does on the religious aspects and bearings of domestic life — I will put before him, as openly as a layman dare, the results of my inquiries at Oneida Creek.

CHAPTER LIV.

HOLINESS.

"While he was yet living at Putney, in Vermont, as a lawyer's clerk, Noyes was struck by that fierce revival of '31, which wrecked so many New England barks. Noyes is said to have suddenly grown grave and moody; all his lights appear to have gone out, leaving him in the dark night, amidst howling storms, against which his puny strength of intellect could make no head. Turning his gaze inwards, he became, as he told me, conscious of sin and death. How could he free himself from these evils? Feeling the world and the devil strong within him, he abandoned law, taking up with the older science of theology. While studying in his new course at Andover, he fell into many temptations, ate and drank freely, and gave way to many other seductions of the flesh. The young divines, his fellow-students in the college, were a bad set, who laughed at revival energies, and sneered at the religious world. Noyes thought he would go away from Andover; seeking the Lord elsewhere, and on opening the Bible, his eye fell upon the conclusive text, "He is not here!" With this warning from Heaven before his eyes, he went away from Andover to Yale College, at Newhaven, where he became a great seeker after truth — not of the truth as it stands between God and man only, but of the truth as between man and man. In the midst of dreams as wild (I infer) as ever visited the brain of an Arab, there was always about Noyes a practical American view of things. He felt that the Divine plan must be perfect; that if he could read that plan, he would find in it an Order of the Earth, no less than an Order of Heaven. What is that Order of the Earth? Not the Pagan law under which we live. He turned for light to the written word. In the Bible, he says, he sought for that rule of life which the schools could not teach him. Pondering the words of the gospel, and conning by himself the writings of Paul, he found in these original documents of the Church a comfort which the preachers of Newhaven had not proved to his soul that they held in gift. Paul spoke to his heart; but in a sense, as he asserts, quite foreign to that in which the apostle had been understood at Antioch and Rome.

Much reading of Paul's epistles led him to believe that the Christian faith, as it appears in the Churches of Europe and America, even in those which style themselves Reformed, is a huge historical mistake. There is no visible Church of Christ on earth. The Church of Paul and Peter was the true one; a community of brothers, of equals, of saints; but it passed away at an early date, our Lord having returned in the Spirit, as He had promised, to dwell among His people evermore. On this second advent, Noyes says that our Lord abolished the old law; closing the empire of Adam, cleansing His children from their sin, and setting up His kingdom in the hearts of all who would accept His reign. Noyes fixes this spiritual advent in the year 70, immediately after the fall of Jerusalem; since which date, he says, there have been one true Church, and many false churches, having His name;—a Church of His saints, men sinless in body and in soul; confessing Him as their prince; taking upon them a charge of holiness; rejecting law and usage, and submitting their passions to His will; and, churches of the world, built up in man's art and pride, with thrones and societies, prelates and cardinals, and popes; churches of the screw, the fagot, and the rack, having their forms and oaths, their hatreds and divisions, their anathemas, celibacies and excommunications. The devil, says Noyes, began his reign on the very same day with Christ, and the official churches of Greece and Rome, together with their half-reformed brethren in England and America, are the capital provinces of the devil's empire. The kingdoms of the earth are Satan's: yet the Perfect Society, founded by Paul, into which Christ descended as a living spirit, never quite perished from out of men's hearts, but, by the grace of God, kept an abiding witness for itself, until the time should come for reviving the apostolic faith and practice, not in a corrupted Europe, a worn-out Asia, but in the fresh and green communities of the United States. Some high and vestal natures kept the flame alive. The day for this true Church came. Faith, banished from the busy crowd, returned to the young seekers after truth at Yale; and the family of Christ, after being corrupted in Antioch, persecuted in Rome, and caricatured in London, is now re-funded at Wallingford, Brooklyn, and Oneida Creek!

In this new American sect,—a church as well as a school,—the rule of faith and the rule of life are equally plain. The Perfectionist has a right to do what he likes. Of course he will tell you (as my host at Oneida tells me) that from the nature of the case he can do nothing but what is good. The Holy Spirit sustains and guards him. Some may go wrong through the old Adam being fierce within them; but a few exceptions do not kill an eternal truth. We hold that a king can do no wrong, though a good deal of scandal, tempered by daggers and actresses, may afflict our royal and imperial courts. A Perfectionist knows no law; neither that pronounced from Sinai, and repeated from Gerizim, nor that which is administered in Washington and New York. He does not live under law, but under God: that is to say, under what his own mind prompts him to do, as being right. The Lord has made him free. To him, the word is nothing: its force having been wholly spent for him at the Second Coming. No commandment in the Ten, no statute on the rolls, is binding upon him,—a child of grace, delivered from the power of the law, and from the stain of sin. Laws are for sinners—he is a saint; other men fall into temptation—he is sealed and reclaimed by the Holy Ghost.

This frame of mind, which is not unlikely to look like rebellion in the eyes of a Gentile, is called by the Bible Communists, a state of submission. In this world you can only choose whom you will serve. You cannot have two masters,—God and Mammon. Earth is not perfect; Christ is Perfect. In confessing Christ, you give up the world, yielding it bodily, thoroughly, and forever. No half measure will suffice to save you; and the whole tendency of American thought (before the War) being in favor of individuals as against institutions, no one felt much surprised on hearing that Noyes and his adherents had made a formal renunciation of their duty to the United States. Others had done the same thing before him; Shakers, Tunkers, Mormons, Socialists, Icarians, and many more. In fact, not a few Americans of the higher class had come to regard the State as a kind of political club, from which they might withdraw at pleasure; but the Perfectionist went far beyond the Socialist, the Shaker, and the Mormon, in his renunciation, for he rejected the law of God as well as the laws of men; the civil code, the statutes at large, the canons and degrees, the Ten Commandments, the Lord's Prayer, the Sermon on the Mount; all his old voluntary and involuntary rules, from his temperance pledge to his marriage vows. Nothing of the old man, the old citizen, was left to him. He denied the churches, he renounced his obligations, he defied the magistrates and the police. In his obedience to God, he cast away all the safeguards invented by man. Noyes had been a teetotaller; on assuming holiness, he began to drink ardent spirits. He had been temperate as a Brahman; he now indulged his palate with highly-spiced meats. He had been chaste in his habits, regular in his hours of sleep; he now began to stay out all night, to wander about the quays, to lie in doorways, to visit infamous houses, to consort with courtesans and thieves. In defending himself against men who cannot reconcile such a mode of living with the profession of holiness, Noyes asserts that he had given himself up to temptation, but the power in which he trusted for protection had been strong enough to save him. He had drunk, and gorged, and wantoned with the flesh, in order to escape from the bonds of system. As he puts the matter to himself, he said, "Can I trust God for morality? Can I trust my passions, desires, propensities, everything within me which has hitherto been governed by worldly rules and my own volition, to the paramount mercy of God's Spirit?" He answered to himself that he could and would put his faith, his conduct, his salvation, in the keeping of the Holy Ghost; and in this confidence, he says, he walked through the house of sin untouched, as the Hebrew children stood unscathed in the midst of fire.

But how, it may be asked, does a man arrive at this stage of grace? Nothing (if I understand it) is more easy. You have only to wish it, and the thing is done. Good works are not necessary, prayers are not desirable; nothing serves a man but faith. You stand up in public, by the side of some brother in the Lord, and take upon yourself a profession of Christ. You say, you are freed from the power of sin, and the stain is suddenly washed from your soul. In this American creed, facts would appear to lie in wait for words, and all that is said is apparently also done. "He stood up and confessed Holiness,"—such is the form of announcing that a lamb has been brought into the fold of Noyes.

When Noyes began to preach his doctrine, some years ago, the spirit of separation was alive and active in every part of New England; for many persons thought that the only hope of staying this impetus of the American mind towards social chaos lay in the principles of association then being tested in such experiments as Mount Lebanon, New Harmony, and Brook Farm. In such a state of confusion, it is no marvel that Noyes should have failed to see that his theory of Individual Action, as he first conceived it, could not work. A man may be a law to himself; but how can he be a law to another man, who is also bound to be a law to himself? Noyes may receive from his own conscience a guiding light; and Hamilton may receive from his own conscience a guiding light: each may be sufficient for its purpose; but how can Noyes' light become a rule for Hamilton, Hamilton's for Noyes', unless by a bargain between the two? If they could not make such a bargain, they must dwell apart; if they could compromise the affair as to these two lights, they came under law. From this alternative they have no escape: on one side chaos, on the other law.

Noyes found himself in trouble the day he began to live with his male and female disciples according to their notions of celestial order—not under law, but under grace; and before the community could exist as a fact, a second principle had to be introduced.

This second principle is called Sympathy; and the office which it holds in the Family is very much like that which the world assigns to Public Opinion. Sympathy corrects the individual will, and reconciles nature with obedience, liberty with light.

Thus a brother may do anything he likes: but he is

trained to do everything in sympathy with the general wish. If the public judgment is against him, he is wrong — that is to say, he is going away from the path of grace; and his only chance of happiness lies in going back to what is most agreeable to the common mind. The Family is supposed to be always wiser than the unit.

A man who wants anything for himself — say, a new hat, a holiday, a young damsel's smiles — must consult with one of the Elders and see how the brotherhood feels on the subject of his wish. If their sympathy is not with him, he retires from his suit. When the matter is of moment, he seeks the advice of a committee of Elders, who may choose to refer it to the Family in their evening sittings.

It was long before this second great principle was introduced as a ruling power, and until it was introduced, the community of Perfect Saints had little of what the world would call success.

CHAPTER LV.

A BIBLE FAMILY.

WHILE Noyes was still a preacher of Holiness, going about among the churches, he made converts of Abigail Mervin (a woman was necessary to him, and Abigail was a female disciple of whom he might feel proud) and James Boyle; and these two early followers were the first apostates from his creed. Abigail seems to have expected an offer of marriage; Boyle had hopes of being elected pope; but neither of these pretensions suited Noyes, who felt averse to wedlock, and meant to be pope himself. They were only the first seceders; for as time wore on, and the true principle of Holiness was understood among his people, the units fell away from the mass. Each man was a law to himself; the spirit operated in single minds; and out of many independent members it was impossible to found a church. No one would concede, no one obey, no one unite. At the end of four years' labor, Noyes stood alone; all his beloved disciples having gone their way; some into the world, others into heresies, many into older sects, from which they had been drawn by him. The press had opened fire upon them. Noyes had been denounced as crazy; a charge to which his conduct and preaching oftentimes exposed him. There were still Perfectionists, but Noyes was not their pope.

Taught by painful trials that ropes cannot be spun out of sand, he turned, as so many others were at that time turning, to the principle of association — with him it must be Bible Association — for a future. Cast adrift from his old friends of New Haven, he went back to his father's house at Putney, in Vermont, where he had been first awakened into spiritual life, and there he began his work of converting the world afresh, by founding a Bible class, and teaching a few simple and rustic persons the way of grace. Some listened to his words; for never, perhaps, since the days of Herod the Great, certainly not since the years preceding the English Civil War, had any people ever found itself in a moral chaos so strange as that which prevailed in the United States. Abigail Mervin had declared, on quitting the sect, that their gospel freedom ran into indecency. The same thing had been said in the streets of Jerusalem and in the streets of London; but while the Gentiles of New York laughed at these stories, the believers waxed in zeal. What were the world and its ways to them? The Putney class grew strong in purpose, if not in numbers; for Noyes having come to see that quality of converts, rather than quantity, was of moment to him, now bent the force of his genius, which was great and original, upon the dozen hearers whom his voice had called together in his native town; until he could transform the Bible class into a Bible Family; in other words, until he had made them ready in soul and body for the great experiments of dwelling in one house, free from the trammels, everywhere else endured, of living under law.

To lodge a family of converts under one roof, the teacher required a large house. A large house, even in Vermont, where the dwellings are built of wood, costs money, and Noyes was poor. His life had been that of a wanderer to and fro; resting-place he had none; and the shepherd, like his sheep, was without shelter from the storm. Among his disciples in Vermont there was one young lady of good family, with present means and some expectations; such a young lady would be a blessing to him in every way, if he could only obtain her as a wife; but then his principles stood in the way. Marriage being utterly against his doctrine of the true gospel life, how was he to get her person and her money into his power? Of course, he could not offer his hand and his heart in the usual way, since she had heard him declaim against wedlock as the sign of a degenerate state. In fact, if he proposed to her at all, — and his need for her dollars was very sore, —he would be compelled to say that he should not expect her to be true to him only, and that he would certainly not engage to be true to her. But Harriet's position was out of the common way. She had no father, no mother, no brother, no sister. Her only kinsman was an aged and foolish grandfather. She had been in love with a young man who wished to marry her, but the old man had interfered to prevent him; on which the girl had fallen sick, and in a fit of remorse her grandfather had sworn an oath that in future she should do as she pleased, and he would willingly abide her wishes. Thus, a way had been opened, as it were, for Noyes to come in with his proposal, which conveyed to her an offer of his hand in the following words (a copy of which has been given to me by himself): —

From J. H. Noyes, to Miss H. A. Holton.

PUTNEY, June 11, 1838.

BELOVED SISTER, — After a deliberation of more than a year, in patient waiting, and watching for indications of the Lord's will, I am now permitted — and indeed happily constrained — by a combination of favorable circumstances to propose to you a partnership which I will not call marriage till I have defined it.

As believers, we are already one with each other, and with all saints. This primary and universal union is more radical, and of course more important, than any partial and external partnership; and, with reference to this, it is said, "there is neither male or female," neither marrying nor giving in marriage, in heaven. With this in view, we can enter into no engagements with each other, which shall limit the range of our affections, as they are limited in matrimonial engagements, by the fashion of this world. I desire and expect my yoke-fellow will love all who love God, whether they be male or female, with a warmth and strength of affection unknown to earthly lovers, and as freely as if she stood in no particular connection with me. In fact, the object of my connection with her will be, not to monopolize and enslave her heart or my own, but to enlarge and establish both in the free fellowship of God's universal family. If the external union and companionship of a man and woman in accordance with these principles is properly called marriage, I know that marriage exists in heaven, and I have no scruple in offering you my heart and hand, with an engagement to be married in due form, as soon as God shall permit.

At first I designed to set before you *many* weighty reasons for this proposal; but, upon second thought, I prefer the attitude of a witness to that of an advocate, and shall therefore only suggest, briefly, a few matter-of-fact considerations, leaving the advocacy of the case to God—the customary persuasions and romance to your own imagination—and more particular explanations to a personal interview.

1. In the plain speech of a witness, not of a flatterer,

I respect and love you for many desirable qualities, spiritual, intellectual, moral, and personal; and especially for your faith, kindness, simplicity, and modesty.

2. I am confident that the partnership I propose will greatly promote our mutual happiness and improvement.

3. It will also set us free, at least myself, from much reproach, and many evil surmisings, which are occasioned by celibacy in present circumstances.

4. It will enlarge our sphere and increase our means of usefulness to the people of God.

5. I am willing, at this particular time, to testify by example that I am a follower of Paul, in holding that "marriage is honorable in all."

6. I am also willing to testify practically against that "bondage of liberty" which utterly sets at naught the ordinances of men, and refuses to submit to them even for the Lord's sake. I know that the immortal union of hearts—everlasting honey-moon, which alone is worthy to be called marriage, can never be *made* by a ceremony, and I know equally well that such a marriage can never be *marred* by a ceremony. You are aware that I have no profession save that of a servant of God—a profession which has thus far subjected me to many vicissitudes, and has given me but little of this world's prosperity. If you judge me by the outward appearance, or the future by the past, you will naturally find, in the irregularity and seeming instability of my character and fortune, many objections to a partnership. Of this I will only say, that I am conscious of possessing, by the grace of God, a spirit of firmness, perseverance, and faithfulness in every good work, which has made the vagabond, incoherent service to which I have thus far been called, almost intolerable to me; and I shall welcome heaven's order

for my release from it as an exile after seven years' pilgrimage would welcome the sight of his home. I see now no reason why I should not have a "certain dwelling-place," and enter upon a course which is consistent with the duties of domestic life. Perhaps your reply to this will be the voice saying to me,—

> "Watchman, let thy wanderings cease;
> Hie thee to thy quiet home."

Yours in the Lord,

J. H. NOYES.

Harriet, left to herself, answered as the preacher wished. In a few days they were united; and Noyes expended her seven thousand dollars in building a house and a printing-office, in buying presses and types, and in starting a newspaper. So long as the old man lived, he supplied them with money to live on; when he died, Brother Noyes came in for nine thousand dollars in one lump. He makes no secret of the fact that he married Harriet for her money; to use his own words, she was given to him as his reward for preaching the Truth.

The first family gathered into celestial order at Putney included the Prophet's wife, his mother, his sister, and his brother; all of whom have remained true to his theory of domestic life. His mother died only a few days before my arrival at Oneida Creek; an aged lady, who went to her rest (I am told) confident that the system introduced by her son is the only true and perfect society of Christian men and women on the earth.

These persons, with a few preachers, farmers, doctors, and their wives and daughters, all men of means, character, and position, went to live in the same house;

setting up, as they oddly phrased it, a branch of the heavenly business in Putney, after a formal renunciation of the Republican Government, and an everlasting secession from the United States.

And now began for them a new life, more daring, more original than that which Ripley, Dana, and Hawthorn tried to follow at Brook Farm. They stopped all prayer and religious service, they put down Sunday, they broke up family ties, and, without separating anybody, put an end to the selfish relations of husband and wife. All property was thrown into a common stock; all debts, all duties, fell upon the Society, which ate in one room, slept under one roof, and lived upon one store. At first they were strict and stern with each other; for written codes being all set aside, as things of the old world, they had no means of guiding weak, of controlling wicked brethren, save that of free criticism on their conduct; a system of government which had yet to become a saving power. The life was somewhat hard. Three hours were spent each morning in the hall; one hour in reading such book of history as might help them to understand the Bible better; one hour in silence, or in reading the Scriptures; a third hour in discussing the things they had read and thought. Mid-day was given to labor on the farm; evening to study, reading, music, and society. One person gave lessons to the rest in either Greek or Hebrew; a second read aloud some English or German writer on hermeneutics; and a third stood up and criticised his brother saint. In the midst of these incessant labors, the old Adam appeared amongst them, and slew their peace. One man ate too much, a second drank too much, a third ran wild in love. Strife arose among the brethren, leading in turn to gossip among their neighbors, to queries about them in the local press, to attacks in the surrounding grog-shops, and at length into suits in the Gentile courts. What they had most to fear in their little Eden was gospel freedom in the matter of goods and wives.

Noyes admits that the Devil found a way into the second Eden as into the first; and that in Putney as in Paradise, the Evil One worked his evil will through woman. When the moral disorder in his little paradise could be no longer hidden, be became very angry and very sad. How was he to bear this cross? A sudden change from legal restraints to gospel liberties, must needs be a trial to the lusts of man. But how could he make distinctions in the work of God? God had given to man his passions, appetites and powers. These powers and appetites are free. Desire has its use and faculty in the heavenly system; and when the soul is free, all use implies the peril of abuse. Must, then, the Saints come under bonds? He could not see it. Aware that many of his people had disgraced the profession of Holiness, he still said to himself, in the words of St. Paul, "Must I go back because offences come?" To go back was for him to tear up his Bible and lay down his work. Such a return was beyond his desire, and beyond his power: so he labored on with his people, curbing the unruly, guiding the careless, and expelling the impenitent. As he put the case to himself:—If a man were moving from one town to another, he could not hope to do it without moil or dirt, how then could he expect to change his place of toil from earth to heaven without suffering damage by the way? Waste is incident to change. His people were unprepared for so sharp a trial; and the quarrels which had come upon them, scandalizing Windham County, and scattering many of the Saints, were laid by him to the account of those as yet unused to the art of living under grace.

Some rays of comfort fell upon Noyes in this hour of his failure and distress. A rival body of Perfectionists, of which Mahan was pope, and Taylor prime-minister, had set up an Eden of their own at Oberlin, in Lovain County, Ohio. Mahan pretended to see visions, to converse with angels, and to receive communications direct from God. Taylor, an able editor and eloquent preacher, made also some pretensions to celestial gifts. Now, between Noyes and Mahan, Putney and Oberlin, there had reigned a fraternal feud, like that which disgraced the two sons of Eve. According to all the Perfectionist prophets, Holiness and Liberty are the two primary elements in the atmosphere of Heaven, — that is to say, of a perfect society; but in the exercise of their daily right of following, each man his own lights, these prophets had come to regard the two elements as of unequal value; so that strife arose between them, questions were debated, and schools were formed. One party, putting freedom before holiness, were known as the "Liberty men;" another, putting sanctity before freedom, were known as the "Holiness men." Putney stood out for holiness; Oberlin for liberty; though both affected to renounce the world, and to admit no tutelage but that of God. Noyes attacked Oberlin in the "Witness;" Taylor answered in the "Evangelical;" and the war of words went raging on for years, until Putney fell away into quarrels; and Taylor had used his freedom in a fashion to provoke the interference of a Gentile court.

CHAPTER LVI.

NEW FOUNDATIONS.

When Putney had become too warm a place for Noyes and his Bible family to live in; not, as he told me, on account of any persecution from the churches of religious Vermont; but solely from the opposition of drunken and worthless rowdies; the Prophet having let his house and farm to a Gentile, moved away from his native town to Oneida Creek; a place which, on account of its beauty, its remoteness, and its fertility, seemed favorable to his plan of trying, by patient industry, to lay a new foundation for social and family life. Mary Cragin, who brought with her George, her husband, and some other friends already tried in the fire, came heartily into his scheme; becoming to this fresh enterprise all that Margaret Fuller would have liked to be, and was not, in the less daring settlement of Brook Farm.

About fifty men, with as many women, and nearly as many children, put their means together, built a frame-house and offices, bought a patch of land, which they began to clear and stock; and giving up the world once more, its usages, its rights, declared their family separated from the United States, from the society of men, even as Abraham and his seed had been separated from the people of Hauran. The new Bible Family announced itself as a branch of the visible kingdom of heaven. Many of the Saints having been at Putney, they had some experience in the ways of grace; and Noyes laid down for them a rule in their new home, which a Gentile would have thought superfluous at Oneida Creek, — the duty of enjoying life. At Putney, said he, they had been too strict; studying overmuch; dealing too harshly with each other's faults. In their new home, heaven would not ask from them such rigors. If God, he asked them, had meant Adam to fast and pray, would he have placed him in a garden tempted on every side by delicious fruit? Man's Maker blessed him with appetites, and turned him into a clover-field! And what were these Saints at Oneida Creek? Men in the position of Adam before the fall; men without sin; men to whom everything was lawful because everything was pure. Why, then, should they not eat, drink, and love, to their heart's content, under daily guidance of the Holy Spirit?

They made no rules, they chose no chiefs. Every man was to be a rule to himself, every woman to herself; and as to rulers, they declared that nature and education make men masters of their fellows, putting them in the places which they are born and trained to fill; another way of saying that God was to rule in person, with Noyes for his visible pope and king. All property was made over to Christ; and the use of it only was reserved for those who had united themselves to Him. The wives and children of the Family were to be as common as the loaves and fishes; the very soul of the new society being a mystery very difficult to explain in English phrase.

Through a dozen years of sharp and feverish trial the society held its ground. War without, and want within, exposed the brethren to temptations, which no body of zealots but a band of New England farmers, artisans, and professional men, could have lived through. Mary Cragin was drowned in the Hudson River, and it was long before a woman could be found to take her place. Noyes made overtures to Abigail Mervin, his first disciple, whom he still loved in the spirit. Abigail would not listen. She is still alive, I may add, and Noyes still dreams of drawing her back into his fold. Sister Skinner became the female leader; but she is now living at Wallingford; and I think that Sister Jocelyn, a poetess, may now be considered as the presiding goddess of Oneida Creek. But as power is only held by sympathy, her spells may be shared by the two singers, Sister Alice and Sister Harriet. I speak as one who has lived under the charm. In spite of their rude fare and their hard life, strange people came and joined them; a Massachusetts preacher, a Canadian trapper, a reader for the London press. Of all these converts to the kingdom of heaven, he who might have been counted on as the man least likely to be useful to such a colony, the Canadian trapper, proved in the end to be the actual founder of their fortunes. As yet, the Saints had given themselves heart and soul to the land, like those Shakers from whom Noyes (as Elder Frederick told me) had learnt his first lesson in social economy; but the arts of growing apples, potting pears, and making syrups, are too common in America for anybody to think of making a fortune by them. The Family did its best; its best was very good. Last year, as I saw by their books, they sold twenty-five thousand dollars worth of preserved fruits. But the lawns and gardens, the stately home, and the busy mills of Oneida, were not made out of apple-trees and peach-trees. They came, in the main part, from the cunning hands of Sewell Newhouse, this Canadian trapper.

One of the great trades of America is that of traps. Traps are wanted of many kinds, for the land is covered with vermin, from the huge bear of the Rocky Mountains down to the common field-mouse; but the Yankee mechanic, so prolific in the matter of cork-screws, sewing-frames, and nut-crackers, has left the manufacture of traps to Solingen and Elberfeld, so that western and northern America have been hitherto supplied with traps from beyond the Rhine. Now, Brother Newhouse, when he settled down to machine work at Oneida Creek, saw, as an old trapper, that the German article, though good and even cheap in its way, might be much improved; and taking the thing in hand, he soon made it lighter in weight, simpler in form, more deadly in spring. The Oneida Trap became the talk of Madison County and of the State of New York. Orders for it poured in; mechanics were employed, forges were built; and in a few months the German article was a saleless article in the New York stores. In a single year the Family made eighty thousand dollars of profit by their traps; and although the income has fallen off since others have begun to imitate this product of the Saints, the revenue derived from the sale of Oneida Traps is still about three thousand pounds English money in the year.

At first thought, there seems to be something comic in the fact of a kingdom of heaven being dependent for its daily bread on the sale of traps. As I walked through the forges with Brother Hamilton, I could not help saying that such work seemed rather strange for a colony of Saints. He answered, with a very grave face, that the Earth is lying under a curse, that vermin are a consequence of that curse, that the Saints have to make war upon them and destroy them,—whence the perfect legitimacy of their trade in traps! It is not in the State of New York, where every man is a pleader and a casuist, that any one is found at a loss for arguments in favor of that which brings grist to his mill.

Anyhow, they made the traps, and then the traps made them.

What may be called the home affairs of the Family seem to have been keeping pace with their outward and commercial progress. The theory of ruling the more disorderly spirits by means of sympathy, was raised from an idea into a science; and the chief business of the evening meetings has now become the evolution of this sympathy as a ruling power by means of free criticism. I was present at one of these meetings, when Sydney Jocelyn, a son of the poetess of Oneida Creek, was subjected to a searching public inquiry. Brother Pitt led the way, describing the young man, mentally and morally, pointing out, with seeming kindliness, but also with astonishing frankness, all the evil things he had ever seen in Sydney—his laziness, his sensuality, his love of dress and show, his sauciness of speech, his lack of reverence. Noyes, Hamilton, and Bolls followed, with observations almost equally severe; then came Sister Jocelyn, the culprit's mother, who certainly did not spare the rod; and after her rose up a cloud of witnesses. Most of these persons spoke of his good deeds, and two or three hinted that, with all his faults, Sydney was a man of genius, a true saint, a credit to Oneida; but the balance of testimony was decidedly against the prisoner on his trial. No man is allowed to reply in person and on the spot. A friend may put in a good word, so as to modify harsh and unfair judgments; but the person under censure must retire from the ordeal to his chamber, sleep on the catalogue of his virtues, so abundantly filled up by his associates; and if he has anything to say either in acceptance or in refusal of the heavy charges made against him by word of mouth, he must put that answer into writing, addressed to the whole community in the meeting-room, not to any individual traducer by name.

On the evening after this testimony had been heard against Sydney Jocelyn, the following letter in reply was read in the great hall:—

To the Community.

I take this occasion to express my thanks for the criticism and advice I received last evening, and for the sincerity that was manifested.

I wish to thank Mr. Noyes for his sincerity, especially in regard to times long past. I well remember when I felt very near him and used to converse freely with him; and I consider those my happiest days. I have always regretted my leaving him as I did. I *loved* him, and I am sure that had I continued with him, I should have been a better man and a greater help to him and the Community. I am certain that my love for him *then* has helped me a great deal *since*, and has been steadily growing ever since, in spite of adverse circumstances, and in my darkest hours his spirit shone forth and strengthened me and helped to dispel evil spirits. I wish to confess my love for Mr. Hamilton and my confidence in him as a leader. I thank him sincerely for his long-continued patience with me and his untiring efforts to bring me near to Christ and the Community.

I confess Christ the controller of my tongue and a spirit of humility.

Sydney.

What, however, struck me most about these criticisms, next to their obvious use in the art of governing men who have set aside the human laws, was not so much their candor as their subtlety. Many of the observations were extremely delicate and deep, showing fine powers of analysis sharpened by daily practice

I should not omit to say, that, although many young men bore witness against Sydney, no young woman had anything to say about him. The elder ladies were free enough, and one ancient dame exhibited a frankness which would have been hard for a Gentile youth to bear in silence. The reason of this was, not that the girls all liked him, and refrained from criticism, but that, as girls and young women, they could have had little to do with him, and could therefore have told none of his faults. But here we are touching on one of the deepest of the many mysteries of Oneida Creek.

The Family has no lawyer, no doctor, in its ranks; on the other hand, it affects to have no quarrels, and to enjoy perfect health. Following the old rule of America—a rule derived from provincial England—the Family breaks its fast at six in the morning, dines at twelve, sups at six in the evening; very much as the Arabs, and the children of nature everywhere, eat and drink, at sunrise, noon, and sunset. A few of the weaker saints eat flesh of bird and beast; the more advanced eat only herbs and fruit. Brother Noyes eats flesh from habit, but very little of it, having proved by trial that it is not necessary for his health. A party of the Saints went up into Canada last fall, under Newhouse, to trap beaver; they had five weeks of very hard life, and came back from the forests strong and well. None of the Family drink wine or beer, unless it be a dose of either cherry-wine, or gooseberry-wine, taken as a cordial. I tasted three or four kinds of this home-made wine, and agree with Brother Noyes that his people will be better without such wicked drinks.

CHAPTER LVII.

PANTAGAMY.

How shall I describe, in English words, the innermost social life so freely opened to my view by these religious zealots of Oneida Creek? To an Arab family I could easily shape the matter, so as to leave out nothing of importance to my tale, for the Arabs have derived from their fathers a habit of calling things by the simplest names. We English have another mood, that of hushing up nature in a fine sense of silence; of spending our curiosity on facts about trees, birds, fishes, insects; while we are carefully putting under dark covers anything that relates to the life and nature of man.

George Cragin, one of Mary Cragin's sons, a young man of parts and culture, above all, of erect moral feeling, fresh from college, where he has taken his medical degree, told me in one of our morning rambles, as he might have told a brother whom he loved, the whole history of his heart—the first budding of his affections—the way in which his love was treated—his sense of shame—his passionate desires—his training in the arts of self-restraint and self-control—(which is the discipline of his life as a religious man), from the moment of adolescence down to the very hour in which we talked together at Oneida Creek. That little history of one human soul, in its secret strivings, is the strangest story I have ever either heard or read. I wrote it down from the young man's lips, as we sat under the apple-trees—that tale of all he had ever felt, and learned, and suffered, in the school of love; told, as he told it, with a grave face, a modest manner, and in a scientific spirit; but I have no right to print one line of the confession which lies before me now. I saw at Oneida Creek a hundred records of a similar kind, though most of them were less complete in detail and in plan. Some day, in the coming years, such records may be gained for science, and become the bases, perhaps, of new theories in physiology and economics. At present they are sealed, and must be sealed. "They are laid up," said Brother Bolls, "these histories of emotion, until society is ready to receive and use them; when philosophers begin to study the life of man as they now study that of bees, we Bible Communists shall be able to supply them with a multitude of cases carefully observed."

The very core of their domestic system is a relation of the sexes to each other, which they call "a complex marriage." A community of goods, they say, implies a community of wives. Brother Noyes maintains that it is a blunder to say either that a man can only love once in his life, or that he can only love one object at a time. "Men and women," he says, "find universally that their susceptibility to love is not burnt out by one honeymoon, or satisfied by one lover. On the contrary, the secret history of the human heart will bear out the assertion that it is capable of loving any number of times, and any number of persons; and that the more it loves, the more it can love. This is the law of nature." Hence, in the Bible Family living at Oneida Creek, the central domestic fact of the household is the complex marriage of its members to each other, and to all; a rite which is to be understood as taking place on the entrance of every new member, whether male or female, into association; and which is said to convert the whole body into one marriage circle; every man becoming the husband and brother of every woman; every woman the wife and sister of every man. Marriage itself, as a rite and as a fact, they have abolished forever, in the name of true religion; declaring their belief that so selfish and exclusive an institution will be spurned by all honest churches the very next moment after the world is rid of the false idea that love is an act of sin.

That I may not be suspected of coloring by a word or tint the actual practice of this strange fraternity, I will give the statement of his social theory, drawn up for me by Noyes himself:—

Brother Noyes on Love.

"The Communities believe, contrary to the theory of sentimental novelists and others, that the affections can be controlled and guided, and that they will produce far better results when rightly controlled and rightly guided, than if left to take care of themselves without any restraint or guidance. They entirely reject the idea, that love is an inevitable fatality which must have its own course. They believe the whole matter of love and its expression should be subject to enlightened self-control, and should be managed for the greatest good. In the Communities it is under the special supervision of the fathers and mothers: in other words, of the wisest and best members, and is often under discussion in the evening meetings, and is also subordinate to the institution of criticism. The fathers and mothers are guided in their management by certain general principles, which have been worked out and are well understood in the Communities. One is termed the principle of the ascending fellowship. It is regarded as better for the young of both sexes to associate in love with persons older than themselves, and, if possible, with those who are spiritual, and have been some time in the school of self-control. This is only another form of the popular principle of contrast. It is well understood by physiologists that it is undesirable for persons of similar characters and temperaments to mate together. Communists have discovered that it is not desirable for two inexperienced and unspiritual persons to rush into fellowship with each other: that it is far better for both to associate with persons of mature character and sound sense.

"Another general principle, well understood in the Communities, is, that it is not desirable for two persons to become exclusively attached to each other—to worship and idolize each other—however popular this experience may be with sentimental people generally. They regard exclusive idolatrous attachment as unhealthy and pernicious, wherever it may exist. The Communists insist that the heart should be kept free to love all the true and worthy, and should never be contracted with exclusiveness, or idolatry, or purely selfish love in any form.

"Another principle well known, and carried out in the Community, is, that no person shall be obliged to receive, at any time, or under any circumstances, the attention of those whom they do not like. The Communities are pledged to protect all their members from disagreeable social approaches. Every woman is free to refuse every man's attentions.

"Still another principle is, that it is best for men in their approaches to women, to invite personal interviews through the intervention of a third party, for two important reasons, viz.: first, that the matter may be brought, in some measure, under the inspection of the Community, and secondly, that the women may decline proposals, if they choose, without embarrassment or restraint.

"Under the operation of these general principles, but little difficulty attends the practical carrying out of the social theory of the Communities. As fast as the members become enlightened, they govern themselves by these very principles. The great aim is to teach every one self-control. This leads to the greatest happiness in love and the greatest good to all. . . . . ."

The style of living at Oneida Creek gives a good deal of power to women, much beyond what they enjoy under law; and this increase of power is a capital point in every new system of social order in the States. Something of this increased power of the female at Oneida Creek, I have seen and felt; and Brother Hamilton assures me there is much of charm and influence in the woman's life, which I have not been able to see and feel. The ladies all seem busy, brisk, content; and those to whom I have spoken on this point, all say they are very happy in their lot. Perhaps there is one exception to the rule: that of a lady, whose name I shall not mention, as she dropped some hint that she might one day think of going home to her friends.

At first, the world waged war upon Oneida Creek, as it had done upon Putney; making jokes against free-love, loading pistols against community of goods. Noyes claims, not only in his contest with Baptist and Congregational preachers, but in his more dangerous conflicts with Madison farmers and herdsmen, that the kingdom of Christ established on Oneida Creek should be judged as a whole. The sexual principle, he says, is the helpmeet of the religious principle; and to all complaints from without, he answers, "Look at our happy circle; we work, we rest, we study, we enjoy: peace reigns in our household; our young men are healthy, our young women bright; we live well, and we do not multiply beyond our wishes!"

By time the enmity of the world has been overcome; the quicker, since the world begins to see that the members of this community, though they may be wrong in their interpretation of the New Testament, are in real earnest as to living the word which they profess. Brother Noyes is now popular in this neighborhood, where the people judge his disciples by the results.

But a prophet may not waste his life upon a little farm, teaching his disciples, by his own example, how to live. Noyes finds that he has work to do on a larger scale and in a wider field: a new faith to expound, an intellectual conquest to achieve; and for these ends of his living as a witness, it is needful for him to reside a good deal in New York, at the centre of all moral, of all commercial, of all spiritual activities and agencies; where the Bible newspaper, called The Circular, is edited and published by his son. Enough for him that he visits the two settlements of Wallingford and Oneida from time to time; received as a prophet, and implored, like the prophets of old, to mediate daily between man and God.

The Family at Oneida Creek consists of about three hundred members, a number which these Bible Communists say is found by trial to be large enough to foster and develop the graces and virtues which belong to a perfect Society. Applicants for admission are refused from day to day. Three or four offers to come in have been refused while I have been lodging at the Creek; the system of life here practised being simply regarded as experimental. The foundations, Brother Noyes tells me, are now regarded as having been laid. When the details have been wrought out, other Families will be formed in New York and in the New England States.

Before I left Mount Lebanon, I had some conversation with Elder Frederick about these people. "You may expect to see the Bible Families increase very fast," said Frederick, who looks upon their growth with anything but a friendly eye; "they meet the desires of a great many men and women in this country: men who are weary, women who are fantastic; giving, in the name of religious service, a free rein to the passions, with a deep sense of repose. Women find in them a great field for the affections. The Bible Communists give a pious charter to Free Love, and the sentiment of Free Love is rooted in the heart of New York."

CHAPTER LVIII.

YOUNG AMERICA.

"We do not multiply beyond our wishes," said Noyes, in summary of the many beauties and advantages of what he and his people call the new Bible Order. "The baby question is the great question of the world," cried Brother Wright, among the Spiritualists of Providence. What do these reformers mean? In a score of different places, people have founded an annual baby show, at which they give prizes to the best specimen of baby-beauty; so many dollars (or the dollars' worth) for fine teeth, for bright eyes, for chubby cheeks, for fat arms and hands, for the thousand nameless merits which a jury of ladies can assert in these rosy yearlings. What do these facts imply? Is infant beauty becoming rare? Has the public mind been roused to a consciousness of the decline? These things can hardly be: since Young America crows and laughs, and is quite as fat, as rosy, and hilarious, as either Young England or Young France. Do the facts suggest that babies are growing scarce on this American soil? If this were the case, a great many people would cry "Amen" to Brother Wright's announcement that the baby question is the chief question of these latter times!

Now, I have been told that one result of the rapid growth in society and in the household of disturbing female creeds, is a fact of which the wiser men and graver women of New England—the great majority of sound and pious people—think very much, though they seldom allude to it in public.

What have I seen and heard in this country, leads me to infer that there is a very strange and rather wide conspiracy on the part of women in the upper ranks—a conspiracy which has no chiefs, no secretaries, no head-quarters; which holds no meetings, puts forth no platform, undergoes no vote, and yet is a real conspiracy on the part of many leaders of fashion among women; the end of which—if the end should over be accomplished—would be this rather puzzling fact:—there would be no more baby-shows in this country, since there would be no longer any Americans in America.

In Providence, the capital of Rhode Island, a model city in many ways—beautiful and clean, the centre of a thousand noble activities—I held a conversation on this subject with a lady, who took the facts simply as she said they are known to her in Worcester, in Springfield, in New Haven, in a hundred of the purest cities of America, and she put her own gloss and color upon them thus:—"A woman's first duty is to look beautiful in the eyes of men, so that she may attract them to her side, and exert an influence over them for good; not to be a household drudge, a slave in the nursery, the kitchen, and the school-room. Everything that spoils a woman in this respect, is against her true interest, and she has a right to reject it, as a man would reject an impost that was being laid unjustly on his gains. A wife's first thought should be for her husband, and for herself as his companion in the world. Nothing should be ever allowed to come between these two." I ventured to ask the lady, her husband sitting by, whether children do come between father and mother; saying that I had two boys and three girls of my own, and had never suspected such a thing. "They do," she answered boldly; "they take up the mother's time, they impair her beauty, they waste her life. If you walk down these streets" (the streets of Providence) "you will notice a hundred delicate girls just blushing into womanhood; in a year they will be married; in ten years they will be hags and crones. No man will care for them, on the score of beauty. Their husbands will find no lustre in their eyes, no bloom upon their cheeks. They will have given up their lives to their children."

She spoke with fervor, and with a fixed idea that what she was saying to me might be said by any lady in open day before all the world; unconscious, as it seemed to me, that while proudly insisting on woman's rights, she and those for whom she spoke were ready to abandon all woman's duties; unconscious also, as it seemed to me, that in asserting the loss of beauty, as a consequence of domestic cares, she and those who think with her were assuming the very fact which almost every father, almost every husband, would deny. Yet, in pious Boston and Philadelphia, no less than in wicked New Orleans and New York, this objection to become a mother in Israel is one of those radical facts which (I am told) must be admitted, whether for good or evil; the rapid diminution of native-born persons being matter of record in many public acts. What my Saratoga friend said to me about his countrywomen having no descendants left alive in a hundred years, expresses the fears of many serious men.

Now, this assertion of the growing scarcity of native-born children in the United States will probably be new and strange to many; since, in England, we are constantly hearing, in the first place, of the rapid growth of the population in America, as compared with Europe; and in the second place, of the high value which is set in that new country on every individual child. In some districts, also, the rule which we find in the New England States, and among the higher classes in Pennsylvania and New York, is not observable. In Ohio and Indiana, and generally, indeed, in the western country, the female prides herself on her brood of darlings, and the Missouri boss, not having a fine lady for a wife, rejoices in his regiment of stalwart sons. Here, in New England, in New York, it is wholly different from what we see in yon healthy and vigorous western cities. It may be only fashion, it may be only frenzy, but for the passing moment, America (I am told) is wasting for the want of mothers. In the great cities, among those shoddy queens who live in monster hotels, among those nobler ladies who live in their own houses, it is extremely rare to find a woman who has such a brood of romping boys and girls about her as an ordinary English mother is proud to give her country. The rule as to number of offspring is rather that of Paris than that of London.

On a point of so much delicacy, I should wish to be understood as speaking with all reserve, and subject to a happy correction of any unconscious errors. A stranger must not expect to see down into all the depths of this mystery of domestic life. Ladies may be shy of debating such topics, and with men who are not their physicians, it is right that they should abstain from conveying their creed by hints. But the fact that many of these delicate and sparkling women do not care to have their rooms full of rosy darlings is not a matter of inference. Allusions to the nursery, such as in England and Germany would be taken by a young wife as compliments, are here received with a smile, accompanied by a shrug of undoubted meaning. You must not wish an American lady, in whose good graces you desire to stand, many happy returns of a christening day; she might resent the wish as an offence; indeed, I have known a young and pretty woman rise from a table and leave the room, on hearing such a favor expressed towards her by an English guest.

Now, what, if this is true, can be the end of such a fashion among the upper classes, except the rapid displacement of the old American stock? Statesman, patriot, moralist, here is a question to engage your thoughts! The Irish and the Germans rush into every vacant space. Is it pleasant for any one to consider that in three or four generations more there may be no Americans left on the American soil? In the presence of such a possibility, have the noble churches, the many conservative schools of New England, no mission to assume?

The tale which seems to be so sadly written on the floor of every room you enter, is also told at large in the census returns. Where are the American States in which the birth-rate stands the highest in proportion to the number of people? Is it found highest in pious New Hampshire, in moral Vermont, in Sober Maine? All fancies, all analogies, would have led us to expect it; but the facts are wholly out of keeping with conjecture. In these three pious, moral, and sober States, the birth-rate is lowest. The only States in which there is a high and healthy rate of natural increase, are the wild countries peopled by new settlers,—Oregon, Iowa, Minnesota, Mississippi, —States in which, it is said, there are few fine ladies and no bad fashions. Strangest of all strange things is the example set to the rest of these States by Massachusetts, the religious centre of New England, the intellectual light of the United States. In Massachusetts, the young women marry; but they seldom become mothers. The women have made themselves companions to their husbands; brilliant, subtle, solid companions. At the same time the power of New England is passing over to the populous West, and a majority of the rising generation of Boston is either of German or of Irish birth.

This rather dismal prospect for Young America is not a consequence of the Germans and Irish put together exceeding the natives in number. Those nationalities are large, no doubt; but as yet they have not turned the scale. The list of marriages still exhibits a preponderance of natives; and it is only when you come to the register of births that the account runs all another way.

Under the constitution of the United States, numbers are strength; numbers make the laws; numbers pay the taxes; numbers vote away the land. Power lies with the majority; and the majority in Massachusetts is going over to the Irish poor, to the Fenian circles and the Molly Maguires. At present the foreigners count only one in five; but as more children are being born to that foreign minority than to the native majority, the proportions are changing every year. In twenty years, those foreign children will be the majority of men in Massachusetts.

How will the intellectual queens of Boston bear the predominance of such a class?

CHAPTER LXIX.

MANNERS.

"WHAT *do* you think of this country?" said to me an English lady, who had spent two years of her life in the Middle States, Ohio and Kentucky. Though I had then been five whole days in New York, I had not come to a final judgment on the virtues of thirty millions of people; so I answered my friend with a cowardly evasion, that it seemed to me a free country. "Free!" cried the lady with a shrug; "you are fresh to it now; when you have lived here three or four months, I shall be glad to learn what you have seen and thought. Free! The men are free enough; but, then, what *they* call their freedom, *I* should style their impudence."

Those words are often in my thoughts; never more than they have been to-day, while strolling through these streets of Philadelphia, now that I have fulfilled my terms and travelled over ten thousand miles of American ground. A lady fresh from May Fair, used only to the ways of well-bred men, to the silent service of her maid and groom, would be sure to fall, like my questioner, into the error of supposing that the only liberties to be found in America are the liberties which people take with you.

All men of Teutonic race are apt to cast big looks on the strangers whom they meet by chance. It is a habit of our blood. The Norse gods had it; and we, their heirs, can hardly ever see an unknown face, an unfamiliar garb, without feeling in our hearts the longing to hoot and pelt. In presence of a strange man, a gentleman puts on his armor of cold disdain, a rough looks out for a convenient stone. We bear this impulse with us on our journeys to and fro about the earth; Englishmen carrying it in the form of pride, Americans in the form of brag. Of course, it is not the way with all. Men of large hearts, of wide experience, of gentle nurture, will neither wrap their pride in an offensive coldness, nor obtrude their power in a boastful phrase. But some of the rank and file, having neither large hearts nor wide experience, nor gentle nurture, will always do so; enough of them, perhaps, to create in a stranger's mind the impression that this English reserve, this Yankee brag, are notes of the Anglo-Saxon race. I shall not say which of these two methods of announcing our riches, gifts, titles, powers, and possessions—our strength, our glory, our superiority—is the more galling to men of another stock; Italians and Frenchmen tell me they have given the palm of offence to our haughty and unbending pride. A Yankee says to them plainly, either in word or look: "I am as good as you are—better;" they know the worst at once. An Englishman says nothing; they have no defence against him; and his silence is both galling and intrusive. Now, we English are apt to judge American shortcomings very much as Frenchmen and Italians judge our own, with the addition of a family pique; so that our cousins of this other side come out from such trials of their imperfections very much tattered and torn.

In an old country like England, where society is stronger than among our cousins in this new home—where personal fancies are held in check by public sentiment, acting in the name of fashion—ordinary men and women are apt to consider smoothness of surface, softness of voice, conformity of style, as of higher moment than they would appear to judges of the stamp of Mill. Of course, no man of the world, even though he should happen to be a philosopher, will despise the charms of a good manner. The lady who sits next to me at dinner, being well-dressed, speaking in low tones, eating her food daintily, smiling on occasion sweetly, does me, by her presence, a positive service. The gentleman across the table, who is always telling the company, in looks and tones, that he is as good as they are—better than they are—takes all flavor from the dish, all bouquet from the wine. Manners may be no more than the small circulating coinage of society; but when these bits of silver have the true mint-mark upon them, they will pass for all that they are worth in every place, at every hour of the day. In the moment of a quick demand a few cents in the purse may be of higher value to a man than a bag of dollars laid up in a bank. What makes a good manner of so much worth as to have raised it into one of the fine arts, is the fact that in the free commerce of men and women, none but the minor debts of society are likely to arise between guest and guest. In the street, in the hotel, in the railway-train, a man's character hardly ever comes into play. What a man is may be of little account to the passer-by; what he does may either gladden that passer-by with delightful thoughts, or torture him into agonies of shame.

The Yankee of our books and farces—the man who was forever whittling a yard of stick, putting his heels out of window, grinding his quid of pig-tail, squirting his tobacco-juice in your face, while, in breathless and unsuspecting humor, he ran, to your amazement and amusement, through a string of guesses, reckonings, and calculations, as to what you were, whence you came, what you were doing, how much money you were worth—as to whether you were single or married, how many children you had, what you thought of everything, and whether your grandmother was alive or dead—that full embodiment of the great idea of Personal Freedom is not so common and so lively as he would seem to have been some twenty years ago. Seeking for him everywhere, finding a shadow of him only, and that but seldom, I have missed him very much; an element of extravagance and humor that would have been very welcome to me in long, grave journeys, which were often a thousand miles in silence. In the wagon from Salt Lake to Kearney, in the boat from Omaha to St. Louis, in the car from Indianapolis to New York, I have often longed for the coming of one of those vivacious rattles, who used (as we have read) to poke his stick into your ribs, his nose into your conversation, to tell you every thing he did n't know, and to pull out your eye-teeth generally; but he no more came in answer to my wish than the witty cabman comes in Dublin, the stolid Pasha in Damascus, the punctilious Don in Madrid—those friends of our imagination, whom we love so much on paper, and whom we never meet in our actual lives!

In the room of this lost humorist, you find at your elbow in the car, in the steamboat, at the dinner-table, a man who may be keen and bright, but who is also taciturn and grave; asking few questions, giving curt answers; a man occupied and reserved; on the whole, rather English in his silence and his pride than Yankee (of the book pattern) in his loquacity and his smartness. Perhaps he whittles; perhaps he chews; assuredly he spits. What impels a man to whittle when he is busy—while he is planing a campaign, composing an epic, mapping out a town? Is it an English habit, lost to us at home, like rocking in arm-chairs and speaking through the nose? I hardly think so. Is it a relic of some Indian custom? The Algonquins used to keep their reckonings by means of cuts and notches on a twig; and when Pocahontas came to England, her followers brought with them a bundle of canes, on which they were to keep accounts of what they saw among the Pale-faces. Whittling may be a remnant of this Indian custom; and the gentleman resting on the next bench to me, without a thought of Pocahontas and her people, may be whittling notes for his election-speeches on his stick. I wonder whether he learned to chew at school? I wonder how he felt when he first put pig-tail into his mouth?

In a railway-train, in a ball-room, in the public street, you have much to do with a man's habits and behavior, not much with his virtues and acquirements.

In my journey from Columbus to Pittsburg, I spent about twenty hours in company with a Missouri boss. Now boss is a master (the word is Dutch, and has gone westward from New York). In London he would have been a capitalist, in Cairo an effendi; in one city he would have had the bearing of a gentleman, in the other he would have had the aspect of a prince. He was a good fellow, as I came to know; but he made no approach in his dress, in his speech, in his bearing, to that elegant standard which in Europe denotes the gentleman. A fine lady would not have touched him with her fan.

Whence comes that nameless grace of style,—that tender and chivalric bearing, which, in rounding off all angles, smoothing away all knots, makes a man appear lovely and acceptable in the eyes of all his fellows? Is it an affair of race? We English have it only in degree; a little more perhaps, naturally, than the Dutch. It is a gift that never comes to us easily and at once; we have to toil for it long, and we seldom win it when we try. No man, says an old adage, has a fine accent, an easy carriage, a perfect presence, whose grandmother was not a lady born; for in society, as in heraldry, it takes three generations of men to make a gentleman. Thus, in our common speech, we imply by a good manner a gentle descent, and by the term high breeding we express our sense of personal charm.

But this common use of language fails to express and explain the action of a general rule. Among Gothic tribes, in whom the tendency towards individual freak is strong, this outward and conceding softness of demeanor may be slow to come and swift to go; it may only come to men who have ease and leisure, brightened by moral culture, and by intellectual toil.

In the Latin, in the Greek, in the Arab, it would almost seem as though it required no time to grow, no effort to improve. An Italian rustic has often a finer manner than an English earl. Why is this so? Not because country habits are a liberal education, as the poets feign; an English plough-boy having no rival in Europe for gross stupidity and awkwardness, unless he can find his mate in that Dutch peasant whose name of "boor" has passed into our language as the fullest expression for lout and clown. Even the Italian, elegant as his bearing always is, cannot stand in comparison with the more supple Greek. A native of Athens, Smyrna, Rhodes, will fleece you with a grace that more than half inclines you to forgive him for the cheat. But he, again, must yield the palm before the easy and unstudied beauty of an Arab's mien; a man whose every gesture is a lesson in the highest of social arts. When you are in an Eastern city, even in an Eastern desert, the question is forever springing to your lips—who taught yon muleteer to bow and smile; who gave that fluent grace to yon tawny Sheikh? A lady, coming into an Arab's camp at night, would feel no dread, unless she had been warned by previous trials: for the Sheikh, under whose canvas tent she may find herself, has, in a perfection rarely seen, that gift of gait and speech which in the west is only to be sought, not always to be found, in men of the highest rank. How does the Bedouin gain this princely air? Not from his wealth and power—a herd of goats, a flock of sheep, are his sole estate; not from his mental efforts—he can hardly read and write. The Sheikh who inspires this confidence, so far from being a prince, a priest, bound by his nature and his habit to do right, may be a thief, an outlaw, an assassin, after his kind, with the scorch of fire and the stain of blood upon that hand which he waves with a bewitching grace. Yet he looks the prince. All Orientals have this nameless charm. A Syrian peasant welcomes you to his stone hut, makes his sign of the cross, and hopes that "Peace will be with you," after a fashion which a caliph could not mend. Ease is the element in which he lives; grace seems to have become his second nature; and he moves with the dignity of his high-born mare.

When you quit the East, you leave some part of that fine air, that flattering courtesy, behind you. Less of it is found in Alexandria than in Cairo; less in Smyrna than at Damascus. Sailing westward, you will lose it more and more; by a scale of loss that might be measured on a chart. Speaking roundly, the gift of seeming soft and gracious, which we call by the name of Manner, declines in a regular order from East to West; in Europe, it is best in Stamboul, worst in London; in the world (so far as I have seen), it is best in Cairo, worst at Denver and Salt Lake. And the rule which governs the ends of these great chains, holds good for all the links between them; the finer courtesies of life being more apparent in St. Louis than Salt Lake; in New York than in St. Louis; in London than in New York; in Paris than in London; in Rome than in Paris; in Athens than in Rome; in Stamboul than in Athens; in Cairo and Damascus than in Stamboul. If I ever go westward to California, I shall expect to find the manners worse in San Francisco than they are at St. Louis and Salt Lake.

CHAPTER LX.

LIBERTIES.

WILL any one learned in the ways of nature say what is the cause of a decline in manners which may be noted at every stage of a journey from the Usbeyah to Pennsylvania Avenue? What is the secret of the art itself? Whence comes this gentle craft, of which the Saxon has so little, the Persian has so much? Man for man, a Persian is less noble than an Arab, an Arab than a Gaul, a Gaul than a Briton; why then should the lower race excel the higher in this subtle test of bearing? Is manner nothing more than a name for the absence of liberty? Is that soft reserve, that bated voice, that deprecating tone, no more than a sacrifice of individual force to social order? Are we polite because we are not ourselves? In short, is a good manner a liberal accomplishment or only a slavish grace?

Two facts may be taken as proved. 1. That charm has scarcely any affection for busy commonwealths. No free people has much of it to spare; no servile nation is without it in abundance. In America, the Negro has it, the Cheyenne has not; in Europe, the Greek has more of it than the Gaul; in Asia, the Persian and Hindoo have more of it than the Armenian and the Turk. 2. It is rarely found among men of the highest genius. Whether in arts or letters, manner means mediocrity: mannerism of style is but a name for the absence of individuality, of invention, of original power. Men who show great force of character cannot show a fine manner, which implies polish, smoothness, and conformity. Hence, men of the higher genius are called eccentrics and originals.

Might not a rule be laid down which should express an approach to the truth in some such words as these: a people has this exceeding grace of spirit in exact proportion to the length and strength of the despotism under which it has been schooled?

I do not say that such will be found the final form of this rule. As yet we have few materials, and no fixed principles, for a science of the Life of Man. But if a large experience and induction were at some future time to show that such is the truth, the fact would serve to explain some points which in our present state of knowledge give us so great pleasure. Men of poetic habits, when they hear of nations falling off in manners as they gain in liberty and power, are apt to grieve, and almost to despair. That nations do fall off in manners with the advance of freedom and prosperity, is one of those facts which are open, obvious, uniform; written in every figure, told in every glance. Go where you list, from Jerusalem to Florence, from Paris to New York, the tale is everywhere the same. The Effendine families in Zion are noticed as being far less affable, now that, after Arab measure, they are rich and free, than when the Holy City was an Arab camp, governed by a pasha of two tails, administering his rough injustice in the Jaffa gate. A Greek is far less winsome in his ways, less sweet and pleasant to have about you, now that he has ceased to be a slave. The Roman Jew, so smoothly spoken, so obsequious to your wish, in the days of yore, has now put on a saucy and audacious air. Free Florence has lost her name for sweet and tender courtesy since she has ceased to gaze into the Austrian's eyes, and make humble love to the Austrian's boot. France threw down her repute for bows and smiles, when she rose up in her wrath to slay her tyrants and break her chains. Yes, with the growth of liberty, the school of manners seems to be everywhere decaying. A Suabian is less polite in Omaha than in Augsburg; a Munster man in Baltimore than in Cork. Fritz will not say "good evening" to you on Lake Erie, Pat will not touch his cap to you in New York. Are not these changes the result of general laws? And if they be, what are those laws?

If it should appear that the fine favor which we call manner is but a note and sign of long submission to a master's will, you may find in the fact some grain of consolation even when a passing rowdy squirts his tobacco on your boots. This negro at the corner will brush them clean; doing his service for you with a soft alacrity, a submissive laughter, to charm your heart. Yesterday, this fellow was a slave, subject to cuffs and stripes, compelled to cringe and fawn. His son will have a way of his own; and his son's son, with a vote at the poll, a balance at the bank, will not be found so meek in spirit as to lie in the dust at your descendant's feet. Like every free man born on this American soil, he will probably say in gait and tone, "Ask me not to serve you,—am I not as good as you?"

It is well to know that the rough liberties for which our cousins have exchanged, as a rule, the deferential habits of their fathers, are of a solid and fruitful kind. If they have sold their birthright of civility, they have not sold it for a mess of pottage. Indeed, they may be said to have made a very good market of their manners; having got in return for them houses, votes, schools, wages; a splendid present for themselves, a magnificent future for their children. They have risen in society; they have ceased to be servants.

The relation of a French cook, of an English butler, of a Swiss valet, to his master, is a thing unknown in this country, whether you search for it on the Ohio, on the Delaware, on the sea-shore. Here you have no masters, no servants. No native white will serve another. Ask your friends in Richmond, in New York, about the birthplace of their domestics; you will find that their serving men and serving women are all either Irish or negro. A lady cannot get a native maid, her husband cannot get a native groom. Tempt a street huckster with as many dollars as would buy you a dozen clerks, and the chances are many that he will say: "I am as good as you; I have the same vote as you; I can go into Congress as well as you; I may be President as soon as you;" and the facts as between you and him are mainly as he puts them. A working tailor lives at the White House. One of the most popular Presidents since Washington died, was a log-cleaver, a woodsman. In this free country all careers lie open. They have always been so in yon Northern States; and, since the War, this Northern rule is fast becoming the law for every part. Even in Virginia there will soon be no mean whites. In Ohio, birth is nothing; in Cincinnati, I have heard it said, that no man has any need for a grandmother. Each man must make himself. Nor does it greatly matter what a man has been some dozen years ago; one year is an age in this swift country; indeed, this liberal dealing runs to such excess, that if a fellow has a smooth tongue, and keeps himself clean, the fact of his having passed a term in Auburn will not weigh heavily on his neck. Morrisey, the New York gambler, once a pugilist, then a prisoner, afterwards a faro-banker, may wear white kid, and give his vote in the Capitol. To pluck, to enterprise, to genius, every office in the land is open prize.

No white native, therefore, need despair so far as to sink into the grade of servant: the position, as he would call it, of a stranger and a slave. If he should fall so low, he would be lost forever in the minds of his former friends, like a Brahman who had forfeited his caste.

Nor do you find among these free citizens of the Great Republic much of that show of deference which in France and England would be understood, on both sides, as the expectation of a silver coin. No native American ever takes a vail. A driver in the street may cheat you, but he will not take from you a cent beyond his claim. No porter will accept a gift of service; no messenger will accept a reward for haste. Sometimes a news-boy will object to receiving change out of a greenback; more than once I have had my couple of cents thrown back into my lap. Thus it happens that no one ever proffers help in your little straits; for no one being employed in looking out for doles, your trouble is not his affair. When you are either young to the country, or careless of its ways, you may have to fetch water to your room, lift your box into the car, take your letter to the post; in short, do every little act for yourself which would be done for you in London for a shilling, in Paris for a franc. Where no man needs your vails, no man watches to do you good. Help yourself, — this is a stranger's motto and necessity in these free States.

Perhaps, the liberty which is more than any other likely to amuse a traveller in this country, is the freedom with which every one helps himself to anything he may want. In a railway-car, anybody who likes it will sit down in your place, push away your satchel, seize upon your book. Thought of asking your leave in the matter may not occur to him for hours. I lent a book to a man in the car at St. Louis; he kept it two days and nights; and then asked me if I was reading it myself. On my saying yes, he simply answered, "It is amusing; you will have a good time." On the Pennsylvania central line, a lady entered into my state-room, on pretence of looking out upon a river; she kept my seat, for which I had paid an extra fare, until her journey ended. If you ask for any dish at dinner, your neighbor, should the fancy take him, will snatch a portion of it from beneath your nose. When I was leaving Salt Lake City, Sister Alice, the daughter of Brigham Young, put up some very fine apples in a box for me to eat by the way; at a station on the Plains I found that a lady, a fellow-passenger in the wagon, had been opening my box, and helping herself to the fruit; and when she saw me looking at her, with some surprise perhaps visible on my face, she merely said, "I am trying whether your apples are better than mine." In the western country, a man will fire off your pistols, try on your gauntlets. Any one thinks himself at liberty to clean his clothes with your brushes, run his hair through your comb, and warm himself in your great-coat.

These things are not meant to be offensive. A fellow gives and takes; lends you a buffalo-hide on a frosty night; helps himself to your drinking-cup at the morning well. The manner is not fine; but the heartiness is pleasant, and you would be unintelligible if you made complaint. Every one you meet has the way which in Europe would be called original.

CHAPTER LXI.

LAW AND JUSTICE.

When Secretary Seward put to me the question which every American puts to an Englishman travelling in the United States, "Well, sir, what do you think of our country?" I ventured to reply, partly at least in jest, "I find your country so free that nobody seems to have any rights." As in all such sayings, there was some exaggeration in these words; yet they convey an impression dwelling on my mind.

No men in the world, not even we English, from whom they derive the virtue, boast so constantly, and with so much reason, of being a law-loving, a law-abiding people as these Americans. Having no State religion, no authentic Church, they seem to cling to the written Law, whether it be that which was fixed by the Constitution, that which has been voted by Congress, or only that which is defined by the Supreme Court, as to a rock in the midst of a storm.

Few things in this free country stand above the reach of cavil. That light which in Europe is said to beat upon a throne, here beats upon every object, whether high or low. Nothing can be done in secret; no one is permitted to live in private. Every man drives in a glass coach, and everybody flings a stone at him as he dashes past. Censure is the world's first duty; in some societies, such as the Bible Communists', criticism is adopted as the only governing power. Life is a Broad way procession. From the elegant frivolities of a lady's boudoir in Madison Square, down to the midnight follies enacted in the cellars of the Louvre, everything in yon city of New York is known, is seen, is judged by public opinion. The pulpit is accused, the press suspected, the government condemned. Capital is assailed and enterprise is watched. Each man thinks for himself, judges for himself, about the most delicate, the most sacred things — love, marriage, property, morality, religion. Law and justice do not always escape this rage for popular debate; but by common assent of minds, they are regarded as the very last subjects to be handled, and only then to be touched with reverential hand.

Whether it be constitutional, general, state, or only municipal, Law is nobly respected by the native American. The Judge of the Supreme Court is treated in Washington with a degree of respect unknown to lawyers in Europe; a respect akin to that which is paid to an archbishop in Madrid and to a cardinal in Rome. The State Judges take the places in society held among us by bishops. Even the village justice, though he is elected by the crowd, is always styled the squire.

This deference to the Law, and to every one who wears the semblance of lawful authority, is so complete in America, as to occasion a traveller some annoyance and more surprise. Every dog in office is obeyed with such unquestioning meekness, that every dog in office is tempted to become a cur. It is rare, indeed, to find a servant of the public civil and obliging. He may be something better, but assuredly he is neither helpful nor deferential. A news-boy will not serve you with a 'Ledger,' an 'Inquirer,' unless he likes. A policeman hardly condescends to show you the nearest way. A railway-guard will put you in this car, in that car, among the ladies, among the rowdies, among the smokers, just as he lists. A crowd of busy and free Americans will stand about, and bear this insolence of authority with a shrug, saying they cannot help it. When coming up from Richmond by the night train, Mr. Laurence Oliphant, myself, and many more, arrived at Acquia Creek about one o'clock; the passage thence to Washington takes four hours; and as we were much fatigued, and had only these four hours for rest, we begged that the keys of our berths might be given to us at once. "I'll attend to you when I'm through," was the only answer we could get; and we waited — a train of ladies, young folks, gentlemen — until the man had arranged his affairs, and smoked his pipe, more than an hour. Yet not one word was said, except by Mr. Oliphant and myself. The man was in office; excuse enough in American eyes for doing as he pleased. This is the kind of circle in which they reason; take away his office, and the man is as good as we are; all men are free and equal; add office to equality, and he rises above our heads. More than once I have ventured to tell my friends, that this habit of deferring to law and lawful authority, good in itself, has gone with them into extremes, and would lead them, should they let it grow, into the frame of mind for yielding to the usurpation of any bold despot who may assail their liberties, like Cæsar, in the name of law and order!

Sometimes, this profound respect for Law gives rise to singular situations. I may name two cases, one of which was told me at Clear Creek, near Denver, the other in Cass Township, Pennsylvania.

Black Bear, a Cheyenne warrior, who had scalped a white man, was arrested by the people of Denver. Across the English border he would have been tried on the spot and hung, there being no doubt whatever about his guilt; but the American people have such lofty regard for the forms of justice, that they will not suffer a murderer to be tried for his life, except under all the delicate conditions of a white man's court. Black Bear was brought from Colorado to Washington, two thousand miles from the scene of his crime; he had clever counsel to defend him; and the chief witnesses of his crime being far away, the jury gave him the benefit of all their doubts. Acquitted by the court, he became a lion in the city, especially among romantic women. He was taken to the Indian bureau; he was allowed to shake hands with the President; pistols and belts were given to him; and he returned to the Cheyenne camp a big chief, appearing to his own people to have been decorated and promoted by the white men, for no other cause than that of having taken their brother's scalp.

William Dunn, of Cass Township, Pottsville, was a manager of mines for the New York and Schuylkill Company; a gentleman and a man of science, with a great command over the coalfields of that picturesque and prosperous region of Pennsylvania. I have spent some days in that fine district, where I heard this story from the lips of his successor. Dunn was going about his duty, in the public street, in open day, when an Irish workman met him face to face, and with an insolent gesture asked for a holiday. "You cannot have it," said Dunn; "go back to your work." Without a word more, the Irishman drew a pistol from his belt and shot him dead. The murderer, taken red-handed, in the public street, standing by the body of his victim, was brought to trial in Pottsville and—acquitted. In that great coalfield, with towns and cities which have grown up in the forest in a dozen years, the Irish are sixty thousand strong. They are very poor, they are grossly illiterate: but every man has a vote, and the sixty thousand vote together as one man. Hence they carry all elections in the coal-field; elect the judges, serve on the juries, control the courts. Among these men there is a secret society called The Molly Maguires, the name and habits of which they have introduced from Ireland. The judge who tried this murderer was elected by the Molly Maguires; the jurors who assisted him were themselves Molly Maguires. A score of Molly Maguires came forward to swear that the assassin was sixty miles from the spot on which he had been seen to fire at William Dunn. Counsel submitted that this was one of the many cases of mistaken identity which adorn our legal annals; the judge summed up the case in the spirit of this suggestion; and the jurors instantly returned a verdict of Not Guilty. That ruffian is still alive. The great company whose servant had been slain could do nothing but engage another in his place. One gentleman to whom they offered the post, replied that he would not take it unless he could be armor-plated.

When you speak of this case to the eminent men of the Pennsylvania bar, they answer that these people cannot be punished, and that you must wait and work for a better state of things. "These criminals," they say, in substance, "are not Americans; they come to us from Europe; squalid, ignorant, brutal; they drink, they quarrel, they form secret associations; in their own country they paid their rent with a blunderbuss, in this country they ask for a holiday with a pistol, and demand an advance of wages with a blazing torch. But what are we to do? Can we close our ports against these immigrants? Should we change our judicial system, the pride of thirty-six millions of solid and steadfast people, to punish a mob of degraded

Irish peasants?" So they allege, with a noble confidence in moral growth, that this evil must be left to cure itself; as they reckon it will do in five-and-twenty years. "The children of these Molly Maguires," says the keen and brilliant mayor of Philadelphia, Morton M'Michael, "will be decent people; we shall put them through our schools and train them in our ways; their children, again, will be rich and good Americans, who will hardly have heard of such a society as the Molly Maguires."

CHAPTER LXII.

POLITICS.

SOCIETY (the voluntary grouping of many units for their common help) is made and held together by the poise and balance of two radical powers in man—akin to those centrifugal and centripetal forces which compel the planets to revolve about the sun—the separating spirit of freedom, and the combining spirit of union. Always acting, and in opposite ways, these forces hold each other in check; that shaking masses into units, this drawing units into masses; and it is only in their nice adjustment to each other that a nation can enjoy political life in the midst of social peace. In all living men, these powers of separation and attraction are nearly equal, like the corresponding forces in all moving matter; but some races of men have a little more of the first power, others have a little more of the second power. The Latin race has a quicker sense of union than the Gothic race; the

Gothic race has a keener love of liberty than the Latin race. Each may be capable of uniting public order with personal independence; but the paths by which they will separately arrive at such an end, diverging from the common line, will reach their goal by loops and zigzags hardly perceptible to each other. A Latin people will dread the liberty for which it longs; a Gothic people will distrust the government of its choice. Compare the structure of a Teutonic Church with that of the Roman Church; compare the political life of America with that of France! Rome has a compactness of organization, to which neither London, Augsburg, nor Geneva can attain; while London, Augsburg, and Geneva have a freedom to which Rome cannot even aspire. In France, again, the tendency of public thought, not of a school, of a party only, but of the solid people, is to sustain authority against the demands of personal right; in America, on the contrary, the action of all political bodies, of all colleges and corporations, of all private teachers, agitators, and philosophers, is directed, now consciously, now unconsciously, towards weakening the public force in favor of individual rights. France has not lost her love of liberty, nor America forgotten her respect for law; for these are elementary instincts in the human heart; without which, in some form of combination and adjustment, society, as we understand it, could not be. But in the large results of thought, in the wide action of politics, one nation is always tending towards military rule, the second nation towards popular rule; France seeking safety in the drill, the discipline, the armaments of a camp. America in the agitations of a pulpit, in the explosions of a press, in which every man has an unlicensed right of speech and thought.

Each of these tendencies implies a peril of its own. If the Latin is apt to sacrifice independence to empire, the Teuton is no less apt to sacrifice empire to independence. In France, the danger lies in too much compression — in America it lies in too much separation — of the political units.

For twenty years before the War broke out, the tendency of men in the United States towards separation had been excessive; not in one society, but in all societies; not in one body, but in all bodies; not between race and race only, but between men of the same race; not in the States only, but in the Churches; not in politics and religion only, but in science, in literature, in social life. Until the War came down upon the nation like a judgment, rousing it from a trance, the moral atmosphere of America had been charged with the fire of secession; almost every man of intellectual force and native genius in the country, either being or seeming to be, driven by the force of some inward spring from his obedience to natural rules and national laws. Society rights, class rights, property rights,— state rights, county rights, township rights,— land rights, mining rights, water rights,— church rights, chapel rights, temple rights,— personal rights, sexual rights — the rights of labor, of divorce, of profession — the rights of polygamy, of celibacy, of pantagamy — negro rights, Indian rights, equal rights, woman's rights, babies' rights: these are but samples of the names under which a common sentiment of division had taken shape and grown into an actual power. What man of mark then raised his voice for unity? Who cared for the central government unless he could mint it into dollars, turn it into patronage and power? Who taught the poor to feel reverence for the law? Were the rich, the learned, the intellectual members of this proud community ever seen in those days at yonder White House? What poet, what scholar, what divine, then made it his religion to respect a freedom which was guarded and controlled by the general vote? A man of genius here and there took office, chiefly in some foreign city; going far away from his native soil, to a place in which he could forget his country, while he made a tale, a poem, a morality, of the messages and memories of a foreign race and a distant age. Irving went to the Alhambra. Bancroft sailed for London. Rich amused himself in Paris. Hawthorne mused in Liverpool; Motley pored over papers at the Hague. Power migrated to Florence, Mozier and Story pitched their tents in Rome. Longfellow, dallying with the Golden Legend, seemed to have forgotten the poetic themes which lay about his home. No one seemed to appreciate American scenery, no one appeared to value American law. For a moment everything brightest in the land lay under an eclipse.

Not a few of the more brilliant men — the younger lights of the New England schools — renounced their citizen rights, and even while they yet lived in Massachusetts, in Connecticut, in Rhode Island, declared themselves by a public act set free from all future loyalty to the United States. It is said that Ripley, Dana, Hawthorne, Channing, Curtis, Parker, some or all, laid down their common rights in the American courts, when they undertook to raise a new society at Brook Farm. Boyle, Smith, and Noyes, were only three in a thousand clever men — born in New England, nurtured in its societies, educated in its schools, licensed to preach its gospels — who seceded from the Great Republic; mocking its defenders, and contemning its institutions. "Ha!" roared Noyes, the idol-breaker, "do you fancy that heaven is a republic, that a majority governs in the skies, that angelic offices are elective, that God is a president, that His ministers are responsible to a mob?" And the crowds who heard him, answered—No!

In the church it was much the same as in the political field. That old and stately church which has the root of its life in the mother country, has long ago ceased to be the popular church of America, if numbers may be taken as a certain test of power; but even this church of an upper class, of an aristocracy, rich, decorous, educated, had not been able wholly to escape that rage for rending and dividing which possessed its neighbors. The preachers struck, so to speak, for higher wages; when some of the laymen, hurt by a display of worldly motives closely akin to those which govern affairs in Wall Street, quitted their fold for that of the Bible Communist, that of the Shaker, that of the Universalist.

The Wesleyan body, numerically the largest church in these States, parted into two great sects—a Methodist Episcopal Church North, and a Methodist Episcopal Church South; a division which was provoked, not caused, by the importance just then suddenly acquired by the negro question. In the northern section of the Methodist church, there was a further trouble and a second split, on account of conscientious scruples as to bishops' powers and laymen's rights; the latter point being mainly raised on the question whether Methodist laymen might sell rum. A new religious body, now of very great strength, the Wesleyan Methodist Church in the United States, grew out of this secession. Indeed, eight or nine sects have been formed out of the original church of Wesley and Whitfield, without counting those seceders who have gone out bodily from the rest.

Next in importance as to numbers come the Baptists; a body, like the Methodists, fired with holy zeal; which was found strong before the world, the flesh, the devil, yet weak in the presence of this seceding spirit. In a very short time this body was divided into Old School Baptists (called by their enemies Anti-effort Baptists), Sabbatarians, Campbellites, Seventh-day German Baptists, Tunkers, Free-will Baptists, with their sub-section of Free Baptists; and into some minor parties.

In the Congregational Church, which prides itself on holding in its ranks the most highly educated ministers and professors in the United States, there arose endless divisions, including Millennialists, Taylorites, and the strange heresy of the Perfectionists, founded by one of their students at Yale College. From the Millennialists, who fancied the world was about to end and the judgment to come, sprang the Millerites, who said it would end on a particular day. The Perfectionists, who declared that the world was already at an end, that the judgment had come down upon us, parted into Putneyites and Oberlinites; sects which threw dirt upon each other, and laughed and mocked when any of their opposing brethren fell into sin.

A great unrest invaded the retreat of the Moravian village of Bethlehem, in the pretty Lehigh mountains; where young men took to questioning book and law; until the Moravians of Pennsylvania lost some customs which had hitherto marked them as a peculiar church.

No sect escaped this rage for separation, for independence, for individuality; neither Unitarian, nor Omish, nor River Brethren, nor Winebrennarians, nor Swedenborgians, nor Schwenkfelders. Perhaps the

Come-outers may be taken as the final fruit of this seceding spirit; since they separated themselves from the older churches, from the dead and dying churches, as they call them, for secession's sake, and solely in the hope of breaking down the religious bodies in which they had been reared. These Come-outers have two articles of faith: one social, one dogmatic; they believe that man and woman are equal, and that all the churches are dead and damned.

Society had to go through these trials; and she cannot be said to have got through her maladies without many a wound and scar; since, in the slackening of all ties and ligatures, men had begun to toy with some of her most sacred truths. Property was attacked. In the press, and in the pulpit, it was said that all private wealth was stolen frem the general fund, that no one had a right to lay up riches, that no man could pretend to the exclusive holding in either wife or child. Doctors took up their parable against the sanctity of marriage; women began to doubt whether it was well for them to love their husbands and to nurse their children. Some ladies set the fashion of laughing at mothers; nay, it became in Boston, Richmond, and New York, a sign of high breeding to be known as a childless wife. Wretches arose in every city in the land, some of them men, more of them women, who professed to teach young wives the secret arts by which it is said, that in some old countries, such as France, the laws of nature have often been set aside. Many a great house is shown in New York, in which resided creatures of the night who imported into America this abominable trade.

Religion, science, history, morality, were thrust aside by these reformers, as clogs on individual liberty. What was a canon, a commandment, to a man resolved on testing everything for himself? Excess of freedom led a few to Communism, a few into Free-love. What, in truth, is this dogma of perfect freedom, except the right of every man to have his own will done, even though his will should take the form of wishing to possess his neighbor's house and his neighbor's wife? Some of these brave reformers, like Noyes and Mahan, seized a religious feeling as the groundwork for their faith; others again, like the Owenites and Fourierites, made a scientific axiom serve their turn; while yet a third and more poetic class, the enthusiasts of Brook Farm, embraced a mystical middle term, making a god of Nature and of Justice. All these schools of practical socialists seceded from the world, renouncing in terms, either express or tacit, their allegiance to the United States.

What noble spirit, it was said, could suffer itself to be enslaved by canons, dogmas, precedents, and laws? Every man was now to be a law unto himself. Liberty was to have its day. The final stage of freedom, as it verges into chaos, is the stage in which no one has any rights left him to enjoy; and in many parts of America this stage of progress had, on the evening of the War, been nearly reached.

Family life was hardly less disturbed by this intruding spirit of separation; disputes, arising on the domestic hearth, being carried into public meetings and female congresses, held to debate the most fanciful points of difference between male and female, husband and wife, parent and child. Women raised their voices against nursing babies, against the sanctity of wedlock, against the permanence of marriage vows. They asserted rights which would have grieved and puzzled such models of their sex as Lady Rachel Russel and Lady Jane Grey. Caroline Dall demanded that woman should have the right to labor in any profession she might care to adopt. Margaret Fuller taught her female readers to expect equality in the married state. Mary Cragin preached the doctrine of Free-love for woman, and practised what she preached. Eliza Farnham urged a revolt of woman against man, declaring that the female is intrinsically nobler than the male.

What a glorious strength of constitution this young society must have had to endure with so little waste the shock of so many forces! What energy, what solidity, what stamina in the young Saxon republic!

CHAPTER LXIII.

NORTH AND SOUTH.

If the negro question lent a pretext to the rage of North and South, the cause of that strife in Charleston harbor which brought on civil war, lay closer to the core of things than any wish on the part of these Southern gentry to maintain their property in slaves. The negro was a sign, and little more. Even that broader right of a State to live by its own lights—to make and unmake its laws—to widen or contract its enterprise—to judge of its own times and seasons—to act either with or without its fellow States—was but a pretext and a cry. The causes which have whitened these Virginia battle-fields (in the midst of which I write) lay deeper still. A planters' war could not have lived a month, a seceders' war could not have lived a year. The lists were drawn in another name, the passions welled from a richer source. No such beggarly stake as either of these engaged a million of English brothers in mortal strife. But when did nations ever close in combat with the actual cause of war emblazoned on their shields? Nations have a way of doing great things on poor grounds; of checking Russia in the name of the silver key, of making Italy on account of one hasty word. Men are the same in every clime. The prize for which the South contended against the North, was nothing less than the Principle of National Life.

What idea should lie at the root of all social habits, all political creeds, in this great republic? In the constitution, itself a compromise, the make-shift of a day, this question had been left an open gap. Every year had seen that opening widen; and sagest men had often said, that such a question never could be closed, except in the old way, by a sovereign act of sacrifice.

On one side of a faint and failing line lay these Southern States, peopled for the most part by a race of Cavaliers; men brave and haughty, the representatives of privilege, education, chivalry; a class in whom the graces which come of birth, of culture, of command, had been developed to a high degree. On the other side of that line, lay yon Northern States, peopled for the greater part by men of Puritan descent; shrewd merchants, skilful artisans, the representatives of genius, enterprise, equality; a class in whom the virtues which spring from faith, ambition, and success, were all but universal.

Here stood the lotus-eater, with his airs and languors, his refinements and traditions; there stood the craftsman, with his head full of ideas, his heart full of faith, his arm full of strength. Which was to give the law to this Great Republic?

In the South, you had a gentle class and a servile class. One fought and ruled; one labored and obeyed. Between these two sections of the Southern people yawned a mighty gulf,—a separating chasm of lineage, form, and color; for the higher breed was of pure old English blood, offspring of men who had been the glories of Elizabeth's court; while the lower breed was of African descent, offspring of the mango plain and the ague swamp, children of men who had held the basest rank even among savages and slaves. No bridge could be thrown across that chasm. No touch of nature, it was thought, would ever be able to make the extremes of black and white of kin. In the eyes of their lords and ladies,—most of all in those of their ladies,—these colored tenders of the rice-field and the cotton-plant were not men; they were only cattle, with the rights which belong to mules and cows; the right to be fed and lodged in return for work, and to be treated mercifully—after their kind. In many of these States the colored people dared not learn to read and write; they could not marry, and hold on truly, man and wife, to each other; they had no control over their own children; they could not own either pigs, ducks, cows, or other stock; nor were they suffered to buy and sell, to hire out their labor, to use a family name. Against each other they had certain remedies for wrong; against the white man they had none. To use the sadly memorable phrase of Chief Justice Taney, a negro had no rights which a white man was bound to respect; in other words, he had none at all.

It is much to say that among men so tempted to abuse of power, there was less waste of life than in any other slave society, even on the American soil. Virginia was a paradise compared with Cuba and Brazil. Some touch of softness in the lord, some gleam of piety in the mistress, had sufficed to keep the very worst planters of English blood free from the brutalities which were daily practised in the Spanish and Portuguese cities farther south. Charleston was not a pleasant place for a negro slave; the law was not with him in his need; oftentimes he had to bear the bitter fruits of a tyrant's wrath. He was only too familiar with the lash, the chain, the blood-hound, and the jail; but still, when weighed against the slave's condition in Havana, in Rio, in San Domingo, his life was that of a spoiled and petted child. The test of a people's happiness is the law of its reproduction. If a race is crushed beyond a certain point, nature protests against the wrong in her own emphatic way. The race declines. Now the negro has been dying away in every slave society on the American soil, save only on that which has been ruled by men of the Anglo-Saxon race. Bad as our rule, and that of our offshoots in Virginia and the Carolinas, may have been, the fact is legible on every part of this continent, in every island of the adjacent seas, that these English planters, and they alone, have given the African a chance of life. We put, from first to last, five hundred thousand negroes on the soil of our thirteen colonies; we made them toil and sweat for us; still, we treated them on the whole with so much mercy, that they are now nine times stronger, counting them by heads, than the number of their imported sires. In Spanish America, instead of the negroes of the present hour being nine times stronger than their fathers, they scarcely count one half the original tale. This is a little fact—recorded in a line; but what tragedies of woe and death it hides! When the great account is made up,—when all that we have done,—all that we have left undone,—is urged against us, may we not plead this increase of the negro under our dominion as some small set-off to our many sins?

A tourist from the Old World—one of the idler classes—found himself much at home in these country mansions. The houses were well planned and built; the furniture was rich; the table and the wine were good; the books, the prints, the music, were such as he had known in Europe. He found plenty of horses and servants; spacious grounds, fine woods, abundant game. In one place he got a little hunting; in a second place a little fishing. Nearly all the young ladies rode well, danced well, sang well. The men were frank, audacious, hospitable. What was unsightly in the place was either far away from a stranger's eyes, or made to look comical and picturesque. He heard of slavery as a jest, and went down to the plantation to see a play. Sam was called up before him to grin and yelp. A dance being on, and the can of punch going round as the negroes hopped and sang, he would go home from the scene merrily confused, and with an idea that the darkey rather loved his chains. In Missouri and Virginia I have seen enough to know how easily tourists may be deceived by the lightness and laughter of a negro crowd. A colored man is plastic, loving, docile; for a kindly word, for a drink of whisky, for a moment's frolic, he will sing and dance. He is very patient, very slow. In Omaha I found a rowdy beating a black lad in the street and inquired the cause:—"me say nigger have right to vote," said the lad; "dis gel'man say nigger ain't folks nohow." The lad made no complaint of being beaten: indeed, he laughed as though he liked it. If the white man had been his master, he, too, would have smiled, and I should possibly have thought it a pretty jest.

The South was made pleasant to its English guest;

for the people felt that the English were of nearer kin to them than their Yankee brethren. A sunny sky, a smiling hostess, an idle life, and a luxurious couch, led him softly to forget the foundations on which that seducing fabric stood.

In the Northern States such a lotus-eater would have found but little to his taste. The country-houses — except in the neighborhood of Philadelphia, where the fine old English style is still in vogue — were not so spacious and so splendid as in the South; the climate was much colder; and the delights of lounging were much less. He had nothing to do, and nobody had time to help him. The men being all intent on their affairs, they neither hunted, fished, nor danced; they talked of scarcely anything but their mills, their mines, their roads, their fisheries; they were always eager, hurried, and absorbed, as though the universe hung upon their arms, and they feared to let it fall. The women, too, were busy with a care and trouble of their own. No idle mornings in the library, in the green-house, on the lawn, could be got from these busy creatures, who were gone from the breakfast-table to the school-room, to the writing-desk, to the sewing-frame, long before the guest had played out his fund of compliments and jokes. It was true that when they could be got to talk about science, politics, and letters, he found them read to the highest point—full of the last fact, the last movement, the last book; bright and knowing people, who let nothing pass them, and with the habit of turning their acquirements to instant use; sometimes making him do service in an unexpected way. But he, an idler in the land, had no enjoyment in their rapid talk. They thought of him little, of their own projects much. When he wanted only to loll and dream, his host had to meet a banker in the city, his hostess had to teach a class in the village-school. He must amuse himself, he was always being told, until the afternoon. There was the coal-mine to see, the new bridge to inspect, the steam-harrow to test. What did he care about coal, and bridge, and harrow! He would smoke a cigarette, and take the very next train for Richmond.

In these sunny Southern houses, with their long verandas, their pleasant lawns, no man was busy, no woman was in haste. Every one had time for wit, for compliment, for small talk. The day went by in gossip. No man there ever thought of working, for to work was the slave's office. Work was ignoble in these cities. Society had said, "Thou shalt not labor, and escape the curse;" and white men would not put their hands to the plough. "Work!" said a stout young fellow in Tennessee to a man from whom he was asking alms, "thank God, I have never done a stroke of work since I was born; I am not going to change; you may hang me if you like, but you shall never make me work." In these sad words spoke the spirit of the South. "In one thing we were wrong," said to me a Georgian gentleman; "our pride would not let us teach. We had scarcely any professors in the South. Our people were well trained and grounded; we had some good scholars and more good speakers; but we had to send into our enemies' schools, to Cambridge and New Haven, for our teachers, whether male or female; and they almost taught our children to be Yankees." Teaching was work, and a Georgian could neither work nor recognize the dignity of work. In one of those passionate storms which sometimes swept across these languid cities, the evils of this borrowed life being clear, it was proposed to found a great University in the South, and to invite, by liberal chairs, the most eminent men of literature and science from Europe, and also from the North; among them, Prof. Agassiz, who was to have been installed their chief. "And how about our social standing?" asked the great professor, from whom I heard these details. There came the rub. The social standing of a teacher in the South! A teacher could not hope to hold any standing in the slave society, and thereupon the proposal to invite the best men to come over from Oxford and Berlin, as well as from Boston and New Haven, tumbled to the ground.

In the Northern cities you had neither a gentle class nor a servile class. In their stead you had men of learning, business, enterprise; men of as pure and lofty lineage as the Southern chivalry, with fresher notions, hardier habits, and a larger faith. The Middle Ages and the Modern Ages could not come together and live in peace; each would be master in the Great Republic,—on the one side Chivalry, with its glories and its vices; on the other side, Equality, with its ardor and its hopes.

Which of these two principles—Privilege, Equality—was to govern this Great Republic?

CHAPTER LXIV.

COLOR.

ONE chance the white man had, and still might have — of living here, in Virginia, also down in Alabama, Mississippi, and the Carolinas, a social and political life apart from his English brother in Pennsylvania, Massachusetts, and Ohio; but the course to be taken by him is one from which it is commonly believed that his pride must revolt, and his taste recoil, — a family alliance with the negro race.

Long before the ugly word miscegenation came into use, and young damsels in ringlets and chignons stood up in public pleading for a mixture of breeds, many sincere, and some serious, men had preached the dogma of a saving quality in the negro blood. Channing had prepared the way for Anna Dickenson. In their flowery prose, the New England teachers had bestowed upon their negro client in the South an emotional nature far above anything that his poor white brother in the North could boast. On the hard and selfish side of his intellect, a white man might be cursed with keener power; the point was moot; but in all that concerned his moral nature, — the religious instincts, the family affections, the social graces, — the negro was declared to be a softer, sweeter, and superior being. He was far more sensitive to signs and dreams, to the voice of birds, to the cries of children, to the heat of noon, to the calm of night. He had a finer ear for song, a quicker relish for the dance. He loved color with a wiser love. He had a deeper yearning after places; a fresher delight in worship; a livelier sense of the Fatherhood of God. These fancy pictures of the negro—drawn in a New England study, a thousand miles from a rice-field and a cotton plantation—culminated in Uncle Tom.

Many good people in the North had begun to think it would be well for these pale and bilious shadows of the South, to marry their sons and daughters to such highly-gifted and emotional creatures, with a view to restoring the strength and thickening the fibre of their race. When the War broke out, this feeling spread; as it raged and stormed, this feeling deepened: and now, when the War is over, and the South lies prostrate, there is a party in New England, counting women in its ranks, who would be glad, if they could find a way, to marry the whole white population, living south of Richmond, to the blacks. Again and again I have heard men, grave of face and clean of life, declare in public, and to sympathizing hearers, that a marriage of white and black would improve the paler stock. In every case these marriages were to happen a long way off. I have met more than one lady who did not shrink from saying that, in her belief, it would be a great improvement for some of the fair damsels of Charleston and of Savannah to wed black husbands. I never met a lady who said it would be well for her own girls to do so.

The War has wrought a change in favor of the negro, who is now a petted mortal in the North, to be mentioned as "the colored gentleman," not as "the damned black rascal" of former times. He rides in the street-cars; he has a right to sit by his white brother in a railway; he may enter the same church, and pray in the adjoining pew. Public men make speeches for him, female lecturers expound him. I have heard Captain Anthony, a New England orator, declare that if he wanted to find a good heart in the Southern States, he should look for it under a sable skin; if he wanted to find a good head, he should look for it under woolly hair. That strange thing was said in Kansas, in one of the cleverest speeches I have ever heard.

The fact is, the negro is here the coming man. Parties being nicely poised, the dark men being likely to get votes, they are even now, in view of that heirship, courted, flattered, and cajoled. During the War the negro proved himself a man:—the black and brown lads who rushed into yon fort (now held by Harry Pierman and his imps) made all their fellows men forever.

Six years ago, as I am told, no lady in Boston, in New York, in Philadelphia, could bear to have a negro servant near her: a black man drank and stank; he was a cheat, a liar, a sot, a thief. I do not find this feeling wholly gone: here and there it may linger for many years; but it is greatly changed; and I have heard very dainty ladies in Boston and New York, express a liking for the negro as a household help. He is neat and willing; quick with his hand; good-humored, grateful. Some of his race are handsome, with the grace and style which are held the signs of blood. Here, in Richmond, and at all hotels from New York to Denver, negroes serve at table, shave and dress you, clean your boots, and wait upon your person. In the many hundreds who have been about me, I have never heard one saucy word, never seen one sulky scowl.

One of the negroes whom we saw in Leavenworth was asked whether he would marry and settle, seeing that he had saved a good deal of money. "No, sar; me not marry: no white lady have me, and me not have white woman who marry me for money." On being asked why he could not court and win a woman from his own people, he exclaimed, "Lord, sar! you not think I marry a black nigger wench?" Yet the fellow was a full-blooded negro, black as a piece of coal.

That the negro is fitted, by his humor, by his industry, by his sociality, for a very high form of civil life, may be safely assumed. Some negroes are rich and learned, practise at the bar, preach from the pulpit, strut upon the stage. Many have a great desire to learn and to get on. Here is Eli Brown, head waiter in the Richmond hotel; a man with a bright eye, a sharp tongue, a quick hand. A few months since he was a slave. He learned to read in secret, and in daily fear of the lash; since he got his freedom, he has learned to write. In this black lad, I have found more sense of right and wrong, of policy and justice, than in half the platform orators of the schools. "Tell me, Eli, do you want a vote?" I said to him in the after-dinner chat, as he stood behind my chair. "Not now, sir," he replied; "I have not read enough yet, and do not understand it all. Sometime I would like to vote, like the others; in twenty or twenty-five years." Is not a man with so much sense fitter for the franchise than a pot-house yelper, who does not know how much he has still to learn?

Last night, I went with Eli round this city; not to see its stores and bars, its singing-rooms and hells; but bent on a series of peeps into the negro schools. They are mostly up in garrets or down in vaults; poor rooms, with scant supplies of benches, desks, and books. In some, the teacher is a white; in many he is either a black or half-caste. Old men, young lads, were equally intent on learning in these humble schools; fellows of sixty pottering with the pen, and flat-nosed little urchins tugging at their A B C. All were working with a will; bent on conquering the first great obstacles to knowledge. These men are not waiting for the world to come and cheer them with its grand endowments and its national schools; they have begun the work of emancipating themselves from the thraldom of ignorance and vice. In Richmond only there are forty of these negro schools.

In the front of men inspired by such a spirit, the planters cannot afford to lie still and rust in their ancient pride. Knowledge is power, and the weaker man always goes to the wall. But though the planter may, and must, prepare himself to compete with a new class on his own estate, does it follow that he must mix his blood with that of his former slave?

The feeling of aversion to the negro as an associate, even for a passing moment in a room, a church, a railway carriage, though it may be softening, as the negro grows in freedom, wealth, and culture, is very strong; not only here, in Richmond, where the negro was a chattel, to be bought and sold, starved, beaten, spat on, by his lordly brother, but in the West and North, in Indianapolis, Cincinnati, and Chicago, far away from the sights and sounds of a servile class. Since the War was closed, a negro has a legal right to enter any public vehicle plying in the streets for hire; but, in many cases, he dares not exercise his right. A cabman would not drive him; a conductor would not let him step into a ladies' car. In passing through Ohio, a State in which the colored folks are numerous, being struck by the absence of all dark faces from the cars, I went forward to the front of our train, and there, between the tender and the luggage van, found a separate pen, filthy beyond words to suggest, in which were a dozen free negroes, going the same road and paying the same fare as myself. "Why do these negroes ride apart—why not travel in the common cars?" I asked the guard. "Well," said he, with a sudden lightning in his eyes, "they have the right; but, damn them, I should like to see them do it. Ugh!" The ugly shudder of the guard recalled a black expression of Big Elk, one of my Cheyenne comforters on the Plains. Here, in Virginia, all the railway companies have posted orders to the effect that, when a negro has paid his fare, he may ride in any car he pleases, subject to the common rules; but, gracious heavens! what negro dares to put his feet on the white man's steps? Sam likes his free condition: at times, he may air his liberty offensively under his former master's nose; but he also loves his skin; and in a land where every man carries a revolver, fingering it as freely as in England we should sport with a cigar-case, Sam knows how far he may go, and where he must stop. Habits are not changed by a paper law; and the day of a perfectly free and friendly intercourse between whites and blacks is yet a long way off.

In Massachusetts and Rhode Island, you will hear it said, in favor of miscegenation, that this scheme for blending races and mixing blood is no new method; but one which had long prevailed in Virginia, Carolina, and Alabama. Your teachers tell you that miscegenation is a fact, not a theory, a Southern habit, not a Northern project. They take you into the streets, hotels, and barbers' shops; they bid you look at these yellow negroes, some pale as Moors, some white as Spaniards; and they ask you to tell them whence come these Saxon features, these blue gray eyes, these delicate hands? They show you a negress with golden hair. Do such things prove that the white blood will not mingle with the black? Sail to Newport, ride to Saratoga. These idling places swarm with colored servants; every man, every woman of whom might be put in evidence of the truth. What is seen in Newport, in Saratoga, is also seen at Niagara, at Long Branch, at Lebanon Springs, at every watering-place in this Republic. North of the Potomac, it is a rare thing to find a pure African black. Many of your house-servants are half-castes, more still are quadroons and octoroons. Broad traces of either English or Spanish blood may be seen in nearly all; in the color, in the carriage, in the contour, in the style. This pale white negro, Pete, has the air of a grandee. Eli, my friend here, has the bearing of a judge. Who knows where Pete, where Eli, got that lofty air? In Virginia, in Carolina, the black squat face, with its huge lips, its low forehead, its open nostrils, is seen in every street. It is not a comely face to look on: though the folks who wear this form and hue are not such brutes as they are sometimes called. Many of them are bright and thriving; Harry Pierman is a fullblooded negro. But even in Richmond these colored people have a large admixture of Saxon blood. Eli Brown is a half-caste; so is Pete; most of these clever lads, our servants, are quadroons. It is certain, therefore, as the New England teachers say, that miscegenation, instead of being a new thing in the South, has been known and practised for many years.

Thus far, however, it has been practised only on one side,—on the male side; and the new plan for mixing the blood of white and black appears to be only a branch of that mighty theory of reform, now agitating and unsettling all society — the theory of equal rights for sex and sex. Hitherto, miscegenation has been open to men, denied to women. Male Saxon life has long been passing into negro veins; and that shrewd observer, Captain Anthony, who said he should look for a good heart under a sable skin, a good head under woolly hair, gave this strange reason for his faith in negro courage and negro talent—that the best blood of Virginia and Carolina flows in the veins of this colored race. For ten generations, he asserts, the youth of this English gentry has been given up to negro paramours; nearly all that time the breeding of slaves for the market has been a trade in these Southern parts. No sense of shame, he says, either prevented a father from giving his heir a pretty quadroon for a playmate, or from afterwards selling the fruits of their illicit love. When, according to Captain Anthony, his youth was spent, his heart was sear, and his brain was dull, this heir of a gentle house was married to a white woman, who bore him children and preserved his name. Is it not clear, asked the speaker, that the strength and freshness of that gentle family should be sought for in negro ranks?

Why, the reformer then comes in and asks, if such things can be allowed on one side, why not on the other? If it be right for a man to love a negro mistress, why should it be wrong for a woman to wed a negro husband? Thus it would appear from a review of facts and sentiments, that this sudden and alarming theory of miscegenation is no more than an effort to make free for all that which is now only free for some; an effort to give legal standing, moral sanction, to what is already a habit of the stronger sex.

But among this stronger sex, with the rare exception of a poet here, a philosopher there, this idea of introducing a fashion of love and wedlock among white women and black men excites the wildest rage. Gentlemen sitting at table, sipping soup, picking terrapin, will clench their hands and gnaw their lips at any allusion to the subject. Americans are not squeamish as to jokes; but you must not jest in their society about the loves of black men for white women. Merely for paying a compliment where it is thought he should not, a negro would be flogged and tarred and hung. No punishment would be deemed brutal and fierce enough for such a sinner. A friend who knew what he was saying, told me in the western country that he had seen a negro seized by a mob for having insulted a white girl; his offence was that of giving the girl a kiss, with an appearance of aiming at a further freedom; and on the girl screaming for assistance, he was collared by a soldier, a native of Ohio, and dragged into Fort Halleck, where he was cuffed and kicked, tarred and feathered, set on fire, skinned alive, and finally stuck, half-dead, in a firkin, and exposed on the open Plains, until his flesh was eaten away by wolves and hawks.

My friend, who told me this story, a Missourian by birth, a soldier in the War, had no conception that I should be shocked by such details, that I should consider the punishment in excess of the offence, that I should think the Ohio soldier guilty of a grievous crime. In the Western country life is lightly held and lightly taken. No one puts the high value on a drop of blood which we of the elder country set upon it. A white man counts for little — less than for a horse; a black man counts for nothing — less than for a dog. All this I knew; and therefore I could understand my friend.

A time may perhaps come, as poets feign and preachers prophesy, when the negro man and the Saxon woman will be husband and wife; but the day when they can go to church together, for the celebration of their marriage rites, without exciting the wrath, provoking the revenge, of these masculine protectors of white women, is evidently a long way off.

CHAPTER LXV.

RECONSTRUCTION.

In the great contest now going forward in every part of this Republic as to the safest theory of reconstruction,—that is to say, as to the principle and plan on which the New America may be built up—every party seems to have put the Union in its front. Under the dome of yon glorious New Capitol, men from the North and from the South appeared to be equally eloquent and ardent for the flag. All speakers have the word upon their lips, all writers have the symbol in their style. Unity would seem to be, not only the political religion of men in office, but the inspiration of every man who desires to serve his country. No other cry has a chance of being heard. Not to join in this popular demand is to be guilty of a grave offence. "We are all for the Union," said to me a Virginian lady not an hour ago, "the Union as it was, if we may have it so; our sole desire is to stand where we stood in '61." So far as you can hear in Richmond, this expression would appear to convey the general wish. North of the Potomac, too, the desire to have done with the past five years of trouble and dissension is universal.

In the new elections, every candidate for office has

been forced by the public passion, though often against his will, to adopt this watch-cry of the nation for himself and for his friends; while he has found his profit in denouncing his enemies and their partisans as disunionists, — a denunciation which, in the present temper of men, is taken to imply all the worst treacheries and corruptions, present and to come; in fact, to clothe a man with such uncleanness of mind and body as lay in the Hebrew phrase of a whited-wall. Union is a word of grace, of sweetness, and of charm. Everybody takes it to himself, everybody claims it for his section. Disunion, a word so musical in Richmond, Raleigh, New Orleans, not thirty months ago, is now a ban, a stigma, a reproach. Its day is past. Republicans call their Democratic rivals disunionists; Democrats describe their Republican adversaries as disunionists. Each section writes the word Union on its ticket, and the shout of this common word from the opposite camps is apt to confuse a free and independent elector when he comes to vote.

Even here, in Richmond, the capital of a proud and fallen cause, in which the streets are yet black with fire, around which the fields are yet sick with blood, there is scarcely any other cry among the wise, the moderate, and the hopeful. A few, unquestionably, cling with a passionate warmth to the memory of the past; but every day, as it goes by, is thinning the ranks of these sentimental martyrs. The young, who feel that their life is before them, not behind, are all coming round to a larger and more practical view of facts. They see that the battle has been fought, that the prize for which they struggled has been lost. Slavery is gone. State rights are gone. The dream of independence is gone. Men who are hopelessly compromised by events — who feel that the victorious

States can never again intrust them with political power—may urge on their fellows the merit and the virtue of despair; but the younger men of this nation feel that sullenness and silence will not help them to undo the victories of Sherman, Sheridan, and Grant. Excepting in the society of women—a class of generous and noble, but illogical and impracticable reasoners—not many persons in the South (I am told) regard the prospect of reunion with a free and powerful republic, just awakening, at their instance, to a consciousness of its colassal might, with any other feeling than a proud and eager joy.

Richmond is not, just now, in a mood of much emotion; since she fell into Northern hands her habit has been that of a proud and cold reserve; yet so soon as the pending elections roused in her a little life, her enthusiasm, such as it was, ran wholly in the form of the ancient flag. At a dinner party given in this city the other day, a politician proposed as a toast, "The fallen flag." "Hush, gentlemen!" said a son of General Lee, "this sort of thing is past. We have no flag now but the glorious Stars and Stripes, and I will neither fight, nor drink, for any other."

From the tone and temper of such political debate as one hears in Richmond, I see no reason to suspect (with some of the New York papers) that this patriotism of Virginia is the result of either fear or craft; for in my poor judgment, no disaster, however dark, no privation, however keen, could have driven these proud Virginian gentry into pleading for a renewal of friendly relations on other than the usual grounds of political science. The return to wiser feelings on the part of these vanquished soldiers seems to have been the natural consequence of events. The life before them is a new life. Slavery is gone, and the hatreds provoked by slavery are going. Men have to look their fortunes in the face, and it is well that they should do it without suffering their judgment to be warped by the disturbing passions so commonly found on a losing side. How are the planters to maintain their place—not in the Great Republic only, but in Carolina and Virginia? At present they are an aristocracy without a servile class. They have great estates; but they have no capital, no mills, no ships, no laborers. They are burdened with enormous debts. They have scarcely any direct and independent intercourse with foreign nations. Worse than all, they are surrounded, in their fields and in their houses, by a population of inferior race. Does it need any more than a little good sense to perceive that the English gentry in the South may find their best account in a partnership with the English citizens of the North, even though these latter should impose on the repentant prodigals a forgiving kinsman's terms?

The blacks are strong in numbers, clanish in spirit; they are fond of money, and have the virtue to earn and save. Can you prevent the negroes from growing rich, from educating their children at good schools, from aspiring to offices of trust and power? They will rise both individually and in classes. The day is not far distant when, in States like Alabama and South Carolina, the race may be swift and hard between the black planter and the white. When that day comes, will it not be well for the white man to have gained for himself some support in the power and enterprise of his brother in the North?

In these semi-tropical parts of the Republic a white man faints where the black man thrives. Nature has, therefore, put the white planter at a disadvantage on this Southern soil. For a dozen years to come, perhaps more, the negroes, who were only yesterday in chains and poverty, may be sorely tried; for they are rooted to the soil; they have neither trades nor callings; they are ignorant of letters; they have very little money; scarcely any of them have friends. Before them stands a world in which they are free to labor and free to starve. At first, they must be servants in the families, toilers on the plantations, in which they have recently been slaves; yet in some cases the negro has already become a planter on his own account, having gained, in a few months, a supply of tools and a lease of lands.

Take the example of my friend Henry Pierman, a negro, who has planted himself out yonder in Harrison's Fort, in a log-cabin, amidst the reek and stench of the great battle-fields. As no white man would rent such land, the lady who owns it, poorer and less proud than she was in former years, has been glad to let a great patch of forest to Henry. The log-hut has but a single room, and in this one room he lives with his black and comely wife, his four young imps, and a brood of cocks and hens. Harry was a slave until Grant tore his way through these formidable lines, when he became free by the great act of war which made all his people free. Happily for him, he had been a domestic slave in one of those rich Virginian households in which nobody cared about the laws. One of the young ladies, more for fun than with serious thought, had defied the police and the magistrate by teaching him to read. Her father being the Governor of Virginia, she snapped her pretty fingers at the judge. Harry read the Bible, and became a member of the Baptist church. Like all his brethren, he is keenly alive to religious passion, subject to dreams and voices, one of which had told him, he asserts, while he was yet a youth and a slave, that he would one day become a free man, would marry, would have children, and would rent a farm of his own. Many years went by before his dream came out, but he prayed and waited; in the end he found that this promise of his youth was kept. So soon as the liberating armies entered Richmond he left his old place, though his master had been kind to him, and wished to keep him as a servant on hire; but the passion to be free was in his veins; voices called him from the city into the fields; and, without money, ploughs, scythes, seed, horses, stock of any kind, with only his black wife to help him, and his three youngsters to feed, he threw himself on the forest land. Last year, his trial-year, was found to be bitter work, but he had put his soul into his task, and he got on. Up early and late, pinching his back and his belly, he was able to send a few onions and tomatoes, a little corn and wood, to market. This produce bought him tools, and paid his rent in kind. By patience he got through the winter months. In the second year his enterprises have extended to a hundred and forty acres, and he has now the help of two other negroes, one of them his wife's father, whom he has lodged in another of these soldiers' huts. One-fourth of his produce pays the rent; the remaining three-fourths he divides into two equal portions, one of which he gives to his negro helpers, the other he retains for himself and wife. Henry is clever, pushing, devout; for his children, if not for himself, he is ambitious. One of his two lads is shortly to begin his school-work; at present he must toil upon the farm. "I heard de angel say in my dream," he said to me with simple faith, "dat I bring up my children in de fear of de Lord; and how man bring dem up in fear of de Lord, unless he teach dem to read and write?"

The field of enterprise for working-men like Henry Pierman is extremely wide. Two-thirds of the soil of Virginia are still uncleared; indeed this old and lovely State is everywhere rich in mines, in waterways, in wood and coal, which a splendid and careless people have left to wait and rot. Each year will see the band of negro farmers grow on these Virginian waste lands; and when the colored people have grown rich and educated, how can they be kept from social and political power? In some States of the South, they are many: in one State, South Carolina, they count more than half the population; so that South Carolina, standing by itself and governed by universal suffrage, would vote itself a negro legislature, perhaps a negro governor. These dark people are growing faster than the pale. In time they will own ships and mines, banks and granaries; and when they have gathered up money and votes, how will the white man be able to hold his easy and safe supremacy in these semi-tropical States unless by union with his white brethren in the North?

Of course, while every hope and every fear may be thus impelling North and South to reunite, each section may still desire to construct the New America on terms best suited to itself. Deprived by the war of their slaves, laden with debts, both personal and territorial, the Southern planters would like to rejoin the ancient league as equals, if it may be, as more than equals. Under the old Constitution they were more than equals, since they voted for themselves and for their slaves; and what they were aforetime they would like to be again.

But Northern statesmen, flushed with their recent

glories, have no mind to put back the sword into its sheath, until they shall have fully secured the objects for which they fought; one of which objects is, to prevent, in future, a Charleston planter from exercising in the national councils a larger share of power than falls to the lot of a manufacturer of Boston, a banker of New York. Such larger share of power the Constitution had given to the Charleston planter, on account of his holding property in slaves; representation in the Capitol being based on population; five negroes counting for three free men; and the masters voting, not for themselves only, but for their slaves. The strife of policy rages for the moment wholly around this point.

The two moderate parties, between which the struggle of the coming years will mainly lie, are the Republican and the Democrat. The Republicans, strong in the North, are weak in the South; the Democrats, strong in the South, are weak at the North; but each party has its organization and its followers in every State of the Republic. They have other points of difference; but the chief contention now dividing them, is as to what guaranties shall be demanded from the rebellious States before they come into Congress and take their chances in the fight for power.

The Republicans say, that all white men in the Union, that is to say, all the voters, should be made equal to each other before the ballot-box; that each man should poll once and for himself only, with no distinction of North or South. The black man they leave out of their account; he is to them as a minor, a woman; having no rights at the poll and in the legislature. This change in the law of voting cannot be made and put into force until the Constitution shall have been first amended. That charter based the power of representation on population, without regard to the number of voters. The negroes counted as people, and their masters got the political profit of their presence on the soil. In the Old America, the planters who exercised this power may have fairly represented the negro mind, so far as negroes had opinions and emotions; but this Old America is gone for ever; the planter can no longer answer for his slave; and his claim by the old law to give this vote on the black man's behalf, must be done away. In future, all white men in the United States must have an equal power at the poll; hence, the Republicans have framed a bill, amending the Constitution so far as to base the representation in Congress not on the number of persons, but on the number of voters. A majority in the new Congress is certain to be of opinion that this bill should pass.

The Democrats assert that any amendment of the Constitution is illegal, revolutionary, needless. They say, and in theory they rightly say, that representation should be based on population; on a great natural fact, easily ascertained, capable of proof; not on a whimsy, a convenience of the day, a mere local act, which may be passed to-day, re-called to-morrow. They clench the doctrine which the moderate section among Republicans profess to have adopted, that a black man, in his present state of ignorance, is not fit to vote; but then they add, that as the black man shall not vote himself, his more liberal and enlightened neighbor, like the electoral classes in a European state, should be allowed to cast his vote into the urn. These Democrats have the great advantage of seeming to stand by the law and Constitution, but their reasoning against the constitutional bill is seen to be futile and unsound. President Johnson and his cabinet are of opinion that this Constitutional Amendment should not pass.

Each party finds a certain amount of sympathy in the hostile camp. The Northern Radicals object to the Constitutional Amendment as illegal and unnecessary; asserting, with the Democrats, that representation should be based on natural population, not on the number of legal voters; asserting, with the Republicans, that all white men should have equal rights in the urn; and declaring, in the face of both these parties, that the negro should be allowed to give his vote for himself. In like manner, the Southern moderates, while they hold to many doctrines which the North will not indorse, are not unwilling to unite with them on the terms of equal rights proposed by the Republicans. This party of peace and compromise is perhaps the strongest, numerically, in the South; but the hopes of more fanatical men have been so hotly fanned by President Johnson and his agents, that calm and reasonable counsels have been heard among the old governing classes with a certain stiffness and impatience.

We need not judge these parties with heat and haste. After her losses in the field, the South may easily persuade herself that she has a right to ask for much, and to take whatever advantages she can of the divided counsels of her foes.

CHAPTER LXVI.

UNION.

THE main obstacle, then, to a Union, such as late events have made possible, and the interests of all parties would suggest, is not the temper of either North or South, but the existence of a paper-law, for which every American has been trained to express a veneration almost equal to that which he professes for the Word of God.

If any human effort of the pen is sacred in the eyes of these people, it is their Constitution. Indeed, a stranger in the land can hardly comprehend the reverence — sometimes rising into awe — with which brave Virginians, practical Pennsylvanians, bright New Englanders, always speak of their Organic law. Apart from the affection borne to it by a great people, that organic law, from whatever point of view it is regarded, fails to impress a student of politics as being the highest effort of human genius. It is less than a hundred years old, and has none of the halo which comes of time. It was not a growth of the soil and of the English mind, but an exotic, drawn from the foreign and artificial atmosphere of France. On the day of its adoption it was no more than a compromise, and ever since that day it has stood in the way of progress in the United States. The principles embodied in it are in direct antagonism to that splendid document, which often lies by its side in the text-books—the Declaration of Independence; for the Constitution denies that all men are free and equal, and refuses to large classes of the people the pursuit of their own happiness.

Who can forget how often, and with what success, that Constitution has been cited in evidence that the negro slave was not considered by the founders of this Republic, as a human being? If all men are pronounced free and equal, by the fact of their birth, it is only too obvious that creatures held in bondage are *not men.* But every one knows that the Declaration of Independence set forth the true and final views of those founders, while the Constitution expressed no more than the political compromises of a day. The very men who signed it wished it to be amended; in the first convulsion which has tried the political fabric of this country, it is found to be the cause of a thousand disasters. It has brought the country to such a stand that years may possibly elapse before the facts which have been accomplished, and which cannot be reversed, can be set in harmonious relation to the paper-laws.

While Americans are busy, unmaking and amending their Constitution, may they not fairly put to themselves the question, What is the use of this record? At best, when the letter of a constitution is true in every detail — true to the designs of God in His moral government of men, true to the life and hope of the people in whose name it is drawn up — it is only a definition of facts. It is a thing of the past; a record of what the people have been, and of what they are. But the act of defining is also one of narrowing, limiting, restricting. Why should the life of a great continent be narrowed down to a phrase? How can a progressive country pretend to limit its power of future growth? By what right may a free commonwealth presume to restrain the march of ideas and events? In a despotic state, where men are neither free nor equal, where growth is not expected, where prosperity is not desired, a paper law, unchanging as that of the Medes and Persians, may have reason for existence; for under such a rule the people can never hope to rise into that highest state of being a law unto themselves. In a country like America, a real constitution should be a vital fact, not a piece of paper, and a dubious phrase. England never had a written constitution. How could she have? Her constitution is her life. All that she has ever been, ever done, ever suffered — these are her constitutions, because they are herself. What would she gain by trying to write down this story in a dozen articles? She would gain a set of manacles. No dozen phrases could express the whole of her vitalities. Some of these are obvious, others latent; no one can remember all the past, no one can foresee all the future. Why not be content to let the nation live? Would any sane man think of making a constitution for a garden, of hanging a paper chain on the stems of plants? Yet men in a free soil have wider possibilities of change in them than trees and flowers. Could anybody dream of devising a constitution for sciences like chemistry, astronomy, and physics? Where you have power of growth, you must have order, method, understanding; not a final theory, not an infallible law.

And what are the advantages derived from a Constitution? Are you afraid that people would forget their principles and betray their freedom, unless they were restrained from wandering by these paper notes? That is the common fear. But see what this fear implies, and say whether all that it implies is just. As men cannot wander from their own natures, their own instincts and passions, you have to assume that your Constitution has a life apart from that of your people; that it is a political fiction, not a moral and social truth. If the Constitution exists in the blood and brain of this bright and tenacious people — if it be the genuine product of what they have done, of what they are — you need not fear its being forgotten and betrayed. If it is an alien statute, what right have you to force it upon them?

In the present state of feeling with respect to the Constitution, I do not think that anybody would be heard with patience who should propose to set the people free, by putting it to a decent end. The time for such a work may come. At present no one dreams of doing more than amending a defective instrument in several places; so as to cast away some of the very worst articles inserted in it by the slave proprietors. Only the radicals propose to bring it into harmony with the Declaration of Independence. But while the political doctors are at work upon it, may it not be worth their while to consider — Whether it would not be better to confine their task to cutting away the obnoxious parts? Why not open the Constitution by removing its restrictions? Why add to a document which they admit to be defective? They know that if this paper barrier had not stood in their way, the differences between North and South would have ended with the defeat of Lee. Why then prepare fresh difficulties for their children, by adding new compromises to the organic statutes?

In a few years, North and South will be one again; state rights will have been forgotten, and the negro will have found his place. A free Republic cannot hope to enjoy the repose of a despotic State; to combine the repose of Pekin with the movement of San Francisco, the order of Miako with the vitality of

New York. Ebb and flow may be predicted of the future; at one time public thought will be found ebbing towards separation, personality, and freedom; another time it will be found flowing again towards union, brotherhood, and empire; but the tides of sentiment may be expected to roll from East to West, from West to East, without provoking a second wreck. That article left uncertain in the Constitution, as to the power of any one State to part from its fellows without their leave, has been now defined by facts. War on that question will not come again; but heats will come, passions will be roused, and orators will take the field, even though the sword may not again be drawn; one side in the fray waxing eloquent on the rights of man, the other side on the power of States. Who shall say which fury burns with the whiter rage? One party will take its stand on personal freedom, the other will take its stand on national strength. These forces are immortal. One age will fight for independence, a second will fight for empire, just as either the Saxon or the Latin spirit shall happen to prevail. When these two powers are in poise and balance, then, and then only, will the republic enjoy the highest share of freedom with the widest share of power.

When the armies came into collision after the fall of Fort Sumter, the true banner of the war was raised, and the battle was accepted on a broader ground. The issue of the fight was then, — What principle shall the Great Republic write upon her flag? Shall her society be founded on the principles of Chivalry, or on the principles of Equality? Shall industry be branded as ignoble? Shall the New America be a slave empire or a free commonwealth?

Under these walls of Richmond the battle of that

principle was fairly fought; with a skill, a pride, a valor, on either side to recall the charges at Naseby and at Marston Moor; but the Cavaliers went down, and the Middle Ages then lost their final field.

When the reign of that martial and seceding spirit came to its close in the midst of rout and fire, the milder spirit of Unity and peace, which had only slept in the heart of these American hosts, came up to the front. A new order was commenced; not in much strength at first; not without fears and failings; yet the reign of a nobler sentiment was opened, and every eye can see how far it is daily gaining in strength and favor; even though it has to contend against craft and passion more fatal than the sword. Years may elapse before this Union sentiment in the South is strong with all the riches of its strength; but the heralds have blown their horns, and the soldiers have raised their flag. Fulness of life must come with time; enough for the hour that the desire for Unity has been born afresh.

Yes; here in Richmond, among these gallant swordsmen of the South, on whom the war has fallen with its deadliest weight—men broken in their fortunes, widowed in their affections—many admit, and some proclaim, that they have made a surprising change of front. They are still the same men as before the war, but they have wheeled about and set their faces another way. Some, it has been said, cannot make this change; they had their part in the past, and with the past they fell. Men whose last act was to burn this city, when they fled, leaving these blackened walls, these broken columns, these empty thoroughfares, as a message, a memorial of their despair, may think they have the right to be heard, and to be considered in these Southern cities; but it is coming to be understood that if the past is theirs, for weal and woe, there is a future before the world in which they can have no share. The victors have set their mark upon them, so that they shall fill no further office of command. Their friends may grieve over this exclusion; but the nation has to live; and the rank and file of the South will not punish itself forever, even for the sake of those who, in their enthusiasm, may have misled it into death. In fact, the tide has turned; the same sea rolls and swells; but the ebb of separation has become the tide of Union.

Though late, a goodly number of these planters see that their fiery haste, their brave impatience, their impetuous valor, had urged them on too fast and far; so fast, that in their rage for liberty they would have murdered law; so far, that in their quest for independence they would have sacrificed empire. In their passion to be free they had forgotten the saving power and virtue which belong to order, balance, equipoise of powers. To gain their darling wish—the right to stand alone—they would have rent society to shreds, and put the world back in its course a thousand years. They see their error now, and would undo their work; so far as such a deed can ever be done. A few still hug their pride and weakness; reading no promise in the skies; and courting the fate of Poland for the South. Others among them may be silent; scanning these crumbling streets, yon Yankee sentinels, those shouting negroes in the lane, with bitter smile; but time is doing upon these sad spirits its healing work. They feel that, having lost their cause, they must yield to nature;—an Anglo-Saxon cannot sink into a Pole.

I do not mean to say that here, in Richmond, the banner of Robert Lee is trodden in the mire: it is not; neither should it be, since that banner gleamed only over men who had armed to defend a cause in which they found much glory and felt no shame. I only say that the banner of Lee has been rolled to its staff, and put away among things of the past, with much of the chivalric error, the romantic passion, of the South, laid up and smoothed among its folds. Good sense, if not fraternal love, has been restored to these gallant people; who see well enough that the past is past, that rage is vain, that the fight is over, that a place in the country may yet be won. At present they are nothing; less than the mean whites; less than their own negroes. The situation cannot last. "Most of our young," said a Virginian to me just now, "are in favor of going in:" that is to say, of compromising the dispute, and taking their seats in Congress: "they do not like seeming to desert their old generals, but they want to live; and they won't stand out forever." These younger men, against whom the victors entertain no grudge, have nearly forgotten the past five years. Youth keeps its eyes in front, and there it sees nothing but the flag.

Hence it comes that in these very streets of Richmond, men who were yesterday on horseback, charging for the Confederate device, are now heard whispering of the Stars and Stripes, with a regret not feigned, an affection not put on. "Our grand mishap," said to me a Georgian soldier, not an hour ago, "was our change of flag; we should have kept the old silk; we should have gone out boldly for the Union; we should have put yon Yankees on the outer side; we should have taken our ground on the Constitution, making our enemies the Seceders; then, we should have won the fight, for all the West would have been with us; and, instead of stamping about these blackened walls to-day, we should have had our pickets at Niagara, our sentries at Faneuil Hall." Perhaps he is right. But is not this regret of the Georgian an after-stroke? Was any such thought as that of holding on by the old flag, of preserving the Great Republic, to be found in the Southern States when the war came down? The rage was then for separation. If wiser thoughts have come, have they not come by trial, in the wake of strife and loss? Those who now put their faith in Union, who look to the Capitol, to the White House, for safety, held in those years by another doctrine; putting their trust in freedom, independence, personality. That dogma failed them; isolation would not work; personality would not pay. Law and policy were against them; the instincts of society were too strong for them. They fought for their scheme of separation; they failed; and, failing, lost both prize and stake; all that for which they had tempted fortune, nearly all that which they had put upon the die.

Happily for the world, they failed and lost; failed by a law of nature, lost by an ordinance of Heaven. No calamity in politics could have equalled the success of a slave empire, founded on the ruin of a strong republic. All free nations would have felt it,—all honest men would have suffered from it; but even with their mistaken cause, their retrograde policy, their separatist banner, what a fight they made! Men who can perish gloriously for their faith—however false that faith may be—will always seize the imagination, hold the affections, of a gallant race. Fighting for a weak and failing cause, these planters of Virginia, of Alabama, of Mississippi, rode into battle as they would have hurried to a feast; and many a man who wished them no profit in their raid and fray, could not help riding, as it were, in line with their foaming front, dashing with them into action, following their fiery course, with a flashing eye and a bounding pulse. Courage is electric. You caught the light from Jackson's sword, you flushed and panted after Stuart's plume. Their sin was not more striking than their valor. Loyal to their false gods, to their obsolete creed, they proved their personal honor by their deeds; these lords of every luxury under heaven, striving with hunger and with disease, and laying down their luxurious lives in ditch and breach. All round these walls, in sandy rifts, under forest-leaves, and by lonely pools, lie the bones of young men, of old men, who were once the pride, the strength of a thousand happy Anglo-Saxon homes. Would that their sin could be covered up with a little sand!

Out on yon lovely slope of hill, from the brow of which the reddening woods and winding waters of beautiful Virginia gladden the eyes of men for leagues and leagues, the pious North has gathered into many beds, under many white stones, the ashes of her illustrious dead; of youths who came down from their farms in Ohio, from their mills in Vermont, from their schools in Massachusetts; the thew, the nerve, the brain of this great family of free-men; who came down, singing their hymns and hallelujahs; giving up ease, and peace, and love, and study, to save their country from division, from civil war, from political death. Singing their hymns, they fainted by the wayside; shouting their hallelujahs, they were stricken in the trench and in the field. New England gave its best and bravest to that slope. I know a street in Boston, from every house in which, death has taken spoil; in the houses of poet and teacher, I have seen

Rachel mourning with a proud joy for the sons who will never come back to her again. These heroes sleep on the hill-side, in the city which defied and slew them; they have entered it as conquerors at last; and here they will keep their silent watch, the sentinels of a bright and holy cause. All glory to them, now and for evermore!

Out, too, in yon swamps and wastes, by the deserted breastwork, by the fallen fort, by the rank river-margin, lie the ashes of a broken and ruined host; of young men, of old warriors, who rode up from the cotton lands of Louisiana, from the country-houses of Georgia, from the rice-fields of Carolina, to fight for a cause in which they had learned to feel their right; soldiers as honest, as brave, and proud as any of their stronger and keener foes. But the strong were right, and the right were strong; and the weaker side went down in their fierce embrace. They fell together; their duty done, their passion spent. Many a tender office, many a solemn greeting, passed between these falling brothers, who spoke the same tongue, who muttered the same prayer, who owned one country and one God They died on the same field, and whitened on the same earth. Still, here and there, some pious hand picks up their bones together, just as the warriors fell in battle, and laying them side by side, leave the two brothers who had come to strife, victor and vanquished. unionist and seceder, to sleep the long sleep in a common bed.

Would it were always thus! would that the pious North, noble in its charity as in its valor, would condone the past! The dead are past offending any more, and the pious tongue, in presence of a soldier's dust, should ask no question of state and party, but lay the erring prodigal by his brother's side. Yon sunny Richmond slope, on which the setting sun appears to linger, tipping with pink the fair white stones, should be for North and South alike a place of rest, a sign of the New America; an imperishable proof of their reconciliation, no less than an everlasting record of their strife.

THE END.

LIPPINCOTT'S PRONOUNCING GAZETTEER OF THE WORLD,

OR GEOGRAPHICAL DICTIONARY.

Revised Edition, with an Appendix containing nearly ten thousand new notices, and the most recent Statistical Information, according to the latest Census Returns, of the United States and Foreign Countries.

Lippincott's Pronouncing Gazetteer gives—

I.—A Descriptive notice of the Countries, Islands, Rivers, Mountains, Cities, Towns, etc., in every part of the Globe, with the most Recent and Authentic Information.

II.—The Names of all Important places, etc., both in their Native and Foreign Languages, with the PRONUNCIATION of the same—a Feature never attempted in any other Work.

III.—The Classical Names of all Ancient Places, so far as they can be accurately ascertained from the best Authorities.

IV.—A Complete Etymological Vocabulary of Geographical Names.

V.—An elaborate Introduction, explanatory of the Principles of Pronunciation of Names in the Danish, Dutch, French, German, Greek, Hungarian, Italian, Norwegian, Polish, Portuguese, Russian, Spanish, Swedish, and Welsh Languages.

Comprised in a volume of over two thousand three hundred imperial octavo pages. Price, $10.00.

FROM THE HON. HORACE MANN, LL.D.,

Late President of Antioch College.

I have had your Pronouncing Gazetteer of the World before me for some weeks. Having long felt the necessity of a work of this kind, I have spent no small amount of time in examining yours. It seems to me so important to have a comprehensive and authentic gazetteer in all our colleges, academies, and schools, that I am induced in this instance to depart from my general rule in regard to giving recommendations. Your work has evidently been prepared with immense labor; and it exhibits proofs from beginning to end that knowledge has presided over its execution. The rising generation will be greatly benefited, both in the accuracy and extent of their information, should your work be kept as a book of reference on the table of every professor and teacher in the country.

www.ingramcontent.com/pod-product-compliance
Lightning Source LLC
LaVergne TN
LVHW021315110826
845150LV00003B/573

* 9 7 8 1 4 2 5 5 5 7 4 0 9 *